Jean Crozier

No Corner Boys Here

VOLUME TWO

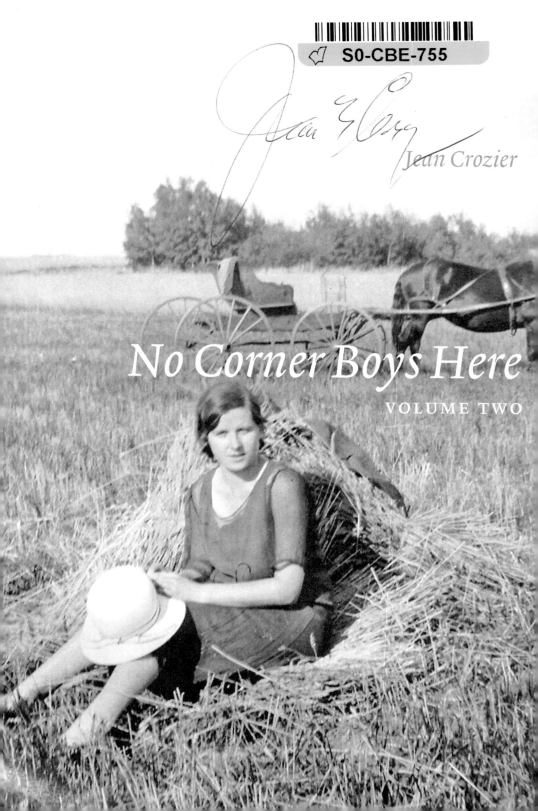

Published by Crozier Information Services, Edmonton, Alberta, Canada.
© Jean E. Crozier 2007
First edition, second printing, 2008.

Website: **www.NoCornerBoysHere.com**

LIBRARY AND ARCHIVES CANADA CATALOGUING IN PUBLICATION

Crozier, Jean
    No corner boys here / Jean E. Crozier.

ISBN 978–0–9784432–0–7

    1. Thurston family. 2. Rogers family. 3. Welsh–Canada–Biography. 4. Immigrants–
Canada–Biography. 5. Frontier and pioneer life–Canada, Western. 6. Canada–
Genealogy. 7. Wales–Genealogy. I. Title.

CS90.T5356 2007   929'.20971   C2007–905208–8

Book design: Alan Brownoff
Printed in Canada by Friesen's, Altona, Manitoba

Contents

The Siblings:
No Corner Boys...or Girls

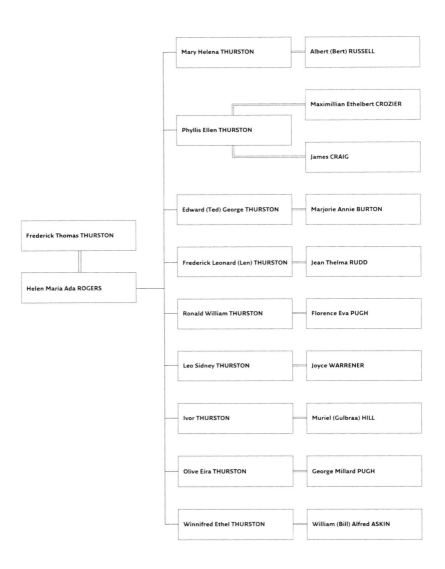

CHAPTER 9

Mary

Mary, the eldest. Determined, cheerful, affectionate, jealous, pious.
She chose to leave Irma for Ontario but yearned
for her parents and siblings.
She sustained a lifelong conflict with one sister
but sought solace with the others.
Her hugs and smiles were readily available.

MARY HELENA, eldest of the nine children, grew to be tall and sturdy like her mother. She was handsome rather than beautiful, her sharply angular nose and cheekbones offset by fine skin and soft hair. Her only ambition was to marry and have her own children; her determination to marry the man of her choice overcame all odds. She was an affectionate woman, but those who dared cross her came up against a blunt force. She could be hell bent on getting her own way or on enforcing her own viewpoint. She envied one of her sisters but got along with the others, became conflicted with her religious community but was called an angel by those she helped. Her determination to return to farming almost bankrupted her family.

Her grandchildren remember the treats: the shopping expeditions, the pies and Welsh cakes, unstinting cuddles and hugs, the surety of her love for them.

Mary has been described as a paragon – loving, pious, generous and charming – as well as the exact opposite. Her character probably included both extremes.

I REMEMBER my Aunt Mary as a multi-faceted woman. Since she lived 2,500 miles away, I knew her mostly through letters and relatives' conversations. Even so, she seemed to have a significant effect on my mother, her next younger sister. As kids, we heard stories about our Auntie Mary and her doings. We learned there was more than the normal sibling rivalry between Mary and our mother. Her own children's attitudes and remarks showed they learned a similar lesson. Separated by such a distance, the sisters had little or no chance to forgive past injustices, to understand one another – or even to develop a desire to do so.

I sometimes wondered how Mary had come to live in Ontario, when she seemed so attached to her parents, her brothers and sisters and their children. Who was this gentle man she married long before I was born, and how had she met him? Why did she seek, and give, seemingly genuine affection to my siblings and I, then write scathing letters to our mother criticizing her parenting skills? How could one person be so different? What was my aunt's story?

MARY WAS BORN at Treherbert, deep in the heart of the coal mining valleys of South Wales, on September 11, 1911, fifteen months after her parents' marriage. She was likely named, according to tradition, after her parents' parents. Her first name was that of Fred's mother Mary. Her second name may have come from Nellie's mother Helen, or perhaps from Fred's sister Alice Helena. There are no photographs of Mary as a baby, not even a snapshot of her in the beautifully hand-crafted christening gown her aunt Alice lovingly created. We know nothing of her birth; perhaps Nellie was attended by one of the valley's experienced midwives, or maybe a doctor was present. Fred would likely have marvelled at the tiny new human being – and then perhaps he went off for a pipe and a pint with his buddies.

Later photographs show Mary as a tall, slender young woman with a sturdy frame. She had fair skin that developed a few freckles; a sharp nose and high cheekbones dominated her face. The widow's peak she inherited from her mother's side defined her hairline and softened her otherwise square face. She had a ready smile, sometimes with that same quirkiness, the same enigmatic appearance as her brothers' smiles.

I ONLY REALLY CAME TO KNOW Aunt Mary after she and Uncle Bert, together with their children Ted, Bud, Pat, and Robbie, returned to the west in 1955. Mary's need to leave Toronto – the largest and most sophisticated city in English-speaking Canada – was, to me, unfathomable. I was a teenager then, open to the welcoming arms of another loving aunt, naive to the complexities of mother-daughter, sister-sister, or aunt-niece relationships.

Today, long after Mary's death, her children speak lovingly of her, as do her grandchildren. Each of them has shared his or her memories of their mother or grandmother. They have saved newsletter articles recounting Mary's kindnesses, as well as the journal Mary wrote while she stayed with her youngest son and his wife in Thailand in the mid-1980's. The memories of Mary's affection for her family, her desire to please her husband and children and grandchildren, are recollections of warmth and caring.

MARY LEFT NO DIARIES and few recollections of her childhood; her journal was primarily a memoir, recollections of life after the family arrived in Canada. She seldom talked of her childhood; her offspring have few if any bits of information about their mother as a youngster.

We know she attended the Romilly Road school in Barry, South Wales but that she was not a scholar. She could hardly wait for her fifteenth birthday when she would be able to leave school. It's easy to imagine one of her school days, a room full of uniformed girls, each at her own wooden desk. The female teacher was probably dressed in a dark skirt and an embroidered cotton blouse. She might have been instructing the class in the intricacies of geography or history, mathematics or English literature when she noticed Mary's inattention.

"Thwack!"

Mary's head would have jerked upright, away from the scribbler in which she'd been doodling, as the headmistress's ruler slammed down. Scholarship brought Mary no joy.

Her parents would not likely object to Mary's school-leaving plea, even though they valued education. Mary would be glad to stay at home with her mother and help with the younger children, or help her father with the dairy cows, perhaps even work in the Welford Farm fields. Or go into service at one of the big houses.

But by the time she finished school in 1926, her family was preparing to emigrate. There was an endless amount of work to be done to get the farm work completed, their belongings sold, and the things they were taking to Canada chosen and packed. Mary's mother remained calm, tending to the children and the housework, regardless of her husband's humour or his growing anxiety. Mary herself didn't know anyone else who had gone to Canada. She had been stunned when her father announced his plan. The children didn't say much to their parents, but they chattered excitedly among themselves.

"What do you think it's going to be like, Ted?"

"I dunno. We had a lesson about Alberta in class today, the teacher had a map, and he showed us the Halifax harbour, and the train tracks going all across the country. He said it would take days and days for us to get to Alberta. Nobody had ever heard of Irma."

"They're probably all talking, about us leaving. I don't care what they say, I think it's exciting." Mary fell into her own bed, leaving her siblings chattering until their father roared his displeasure.

Mary on the left, with Phyllis in her Girl Guide uniform and a young sibling, possibly Ivor, at Welford Farm, c.1924.

Their belongings were disposed of by auction. The farm implements were sold off in the late fall. At a second sale in early spring, their household furnishings were dispersed, most of the delicate china and crystal, the furniture and even their few personal possessions. A decision had to be made on each item – only the most essential things could be taken. There were strict limits to the allowable baggage weight. Almost none of the beautiful glass or crystal items, the china and silver, furniture or pictures would go to the new home.

"Ma-Ma-Ma-Ma-Mary, now you mind those little 'uns, Phyllis is busy with the accounts, m-m-m-m-mind they don't get in the way," Mary's father commanded, his gravelly stutter even more pronounced than usual.

That day Mary's thoughts were only partly on the immediate needs of her five younger brothers. Daydreams intruded, thoughts of Canada where fruit trees blossomed, wheat and oats stood golden in the fields, and vegetables grew as big as your head, according to the man in the immigration caravan.

"Will it be warm?" she wondered. "I wonder what our house will be like? Maybe I'll have a room of my own. I wonder if there'll be Indians? And I won't have to go to school."

❧

LESS THAN A MONTH after the auction at Welford Farm, the family disembarked the westbound train at Irma, Alberta. It was 7:00 p.m., and the daylight had almost faded. From the wooden platform they could see no trees and only a few buildings. The name 'IRMA' was emblazoned on a wooden sign suspended from the station roof. The village bore little resemblance to Dinas Powys or Porthkerry, or the larger towns of Cowbridge or Barry in South Wales.

Mr. Davis, the land agent, met the family and guided their steps across the road to the hotel where Mrs. Shaw, the owner, re-opened the dining room and provided them with a full supper of meat and potatoes, pie for dessert, tea with milk and sugar.

The next morning, Mary awoke in an unfamiliar but comfortable bed. Phyllis was already up and getting dressed. The boys' voices carried through the thin wall.

"Phyl, Mary, it's morning. We've been awake for hours. Let's see if we can have breakfast yet," coaxed one of the brothers, likely Ted, who was always looking for food.

The family assembled in the dining room for breakfast, hot porridge with cream, thick slabs of toasted bread with butter and jam, a pot of tea. The children ate quickly. Not even Leo dawdled over his food.

"How can Mum possibly be so calm," wondered Mary, "she's already nursed Olive, now she's making sure Phyllis and I and the boys have breakfast along with Dad."

The door opened and in came Mr. Davis, the man who had greeted them at the train. " 'Morning, Mr. Thurston, Mrs. Thurston, how's our new Canadian farmers?" he asked cheerily. "Done your breakfast yet? Well, come then, climb into the wagon and I'll take you out to your new home."

'Dapper Dan' as they later found he was nicknamed, led the family outside; his wagon and two-horse team of Clydesdales was tied to a hitching post at the hotel entrance. The horses' winter coats still clung raggedy-thick around their bodies. "Here now, let me help you up," he said to Nellie as she hesitated for a second at the wagon's high step. "This big girl here can hold the baby for a moment."

Nellie climbed in, Davis handed the baby up to her, then all the children clambered up, first the little boys, then the bigger ones, finally Mary and Phyllis. Fred filled his pipe and lit it as soon as he was settled in the seat beside Mr. Davis. The children's eyes grew big as the wagon left the village behind and headed out over the trail. All around them lay muddy fields and remnant snow pockets, near-emptiness where the horizon stretched for twenty-five or thirty uninterrupted miles (40 or 50 km). A few shrubs edged the hollows. The only trees were in clumps dotted here and there across the landscape. There were no birds, no rabbits, no greenness.

Mr. Davis guided the horses across country from the village, then onto the road past the slough and north for a couple of miles. And there it was, their new house, a grey-weathered building, wooden, atop a small hill. A wooden barn stood close by. They'd seen no other buildings on their journey from the village.

The family gazed upwards in silence, their eyes taking in the huge sky, the wide open fields with no other houses, the last bits of greyed snow still lying upon the cool ground. They were home. Their long journey was over and their new life had started.

I can only imagine the thoughts that ran through the children's heads. They all remember the adventure side, the excitement of going to a new country, a place where there was none of the class system that was so entrenched in the Wales of the 1920's. But they were used to stone buildings, small neat fields, tidy hedgerows, paved roads, and lots of people. The Alberta they came to was a big open land. The village of Irma had one muddy main street, wooden buildings, and a communal well to supply drinking water. The population was perhaps 200 people; most of the settlers had come from somewhere in

Britain, many of them established on land granted as a reward for military service.

❧

"THIS IS MY BED, Phyllis, yours and mine," Mary called as she found a straw-ticked mattress on one of the two beds in the larger bedroom.

Nellie looked at the two beds. "You and Phyllis will sleep here, and Leo too. Ted will sleep on the couch in the other room. We'll put Len with Ron and Ivor in this bed. Olive will stay with Dad and I. The linens will be here soon."

The big trunks of clothes and linens and blankets, the boxes of dishes and other household goods, as well as Fred's farming tools, were soon brought from the station. There was a scramble to find places to put things. Cupboards were scarce.

"Look, Phyllis, there's a pantry with shelves for all the kitchen things, and there's stairs here under the trapdoor in the middle. Oh, it's dark down there," said Mary as she continued to explore the house. "I wonder if there's mice? Or rats? We'll have to get a cat, Mum."

Phyllis and the four older boys started school within a few days of their arrival in Irma, leaving only Ivor and Olive at home. Mary worked beside her mother in those first weeks. She hauled water from the slough to scrub the floors and walls. The house, originally homesteaded by George Graham, had stood vacant for several months. The mice had moved in for the winter. Their droppings were in the cupboards and corners, even right in the middle of the front room. Spiders had built webs – stringy webs that hung down from the ceilings, intricate webs in the corners, some with lifeless flies still ensnared.

"Look Mum, there's pussy willows down by the slough, like we had back home," said Mary one day, "I wonder where the oranges are?"

"Cal Goodale laughed at Dad yesterday when he asked about oranges," replied her mother. " 'E said that was a story the immigration people told. They collect a commission for every family they sign up to come to the prairies. Cal said he'd heard they told some pretty big stories, but there's not much fruit here, only berries. Dad never did believe nowt about those stories of oranges."

Mary's father bought a cow from a neighbour, a range cow, nothing like the pedigreed dairy cattle he'd had in Wales.

"That'll do, we won't 'ave some'at to sell. There'll be milk and cream for our table, that's all," Fred announced at dinner one night.

At first, the family kept all the milk for their own use. Then, within a year or two, they purchased another cow or two, bought a separator and Mary learned to operate it. She collected the skim milk in a pail and siphoned the cream into its own can. They bought a butter churn from McFarlane's General Store, Mary took her turn at churning and Nellie sold the butter door-to-door in the village. The remaining cream was shipped by rail and sold to the Viking dairy co-op. Fred and the boys built a chicken house, and Nellie bought a hundred little chicks. Perhaps she also bought a few grown hens from one of the neighbours, brown-feathered birds like the ones she'd raised in Wales. The family needed eggs for its own immediate use, for eating as well as baking.

Fred and Nellie sought the best bargains for any essential purchases, making do with what they had. They planned for the time when they would farm their own land. This first year, the Thurston fields may have lain fallow, with the boys harrowing it a few times over the summer to keep the weeds down. Or, perhaps, they rented the land out that first year, no-one seems to remember just what path Fred took. For the family had a full year to decide whether or not to stay in Canada – and why use their precious cash to buy equipment that might have to be discarded a few months later? Renting the land out would give them a little more cash. What little money the family had was hoarded carefully.

"Nobody seems to have much money here," thought Mary, "and there's no big landlords' houses either. I hope I can find a job. I saw a pretty blue dress in the Eaton's catalogue yesterday." The neighbours had told them about the T. Eaton Co. Ltd. of Winnipeg, how to get a catalogue, send in an order and some money, then await delivery.

"M-M-M-M-Mam, Mrs. Shaw wants help in the hotel. She'll pay $25.00 a month," Dad said one day after he'd been to the post office to pick up the precious letters from Wales. "Mary can start tomorrow." Turning to his eldest daughter, who was standing beside her mother in the kitchen, he ordered, "You mind you do what she tells you; that wage will pay for the groceries."

"I will, Dad, I'll do my best." Mary was excited at the prospect. "I'll do whatever Mrs. Shaw wants me to. Maybe there will be more settlers like us, do you think, from Wales?"

Mary walked into town the next morning, and arrived at the hotel before 7:00 o'clock. "This is where you'll sleep," said Mrs. Shaw, as she showed Mary to the tiny little room that was to be hers. She'd be able to go home once a week on her day off.

Summer was a busy time for the hotel. New settlers were coming through, and there were land agents, salesmen, and the occasional lone traveller. Mary swept floors, made beds, emptied the despicable thunder mugs[1] from under the beds, cleaned out the washbasins and filled the pitchers in each room. She hauled water from the well and poured it into the tub on the coal and wood stove, did the laundry in the hotel's hand-operated washer, and hung the sheets and towels on a line behind the hotel. She placed a poplar pole securely under the centre of the line, so it didn't drag the clean washing into the mud. Ten- or twelve-hour days were standard.

"What's the matter, Mary, aren't you feeling well?" asked Mrs. Shaw as Mary washed the breakfast dishes slowly, her face a mask of unhappiness.

"I have a bit of a headache," replied the teenager, "and my stomach aches." The pangs of female adolescence often multiplied after a day or two away from home. Besides, she'd taken her wages to mum and thought she'd saved enough to buy the blue dress from the catalogue. Instead, Fred needed her entire wage. The blue dress would have to wait. "It's my money," Mary thought in typical adolescent pique. "I don't see why I can't keep at least some of it. It's not fair."

Mary learned to cook green beans that had been salted and stored in a crock over the winter, and she learned to soak salt pork before she cooked it for breakfast. She picked root vegetables from the bins in the cellar, where they were stored all winter, and she learned to snap the sprouts from the potatoes before she peeled them.

"Gotta get these carrots used up before they turn rotten, and the potatoes – look at those sprouts growin'," said her employer, "they'll be startin' to soften up pretty soon. You can cut out those rotten parts and boil the rest. We'll have mashed potatoes on the menu tonight, with that beef joint."

Mary did as she was told. "Boiled vegetables taste different here," she thought, "kind of salty but a bit odd." The highly alkaline well water imparted a different flavour than she'd been used to in Wales. The tea and coffee were so dark they stained the farmers' teeth, although few people over forty still had their own teeth.

Mary worked for Mrs. Shaw until the early summer influx of new settlers slowed to a trickle, then she worked for one neighbour after another. Sometimes there were children whose mother needed help. Other households simply had more tasks to be accomplished than the family could handle.

Child care was Mary's favourite job. She could always divert a child's attention, or find something to amuse or excite a youngster. "Come on, Jack," she might have said to an unhappy child, "let's go and find the kittens." And off they'd go to the barn, the child's hand in Mary's; soon the unhappiness would have been forgotten.

The summer passed and fall came. The shortening days were not unfamiliar, as Irma lies close to the same latitude as Wales. But unlike the old country, fall in Alberta brought coloured leaves along with the ripening grain, frosty windows and ice on the animals' water troughs.

Mary spent much of her salary on warm clothing. Nellie knit mittens and scarves for all of them, her fingers flying even in the dim light of the kerosene lamps. There would be no electric lights on North American prairie farms for another quarter century.

Mary learned to shoot, and undoubtedly rid her parent's farm of at least some of the pesky gophers. c1933

"I'm so cold," Mary cried one day, "nobody ever told us about this cold. It was supposed to be warm and sunny here." She stood close to the stove in the middle of the kitchen floor, held her hands over it, tried to warm her feet and get her body close to the heat at the same time. "I can't stand this," she thought. "I've got to get something else on. What can I find to wear?" She rummaged around in the small cupboard where she and Phyllis stored their clothing. She found a soft woollen sweater. It didn't look like hers but it would be warm. She put it on then covered it with an old shirt.

"She used to take my clothes and wear them without asking, then she'd put them back dirty or torn, and never even tell me. Mum and Dad never believed me, they just thought Mary could do no wrong," my mother told me more than once. I wondered, later, about the dynamics between the sisters, the older one's charming demeanour and the younger sister's rebellious response, and their parents' role in the sisters' disharmony. I didn't ever hear Mary's side of the story.

Over the next ten years, Mary worked at many of the area farms, some in the Irma district, others a little farther afield, some south of town, even as far down the line as Kinsella and Sedgewick, 40 miles (64 km) away. She returned home for her days off, between jobs, and when another pair of hands was needed on the Thurston farm. She learned to use a small-bore rifle, a .22, and used it to keep the gopher population at bay.

Live wasn't all work. There were plenty of young men and women in the district who loved to dance, play ball, picnic, and prepare theatrical presentations. The 'MerryMakers' were aptly named.

"Come on Mary, the MerryMakers need you for this play we're doin'," called one of the Goodale boys from his horse as he came upon Mary walking home from Irma.

"Oh, do they? What's the play? Well, that would be fun. When's the practice?" she asked.

"Tomorrow night, up at the Alma Mater hall, 7:00 o'clock, bring your raggediest jacket. You'll need it for your part," and with that young Goodale was off.

None of the MerryMakers' activities needed much money, and none of the group's members had any spare cash.

It wasn't a Goodale boy, though, that caught Mary's eye. Rather, it was Bert Russell, the eldest of four children, a tall, slender man, soft-spoken and gentle, unlike his father. His family had a farm not far from Sedgewick, a few miles south of Irma. Mary had worked for a neighbour family. Perhaps Bert came to visit, perhaps he helped Mary's employer; there weren't many neighbours and they all knew one another.

In later years, Mary's sons told stories of their grandfather, the years when he lived with them in Ontario, his difficult disposition and dictatorial manner, their admiration for their mother's ability to handle the old man. My cousins alluded to their grandfather's harsh treatment of his children when the family lived in Alberta, the verbal and physical abuse he delivered. And they described the way he pushed Jessie, his wife, to abandon Bert and his siblings and return to her family in Oswego, New York.

'Peg Leg' Russell used to come to our house whenever he was in Edmonton. He'd get off the bus at Whyte Avenue and walk the 5 blocks south. My sister and I were fascinated by his wooden leg, but we never found out where his own leg had gone. c1944.

"He brought this other woman home to the farm," said my cousin. "And he expected his wife to live there with her."

"She can help you with the housework," he is reputed to have told Jessie.

There are rumours, too, of harsh treatment meted out to the Russell children...

Each fall, the Russell family left the farm to the snow and the cold, the wind and the coyotes' howls. Bert's father, 'Peg Leg' James Russell, was from the small Ontario town of Durham, north of Toronto. He returned to Durham every fall, and spent the winter making harnesses for the farmers' big work horses. When spring came, James Russell returned to his Alberta farm and peddled his products to the area farmers.

"You sure had to check out that harness, too," laughed one of my uncles, long after Peg Leg Russell had sold his last set of traces. "Them things, why you never knew if the two reins would be the same length, or the chains all made of the same stuff. He peddled that harness around here for years."

Bert wasn't long past adolescence when he became involved with a young woman. Their marriage was difficult at best. Then Mary entered Bert's life.

"We're not together, Mary," Bert told her during one of their long talks. "It didn't work at the beginning and it won't work now, or ever. But to get out of it, that won't be easy."

"We'll find a way, Bert," said Mary. "Do you know anyone in Irma who's been divorced²? Yes? Maybe we could find out how he did it."

It's difficult, now, to imagine the stigma of divorce in the Canada of 1934. The churches, both Protestant and Roman Catholic, vehemently opposed divorce. So did the politicians. Most Canadian couples stayed together, happy or not, in spite of even the major problems caused by alcoholism or abstinence, poverty or wealth, domestic violence or incompatibilities. Mary and Bert must have cared deeply for one another to have contravened the social norms of the day. I remember watching them, thirty or forty years later. Their respect and affection for one another remained so obvious, clear to see and hear.

I WONDER HOW Mary broke the news to her father, that gruff and minimally-educated Welshman, the upright churchman, the deeply-principled and authoritarian parent. Perhaps the conversation was something like this:

> "Dad, Bert's divorce has gone through. The final decree has been issued. Now we can get married. I'm twenty-six-years old, Dad, I know what I want." Mary was in tears. Her parents liked Bert Russell, but they believed in marriage, permanently and forever: 'in sickness and in health', just as the Prayer Book said. Divorce was not for their daughter.

"Mum, I'll write, and we'll come back, we won't stay in Ontario, I couldn't stay away from you and Dad and the rest of them," she said that day in late May. Her brother Ron drove her into town to catch the afternoon train a few days later.

Mary had scrimped and saved for months to buy her $45.00 train ticket. It was 1937, paying jobs were hard to find, none of the neighbours had much money and they often paid her in food, not hard cash. Sometimes she agreed to work for part produce, part cash.

The train fare didn't include a berth. Mary sat up for the three long days and two nights to Toronto. She carried her own blanket and pillow, and a basket of food, thick slices of bread and butter wrapped in waxed paper, some cold chicken, a saskatoon and rhubarb pastry and some dried apples. There was tea with a bit of lemon in a two-quart sealer. What went through Mary's mind, I wonder, as she watched the prairie landscape change to the rocks and lakes and trees of northern Ontario? How did she manage the conflict between her family's beliefs and her own desires, her love for her parents and siblings and her love for Bert Russell? It can't have been an easy journey. The long trip was worth it, she'd always known that.

"How did they take it, Mary? Were your Mum and Dad very upset?" asked Bert, his voice and his eyes gentle and solicitous.

"Oh Bert, I hated leaving them, but I want to be here with you. And we'll go back, won't we, Bert? We'll go back there to live after a while?" she said, anxiousness for her parents mingled with the joy of being with Bert.

"We'll work it out. We'll go back some day."

Bert's father had loaned him the car for the trip into Toronto. The young lovers drove to the Lake Ontario waterfront and parked. They meandered the paths that bordered the shoreline. Mary marvelled at the size of the city behind them, the tall stone buildings, the wide paved streets, even the streetcars and the traffic lights. It was all so different from Irma, and even Edmonton, with its population of 87,034. Here in Toronto there were close to 900,000 people. But who cared? Bert was the centre of Mary's universe.

They were married in the United Church manse in Durham, Ontario on the evening of June 7th, 1937. The bride was beautiful. That afternoon, in the beauty parlour, Mary paid fifty cents for a luxury shampoo. Then the hairdresser 'marcelled' the bride's shiny dark hair: set it in deep, undulating waves, using a process named after the famous Parisian hairdresser, Marcel Grateau.

Earlier that spring, Bert had rented a one-bedroom cottage and planted potatoes in the garden behind it. The young couple arranged their belongings in the cupboards: their clothes and shoes, combs and brushes and books, the household goods Mary's friends had given her at the shower they'd held before she left Irma. There were rose bushes in the flower beds, similar to the beautiful rosemunde blossoms Mary remembered seeing in Wales.

"I'll pick the red one today, Bert, won't it be pretty, there's a little vase in with those things they gave us at my shower in Irma," she said, absorbing the rosy fragrance.

Soon, Mary stopped picking roses. The fragrance upset her stomach.

"What is it, Mary, are you sick?" asked Bert, coming in from the harness shop one smotheringly hot day in late July. And she was, but it wasn't anything the doctor could cure. Mary had become pregnant almost immediately after they were married. Heat, humidity, and morning sickness were a horrible combination.

Mary revived as the cooler fall weather settled in. She borrowed a sewing machine to make flannelette diapers and nightgowns for the baby who was to arrive in early spring. She cut the soft fabric into squares, 36" (1 m) each, and stitched a hem on all four sides. There was enough fabric for twenty diapers; she'd make another twenty after Bert got paid the following month. Then she started on the night-gowns, open at the back, fastened with a button at the top, or with bias tape. She embroidered a little emblem on the front of each gown. Every item had to be washed, even though she'd washed the fabric before sewing it. All the sizing had to be removed, leaving the fabric soft so it wouldn't irritate the baby.

"It's so scary, Bert, being here without Mum or anyone from back home. Mum didn't have an easy time, you know, with the babies, I remember the day Winnie was born out there on the farm at Irma, and that was her ninth." Apprehension showed in Mary's voice.

Mary and Bert's eldest son, Ted, was the first in his generation to wear the christening robes made for Mary. Summer 1938.

Young Ted looks as if he's trying to escape his father's hold – perhaps a portent of things to come! Durham, Ontario, summer 1939.

"Would you like my sister Peg to be with you?" asked Bert.

"Do you think she would come? She's been with other women hasn't she, when their babies were born?"

Peg arrived a few days before the baby's birth on March 24, 1938. But she had to do more than catch him. Ted's was a breech birth, bottom first, "folded up like an accordion" his aunt told him later. By the time his head emerged, his little body was blue and starved for oxygen. Peg blew her breath into the baby, cleaned him, and warmed him – and he survived, the first grandchild for Fred and Nellie Thurston. Mary eventually recovered from her arduous, painful delivery.

The new baby was named James Frederick, after both his grand-fathers, but his nickname was Ted. He was a long and gangly baby, and he grew to be a tall, slender adult with the sharp nose, high cheek-bones, and the thick auburn hair common in the Thurston family.

The tiny cottage seemed smaller with the new baby and his things -- diapers, clothes, a cradle, baby powder and soap. Mary hung the baby's flannel diapers everywhere to dry – outside in the humid spring air, inside to finish drying and to get warm.

"If we were in Alberta, these diapers would be dry in an hour. They'd fly in the breeze and the sun would dry them so fast," thought Mary as she tried to keep her home tidy, her husband happy, and her baby dry. Soon they moved into a larger house, one with a couple of extra bedrooms, which they'd fill with boarders to help pay the rent.

"Yes," said Mary to the young man at the door, "we do have a room available, and we would give you all your meals, and I'd do your laundry too." Their first boarder moved in. Mary kept them all fed on $1.00 a day, purchased groceries supplemented with the garden veg-etables she tended. Her roses were beautiful: red, pink, yellow, and white blossoms with long stems.

As Mary took care of her husband and son, her house and her garden, automotive technologies were advancing rapidly and world politics were becoming chaotic.

"There's not much money this week, Mary, but there's not a lot of harness being bought any more. The farmers are really going into tractors, you know, it makes their work so much easier. I don't know what Dad is going to do. But I think I'd better look at something else. War's coming on for sure, there's a lot of programmes being offered to get people trained to build aircraft and armaments," said Bert, concern showing in his voice, his forehead buckled into a frown. For them, as for many others, the prospect of war had both a horror side and a side that could give them a much-needed economic boost.

Within a short time, Bert began work with Victory Aircraft Ltd. at Malton, just outside Toronto. His income had never been higher.

"Why don't you take Teddy and go back to visit your parents for the summer, Mary. He's two-years-old now, we've got a bit of money and I think it would do you good," Bert said after he'd opened his pay envelope in the spring of 1940. Mary leapt at the thought – to be able to see her mum and dad and show them their grandson. It had been three years since she'd left home. They wrote regularly but still…

Mary's return trip to Irma by train held a different excitement than had her eastern journey. Young Teddy ran up and down the aisle as the train swayed back and forth, his mischievous ways a welcome diversion for the often bored passengers. Mary was excited but exhausted after travelling across the country with a toddler, three days and two nights on the train. As the train crossed the Fabyan trestle west of Wainwright, then slowed down as the Irma station came into view, she searched for a familiar outline.

"There, Teddy, look, there's your uncles." She guided the little hand in a wave, her excitement rising with every minute.

The conductor helped them off the train. Ron and Ivor had come to get her, their faces freshly shaved and their dark hair slicked back. Clearly they were more prosperous than when she'd left them.

"Ron, Ivor, let me look at you. Teddy, say hello to your uncles," directed Mary, trying to extricate Teddy from the folds of her skirt.

It was summer time, and as they drove along the dirt road toward the farm, the wheels tossed up sworls of dust. The smell of sweet clover, timothy and alfalfa almost overwhelmed Mary. They reached the driveway, the long sloping hill leading up to the house. Fred and

Mary and her son Teddy are here with Winnie and Phyllis' daughter Maureen, in Edmonton, c1941.

Nellie met their daughter and young grandson at the door, tears in their eyes and smiles on their faces.

" 'ark now, ah, isn't he a fine wee boy, Mary, " said her mother. "Come on, now, it's been a long ride. The kettle's boiling. We'll have a cup of tea. Here, you fix up some cookies for Teddy." Nellie handed Mary the tin of round oatmeal cookies and a pot of dates that had been diced and stewed slowly till they'd become thick and smooth. Mary spread the date butter on a cookie and covered it with a second round. The treat became Teddy's favourite.

Mary wondered if her father had truly got over his anger at her decision to marry Bert. Nellie had written every week, her letters carried news of crops and weather and church and family. She'd never asked about Bert's divorce. Not likely mum or dad had forgotten about it, though. Mary never knew much about her parents' private conversations. Only the sound of their muffled voices could be heard through the bedroom wall each night as they lay in bed.

"Dad seems okay," thought Mary, "maybe he's over it."

The month passed quickly. Teddy played in the fine-grained soil outside the house, let it run through his hands and into all the wrinkles and folds of his overalls. A fair sample of prairie soil made it into his mouth. Teddy chased the chickens, and wailed loudly when one obstreperous rooster pecked at him.

Mary rode the train to Edmonton some time that summer, maybe to shop, maybe to visit her sister Phyllis, maybe to treat her youngest sister with a trip to the city, or maybe for all those reasons.

Mary helped her mother in the kitchen, made tea several times a day, prepared lunch to take out to the fields where the boys were haying, hauled water and did the laundry. They baked pies filled with rhubarb from Fred's garden mixed with one of the remaining jars of saskatoons. Familiar smells wafted from the oven as the pies and home-made bread baked, or the beef roasted for dinner.

"But the heat," thought Mary, as she washed the dinner dishes. "I'd forgotten how hot this stove makes the kitchen. And it's already over 80°F (26°C) outside." It was a shock, returning to where there was so much hard work to do, with no electricity to pump the water or to provide heat for cooking or light to brighten the dark places. Her home with Bert had electrical power and running water, with a paved street and shady trees in front.

The summer passed quickly.

"I'll write, Mum, keep sending letters, please Mum, we'll be back here to live some day." Mary was gone again, back to Bert and their home in Ontario, back to the electricity and the paved roads and the larger towns with their spired churches and brick buildings and beautiful rose beds.

Soon another baby was on the way. Mary's second pregnancy was easier than the first one, and so was the birth. Baby Albert arrived on June 2, 1941 as the summer's heavy humid air descended. Named for his father, he soon became known as Bud. He grew into a tall young man with a square jawline and his father's build.

Mary and Bert moved to Brampton, close to the Victory Aircraft Ltd. plant where Bert was one of several hundred men building the Lancaster bomber[3]. Many of them were young fathers, others were older men who would have signed on for armed service duty if they'd been able. In the early years of the war, during the Battle of Britain and the European campaign, Bert's work days often stretched to twenty hours. Hundreds of Lancaster bombers were needed, and they rolled off Canadian production lines with speed and quality.

There were women, too, working in the plants. 'Rosy the Riveter', the poster girl, exhorted women to get out of their kitchens and support Canada's war effort by building airplanes, assembling gas masks, and packing weapons. By 1943, 261,000 women were employed in war-related manufacturing. Their jobs ended as soon as victory had been achieved. The women were again relegated to the kitchen so the men would have paying jobs.

Mary took care of her two baby boys, the lonely days and evenings and sometimes nights without her husband eased by his pay – $45.00 a week – likely more money than either she or Bert had ever known. They bought a car, and Bert drove some of his fellow workers to the plant. They shared both expenses and gasoline ration coupons, the 'tickets' issued to each family during WWII to control meat, butter, oil and gasoline sales.

Mary's desire for a daughter was fulfilled when Patricia Mary was born on March 7th, 1943.

YEARS LATER, long after Mary died, my cousin Pat told me she'd always felt special, the only girl in a family of four children. She and her mother were constant companions. Mary did her best to get Pat everything she wanted. There was never any question about Mary's love for her daughter, or her daughter's love for her mother.

BERT WORKED AT THE PLANT, Mary worked at home. In addition to child-care and housework, Mary took charge of the family's banking. She walked or rode the bus to deposit Bert's cheque, and precisely calculated the account balance. In those days, long before automated bank machines, bank clients could deposit or withdraw money at one location only. There, the teller manually entered each transaction in a small book and added or subtracted the amount; the entries and the totals were hand-written. Mary checked every entry. An error of even a penny sent her back to the teller for correction.

"Now, I think there should have been an interest payment made to us this week, shouldn't there?" she asked the teller, who in turn checked and corrected the steadily-growing total. Mary and Bert could hardly believe their eyes when the account balance reached the $1,000 mark. By war's end, they had saved $2,000.

"Oh Bert, we'll be able to go back to the farm now." Mary was ecstatic, but her husband showed less enthusiasm. He'd become used to running water for washing and laundry, electricity for lights and tools, stores close at hand, paved roads, and lots of people around. There was a little shoe repair shop in Port Credit that seemed much more interesting – and far less risky – than farming. Shortly after war's end he bought the business and transferred his harness-making expertise to shoe repairs. The war had produced long lists of consumer shortages, from coffee to leather to steel. Brand new shoes were scarce and expensive. The shoe repair business did so well that Bert sold it within a couple of years at a good profit.

"Now," thought Mary, "now maybe we'll be able to go back home to the west."

In the meantime, Mary's brothers' lives had taken some interesting turns. Len, the second eldest brother, had also left the farm and come to Ontario in about 1940. After he'd recovered from an almost fatal accident in a Hamilton steel plant, Bert had helped him get work at Victory Aircraft. Len met and married a beautiful, impish young woman named Jean Rudd. Mary's middle brother, Ron, joined the army in 1941 and was stationed in London, Ontario when the war ended; he would be demobilized in Alberta.

Mary badly wanted to return west. Both Bert and Len needed jobs. At Mary's urging, they agreed to look for work or opportunities in

Alberta. Mary took the two younger children and travelled with Ron by train to Irma. Len and Jean and their baby son John stayed with Bert and seven-year-old Ted. They drove west in Bert's car along the American route south of the Great Lakes, then across miles of gravel and some paved roads. It would be twenty more years before Highway #1, the TransCanada Highway, would be built.

Fred and Nellie received Mary and the two little ones with much joy, and by the time Bert and his entourage arrived, Mary and the children were happily settled in. Once again, Mary's hopes for returning to her family rose. She prayed every night. She accompanied Len and Bert on their possible-land-buying forays around the district. After just a few days, both Bert and Len had seen enough. They had no wish to return to the back-breaking, risky business of farming, and there was almost no manufacturing anywhere in Alberta.

Perhaps she and Bert walked the yard the day of the decision. "Mary, there's nothing here for us. Everyone is predicting lower prices for farm produce now that the war's over and there's no soldiers to feed. There's no point in farming if we can't make a living at it. And manufacturing – well, there isn't any. That's all I know how to do – farm or work in a plant. All those soldiers are going to be coming back home, they'll have first priority on the jobs. We just can't make a living here, Mary."

Bert held his wife closely as she shed bitter tears.

"Never mind, Mary," said Jean, who had never before been to a farm that had no electricity or running water, and where the fields were so huge. "Why would you want to live like that when you can be comfortable in Ontario?"

"You don't understand," sobbed Mary, "it's so far away."

Within days, the two families were back in their Ontario homes.

Bert and Len searched for a way to support their families. They decided to go into trucking, buying and hauling manure and sand and soil to Brampton's famous greenhouses. They bought two used Reo trucks from an acquaintance of Len's. In summer, they hauled for the greenhouses. In winter, they cleared streets and parking lots.

Mary lived for her husband and children; she was happiest surrounded by her sons and daughter. Ontario, c1945.

The business entailed hard work and long hours, but it was a money-maker. Mary's younger brother Leo worked with them in the summers during his years at St. John's Theological College in Winnipeg.

Mary took care of her children and her home, she cooked and sewed, raised vegetables and flowers, and made sure there was good food and comfortable surroundings for her husband at the end of his work day.

For Mary, church attendance was an integral component of child-rearing. Mary had confirmed her faith according to Anglican tradition before she left Wales. She and Phyllis joined the Women's Auxiliary (W.A.) of the church while they were still in Irma, and were active members throughout their lives. Mary's election as both secretary and press secretary of the organization were reported in the *Irma Times* of Friday, January 6, 1933. Once married, Mary continued to support her church.

Mary attended the Anglican church in Durham, regardless of the fact that the church didn't, at that time, sanction her marriage. She encouraged Bert to join her in the church but neither cajoling nor coaxing were successful with him until a few years before his death. She took her children to church wherever they lived, in Durham and in Brampton, then later on in Cooksville. She dressed the children in their Sunday best and took them to church on the bus or had Bert drive them. Mary continued her membership in the Women's Auxiliary (later renamed the Anglican Church Women) and served in the Altar Guild and the choir and an assortment of other church-based organizations and activities. The church became the centre of Mary's social life and the focus of her energies outside the family.

"YOU KNOW, MARY, there has to be a better way to make ends meet. I don't want to spend the rest of my life hauling manure," grumbled Bert after a particularly tough week. He'd had to deal with the old Reo's mechanical problems and had put in long hours. Although Bert worked hard, his brother-in-law was even more driven to succeed. It was becoming increasingly difficult to find dry manure close to Brampton and the additional miles of hauling reduced their profits.

There were still plenty of post-war shortages in Canada, including that of American-built cars. The economy was recovering and Canadians clamoured for consumer goods. Everything from phones to refrigerators was in short supply. But British cars were being built and imported, and when Bert found an opportunity to get into that business, he moved quickly.

They bought a building in Cooksville, a small town south of Brampton, and created Russell's Garage Ltd. with first one then two service bays, and a Cities' Service Ltd. gas and oil dealership. The family lived in one part of the building, and transformed their living room into a display centre for British Motors Corporation vehicles. Instead of a chesterfield and chairs, the room held Morris Minors™, Oxfords™ and MG™'s, as well as Riley™'s. Later on, after the business grew, Bert also took on a Rambler™ dealership for American Motors Corporation. He spent most of his waking hours in the garage.

After the war, Bert opened a British car dealership and service garage. c1948.

Mary took her children to see Toronto's Santa Claus parade, then to visit the jolly old man himself. Ted and Bud, c1944.

Although he wasn't a licensed mechanic, he knew cars. And he always hired qualified tradesmen.

Robert, their fourth and last child, was born on July 20th 1949. His parents expanded the house and the garage, put in a real showroom and retrieved their living room. Mary spent all her time looking after her children or attending to church activities. Her sons and daughter generally got what they asked for, if not the first time, at least by the second or tenth asking.

The house had two storeys, and was surrounded by trees and fields. There was dirt in the back yard for toddler Rob to move with his toy trucks and diggers.

"No, no, no, Mommy, I have to move the dirt today," he sobbed one evening when Mary took him in to bed. He was a determined child, and was heartbroken at having his earth-moving job interrupted before he'd completed his 'work'.

"There, there, now, it'll still be there tomorrow," soothed Mary, astonished at her son's distress. Sometimes his tears gave the desired results, as Mary allowed the little boy to spend an additional few minutes with his toys.

Mary made time to play with her daughter, who had few playmates of her own in semi-rural Cooksville. Pat's childhood was replete with tea parties, when she dressed up in her mother's cast-off clothes and shoes, sat her dolls at the table, and poured tea into china cups. Mary became 'Mrs. Villa', and shared tea and cookies with her little 'grown-up' daughter. They had adult conversations. Pat listened to her mother's stories of life on the farm.

YEARS LATER, Pat recounted her memories of her mother, the roses she grew, the Christmas cake she baked, the trips into Toronto to watch Eaton's splendid Santa Claus parade.

My husband Ron and I were in Mississauga with Pat, her husband Fred, their son Chad and their daughter Shawna, a decade or more after Mary died. I wanted to talk with Pat about growing up in Cooksville, her memories of her parents, and of visiting our grandparents, aunts, and uncles in Alberta.

"Oh Jeannie, it's so good to see you. Now can I make you a cup of tea? How about a cookie? Your room's down the hall, here. This used to be Mom's room, she shared it with Shawna. Let me know if you need anything." Like her mother, Pat spoke with gentleness and affection.

"Look at this plant, Jeannie," Pat said, touching one of the shiny green leaves of the hoya vine that clung to the wall above the stairs. "It blooms every year at Easter time, every single year. And you know, it only started to do that the year Mom died. It had never bloomed before. I think she has something to do with it."

Pat told me about her childhood in Cooksville when her mother was often her only playmate, her experiences when she visited in Irma, and her adult relationship with her mother.

"Mom was such a help to me, Jeannie. You know, when Chad was a baby he had colic, and Mom would lie down and put him on her stomach, and he'd settle right down. I've had so much trouble with nervousness and depression, my doctor put me on Valium years ago and wouldn't let me go off it so now I've really got a long way to go to recover. I don't know what I would have done without Mom all those years."

Mary's Ultimate Fruitcake

Preparation time: 1 ½ hours
Standing time: Overnight
Cooking time: 30 min.
Baking time: 3 ½ hours
Makes: 11 ½ lbs. (5 ¾ kg) fruitcake

Ingredients
8 oz. (250 g) whole blanched almonds, about 1 ¾ cups
4 oz. (125 g) slivered blanched almonds, about 1 cup
15 oz. (450 g) seeded raisins, about 2 cups
12 oz. (375 g) seedless raisins, about 2 cups
8 oz. (250 g) currants, about 2 cups
1 lb (500 g) cut citron peel or mixed peel, about 2 cups
1 lb (500 g) pitted dates, about 2 ½ cups
2 - 375 ml bottles red maraschino cherries
¾ cup brandy or cognac
19 oz. can crushed pineapple, about 2 cups
2 cups granulated sugar
1 cup strawberry jam
¼ c. brandy or cognac
4 cups all-purpose flour
2 tsp. ground cinnamon
½ tsp allspice
½ tsp ground cloves
1 tsp salt
1½ tsp baking soda
1 lb. (500 g) butter, at room temperature
2 ¼ cups granulated sugar
12 large eggs

The night before
1. Measure almonds, raisins, currants and citron peel into a large bowl. Thinly slice dates, using a sharp knife, and add to mixture.
2. Drain cherries, saving ¼ cup juice, and slice thickly. Stir cherries into almond mixture along with ¾ cup brandy. Cover tightly and leave at room temperature overnight. Stir occasionally.
3. To save time, cook pineapple mixture the night before baking day (mixture must be cool before being added to batter), as follows: In a heavy-bottomed saucepan,

combine crushed pineapple with its juice and 2 cups sugar. Cook, uncovered, for a half-hour to reduce most of the liquid. Stir frequently near the end of cooking to prevent burning. Remove from heat. Stir in jam and ¼ cup each of maraschino cherry juice and brandy. Cover and refrigerate.

Baking day
1. Choose pans that are at least 3 inches high. Finished batter measures 24 cups and fits in a set of 3 graduated wedding-cake pans (a 7 ½ inch, a 5 ½ inch, and a 4 inch square pan) and an 8 x 4 inch loaf pan. When baked, each cake will be 2 ½ inches high.
2. Lightly grease each pan, then line with heavy brown paper or aluminum foil, dull-side out. Grease paper or foil well.

Baking
1. Preheat oven to 275° F. In a large bowl, sift or stir flour with spices, salt and baking soda until well blended. Sprinkle one cup of this mixture over fruit and almond mixture and toss with your hands until all fruit is coated lightly.
2. Measure butter and 2 ¼ cups sugar into a large mixing bowl. Beat with an electric mixer at medium speed until creamy. Beat in eggs, one at a time. Continue to beat at low speed. Gradually beat in ⅓ of the flour mixture, followed by half the pineapple mixture. Repeat additions, ending with flour mixture.
3. Pour over flour-coated fruit and almonds. Mix with your hands until fruit is coated evenly. Divide evenly between prepared pans, leaving a 1-inch space at the top of pans for batter to rise. Smooth surface.
4. Bake in preheated over for 3 to 3 ½ hours, depending on size of pan. After cakes have baked for 1 hour, lay a large sheet of heavy aluminum foil over top of pans to prevent crust from darkening. A small loaf takes about 2 ¾ hours, the 7 ½ inch square cake needs 3 ½ hours. Cakes are done when they're fairly firm to the touch in the centre and a skewer inserted in the centre right to the bottom comes out clean.
5. When cakes are done, remove from oven and place pans on a cake rack to cool for 15 to 30 minutes. Then, turn out cakes. Carefully peel off paper and cool cakes completely on a rack.
6. To store, wrap cakes in a brandy-soaked cheesecloth, if you wish (this is not essential, as the cakes are very moist). Wrap in foil and store in the refrigerator or a cool place. Cakes will keep well in the refrigerator for months.
7. To ice fruitcake, cover top of cake with ¼ inch layer of marzipan or almond paste and finish with ¼ inch layer of Festive White Icing.

Per ½ ounce serving: 55 calories, 0.7 g protein, 0.2 mg iron, 8 mg calcium.

As Pat talked about her mother, the depth of their relationship became increasingly obvious. Pat had relied on Mary for advice, for help in child-care, and for day-to-day companionship.

"How fortunate she is," I thought, "to have had her mom so close, and to have had such a good relationship with her."

Pat didn't say much about her mother's determination. Mostly she remembered the good things. Pat told me about the day she and her mother took her to Toronto; Mary was the only person in the crowd who helped a woman struggling with a stroller and a child, to get down from the streetcar. Or the many times when Mary reassured her daughter that "whatever happens to you, come home and we'll discuss the situation. No problem is ever too big that we can't work it out together".

"There aren't many mother-daughter relationships that are so caring," I thought, that day

AMONG PAT'S INDELIBLE MEMORIES are those surrounding the family's return to the West. The year was late 1954 or perhaps early 1955. Pat had just entered adolescence.

"Bert, we'll all work together, we'll be able to farm again, " Pat remembers hearing her mother say. They were in the midst of another discussion about going back to the Alberta farm life that Mary believed Bert had promised her.

"It's the air, Bert, you know what it's like, dry and clear, not this heavy humid air that's here. And the boys and Pat, they need to have their grandparents close. We've got some money now, and it wouldn't cost that much to get set up. My brothers will help us; you know how they all work together. Please, Bert, it's time to go home."

It wasn't as if any of them were strangers to the farm. Mary had taken the children out to visit every summer, and they'd loved the time they'd spent in the central Alberta countryside. The boys and Pat had stayed with their grandparents, and with their uncles and aunts: Ted and Molly, Ron and Florence, Olive and George.

"Mom, will we be able to pick saskatoons?" asked Pat.

"Of course," enthused her mother, "I'll show you where I used to pick saskatoons and pincherries and chokecherries."

"Oh, that'll be such fun, and then we can make them into pies, can't we, like Gran does?" replied her daughter.

"I'll bet I could make some money raising beef, Mom, couldn't I?" asked Bud, who had his own stash of money that he'd saved from his paper route in Cooksville.

Seventeen-year-old Ted was quieter. He'd been out to the farm several times, and he loved being with his grandparents, aunts, uncles, and cousins. But he had developed his own social life in Ontario, friends that he hung out with and who shared his passion for hot cars and good times. He wasn't as enthusiastic as were his siblings.

Still, he thought, "I'll go for Mom's sake, and Dad's. They'll need help getting this thing off the ground, and they've always helped me whenever I needed them."

Len agreed to lease the garage business, including the car dealership. Mary began sorting and packing in the spring of 1955. Bert and Ted scrubbed out the well-used Reo truck, removed every trace of dirt and manure, then drove it up the driveway. Bert closed in the truck box to transport their belongings. By the time the children had finished school in June, the boxes of winter clothes and other lesser-used items were already packed and shoved into the front of the truck box. In went the garden tools and toys, the toaster and the electric frying pan and the curling iron, the radio and the record player. Finally, the appliances they used most frequently – the electric stove and the refrigerator, the piano and the television. They closed and locked the doors, and tied Bud's bicycle onto the back.

All the weight was on the back of the truck. It would be tough going when the wind blew or the road was rough or when the truck had to negotiate hills and dales...

"We've done it, Bert, it's all loaded. I've packed lunch. How far do you think we'll be able to go today?" Mary was anxious and the kids were excited. The little dog raced around, barking excitedly, determined to not get left behind.

In the mid-1950's, the family returned to an Irma farm. They packed their belongings into the old Reo truck, and tied Ted's bicycle on behind. c1955.

Ted folded his tall body into the dark blue Morris Minor™, Mary joined him in the front seat, Pat and Rob and Beanie the Pekingese dog were in the back. Bert drove the truck with Bud beside him.

"Oh my, I wish I'd learned to drive, I'd be able to help you out, Ted," said his mother, but she never had learned, and never would.

I've driven across Canada more than once, but not the Canada of 1955, when highways were narrower, hotels and motels and restaurants unlike those of today. It's a big trip from Toronto to Irma, Alberta, 2,500 miles (4023 km), four days' travel with one driver in a good car. I would do the trip again, but only with a cellphone available and a credit card in my pocket. Neither convenience existed in 1955.

Their route took them around the north end of Lake Superior, through the town of New Liskeard. There was a stop light at the bottom of the hill where the highway made a sharp right turn. The brakes on the old Reo failed as it headed down the hill toward the light. The overloaded truck careened past the stores and through the intersections. The residents scattered.

Bud sucked in his breath; he was glued to the passenger seat. There were no seat belts. Bert's face became pale, his eyes wide, his fingers on the wheel white-knuckle-white.

"That was a close one, Bud." Bert maneuvered the truck to a stop beside the highway on the other side of town. His hands shook as he wiped his brow. After a few minutes he and Bud hiked into town to arrange brake repairs.

Two days later, as they reached the Saskatchewan prairie, a ferocious thunderstorm developed. The black clouds dumped rain and hail in a wide swath, cars and trucks sought shelter behind the wooden grain elevators that towered above the flat land in every village, often only ten or fifteen miles apart. Bert and Bud stayed inside the truck, unable to hear one another for the din as the hailstones pounded the Reo's metal cab. Eventually, the hail and the rain abated; within a few more minutes, the sun was out and a rainbow appeared across the horizon.

By then, the two Russell vehicles had become separated. Bert reached Regina, halfway across Saskatchewan. The little Morris Minor was nowhere to be seen, even on the flat prairie where a person could see for miles.

"Where's Ted and your mother, Bud? I haven't seen them for hours. There must have been an accident. We're going back." He turned the old truck around and drove most of the way back to Winnipeg, a distance of perhaps 500 miles (800 km), looking for his wife and family in the little dark car.

"Oh, Bert, we were fine, Ted's a good driver," soothed Mary after they'd been reunited. The two vehicles stopped beside the road. Mary pulled out the little stove and made tea, and they ate the few Welsh cakes and pastries left in the tins.

The next day, they drove into Olive and George's farm north of Edgerton, stayed overnight and went on to Irma the following day.

"We're here, Mum," said Mary, tears running down her cheeks. "We've got here safely, oh, it's so good to be home." Fred and Nellie had watched as the two vehicles drove up the hill from the main road, turned around in the big farmyard and pulled up outside the little grey Insulbrick™-covered house. The adults, the children and the dog tumbled from the tiny car and the rattling truck, relieved to have reached their journey's end.

"Don't you let that dog chase the chickens, now," cautioned Mary's father. "We don't want dead hens or turkeys."

"We're back where we belong," thought Mary as she helped her mother set out the tea, spread date butter on the oatmeal cookies, and place cheese and crackers on a plate.

Mary and Bert had pinned their hopes – and their finances – on a good crop that year. But it had been a wet, rainy spring and Mary's brothers had been able to seed only about twenty acres for their sister and brother-in-law. They would have to find some other source of revenue until the farm could produce a steadier income.

Their new property, a partly broken half-section, was half a mile north of Fred and Nellie's farm. Since the only building on the place was an old, vacant house, Mary and Bert bought Ron's old house (he'd built a new one) and hauled it up to their property.

"Oh, that will be fine, won't it," said Mary as she watched the house being skidded along the road. Ron drove the tractor, Ted and Ivor guided other vehicles around the moving home. Bert poured a foundation, and the house was set onto it. It was a start. Bert set his sons to tearing down the old house on the west quarter section. Then he recycled the boards, carefully incorporating them into the renovation and addition to their new home.

While the house was being readied for use, Ted and Bud slept in the truck box which they'd removed before selling the old Reo to a neighbour.

Fred witched for water, but found only a low-flowing aquifer. The driller from Wainwright went down 300 feet to find good water, anther unexpected expense.

They built an outhouse and got used to using it before the weather turned cold.

"How about if I buy a couple of cows, Grandad?" asked Bud. "They could pasture out for the summer and if I bought pregnant ones, I could have a couple of calves in the spring." Bud knew there was money in beef. His uncles taught him how to keep the cattle healthy and marketable.

While Bud loved the farm, his older brother was less enamored. "I've had enough of this," Ted announced that fall. He'd been working hard all summer, tearing down the old house, lugging the lumber to the new place, helping with fences and construction and even the garden. Now the weather was closing in, the outhouse was cold in the morning and at night too. There was never any hot water to bathe in, there wasn't any TV, and there was no money.

"I'm going to the city. I'll get a job as an apprentice mechanic. I've already done one year. It's time for me to make some money." Ted found a job at Minns Motors Ltd., a British car dealer on the city's south side. Most of his salary went for food, lodging, and warm clothes. He was a frequent guest at his Aunt Phyllis's dinner table and I occasionally spent a weekend with Aunt Mary and Uncle Bert at the farm. They always welcomed my siblings and I warmly.

Years later I learned that my adolescent complaints to my cousins and their mother produced unexpected results. "She used to write letters to me," mom said, "letters telling me what to do, how to raise you kids, telling me that I was doing it all wrong." I can only imagine the letters and the responses. The relationship between Mary and Phyllis simmered and flared, probably with no thought of mutual support, assistance, or understanding. My siblings and I knew nothing of the letters. To us, Mary was another of the aunts and uncles who offered love and understanding to the city kids.

That fall, Pat and Bud and Rob rode the school bus for the first time in their lives. They tried to fit in with the kids who were used to driving tractors and milking cows but who had never seen a television or high-rise office tower, boys and girls who knew the price of oats and wheat and beef but had never watched television or dined in a nice restaurant.

Winter closed in and Bert was forced to stop work on the house. There was little money left for more renovating. Bert found a job in Wainwright, 18 miles (28 km) away. The winter was bitterly cold, and Mary worried as Bert drove back and forth to his night shift as a steam engineer.

"Well, there aren't any choices, Mary. We've had so many expenses we hadn't calculated on," said Bert, "and there's practically no work here. This isn't like Cooksville or Brampton, where there are lots of plants. That place in Wainwright is the only place where I can get a decent-paying job. There's no other way."

It was the coldest winter on record, with huge snowfalls. The drifts beside the road grew to eight and ten foot heights as the graders plowed a path for the school bus. Temperatures frequently dropped below -30° C. The Russell house had no furnace, only a wood and coal heater and a propane stove. On cold mornings, Mary sometimes lit the propane stove, then crawled back into bed to wait for the house to warm up. One day, the match burned out before the propane caught fire. There was no noise, no warning, before an explosion of unburned propane boomed through the little house. The dishes rattled on the cupboard shelves, and cutlery jumped in the drawers. A few glass jars, left too close to the edge of the pantry shelves, fell to the floor and broke. Particles of wood shaving insulation floated gently down from the rafters and landed on the freezer, the refrigerator, the record player and television, each of which sat blankly along the wall waiting for electricity.

After the initial shock, Beanie the dog ran in circles, barking at he knew not what. Mary and the children cowered in their beds for a few moments, too stunned to move. The explosion only became humorous years later.

In the spring they seeded 150 acres, built pig pens, and fenced the pasture land. They bought Ron's old John Deere™ tractor and borrowed a plow. The winter's outrageous snowfall had left plenty of moisture in the soil. The spring sun shone and warmed the redolent earth, and the grain sprouted readily, as did the garden vegetables. Bud's calves had become healthy, 1,000 lb. (454 kg) steers and heifers. By July there was a beautiful crop of wheat in the south field, taller than Bud's knees, headed out with big fat kernels atop each stalk.

"Look at it, Bert, isn't it beautiful? We'll be okay with this crop, won't we? We'll have enough money now, maybe you won't have to work in Wainwright this winter," Mary and Bert stood close together, watching as the breeze created waves across the thick green crop. Mary's dream had become a reality.

On the last weekend in July, Ted came home from the city as he usually did when his folks needed help. He and Bud went into town in the little Morris Minor™. They saw the black clouds building and were inside Carl Anquist's John Deere™ dealership when the storm hit. They watched in awe as the huge drops fell, driven by ferocious winds. The sky was blacker than black. The rain was like a wall of water.

"What's happening at home?" Ted shouted above the storm's raucous din. "We'd better get out there."

They turned the little car north and drove back out to the farm, down the now-muddy road where the water still sheeted off into Milburn's slough, up the hill along their grandparents' place. The fields were white, covered six inches deep in golf-ball sized hail stones. There were no leaves on the trees, even the bark had been stripped off. No green, no flowers, no sweet clover or even pigweed was visible. The brothers were speechless. Slowly, they drove the remaining quarter mile to their house. The yard was white. Not a blade of wheat remained standing in the field.

Inside the house, Mary held Pat as they sobbed together. Tears released the aftermath of fear, the crashing letdown after their frantic efforts to keep the storm out of the house. They'd held blankets and pillows over the windows, their ears unable to hear the shouting to one another over the horrible howling storm.

"We're finished," said Bert, his face ashen.

A prairie hailstorm is almost unbelievable in its violence and its focus. There can be a run of several hot days, where the sun beats down harshly and sucks up all the moisture from the land and the lakes. Each tiny drop of moisture becomes coated with dust – and as they gather together in the sky, a dark almost purple-black cloud forms. Within the thunderhead cloud, air currents swirl violently, tossing the bits of moisture upwards sometimes ten miles to where the air is cold. The hailstones that form may be as small as peas or as large as golf balls. Occasionally they reach baseball size.

The hailstones, usually driven by strong winds, create utter devastation. Vegetation cannot withstand such an onslaught. Cars, houses, roofs, and signs are ripped to shreds, or at the very least are left with large dents. The storms usually cut a narrow swath, seldom more than a quarter of a mile wide, and perhaps a couple of miles long.

Fifteen minutes after the hail has wreaked its havoc, the sun again shines brightly, the temperature rises to normal summer values, the sky clears – and the vegetation that has been pelted against the ground begins to rot. Within a day or two the putrid smell is pervasive, as it was a few days later, when the Russell family climbed into the truck and Ted's car.

Mary cried as they passed her parents' home. There was no point in stopping. Her parents had escaped to Edmonton for the day, driven away by the stench of rotting vegetation.

There are few things more devastating than a prairie hailstorm. Seldom more than a half-metre wide and perhaps a kilometer long, its toll is sudden, violent, and absolute. A few minutes earlier, the Russell's grain stood tall and strong. 1956.

Another view of the hailstorm that destroyed the Russell's crop.

1956

Hail storm at Irma –
worst in living memory killed
birds on sloughs - chickens etc.
Terrible thunder - Ivor heard it in Irma
but Mum + Dad did not hear the thunder
because of the roar & noise of the
hail storm.

Mary's description on the back of the photo.

They were back in Cooksville in four days. The children bunked with friends until September when they were able to get back into their old house. Bert and Ted found jobs. Once again, the electrical appliances worked. Mary busied herself re-making a home.

❧

IT'S HARD TO IMAGINE the devastation caused by such a hailstorm, the total destruction of a life, a plan, a dream in just five or ten minutes. We remember life by events, markers of significance or of trama. "Where were you when Kennedy was shot?" we ask one another. Or, in conversation with another Edmontonian, we'll say "Where were you when the 1987 tornado struck?" Our parents might have asked one another "Where were you when the bomb hit Nagasaki?" For every generation there is devastation, a tragedy beyond the scope of everyday imagination. So it is with hailstorms. The tears welled up and spilled from my cousin's eyes as he described the annihilation of his family's dream and its property, that long-ago day in July. Some memories never fade.

THE FALL COLOURS were glorious in southern Ontario that October – brilliant red sugar maples, bright yellow birches, almost maroon-coloured sumacs. Pat arrived home from school one day to find her home rearranged. "Oops, Mum and Dad must have had a fight," she thought. "All the furniture's been moved again. She always does that when she's mad at somebody." Pat seldom knew what caused her mother's distress.

Len's lease on the garage ended, and Bert regained the business. Ted completed his mechanic's apprenticeship at the garage. Bert often worked all evening, even on Saturday nights. The family had little social life, indeed, the children seldom had much time with their father. But on Sunday mornings, Mary or Pat often made toast and tea and carried it up to the big bedroom. The children climbed into bed to share breakfast with their parents. "Roll it up," was Rob's way of asking for jam on his toast and then to have it folded over. Mary took the children to church. Bert enjoyed a few peaceful hours alone.

WHILE MARY KEPT HOUSE, Bert focussed his energy on building his automotive business. All the children worked in the garage, or at the front end pumping gasoline, as they grew into adolescence. Soon Bud finished high school and was ready to take his place in the family business.

"Mum, I've already talked to Dad, I'm going to enroll in the apprenticeship program and get my mechanic's papers, and come work at the garage," said Bud, knowing his mother would be pleased that he wanted to work with Bert.

"Well," his mother chuckled, "you'll still have to help Pat sometimes when she needs time off from pumping gas on Saturdays." The pleasure she felt at having her second son come into the business was mixed with apprehension. The dissension between Ted and Bud always simmered, frequently flared.

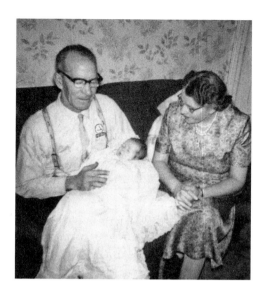

Ted and Ethel's first child, Lynn, born in February 1961, dressed in the same christening gown worn by her father and grandmother.

"How will they be able to work together?" Mary wondered, "I hope they don't argue in front of the customers."

Bert's pressures eased as his sons took on increasing responsibility for the business. Ted completed his auto mechanic's training; Bud soon followed the same route. The garage was busy.

Occasionally, Mary was able to persuade her husband to take an hour or two off for a picnic lunch and a drive. By the late '60's all Mary's children had left home: Ted and Ethel were married in May of 1960, Bud and Wendy in November of the same year, Pat and Fred were married in 1966. Rob went away to university.

The friction between Mary's two elder sons simmered only slightly below the surface. Ted got a job in his Uncle Len's machine shop in Brampton. In 1968 Bud took over the garage. Bert retired.

Mary and Bert bought a new home on Sharon Crescent, not far from the garage. Mary dreamed and re-designed, Bert hammered and nailed till they were both satisfied. In this new home, the kitchen was at the front. Mary could watch out over the neighbourhood while she cooked, just as her mother had done on the farm. Heavy red velvet draperies and off-white sheers covered the living room windows that overlooked the back yard. Mary's rose gardens encircled the house.

"OH, HOW ARE YOU, you found us alright. Now, come in here, you must be so tired, it's almost midnight," said Auntie Mary as my husband and I and our four daughters stumbled in. It was the July 1st long weekend, 1972. We hadn't considered running into unending lake-bound Toronto traffic when we scheduled our cross-country journey. We were all cranky with exhaustion when we finally reached Sharon Crescent. The welcome was so warm, Aunt Mary and Uncle Bert took us into their home, showed us to our rooms, and made tea and toast.

We showered off the grit we'd accumulated during our three-day camping trip from Edmonton, enroute to Nova Scotia. We relaxed and enjoyed being pampered.

"Would you like to see Niagara Falls?" asked Aunt Mary.

"Oh, wouldn't that be great, the girls have never seen the Falls." We would drive to Niagara Falls that afternoon, go underneath the falls dressed in bright yellow slickers, watch with awe as the water pounded over the rock and sprayed up on our glasses.

"Can we go barefoot?" asked one of my daughters.

"Of course you can go barefoot," Mary replied before I could say anything.

"Oh no, they can't," I said, determined that my children display correct behaviour, not look like western bumpkins – or get glass in their feet.

My aunt seemed so kind and loving, so ready to give and receive affection, so warm and genuine. And I always felt so guilty when I disagreed with her, or when my perceptions or opinions opposed hers.

But that day, we were grateful for the warmth of our welcome, and appreciated the chance to break our cross-Canada trip with a few days in a real house. "Thanks so much for having us," I said as we left the next day, with hugs all around. Auntie Mary and Uncle Bert had always been generous with their hugs.

Mary and Bert had more free time after Bert retired. Here they are with their daughter Pat and Mary's parents, at one of the then-popular drive-in restaurants. c1960.

ALMOST EVERY SUMMER after Bert retired, he and Mary went west. Sometimes they'd take a trip with Mary's parents. Other times they went to the mountains with Leo and Joyce or with Olive and George.

The news from the west in the late '70's was disturbing. Fred's lungs could not be kept clear of fluid. He'd been diagnosed with chronic bronchitis and emphysema, and his heart was aging. Mary could not believe her father had emphysema and needed a breathing apparatus.

Nellie's health also was deteriorating; her arthritis continued without remission. She was in constant pain, her fingers became increasingly crooked and her body shrank, changing her from the strong woman she'd been into a tiny, bent, almost weightless woman.

Mary's siblings telephoned when their father was hospitalized in the spring of 1978. Initially, they expected him to return home to Chacutenah Manor. Their expectations weren't fulfilled.

Mary didn't make it to her father's bedside before he died. She stayed in Irma afterwards to help pack her parents' things. Nellie did not want to stay in the Manor. She opted to live with Olive and George on their farm north of Edgerton. Mary and Olive sorted through the lifetime of collectibles, the copper kettle and the candlesticks, the few remaining crystal goblets their parents had brought from Wales in 1927, the cups and saucers, the pewter teapot with the strawberry on top and all the other things that had surrounded their parents. It was a difficult job.

Fred's funeral was only the first. Others would soon follow.

Bert wasn't feeling well throughout his father-in-law's funeral and the subsequent days at Irma. He left Mary to help move her mother, and flew back to Ontario alone. Ted picked his father up at the airport.

"Well, you're not looking so good there, Dad," said Ted, concerned and shocked at his father's appearance, "what can I do for you?"

"Nothing much," responded Bert. "I'll get to the doctor tomorrow." Within weeks, he was in the Mississauga Hospital, diagnosed with cancer in his liver and pancreas.

"Bert, I'll pray, we'll pray together, maybe we can beat it," said Mary as waves of panic and shock engulfed her. "Let me get you some tea, would you like some Welsh cakes, or some soup, how about some soup, it would make you feel better."

Nothing made him feel better. Mary watched helplessly as her husband grew weaker and sicker. Bert died on August 8th, 1978.

Mary never got used to being alone. Neither did she get used to losing her father. And in 1979, the first of the Thurston siblings died. Ivor, the youngest brother, succumbed to liver and pancreatic cancer, just as Mary's husband had done.

DEATH WASN'T THE ONLY DISASTER Mary had to face alone. Bert wasn't there to comfort her late in 1980 when she returned from her doctor's office. He had found a lump in one of her breasts. She received the biopsy results a few days later.

Mary and Bert's family gathered closely around following Bert's diagnosis of cancer in mid-1978. They're shown here on a sunny day in the backyard, with Pat and Rob in one photo, Ted and his wife Ethel in the other.

"Pat, it's cancer," she said, her eyes full of terror, the fear of a woman whose husband had succumbed to cancer only two years previously. "They've booked me for surgery."

"Mum it'll be alright, I know they'll get it all. And we'll take care of you, Mum, don't you worry," responded Pat.

It wasn't alright. There were problems with the surgery, the mastectomy didn't drain properly, and the wound became infected. Eventually it healed. Within a few months, Mary's solution to her lopsidedness was to have her other breast removed.

Mary was back in Alberta the following year for yet another family funeral. Mary and her siblings had watched as their mother's health diminished. Nellie died on April 25, 1981, three years less three days after Fred's death.

Mary and Olive consoled one another; the two sisters had drawn closer and closer as the years passed. They sorted their mother's possessions, decided who would receive the cups and saucers, the few crystal wine glasses remaining from the set brought from Wales, the pewter teapot with the strawberry on the lid, the picture of Caerau church where they'd been married, the momentos and souvenirs of a lifetime.

"Olive, I know it's God's will, but it's so terribly hard," said Mary, tears coursing down her cheeks, "first Dad, then Ivor, then Bert. And now Mum. It's so lonesome."

"You can come out and visit whenever you want to, you know, Mary," said Olive. "And stay as long as you want, we don't have a lot of excitement out here, but I think you'd be comfortable." The sharpness of their grief eased a little as they reached out to one another.

Mary returned home. She continued to live in the house she and Bert had so lovingly renovated. She attended church, tended her roses, and spent days with her daughter and grandchildren. Nothing helped.

"Ted, I can't go on, I can't live alone like this, in this great big house. The gardens are so much work. I just can't bear the silence. It's so empty without your father," said Mary. "I think I'll sell the house to Pat and Fred."

"What do Pat and Fred think?" asked Ted.

"Well, they think it's a good idea," responded his mother.

Pat and Fred bought the house and had an addition built on to give Mary a mother-in-law suite.

"Pat, I hope this works out alright for you. I just don't want to be alone yet," Mary said, quietly.

"Oh, Mom, you know it'll be fine. We've got space here, and we really like having you around, you know," answered Pat, "and Shawna really, really wants to share the bedroom with you."

Mary lived on at Sharon Crescent for ten years. Then, she chose to move into her own apartment. It would be the first time she'd ever lived alone.

"It's the coming home to an empty place, Jeannie, that's when I feel most alone," said Mary one day during a visit to Alberta in the mid-1980's. I'd been divorced myself by then, and had transitioned from life on an acreage to a walk-up apartment, then to my own house. I understood loneliness.

"I know, Auntie Mary, that instant of opening the door, knowing there's no-one to greet you or for you to greet – that's really tough, isn't it?" The emptiness of a home with no-one in it had never changed for me. "I always leave the radio on, so there'll be music playing when I open my door. Maybe that would be helpful."

"Perhaps," said Mary, doubtfully. Vulnerability surrounded her, a widow without a shield, an aging woman without protection.

❧

"MOM, HOW ARE YOU?" Rob's gentle voice, so much like his father's, was on the phone from the Philippines. It was spring, 1982. Rob had been in the Philippines for several months, working as a quality control inspector at a nuclear power plant under construction just outside Manila.

"What are you doing these days? Would you like to come over here for a while? I'd sure like to see you, and I've got a surprise – Jenny and I are getting married next month. Can you come over for the wedding?"

It was a welcome relief for Mary, a chance to get away from Toronto, and to spend time with her youngest son. He'd been working at off-shore jobs ever since he'd switched from x-raying humans to non-destructive industrial testing. Mary wondered if he would ever come back to Canada. The thought of a new daughter-in-law was a surprise.

The flight from Toronto to Manila was long and tiring, but on arrival it was easy to pick out her auburn-haired son. Rob was head and shoulders taller than the excited crowd of short, dark-haired Fillipino residents gathered around the exit, each one waiting to greet relatives returning from jobs abroad.

"Mom, it's good to see you. Let me take your bags. Meet Jenny, Jenny meet my mother," he said to the tiny, beautiful woman at his side.

"Oh, it is so good to meet you, Mom," said Jenny. "Welcome to the Philippines. This is a beautiful country, maybe it will be hot for you, but our house has fans. You will be fine, I hope. We will do our best to make you happy."

Mary stayed for several weeks. It wasn't the last time she would visit Rob and Jenny in a far-away land.

BACK AT HOME, Mary continued to spend much of her time with Pat and the grandchildren.

"I remember grandma baking a lot, she took care of us when my parents were busy, and she'd take us shopping at the mall. She said she liked doing that, she couldn't do it when she had a family so she enjoyed spending on us grandchildren. She was such a happy person, relaxed, casual, good to be around. If something broke or fell, she'd brush it off," recalls Pat's son Chad.

Ted and Ethel's daughter Cheryl remembers her grandmother travelling to the Holy Land and the Philippines, and to Grande Prairie after Cheryl and her husband moved there in 1981.

Right: Mary's youngest son, Rob, married Jenny Rapadas in the Phillipines on May 3, 1982. They welcomed Mary into their home and their lives.

Bottom: The 1985 family reunion: Phyllis, Ted, Olive, Len, Mary, Leo.

Mary visited with her siblings in Irma and Edgerton, was an enthusiastic participant in the first family reunion in 1985, wrote letters and made phone calls to her relatives in Alberta, reached out and offered her love to friends and family.

IN THE WINTER OF 1987, Rob bought his mother an airplane ticket to Thailand, where he was working at the time. Mary hadn't been feeling well, but she was anxious to see her son, her daughter-in-law and the children, Albert (A.J.) and Robert (Jamie); Jenna would not be born until three years later.

Again, Mary stayed for several weeks. She helped Jenny in the kitchen, played with the grandchildren, and basked in her son's attention.

Pat and Shawna collected Mary from the airport when she returned to Canada. Pat recalls looking at her mother and thinking: "She has cancer." Her words conveyed only concern, though, as she asked Mary about her pallor, the yellow tinge of her skin, her apparent fatigue.

"The women in Thailand are all like this," said Mary, "they told me they don't have enough protein in their diet." Pat was not so sure. She took Mary to her apartment, made sure there was food and that Mary was secure, then left her to again get used to the apartment.

A couple of months later, sometime in May, Mary appeared at Pat and Fred's house on Sharon Crescent. She'd been at her regular weekly bowling league when something unexplainable had happened. Mary was visibly shaken.

"What was it Mom?" asked Pat.

"I don't know, Pat, but it's horrible. Scary. I was in the washroom at the bowling alley. I got all mixed up. I didn't know where I was or why I was there," said Mary, her voice shaky and tears ready to spill from her eyes. "Someone helped me, she got me onto the bus, but Pat, nothing looked familiar. I thought I was lost. The bus driver helped me when I told him that I wanted to get here to Sharon Crescent. He even got out and helped me off the bus, and then he showed me how to get here."

It was easy to see Mary wasn't herself. "Come on, Mom, the doctor can see you right away," said Pat after she'd called the doctor's office. For the next few days, Mary stayed with Pat and Fred. Pat took her mother to the neurologist.

"No, she doesn't have Alzheimer's disease," he said, but he couldn't tell her what Mary did have. Pat took her mother to the oncologist.

"She has cancer in the top of her stomach and the bottom of her esophagus," was the diagnosis. "She must have surgery. It will give her a 50% chance of survival." There were no options. Mary's potassium levels were seriously below normal; she was hospitalized for observation and to restore her body's mineral balance. Her sister Olive flew in. There were complications, haemorrhages, and intensive care wards.

"No more surgery," Mary said.

She pulled through, was discharged and went home to Pat and Fred's. It was a long, hot summer. Water condensed and ran down the outsides of drinking glasses and the pitchers of lemonade and water. Perspiration dripped and drizzled all day and most of the night. Pat and Fred installed an air conditioning unit in the bedroom Mary and Shawna shared.

Mary never once complained.

Eventually the weather cooled. The maple leaves turned to red and the corn husks dried and yellowed in the fields. The neighbours decorated their front porches with corn stalks and scarecrows, orange pumpkins and brilliantly-coloured leaves.

Mary didn't get better. She told Pat and Fred one day that she didn't feel well. They called 911. The ambulance took Mary to hospital.

The oncologist greeted them and said privately to Pat, "You know your mother has bone cancer."

"No," Pat's brain shrieked silently. "No, that can't be true. She's my mother. . . no, this can't be happening to her." But it was.

"No, no, I didn't know," Pat said to the doctor. "None of us knew. She always took care of us. We'll take care of her."

Mary went home with Pat and Fred. She watched and took part in Christmas preparations, went to church every Sunday, and made

Christmas cake with Pat. She filled the freezer with rhubarb pies and apple pies, and butter tarts just like her own mother used to make.

MY COUSIN TED PHONED to let me know of his mother's condition. A few days later, Mom joined my sister and I for dinner with our brother Mike and his wife Donna.

"Mom, Ted told me that Mary's situation is really bad. They don't expect her to live much longer." I recounted Ted's phone call with difficulty.

Mom flew to Ontario a couple of weeks later.

"She told me she'd always been jealous," my mother told me. "I was so good in school, and then later I could afford to buy the kind of things she wanted, silk stockings and nice clothes. . ." Perhaps the reconciliation was mutual; it would be unusual for all the imperfection to be on one side.

My heart ached for these two women, each with her own strengths, each with her own weaknesses, each with her own need to love and be loved.

ALTHOUGH MARY kept her apartment, she never lived in it again for more than a few days at a time. It was handy, though, for her visitors, as a place for her siblings to stay when they came to see her. Ted and Molly came, Leo and Joyce, Olive and her daughter Linda and her two daughters. Winnie's daughter Ann and her husband Keith came. Phyllis's visit in January gave the two sisters an opportunity to address three-quarters-of-a-century-old hurts, the last chance for them to neutralize a lifetime of conflict. Mary's children and grandchildren were always around, ready to help their mother and grandmother, eager to do anything they could for her.

In mid-April, Mary was back in hospital. The pain-relief drugs caused hallucinations. During one such experience, Mary fell out of bed and badly injured her face. Her eyes were blackened and her nose and cheek bruised.

On Sunday, the minister visited and gave her communion. Her granddaughter Cheryl was with her. She watched and listened as her grandmother picked up Cheryl's hands in her own, held them gently, compared the softness and the wear, the colour and the scars. "How wonderful, the old and the new," she said. Her voice held both love and the wonder of life.

Mary was joyful, not afraid of death. Her doctor told Pat, "I've never seen anyone quite like this before."

"You look beautiful, Mom," said Pat, as she sat beside her mother, feeling and seeing the aura of peace that surrounded the woman who had become so frail and ill.

"Yes, and I'm going to die," responded Mary.

She slipped away on Mother's Day, May 14, 1989. Her ashes were interred at St. Peter's cemetery, Erindale, in Mississauga, Ontario.

CHAPTER 10

Phyllis

Phyllis, the most academic of the siblings. Driven to succeed.

A woman who selectively revealed her many facets.

Easily hurt. Aggressive, submissive, affectionate, reserved. My mother.

PHYLLIS ELLEN, the second Thurston daughter. Her middle name came from her mother, or so they thought at the time. She is shorter than her siblings, slender as a young woman but less so in mid- and later-life. She has a sharp nose, delicate skin, and snow-white hair that once was deep auburn. Even as kids we admired her long slender fingernails with the half-moon at each base, and we watched as she pulled her nail file from her purse and cleaned under each fingernail every time we got on a bus or into a car. My mother has always been well-groomed.

Phyllis Ellen is an exceptionally intelligent woman whose search for knowledge, love, approval, friendship, excitement, adventure, and belonging has never ceased. Her adolescence was interrupted by her family's emigration; years later she could remember every trail, every building, every relative in her beloved Wales. She never forgave her father for bringing her to Canada.

Widowed, she supported four children, alone, for eight years. She married a bachelor when her younger children were entering adolescence because "Colleen and Michael needed a father", and tried to become a farm wife in the most traditional sense.

She was a teacher whose students' drawings always showed her with an immense smile. She was a collector whose travel photographs filled slide carousels, albums, and boxes. For decades, her basement housed boxes and boxes of stuff, precious only to her.

Phyllis seldom accepted the status quo. She rebelled against her father's authority. Her demeanor is sometimes reticent, sometimes combative. Her ready smiles conceal a lifetime of unremedied hurts and injustices. Perhaps she also learned the adage that 'laugh and the world laughs with you, cry and you cry alone'.

She rejoiced, on her ninety-second birthday, when she received a two-year extension to her driver's license.

Daughter, sister, mother, wife, widow, grandmother and great-grandmother, teacher, community worker, volunteer.

"I always wanted more," my mother told me. "The others seemed satisfied with what they had, but I never was."

HOW ON EARTH can I write about my own mother?

"I wouldn't touch that one with a ten-foot pole," said my brother.

"Well, you'll just have to do it, Jeannie, just like you're doing for everybody else," said my sister. "You can do it."

How can I describe this woman who wanted so much but was often unable to bring her dreams to reality? Who left Wales as a teenager and maintained she never did love her new homeland as she had the old one – but who remained in Canada the rest of her life?

How can I be objective about a woman who mouthed the words of gender equality but who seldom heeded her daughters' views, who questioned her granddaughter's need to go to university ("She'll just go off and get married anyway, why waste the money?") but accepted her son's views and edicts without question. ("The girls sometimes had a rough time," he said. "She always handled me pretty much with kid gloves.") Phyllis only accepted assistance from a woman if there was no man available; she automatically assigned absolute validity to the things her (always male) doctor / bank manager / hair dresser / minister / store owner / principal / realtor / investment dealer said. After their parents separated, she told her grandsons (to my sister's chagrin) that they were now "the men of the house".

"What does that mean?" I wondered. "She ran her own household for years while we were kids, does she think she didn't do a good job? Does she believe her own daughter is incapable of owning a house and managing to be both parent and employee? Or is she just trying to make her grandsons feel important?" There never seemed to be an answer to these anomalies.

How can I offer my own perspective on her life, her relationships with her parents and her siblings, her husbands and her children? Was it her need to always want more that prevented her from accepting my sisters and I, our spouses and children, as we were and are?

How can I describe a woman I know only in bits, the small slices my sisters and I were allowed to see?

My daughters and I laughingly admit that we do, at least in part, become our mother, like it or not.

At times, I can hear her voice in my own, feel the unresolved hurt she experienced at her parents' hands in my own sense of injustice. Probably neither my mother nor I see ourselves as others see us. She brought joy, peace, warmth, and love to the lives of others. But for some of those who cared the most about her – her parents, her daughters, her sisters – she was and is an enigma, a woman who covers her feelings and her desires beneath a veneer of perfection, a woman whose parents were, themselves, unskilled in resolving disputes, addressing rivalries, or reaching negotiated peacefulness. They were also parents who, I suspect, seldom stood up for their non-conforming daughter. How, then, could she ever learn to love herself?

Every now and then, when my siblings and I were children, our mother let us leaf through her photograph albums. We especially loved the old one with black pages. The photographs inside were little square things, some sharp and clear, others blurry and indistinct. Four black photo corners held each photograph to its page.

There were a few photographs of Wales, taken by other people, before mum had her own camera. Those photos meant little to us at the time. We preferred to look at the Canadian photos of our mother. There she was, a beautiful, slender young woman on a picnic with a former fiancé, or beside the car she and her girlfriends drove to Seattle in the midst of the Depression. The album holds photographs of her siblings – Olive with a young lamb, Winnie in her overalls, Ivor on his horse. Pictures of the boys – she never called her brothers men even after they'd grown up – working with the threshing crews, or skating on a frozen slough, or on their own wedding day.

They are black and white photographs, the earlier ones taken with an old Kodak box camera, later ones with the bellows camera whose firm but gentle click signalled the shutter's operation. Important and not particularly significant events are recorded on film, portraits of parents and siblings and friends smiling for the camera. The photographs don't record domination or submission, defiance or acquiescence, discord or unity. Images of my people and their landscapes captured at a particular moment tell part of the story; what else was going on, what happened after the shutter clicked its final shot? Only in later years did I ask questions, probe into my mother's life, inquire about the things that had made her happy, and the experiences that were responsible for her pain, the anger that lurked just under the surface. I wish I'd asked the questions earlier.

The photographs provide a visual image of mum's life, the parts she is willing to share, the people and places she has been. As she ages, she tells me more of the day-to-day details, the colour parade, of her

The Girl Guide camp at Boverton, South Wales – Phyllis's last summer in Wales. The handwritten caption is so clear – Phyllis's writing remained the same throughout her life.

Phyllis and her fiancé Jack Rossiter in the summer of 1935, at the Thurston farm.

Right: Winnie, the only 'Canadian' child, in 1933. The girls are always pictured wearing dresses, not pants – and those were the days when everything was ironed using sadirons heated on the stove.

Bottom: The boys all rode horseback; two of Phyllis's brothers in about 1935, perhaps Ted and Len.

Phyllis was confirmed in the Anglican Church in Irma, 1929.

activities and her story. My siblings and I listen, fascinated, intrigued by the details.

❧

"THINK BACK to when you were a child, Mum," I asked. "What's your earliest memory?"

"Well, my goodness, you wouldn't know about chilblains[4], but anyone who grew up in England knew about them. Your feet and hands get cold and stay that way for a long time. We didn't have central heating, and the dampness made things so cold. My feet would get so sore. Chilblains are terribly painful things.

"That's my first memory, I think I would have been about three-years-old, we lived in St. Agnes then, and I remember Grandpa holding me on his lap in front of the fireplace rubbing my feet and crooning, 'There, there'. He knew how much those things hurt."

It was good to hear mum speak kindly of her father, a man she'd once told me was a stubborn, bigoted tyrant. He did not accept others, at least not as a young man. I can't imagine the hurt he must have caused when he accused mum of putting on airs. As grandchildren, we never saw that side of him. Perhaps he mellowed as he aged, as most of us have.

"He wasn't always kind and gentle like that. We kids were afraid of him. He'd come up those stairs at Welford Farm with his slipper in his hand, and oh boy he'd give it to us. He'd go to the boys' bedroom on one side of the stairs, I could hear him whacking them. And then he'd come over to the girls' room. He was really cruel sometimes."

"Let's talk about the places you lived, Mum. I know you remember Welford Farm, but do you remember the homes you lived in before that?"

"I can remember those places just as if we still lived there," mum said.

"I think I was about three or four when we lived at St. Agnes in Cornwall. The house was named Rosemundy Villa and it was on two levels; its garden was down below the road. And then we lived at Stone Farm in Sidford, where Uncle Leo was born. The house isn't there any more – I tried to find it on one of my trips over there, but it had been torn down. When we were in Cornwall, at Redruth, we lived on Stanwell Road. And remember, when I took you to England in 1981, we went to the house at Bickwell Valley, the one with the thatched roof. I loved that place, my bedroom was upstairs, it was so warm and snug. We moved around so much, I think that's why I never had an accent."

"How did you feel about moving around like that, Mum? Wasn't it a lot of moving for that time? I always thought that people in England were pretty stable – remember when we went to see the woman who babysat you in Sidmouth, I think it was, she still lived in the house she'd been in for seventy-five years. I remember being astonished that a person could live in one place for that long!"

"Children weren't consulted in those days, you just went where your parents took you and you didn't question what they did. We had to move to be close to grandpa's work, I guess, that was when he was cutting timber and they'd cut everything they could and then move on. He ran a portable lumber mill then for a contractor named Howell or Howells.

"I must have gone to school in St. Agnes, and in Sidmouth and Sidford. I can remember going to baby school, I was only about four-years-old, and we started to learn French when we were just little things – real Parisian French, not the stuff we learn here.

"Then we moved to Welford, about 1921 or 1922 I think. The house faced the sea, on the north side of the road to Barry, maybe four or five miles (8 km) from town. We all went to the Romilly Road School, the boys and the girls in separate sections, not mixed together the way we do here. The boys had men teachers, and the girls had women teachers. I guess we played together at recess or at noon, but we didn't have classes together."

"Did you like school, Mum?" I asked. My mother had always had high academic expectations of her own children. When I questioned her once about why she'd never praised the excellent marks my siblings and I obtained, she said I shouldn't need to be praised for something that I just ought to do.

"Oh, I loved school," she replied. "The worst day of my life was when Grandpa told me we were coming to Canada. I'd sat for a special exam, there were 2,000 of us girls and I came in second, second out of 2,000, can you imagine? And I won a four-year scholarship to go to the Barry County Girls' School[5]. I only used a year and a half of the scholarship. I wanted to stay there when they came to Canada, but Grandpa wouldn't hear of it. The rest of them didn't care: they could go to school anywhere. I never forgave him for that."

It's difficult to fully imagine the depth of anxiety, of betrayal, mum must have felt. Her situation then was so different to those we experience today in this country. We have ready access to good schools, to universities and colleges, institutions where we can excel academi-

Phyllis's friends at the Barry County Girls School, 1926; the daffodil symbol on the girls' uniforms signifies they belong to 'Cadoc House'

cally and form lifelong friendships and professional relationships. In the Wales of mum's childhood, attendance at a school such as the Barry County Girls' School provided an assured road to academic and social success.

"Mum," I said, wanting to divert her from the painful memories, "tell me what school was like. What did you study?"

"Oh, we took such interesting things. Geography and algebra, and English literature, and French. We learned Latin and Welsh too, and I'd started taking German lessons. And gym – I loved to climb ropes, I could shinny up those ropes faster than anyone else in my class. They said I was just like a monkey. We used to play field hockey, that was such a good game, fast too, and I could run. And tennis. I was a real athlete in those days.

"They taught us all sorts of fine arts and hand-work, painting, drawing. I was awarded a certificate from the Royal Society of Art Masters for a painting I did. Wish I still had it, but I guess it wasn't stored away safely.

"They taught us to embroider too, delicate work on beautiful fine fabric, cotton lawn I expect it was. The teachers all wore white blouses in school then, you know, and they'd wear fine cotton camisoles. Well, this one teacher liked my work so much, she used to have me do the embroidery for all her camisoles. Fine, fine little tiny stitches, some of it was cut-work, you know what that's like, a design in close-together stitches then a shape cut out of the middle. You had to be so careful not to cut the stitches.

"And I had a violin. I was taught to play it at school, not in a class but by myself in a little room. Oh, I loved that violin and I couldn't bring it with me to Canada, I had to leave it behind, Grandpa said there wasn't room for it. I brought practically nothing but a few clothes with me.

"At school, we all wore uniforms and we were divided into 'houses' – just like the boys and girls in the Harry Potter books the kids all read now. My house was Cadoc. Its emblem was a bright yellow daffodil. We wore a blue serge tunic with three pleats coming down from the yoke, a belt at our waist, and the daffodil emblem was sewn on the yoke. In the summer we wore a blouse made of a silk material we called 'Jap-shan', like shantung [a light shiny silk fabric] and in the winter we wore a green cashmere sweater – we called it a 'jersey' – long sleeves with a turned-down collar."

"So much sadness for her," I thought. "I wonder if she would have harboured such resentment if she'd been allowed a choice of coming to Canada then, or later. Or if her memories of the beautiful country and loving relatives would be different if she'd become an adult before coming to Canada. Or, possibly, if there had been a school here of the same calibre as the girls' school she attended over there."

Who knows what would have happened to Phyllis had she been allowed to remain in Wales. She was only thirteen-years-old. She became caught up in the thrill of the emigration venture, along with the rest of her siblings.

"We were so excited: no one in Wales knew anything about Canada, let alone Irma, the village closest to our new farm.

"I remember the sale we had, of all the household things. We'd had a sale in the fall of the farm stuff, the cattle and the dairy equipment. Then we had another sale in the spring, before we left.

"Grandpa asked me to keep the accounts, and I had a big ledger that I wrote everything down in, the price each item was sold for, maybe even who bought it. The beautiful things, china and glassware went for a song. We kept those accounts for years, then one day, I guess Grandpa was cleaning out his desk, and he tossed it out. I can't believe he'd do that, but he did." Her eyes and voice were sad.

"You and Aunt Mary stayed with your Uncle George and Auntie Marie in Caerau, didn't you, the night before you left Wales? And the rest of them all stayed with Uncle Bill and Aunt Bessie at Dinas Powys? I guess you must have re-connected on the train, because I know you caught your ship at Liverpool."

"I guess we must have, I don't really remember. But I remember a reporter taking our picture right on the train station platform. He was from the *Western Mail*. I wish I could get a copy of that photo."

"So would I, Mum. I tried when I was in Wales, but I wasn't successful: the microfilm with that photo has been lost."

My mother remembers the trip across the ocean, then the week or so it took to get to Irma, by train, from Halifax. And she remembers the dinner they ate that first night in Irma, at Mrs. Shaw's hotel.

"She was so kind, she opened up the dining room and fed us all. The train got in after the hotel's regular supper hour was over. But you know, she brought all kinds of food, meat and potatoes, and then she brought us each a little bowl of yellow kernels. We didn't know what it was, so Grandpa asked her. It was corn! We'd never eaten it before; in Wales we only used corn to feed the cattle and pigs. Grandpa didn't touch his, and he never did eat corn. He grew it for the rest of us, though, after he got used to the idea."

Once the family was settled into the little house up on the hill just north of Irma, Fred and Nellie put their children back into school. Nellie walked Phyllis and Ted, Len, Ron, and Leo to school that first day.

The Irma Public School was built in 1912, a wood frame building, with two rooms on the main floor and another room in the basement.

Grades one to nine were taught, with boys and girls together in the same room. Some students rode their horses and put them in the school's barn. Others walked every day, regardless of the weather or the frigid temperatures.

In 1921, the Irma High School opened, the first consolidated high school in Alberta. It brought together students from all the surrounding school districts, to study together in separate Grade 10 and 11 classes, later expanded to include Grade 12.

An annual event was the visit of the school superintendent, who arrived by train[6] at noon, spent the afternoon visiting the classrooms, then went on to Wainwright the next day.

"The school superintendent said he'd never heard anyone speak French as well as I did," Mum told me. Her remembered French was still good enough that she was able to help me with my French-language homework when I was in high school, a quarter-century later. But what good was excellent French, in a community where few if any other people spoke the language, and most people were focussed on simply making a living on their farms?

Phyllis graduated from high school at a time when earning a living at anything, farming included, was extremely difficult. Not only had the Depression plunged western Canada into the worst economic downturn of its history, but women were still subject to very limited career opportunities. Nursing was acceptable, teaching was possibly better but country schools didn't pay very well.

Most of the young farm women simply went to work on other farms and waited until a likely-looking young man came along to marry. Some girls went to one of the province's three agricultural colleges – the Vermilion School of Agriculture (VSA) was closest to Irma – where women's classes were held in home-making, sewing, canning and poultry-raising. Secretarial classes were added later, probably after the war.

Phyllis chose to become a teacher, and opted to take the one-year program at Camrose Normal School. At the time, there were three

Top: Camrose Normal School (CNS), about 1931; it was here that Phyllis learned to teach.

Right: Phyllis with her baby sister Winnie; perhaps Fred and Nellie took a day or two off from the farm to deliver Phyllis to the Crossley home in Camrose, where she boarded while she attended Normal School. 1931.

Normal Schools in Alberta – one each in Camrose, Calgary and Edmonton. It would be another decade before teacher training was fully transferred to the University of Alberta.

"Why did you go to Camrose, Mum?" I asked. "Why there rather than Edmonton? And how did you pay your fees?"

"I guess because it seemed closer than Edmonton, and it was a small town, not a city. Grandpa paid my fees, but I had to pay him back. And I had to pay my hospital bill too, as soon as I'd graduated."

"What hospital bill?"

"Well, I'd had my appendix taken out when I was in high school. I'd got sick in the night. Gran had to take me to the doctor in Irma, and he operated at the Viking hospital. Then I stayed with the principal in Irma afterwards, since I wasn't able to walk that distance from the farm, back and forth to school. I had to finish the year, of course. High school only went to Grade 11 in those days, then you could go to

Normal School. That's what I did. And I paid the hospital bill with my first few paychecks after I graduated from Normal School and started teaching."

I shook my head at the differences in both health care and in education from that time until more modern days. There was, and is, so much of mum's life that she's never really talked about. "Did you board out when you went to Camrose, or was there a residence?"

"You know my friend Edith Crossley, who lives in Edmonton now? Well, I boarded with her and her parents. Her father was in the Alberta Provincial Police[7], and the jail was at the back of the house! They were so good to me, he was just like a father, not harsh like Grandpa, but so kind."

Every now and again, my mother drops comments about "the time when the three of us women drove to Seattle" or "the week we drove that old Model-T Ford up to the Peace River country". Those trips must have taken place when she was at Normal School, or perhaps shortly after she graduated and began earning a salary. A battered old suitcase stored in Mum's basement holds photographs of the trips.

Mum's available cash and time for travelling were quickly and severely curtailed by the Depression. She poured all her energies into teaching. Both the monetary and the academic rewards were marginal.

A few parents in the rural school districts really wanted their children to learn. Other parents sent their children to school only because the law demanded attendance up to age fifteen, or completion of Grade 8, whichever came sooner. Although the federal government had carefully set aside land for schools, and the provincial government set the curriculum, achievement of excellence – or even a satisfactory passing grade – was up to the students and their parents.

On the prairies, school lands were identified with the initial survey. Sections 11 and 29 in each 36-section township were set aside as school lands. A typical rural school district drew its school population from an area measured four miles by four miles (6.5 km); the schoolhouse was built in the centre of the area.

Top:Phyllis and her friends in Seattle – young women from the prairies enjoying the simple pleasures of running water and lush gardens.

Bottom: Phyllis with her friend Anne, somewhere on the road between Irma and Seattle, Washington. Summer 1935.

This photo could easily be a picture of Phyllis's daughters Colleen or Maureen – even the gestures were inherited.

The rural schools were small – usually just one room, sometimes with a useable basement. Some schools had a small house, a 'teacherage', for the teacher to live in. Most of the time, however, the teacher boarded with one family after another, month by month, and part of her pay was the board she received.

There was usually a barn on the school property, and a boys' and a girls' outhouse. The schools had desks with folding seats, various sizes to fit children from age six to size big – a few children attended school beyond age fifteen, or were almost fully grown by then. There were blackboards, a water pail with a dipper[8] from which everyone drank, a washbasin and a slop bucket. The wash water was used by all or most of the children before being dumped into the slop bucket, to be poured out on the ground at the end of the school day. There was a teacher's desk and chair, and a stove that ate wood and returned little heat. The teacher's job consisted not only of teaching the children, but also of pumping water, lighting the fire before school started, making

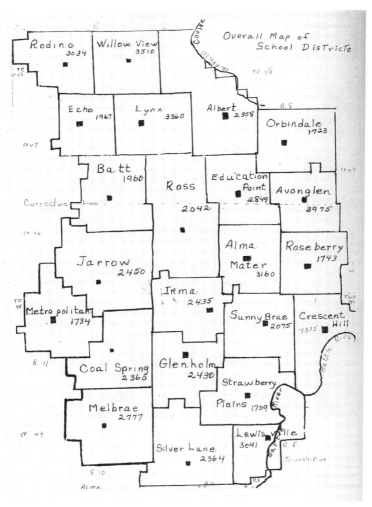

The school districts in the Irma area; Phyllis taught at Sunny Brae during the Depression years, Olive taught at Metropolitan School a decade later.

sure the barn was cleaned out and the outhouse holes received periodic doses of lye, also that someone was called in to clean the chimney pipes as needed.

Phyllis's responsibilities as a teacher would not be quite the same as were those of her teachers at the Barry County Girls' School. Still, Phyllis was lucky. Just as she graduated with her teaching certificate, the Sunny Brae school southeast of Irma reopened. The school had been closed for several years, because less than the requisite six school-age children lived in the district. Phyllis applied for the teacher's job, was hired, and taught there for five years. Her starting salary was $840.00 for ten months. A year or two later, as the Depression deepened and crop prices dropped, her salary also dropped – to $700.00 for the year.

It's hard to imagine a more dream-dashing situation for a beautiful young woman, nineteen-years-old, educated in a well-developed, structured system. In the rough prairie school, many parents wouldn't have known fine cotton lawn if they'd seen it. The separation between mum's youthful skill-development with a fine needle and the skills desired by the local parents could hardly have been greater. A yawning abyss loomed between Phyllis's ideals and the realities she faced at the Sunny Brae school.

Phyllis boarded with one family this year, another family the next year. One farm wife gave her jam sandwiches every day for lunch. She hated those sandwiches but didn't know how to say so.

"You didn't eat your sandwich?" queried the landlady.

"No, I wasn't hungry," Phyllis replied. Most weeks she heated canned soup on the pot-bellied stove and ate that for lunch.

The little school never had more than twenty students, distributed unevenly among grades one to nine. Phyllis was there every day, rain or shine, hot sun or bellowing blizzard.

"I remember one winter day, I froze my feet so badly they ached for months. It was -40° outside and there was a wind blowing, but I had to go to school. I was afraid that if I didn't, some of the students would show up and not be able to get inside.

Top:Sunny Brae school, about 1932 – a typical, clapboard country school, uninsulated, alone on the prairie.

Right: The children made their own fun – black poplars grow rapidly, withstand cold weather, and make great climbing trees.

Peek-a-boo!
Sunny Brae. 1933.

Phyllis and seven of her students at Sunny Brae, 1935.

"So I walked to school. I was boarding about a mile or so away. The snow had drifted in over the steps, but I got up to the door and unlocked it. There was some fire wood inside, and I chopped some kindling and got the fire started. It was as cold inside as it was outside, and I couldn't get the place warm before my feet froze. What a day that was. And you know, not one student showed up. I'd done all that for nothing."

Every Friday afternoon she walked the five miles west from Sunny Brae to Irma, stopped in at the restaurant for tea and to visit briefly with the owner, then marched the remaining three miles home. One of her brothers drove her back to her boarding house on Sunday night.

Phyllis took much of her salary home to her parents. With her first cheque, she bought them a radio, battery-operated, Viking brand, from the Eaton's catalogue. "Now you won't have to go to Barber's to hear the King's Christmas speech. And you'll be able to hear the grain prices when when they come on at noon, and the cattle prices, and the news."

Fred accepted the radio. His daughter recalls receiving minimal thanks for this gift she had thought would be so special. Neither does she remember any gratitude for the tax payments she made on her

Phyllis in winter, 1935 – she walked home every Friday after school.

father's coulee land – a quarter section of pasture land on the south side of the highway that would have been taken for non-payment of taxes if she hadn't paid the outstanding bill.

Phyllis occasionally took her younger sisters to the city on the train and bought them dresses and treats. She was able to set aside a little money for herself. By 1937, five years after graduating as a teacher, and with the Depression beating all economic sense out of the prairie's farmers, Phyllis resigned her position. It is unlikely there would have been a paying position that fall, anyway.

Before Phyllis handed in her resignation, she had agreed to work as a companion to the woman who ran the village café. They had become friends when Phyllis stopped in the café for tea on her Friday afternoon walks home from Sunny Brae. The young woman's husband had suffered a ruptured appendix and died suddenly, leaving her with five young children to raise. Phyllis accompanied the widow and her children to Vermilion.

"Why Vermilion, Mum?" I asked.

Phyllis with Max, 1937 – he didn't wear overalls.

"I don't know if she had family there, or what. That's where I was living when I met your father, you know. He travelled around the province as a salesman for Investor's Syndicate. He was so kind, well-dressed, and always a gentleman."

"He was a lot older than you, though." I waited, wondering what a beautiful, slender, popular young woman might have seen in Max Crozier, a man older than her own father.

"Well, he was. Maybe I was looking for a father figure, someone who would be kinder than Grandpa." Behind her eyes I could see the wheels of memory and analysis twining together.

Perhaps mum was also looking for a more genteel way of life than she could find on a farm or with a farmer. My father wore fine clothes, a three-piece suit with a tie and a nice shirt, a hat and overcoat when he went out. His wardrobe was a world apart from the overalls and boots worn by the Thurston boys. Rather, it was similar to the garb of the uncles in Wales, whose gardening attire was more formal than the prairie farmers' Sunday-go-to-church clothing.

Somehow, the widow from Irma got back on her feet; Mum doesn't remember the details. Phyllis moved to the city with Max, the man who would be my father. The Depression continued. There were few customers for Max's mutual funds. Unemployment Insurance had not yet been created. Poverty was rampant. The couple rented a one-room apartment somewhere near 107th Avenue and 100th Street, and set up housekeeping with a bed and a gas stove, a couple of chairs and a table.

My father must have left Investor's Syndicate, perhaps to find work that would keep him in the city. He sold the car, their only asset. The handsome, nearly-new vehicle brought $60.00.

Without a vehicle, they had to rely on a friend to take them to the hospital on December 27th, 1938 when the temperature was -60°F (-51°C) and an ice fog covered the city. Phyllis and Max's first daughter, Maureen Ellen, was born that day.

When I asked Mum to remember that time, she struggled to recall long-forgotten images. "I think I've purposely blocked out this memory," she mused. "It was such a traumatic time. We were desperately hard up. Sometimes we ate and sometimes we didn't. I had a very nice long, fine wool summer coat. We had no food, and I was trying to nurse a baby so I took my coat and called in at all the second-hand stores at the top of 101 Street to see if I could get something for it. Even when my asking price was 50 cents, I was not successful, and I returned home with my coat. I had it for many years, and I think I eventually cut it up to make children's clothes."

"It's hard to imagine the Depression, if you've never lived through one, Mum. What did Dad do, after he'd sold the car?"

"Oh, he tried all sorts of things. He even tried selling doormats made out of old car tires – the term 'recycle' hadn't even been invented then! Before the Depression, he'd been very successful selling men's wear, he and his brother Norman. There just weren't any jobs during the 1930's and nobody much was buying anything either. Food was cheap

– tomatoes were three for a quarter, tea 10¢ for a 2 ounce package, eggs were 10¢ a dozen, bologna 5¢ a pound. We ate so much macaroni and rice that for years I got ill at the sight of it.

"One day, I'd taken Maureen out for a walk, we'd moved by then, close to the Gyro [now Giovanni Caboto] Park on 95th Street north of 109th Avenue[9], close to St. Stephen's Anglican Church, where I went. I was expecting you, Jean, it must have been the spring, because you were born on May 2nd. And you know, the nuns from the convent beside St. Stephen's came to our place one day. They brought a whole layette, hand-knitted jackets, diapers, and things, and a beautiful pink satin bunting bag lined with blue flannelette. I just sat down and wept, I was so grateful.

"And then, when labour started, your dad had to get us all the way over to the University Hospital. He made some kind of a deal with a taxi driver, and then afterwards he walked all the way home. Or maybe he walked home the next day, because I lost so much blood giving birth to you – you were a 9 pound 13 ounce monster – they had to give me a transfusion. Your dad lay on one bed, and I lay on the other one, and they hooked us up together, and his blood ran right into me. Not like they do it now."

PHYLLIS AND MAX and we two little girls moved several times in the next three or four years. "One time we were evicted because we couldn't pay our rent. We didn't have much, but the landlady kept almost all our belongings," Mum told me.

In 1940 or perhaps 1941, they rented a suite, the top floor of a house, on 92nd Street and Cameron Avenue – an area in the river flats between the Dawson and Low Level bridges. The house had a balcony big enough for Maureen and I to ride our tricycle.

By then, the situation had changed in Edmonton. The country had already begun to recover from the Depression when World War II was declared in September of 1939. The city was soon full of servicemen. Canada was the headquarters for the Commonwealth Air Training

View from the house on Cameron Avenue, looking southeast over the Riverdale community – now a very desirable, inner-city community.

Maureen and I having tea on the balcony, not long before we moved to our own home.

Edmonton's city airport was transformed during World War II when it became a major component for training and for the U.S. Army and Air Force as they built the Alaska highway and the CANOL pipeline.

Program; hundreds of young student airmen developed their flying skills in the blue Alberta skies.

Americans also came by the thousands, servicemen and civilians. Edmonton was the jumping off and supply point for construction of the CANOL pipeline from Norman Wells, Northwest Territories to Whitehorse, Yukon Territory, built to provide an assured supply of oil for Americans in Alaska. Edmonton was also the supply point for men and materials building the Alaska Highway, 1500 miles (2,333 km) of military road pushed through the northern prairie, then boreal forest and muskeg from Dawson Creek, British Columbia to Big Delta, Alaska in response to the Japanese threat off the west coast.

Edmonton's housing market boomed. Max became a licensed real estate salesman. M. E. Crozier Agencies Ltd. prospered. Max rented office space from a Mr. Mann, whose Marcus Coal Company operated from a bright yellow, clapboard building on 104th Street, just south of 104th Avenue [Telus's red brick telephone building is now on the site]. After Mann's death, Max bought the coal company from the widow.

Phyllis, Max, Maureen and I in front of our house on 77th Avenue – our father always dressed like a gentleman.

"Oh look, Max, there's a coyote," Mum pointed to a duff-coloured animal in the field. We were on our regular Sunday drive – a time when Max dropped in to collect debts from his coal and wood clients, people who hadn't been able to pay for their fuel when they bought it. Those drives took us all over the city. Sometimes we stopped at the airport to watch the planes land and take off. Other times we visited friends who lived on an acreage in the area now known as Valleyview, just above the Valley Zoo – it was in one of those fields that we saw coyotes or deer.

"Your dad was so soft-hearted, you know. He'd let anybody with a sob story have coal, and then he'd have such a hard time collecting. There were thousands of dollars outstanding when he died."

While coal and wood sales were a difficult way to make a living, real estate sales were much more lucrative. Max was ready to buy when an appropriate property came on the market. He'd found a home for his family.

"It's just a shack," he told gran and grandpa, "but it's ours."

The house was on 77th Avenue between 89th and 91st Streets – the furthest block in the city's southeast to have water and power, telephone and sewer. My siblings and I grew up in that house, which sat on one lot and had two vacant lots on its west side and one on the east.

Phyllis and Max fixed up their house. They had running water installed, and kitchen cupboards. They ran a natural gas line into the previously coal- and wood-burning stove and put a gas-fired heater into the living room. Within a few years, they raised the house and poured a foundation and basement floor, then built a bedroom downstairs.

Our family expanded: Colleen was born in 1946 and Michael in 1948. Mum's albums hold images of Maureen and I with our young siblings, Colleen as a curly-haired child with dimpled cheeks, Mike a very chunky little boy with coarse auburn hair.

"I almost died when Michael was born. I'd carried a basket of laundry upstairs - your Dad told me not to but I thought I could. Michael was born six weeks early, he was so tiny. Not like he is now! And he had that red birthmark on his leg, remember? The doctor said if it ruptured, Michael could bleed to death. I had to take him in for several treatments when he was still a baby."

We lived a normal life – our father went to work every day; our mother stayed home and took care of us and the household. She made all our clothes, baked bread and pies, and cooked delicious and wholesome meals of meat and potatoes and vegetables.

On the very coldest days of the winter, our father drove us to school in his old Buick™. We walked home, or took the bus. Sometimes the smell of fresh bread or of slow-cooked beef stew wafted our way as we neared home.

Max was home every evening. Mum changed her clothes before her husband got home, brushed her hair and put on a clean apron. She always had supper ready for him, sometimes with us kids already fed. She would mix an Old Fashioned for him, and he would sit on his chair in the kitchen, talking as mum set the table.

Top:Curly-haired Colleen on our front lawn, 1947.

Bottom: Mike, born prematurely but who soon grew into a sturdy little boy, 1949.

Mum and dad at a Realtors' Convention in Calgary, 1949 – one of the few times our parents went away without us. Mum is in front, right centre, wearing a long coat with a fur collar; dad is on her left.

Mum never wore slacks in those days. She sewed and wore cotton housedresses, covered by a full-front apron, just like her mother's. Mum's hair was a deep auburn colour, long and shiny; kept in braids twined around her head.

"You had such beautiful hair, Mum. Remember how we used to like brushing it for you? You'd sit on that little leather stool and we'd close the blinds, then Maureen and I would brush and brush, and watch as the static electricity made sparks fly!"

" I know you used to like brushing it, but that hair gave me such a headache. It was so heavy. Your dad didn't want me to cut my hair, though, so I kept it long for him."

We were practically never left with a babysitter. "We'll have time to travel when they grow up," our father said. The only time I remember my parents leaving us was in about 1947, when they went to a real

Our old Buick outside a cabin in the mountains on one of our two family vacations.

Here are Maureen, Colleen and I with our father at Yoho National Park, about 1949.

estate convention in Calgary. Gran came and stayed with us, at our house. I remember that weekend as such a treat, although the details of what we did are lost.

We took two family vacations.

In the summer of 1949 we drove to Banff and Jasper and out to Radium Hot Springs. My brother was a baby then, and spent most of the time in an ingenious hammock slung behind the front seat. The ropes at each end of the hammock were tied to a piece of right-angled sheet metal inserted into the window slot on either side of the car. Seat belts were not to be invented for another thirty-some years.

When we arrived home, our father went to the Blue Cross Animal Hospital to retrieve Cookie, our pudgy Border collie whose ears could detect the noise of a candy wrapper from a hundred yards away. Dad returned alone, his shoulders sagging and his head bowed. "The vet said Cookie thought we'd abandoned her, she stopped eating and just died," he told us. There was no longer any joy in our holiday.

The next year, we took a more extensive vacation, still in our old 1938 Buick. We drove the Big Bend highway west through the mountains to the coast, took the ferry to Vancouver Island (I had tonsillitis again and couldn't go out on deck), drove down through Washington State and to Bonner's Ferry in Idaho, through the Crowsnest Pass and home to Edmonton. I remember the ferns along the Big Bend highway[10], the many stops on hills and desert areas to let the over-heating old Buick cool down, Victoria's Butchart Gardens and the Grand Coulee Dam.

My mother, on the other hand, remembers Golden, British Columbia: "...before we arrived at Golden, going through the Kicking Horse Pass, we had the most awful experience. The road allowance was carved out of the mountainside – a one lane road with an occasional place to meet oncoming cars. In some places, where the road could not be carved from the mountainside, whole trees were pushed into holes drilled in the rock – horizontally – and cars passed over them. There were no guard rails. On the outside there was a drop of hundreds of feet down to the Kicking Horse River, and I said that I would never go that way again. I was so terrified. I never did, until many years later when a proper road had been built."

We didn't know that trip would be our last.

Back home again, the peas and beans were waiting. My mother had grown up with gardening. My father, on the other hand, probably had not – he'd come from a hotel-owning family, business people, not farmers. He learned the intricacies of planting and watering, hoeing and hilling, weeding and thinning after we moved into our house on 77th Avenue.

My parents sold the furthest west lot in our property in about 1948, and the lot east of our house about a year later. The remaining lot was where we grew carrots and potatoes, peas and beans and beets and cucumbers and cabbage. My father even tried growing peanuts one year. Mum canned everything, jars and jars of vegetables. She made pickles – dill, mustard, sweet mixed, and even pickled onions. She made jams and jellies from the raspberries in our back yard, Concord grapes and Damson plums from British Columbia. She bought and canned fruit, peaches and pears and apricots and prune plums. No saskatoons were ever canned or made into jam at our house.

We had a comfortable home, food on the table, clothes that fit, a car, whiskey and Angostura bitters in the corner cabinet, and enough money to pay the bills and to indulge in an occasional ice cream cone. We were all healthy, my older sister and I were doing well in school, our younger sister was a sturdy child and our brother a healthy toddler. Then disaster struck.

In November of 1950, my father's car was hit, head-on, by a truck on the old one-way bridge just outside Fort Saskatchewan, a few miles northeast of Edmonton, where he had shown a property to a client.

The client wasn't injured. My father suffered a broken leg, lacerations and bruises and cuts. He was no longer a young man – he'd been born in 1879.

After he was released from hospital, he limped about the house on crutches, hauled his heavy plaster-of-paris cast as best he could, tried to recover, railed against the salt substitute he used when regular salt caused fluid retention. That was 1951, and the best medical doctors still prescribed long bedrest for almost every ailment – measles, colds, childbirth, and broken bones.

His heart began to suffer. It gave up in the middle of the night on March 28, 1951. He was seventy-one years, ten months and thirteen days old when he died, although we kids didn't know his age then.

My mother was a widow, not yet thirty-eight-years-old. We children were fatherless.

My Aunt Winnie was there that night. She'd been boarding with us for a while, and I remember her taking us to the bedroom in the basement. "I didn't want you to see the undertaker come," she told me years later.

My siblings and I didn't go to the funeral. Instead, we stayed with the neighbour across the street and went home after our father's body was buried in the city's 107th Avenue cemetery. Gran and grandpa and our aunts and uncles gathered in the living room, silent and sad. Mum was in the bedroom, the front one right off the living room. Grief-stricken, she lay alone on the bed that had been hers and our dad's. We had never before heard our mother cry.

"I kissed him," she sobbed. "He was so cold."

Maybe no-one knew what to say to us. We certainly couldn't voice our fears. How could we ask who would take care of us? Who could tell us what our lives would be like? My sisters and brother and I remained silent, isolated in separate tents of grief, enveloped in voiceless confusion.

We'd lost our father. The person mum dressed up for every day before he arrived home for dinner. The man who sat in his chair beside the stove and sipped his daily Old Fashioned while he and mum discussed the day's activities. We'd lost the man who owned and drove the car. The father who cooked Sunday breakfast of sausages and eggs and toast and coffee in that funny two-tiered Silex coffee pot. The fisherman who cut the anglers' fly pictures from his Old Gold cigarette packages, and fastened them into a small black album.

We lost our choice of eyeglasses – provincial Mother's Allowance would only pay for the cheapest, ugly, pink plastic frames. No longer could we choose which firecrackers to buy for the May 24th and July 1st holidays – there were no more firecrackers for any occasion. We lost the smell of home-baked bread as it wafted toward us after school on cold winter days, the delicious scent of stew when mum cooked it in the big Dutch oven on top of the stove. There were no more Sunday drives in the country or trips to watch the planes land and take off at Blatchford Field.

Our mother didn't discuss her loss.

Neither did she discuss our finances.

"You won't be able to take dancing lessons any more," she told me. That change was only one of many. I later learned there was no life insurance, no money, and little hope of collecting the outstanding debts.

Within a couple of months, mum started work at the provincial Department of Education Exams Branch. Her pay was bottom-of-the-barrel, entry level, far less than was needed to support a woman and four children. My older sister babysat most weekend evenings, as – within a couple of years – did I. The postwar baby boom was on and the neighborhood was full of young families. Half our babysitting pay went into the kitty, theoretically for extra treats, realistically to buy necessities such as shoes for our growing brother.

I can only imagine the stresses life held for our mother in those days. A woman suddenly widowed, four young children to support, no life insurance, her only assets a bit of property. No money, no time to grieve, bills to pay, food to buy, no time, no freedom, no future.

Our neighbour, Mrs. Brown, took care of Colleen and Michael until I got home from school. The Rotary Club brought a hamper of food at Christmas time, a strong wooden box with carved-out hand-holds, filled with canned vegetables and a Christmas pudding, a bag of Mandarin oranges, potatoes, and a turkey. My brother still has one of the box ends, preserved in a shadow box frame, complete with a plaque that declares 'Never Forget'. My sister remembers that in those years, "You were the one, Jeannie, who handed out kisses and hugs, band-aids and cookies."

The only assets mum had were the house and its two lots. She sold one-half of the remaining vacant lot in the early 1950's so she and our western neighbour could each have a decent-sized piece of land – the lots were only 33' (10 m) wide. Then she sold the garage to the same neighbour, since we no longer had a car. He hauled it over to his side of the lot line. The money was used to buy our first refrigerator, a natural gas-powered Norge, a replacement for our old icebox.

WITHIN A YEAR of our father's death, mum moved from the Exams Branch to the Correspondence School Branch, housed in a red brick building on 122nd Street and 104th Avenue. It was an hour's bus ride each way from our house. She left home at 7:30 a.m. and got back at 5:30 p.m. On those nights when she cashiered at the Roxy Theatre on 124th Street, two or three times a week, she would not get home until 10:30 p.m. or even later.

Maureen worked at the Army & Navy Department Store part-time, she and I babysat, and we both delivered flyers – a job I hated passionately.

Life as a single mother was at least as difficult then as it is now. Parent-child conflicts populated our household.

"No, you're not wearing lipstick, Maureen, you're not old enough." Angry voices again, mother and daughter conflict. My brilliant sister, who had been promoted from Grade 4 into Grade 6 without doing Grade 5, dropped out of school in the middle of Grade 11, and immediately left home. She was just fifteen years old.

Maureen seldom found an easy way to do things. Her behaviour was confrontational, her social skills undeveloped. Why couldn't she just have put her lipstick on when she got to school and take it off again before mum saw it? "She wouldn't cuddle, even when she was a baby," Mum told me years later.

"I remember your sister," said my school counsellor when I was about thirteen. "Her written work was absolutely superb, but socially she just couldn't seem to get along."

Years later, long after I'd become an adult and turned to counselling, myself, I learned that it's common for one person in a family to carry an entire family's load of dysfunctionality. Was that my older sister's role, to bear the brunt of the whole family's problems? Had it also been my mother's role, in her own family, a generation earlier? So much to think about, so many issues left ragged, untended and raw.

Although there was one less mouth to feed after Maureen moved out, mum's pay at the Correspondence Branch was still barely enough to go around. And, I suspect, mum was hugely bored with the work of a clerk. She wanted more and better.

The first baby boom children entered school in 1952. Within a year or two, they crowded the classrooms. New schools were built, especially in areas such as ours. Teachers were in short supply but mum's Camrose training did not meet 1950's standards. In desperation, the University of Alberta developed a six-week upgrading session in summer school. Mum leapt at the chance, and spent the summer of 1954 in school. I have no idea how she found the money to keep food on our table while she attended university and put in her first month on the job.

For six weeks, she got up at 5:00 a.m., had a hurried breakfast, reviewed her day's assignment, and caught the bus to university for 8 o'clock classes. We took care of ourselves. When mum arrived home, she was faced with a bounty of garden produce as well as her daily class assignments.

The beautiful black-loamed garden grew magnificently that year. It produced peas by the washtub-full, beans enough to burn, potatoes and carrots and beets and flowers. More than once, my siblings and I shelled peas till bed-time. Then Mum filled jar after jar with peas or carrots or beets, filled the jars with boiling water and a bit of salt, and plunged them into boiling water for the requisite three-hour sterilization period. While the vegetables boiled, Mum did her homework.

Armed with her new diploma, but fearful after her years away from the classroom, Phyllis sought a position with the Edmonton Public School Board.

"Now, you'll be just fine," encouraged the superintendent, "some of our best teachers are women who have taken time out to raise a family. They understand what children need. I'll put you in a school close to home."

And that's what he did. Phyllis was assigned to the staff of the new Avonmore school – except that the school hadn't yet been built. All the Avonmore students, and their teachers, were housed in the King Edward Park (now named Donnan) school on 78th Avenue and 87th Street. The Avonmore students went to school in the afternoon, the King Edward Park students attended in the morning. Finally, shortly before Christmas, the Avonmore School was finished. Phyllis marched her Grade 1 students to their new school, six blocks away. Each child carried his or her books and scribblers, pencils and erasers. Along the sidewalk they marched, in pairs, excitement and trepidation mixed together as they began another journey.

In the meantime, and in addition to the rigours of re-entering the classroom, Phyllis attempted to continue her education by correspondence, encouraged by her summer school instructors. It was too much.

"Here again, my ambitions were thwarted. If it hadn't been for you kids, I would have gone on to get an education degree. But I couldn't do it, it was just too much to teach all day, take care of you, and go to university at the same time. So I taught the same grades, with the same number of children, as the other teachers, but my pay was just a fraction of what the others made."

PHYLLIS TAUGHT Grade 1 or Grade 2, sometimes a combined Grade 1/2, usually with thirty or so little ones. In good weather, she rode her bicycle to school, a rust-pocked old black thing with a basket on the front in which she carried all her teacher's stuff.

It was the embarrassment of all embarrassments – my mother, a teacher, a woman who was supposed to be proper, she who had always made sure her children followed the rules, who was overly (we thought) concerned with what the neighbours would think, riding a bicycle, her skirt flying around her knees. Please. I was fourteen.

The Avonmore teachers didn't seem to think their bicycle-riding associate was particularly odd. They were a close-knit bunch, Helen Young, Gerry Grover, Cob Corneliuson as principal, Annie Roberts as vice-principal, several others. They taught together and laughed together. And they partied at our house – it was the era of party games, get down-on-the-floor push-the-egg-with-your-nose races, or clasp-the-wiener-between-your-knees-as-you-run-across-the-room competitions. Someone would be declared the winner, and they'd all collapse with laughter.

"At last," I thought then and still believe the truth of it now, "my mother has found a group of people with whom she fits, people with similar interests, similar education, a like-minded desire to enjoy life." Those associations continued, even after mum left Avonmore School – several of the Avonmore crowd attended Phyllis's seventy-fifth birthday party, and appeared again to celebrate her ninetieth birthday.

There were non-school friends in Mum's life too. Occasionally, a single man entered her life. My favourite was probably A. K. Olive, father of Mum's associate from the Correspondence Branch. He was well-known in the province as the gentleman who founded and managed the Alberta Treasury Branch, the provincially-chartered bank established in the 1930's to provide financial support when the federally-chartered banks refused to issue mortgages or loans to Alberta farmers.

He was a widower and he had a heart condition. He came for dinner occasionally, including one September day in the mid-1950's. It was mum's birthday, and I'd made her a cake. With lots of candles. The right number for her forty-something age.

"What have you done? What are all those candles for? There's far more candles there than I need." Her anger surprised me.

"Why is she so mad?" I wondered with early-teen naivete. I hadn't meant to do anything wrong or hurtful. "That's the right number."

Mr. Olive (for we never called him anything else) and Mum had planned to marry, she told me several years later. A midnight phone call signalled the end of that dream. The sudden heart attack had killed him almost instantly. Phyllis put on a brave face and went to school as usual in the morning, the ultimate in the stiff upper lip philosophy. Another round of thwarted dreams.

A COUPLE OF YEARS WENT BY, Phyllis continued to teach, we kids grew into adolescence. I made my way through high school. I began to worry about my mother's future, what she would do after I, then my younger sister and brother grew up and left home. Mum, of course, was pretty old – she must have been all of forty-four or so! And then... a new man began to appear at our house for supper, or to take our mother to a movie...

On one of her visits home to Irma, Mum had run into Jim Craig, a former neighbour. Mum remembered him as the young man who often stopped to give her and her siblings a ride to or from Irma when she was a girl.

"I didn't know him very well then, of course. I was so shy, he'd stop and I would just get in and sit in the back of the wagon while he drove the horses.

"His father was a crackerjack carpenter," Mum said. "He homesteaded that land north of us at Education Point about 1908. He used to leave his wife and children up there alone for months on end. He spent a year in Edmonton working on the new Alberta legislature building." Mum shook her head as she told the story.

"Jimmy was the only son, he had three sisters, but his father put him in charge of the farm when he turned thirteen. He was kept out of school to plow and to harrow, sow the crops and cut the hay, regardless of the truant officer's displeasure. There was just no time in his parents' thinking for higher learning, or for baseball (the joy of most prairie farm boys), for games or socializing."

Jimmy never did return to school. He farmed, his sisters attended school, his father did carpentry, his mother kept house. When the girls reached high school age, around 1934, the family moved closer to town, onto a quarter section about a mile and a half north of town. The new farm was right across the road and a quarter mile south of the Thurston farm home.

The Craig sisters grew up and left home to work or to marry. The parents moved into town. Jim stayed on the farm and raised grain – hard western wheat, golden oats, long-bearded barley, frothy canola, and sometimes rye. He didn't raise cattle or sheep, chickens or pigs. Why would a bachelor need livestock? Rather than spending his winters alone on the farm, Jimmy went to Edmonton and spent his days stacking and handling lumber for the Monarch Lumber Co. Ltd.

The winter nights in central Alberta are long, and the life of a bachelor can be lonely – as can the life of a widow. Jim welcomed some companionship when he had finished his days at the lumber yard. No doubt he also enjoyed mum's cooking – her pies are the best. Jim became a frequent visitor at our house.

Television was still pretty new in Edmonton, and our budget didn't stretch to a TV set. Jim brought his TV to our house. Mike and Colleen watched Lassie and Rin-Tin-Tin, The Lone Ranger and Zorro. Soon Jim became as permanent a fixture as the television, except that he went home at night.

"Jean, Colleen, Michael (Mum never, ever called my brother Mike), come downstairs, I want to tell you something." Mum preceded us down the basement stairs, into the bedroom, and sat us down on the beds. "Jim has asked me to marry him, and I've accepted him. What do you think of that?"

I don't actually know how Colleen and Mike felt at the time, although I suspect they simply believed they had no choice. I was happy for mum, glad that she'd found someone to share her life with, relieved that she wouldn't be growing old alone, certain she would have financial and social security with Jim. I had some reservations – Jim had never married, never needed to develop parenting skills, his education and interests were very different than Mum's. I assumed they'd work it all out. In the meantime, I was planning my own wedding, to take place in the spring of 1959.

I wonder, now, why mum and Jim didn't tell us, together, abuot their marriage plans. Surely they didn't think it would be a surprise. Neither, I'm sure, did mum consider the similarity, between her decision to marry Jim and move herself and her children to Irma, with her father's decision to move from one country to another and to take her and her siblings along.

On July 11, 1959, Mum and Jim Craig were married. Their friends Edith Wiltse and Don MacKay witnessed the ceremony. Only my siblings – thirteen-year-old Colleen and eleven-year-old Michael – and I, along with Edith's husband Jack, were invited to the ceremony and to share the wedding feast at the Corona Hotel. Forty-six year old Jim had acquired a wife, three daughters, a son-in-law (I had married in May and he was working out of town at the time of mum's wedding) and a son.

"Not bad for a prairie bachelor," I told him. He laughed. Jim had always been one of gran's favourites.

Mum, Colleen, and Michael moved into Jim's little wooden house, the one his parents had built several decades earlier. Jim had been living mostly in the back part – the kitchen and the bedroom. The living room had made a fine storeroom for firewood and the front bedroom for other stuff. There was no power, no running water, and the toilet was in that little house down the way. Colleen and Mike went to school on the bus. Mum raised chickens, Jim bought and raised cattle. The farm became a year-round operation.

Mike and Colleen, on the other hand, wanted horses to ride. Failing that, they rode the cattle – but only when their stepfather was out of sight.

Mum and Jim Craig were married July 11, 1959; here they cut their wedding cake, with their attendants, Don McKay and Edith Wiltse.

Mum again became a full-time housewife. She and Jim built a new home in 1964, a bungalow with a real bathroom, electric lights, a natural gas stove, and plenty of room. Mum baked pies and cakes, cookies and squares. She roasted beef and chicken, canned and froze fruits and vegetables, made jars and jars of jam and jelly. She joined the Women's Institute, the Anglican Church Women, and the Order of the Eastern Star. She sewed clothes and curtains, mended Jim's denim overalls and darned his woollen socks, learned basketry and photography, refinished furniture and headed up the committee that produced *Down Memory Lane*[11].

Mum was home again to her family. Her brother Ron lived a mile south, her parents were across the road and up a quarter mile, her sister Winnie was another mile north, their brother Ted lived half-a-mile past Winnie's. Brothers and sisters, spouses and children, more than twenty Thurston family members lived within a five-mile stretch. Their sister Olive lived forty miles east and Leo, their minister brother, occupied the rectory in several Alberta parishes. Len and Mary had struck out for Ontario in the 1930's.

The farmhouse in mid-winter, hoar frost on the trees and the pale prairie sunshine casting shadows over the snow.

My first daughter, Jennifer, was born in 1960, and was soon joined by three sisters (Joanne, Beth, and Kate) as well as David, my husband's son from his first marriage. They were curious about the cattle, the pigs, and the chickens, the dog and the barn cats.

We tried to get down to the farm for special occasions, for birthdays and anniversaries, sometimes just to visit.

"Now, don't let the children run out there and shout," Mum ordered during one of our visits to the farm. "The cows will get scared and run through the fence."

The cattle seldom saw children and were as curious about my youngsters as they were about the cattle. We stood on the back step and gazed at the cattle as they bunched up against the fence.

"Can I feed the chickens, Gran?" asked one of my girls.

"No, you hadn't better go in the chicken house. Colleen will take care of the eggs.

"I guess you could put these crusts of bread in the dog's dish. Don't try to play with her, though, she's not used to children and she might bite.

"Those are barn cats, now. They're not used to kids. You'll never be able to catch them, and if you did, they'd just scratch you.

"We'll have some tea in a few minutes, and some cookies. You'd like that, wouldn't you?"

❧

YEARS LATER, I queried mum about the thirty-five years or so she'd spent on the farm.

"What did you like about it, Mum? It was such a huge change for you, after living in the city for twenty years, the services there and your friends."

"Well, there's something about farm life that can never be equalled. I could wander around dressed as I pleased, sit outside and listen to the birds sing, watch the pheasants as they picked up grain near the back door, hear the coyotes howl at night, and gaze at the brilliant display of Northern Lights."

Mum chatted about her social life in the country, the associations she belonged to, friends and neighbours in the community.

Although she maintained her love for the farm, perhaps she found the days alone too long, the isolation too lonely. Whatever the reasons, her decision to retire from teaching when she and Jim were married was about to be revised.

Donald Gunn, mum's good friend, was principal of the Irma School. Its students are bussed in from all the former local school districts for miles around. Some of them spend an hour or more on the bus, each way, every day. The Irma School accommodates students from kindergarten to Grade 12.

"Phyllis, I need a teacher, a good one, like you. I thought we had all the teachers we needed, but I've just had a resignation and I don't know where to turn. I know I said I'd never ask you to teach full time, but you know, those children need someone like you, a motherly person who'll make them work hard but who will love them at the same time."

Donald had been a good teacher. He was a good principal. And he was a very persuasive man.

"Well, I'll have to talk it over with Jimmy, Donald. I don't know how he'd like having to get his own dinner. I guess I could get a plate ready for him so all he'd have to do would be to warm it up. He'd probably like me to have real money coming in! I'll talk to him, Donald. When do you need to know?"

"Well, the sooner the better..."

Mum was happy again. She taught in Irma for three years.

Then there was a problem at Albert, the last remaining district school, 15 miles (24 km) north. Mum agreed to take on the school and its multiple grades. In winter, the road was icy, sometimes with black ice that couldn't be seen until the car was upon it, slithering and sliding, closer and closer to the ditch. Mum drove white-knuckled, aware that the houses were at least a mile apart and the road was not well-travelled. She always carried a candle and a chocolate bar or two, blankets and heavy clothes, just in case. Cell phones would not come into existence for another twenty-five years.

For ten years after the Albert experience, Mum drove the eighteen miles (28 km) back and forth to Wainwright, five days a week. Surrounded by darkness both in the morning and at night, sometimes with snow blowing, sometimes with ice on the highway, she piloted her car back and forth, back and forth. She covered one hundred and eighty miles (290 km) in a week, over 5,000 miles (8,000 km) in a year, over 50,000 miles (80,000 km) in a decade to teach Wainwright's grade four children. And they loved her for it.

"Hi there Mrs. Craig, how are ya? Yep, this is my little girl, I've got two more of 'em at home, and a boy too!" The tall young man smiled down at my mother, as he and she stood on Wainwright's main street. The entire community was populated with her former students.

Both Colleen and Michael left home for university in the mid-1960's.

And Mum began to travel. For the first time in her life she had both the money to indulge her desire, and time when she wasn't completely responsible to, or for others. She wanted to discover other countries, the sights and sounds and smells of foreign places. Occasionally she took one of her children or grandchildren with her.

In 1967, Canada's Centennial year, Mum offered to pay my fare and living costs if I would accompany her to Montreal. The World's Expo – Expo 67 – was celebrated in our country that year. It was Canada's coming of age, the year when we woke up and realized that we lived in a wonderful country, a nation that had its own distinct personality, a country that was respected around the world, a dominion well on its way to developing it own cuisine, culture, and identity.

"Peggy Smallwood's husband Cliff will arrange our visits to the best pavilions at Expo," Mum told me. "You remember, he's the Member of Parliament for this area. Peggy'll take her son Bob, he's fifteen, younger than you, but I think you'll get along okay."

I made arrangements for someone to take care of my little daughters, my stepson and their father. We travelled across the country by train, the first time I'd ridden a train since my summer days at the farm. In the intervening years, diesel engines had replaced the steam powered trains I'd loved, but the familiar clickety-clack, clickety-clack of wheel on rail still echoed through the night.

At the Expo site on Montreal Island, we were ushered into VIP lounges, entered the pavilions at pre-arranged times, and escaped the lineups of rain-soaked tourists, all thanks to mum's Member of Parliament. We saw a film of the first heart transplant (by Christian Barnard, in South Africa). We went to the theatre with 360 degree movie screens and watched the RCMP's musical ride totally surround us. We ate Montreal smoked meat stuffed into hot rye buns, and we drank Italian red wine from paper cups – much to the chagrin of the sensual Italian man behind the counter, who had run out of clean wine glasses.

On the north shore, in downtown Montreal, stood Place Ville Marie, at over thirty stories the tallest building I'd ever seen. It's middle section was encased in cloud; only its upper and lower floors were visible. It was an awesome sight. We caught our train to Toronto below the partially shrouded tower.

"Phyllis, Jeannie, here you are. How was your trip? Did you enjoy Expo? I'll bet you'd like a cup of tea. We'll just get your luggage, and then we'll go home. Pat will have the tea kettle on for us I expect." Mum's brother Len and sister Mary picked us up and took us home to Cooksville.

"You haven't seen Niagara Falls, have you Jean? We thought we'd take you there tomorrow if you'd like. We could have supper in the revolving restaurant. It's so lovely to look out over the Falls, especially as the sun sets."

Mary and Bert enjoyed taking their guests to see the famous Falls. We stayed at their home for a couple of days, visited with children – Ted and Ethel in Streetsville, Bud and Wendy in Cooksville, Pat and Fred also in Cooksville, Rob was away at university.

"How about if I come and get you and Jean tomorrow, Phyllis, we could go for a drive. I'll take you back to Mary's after supper." Len was on the phone from Brampton, about fifteen minutes away.

"Oh, look at those red leaves, Len, it's just so beautiful. These woods remind me of England, we didn't have red maples over there, but the size of the trees, they're so big, and all different kinds." Mum and Len reminisced in the front seat while Len's wife Jean and I chatted in the back. We drove through the Humber Valley, along roads bordered by gray, weathered rail fences, hillsides brilliant with sugar maples, their broad red leaves an astonishing contrast against the yellowed fields.

By the time we got back to the prairies, the harvest was in and winter was on its way. Michael was in university, Colleen was working in Edmonton; Jim was on the farm.

The next February, my sister married and moved to Chicoutimi, Québéc – a distance of over 3,000 miles from Edmonton. The following summer, my five-year-old daughter Beth came to me with tears in her eyes: "Mummy, why doesn't Auntie Colleen love us any more?" she asked. How can one explain to a child that love continues even when the favourite auntie is so far away that she can no longer visit?

MUM CONTINUED TO TEACH. "I'll teach until Michael's finished university. I want to have enough money, in case he needs some," she said.

Mum and Jim were there when Mike graduated from university with a Bachelor of Education in 1970, and then when he graduated from law.

"Well, of course he graduated with honours," Mum said, proudly. It was a grand day for my brother. We were all proud for him.

I REMEMBER the first time mum returned to England and Wales. Fifty years had passed since her father had brought her to Canada.

We all knew of our mother's longing to see Britain again, to relive the happier days of her girlhood memories, to walk the familiar paths to school and to church, to visit the homes where her roots seemed still embedded, and to visit with aunts and uncles and cousins she hadn't seen in fifty years. We wondered how broad would be the gulf between the memories of a fourteen-year-old girl, forced to emigrate, and those of a middle-aged woman who by then had been married twice, borne four children, taught school, and forged a solid place within her community, but who still pined for the Wales of her dreams.

I recall being worried that the intervening years and urban development would have destroyed the country of her memories. It hadn't occurred to me that the homes she'd lived in were already over two hundred years old in the 1920's, so the ensuing fifty years brought about few changes. In Britain, as in Canada, the cities grew while the villages remained fairly constant.

Mum was not disappointed. Rather, she seemed to have great difficulty in settling again into life in rural Alberta. By the time she arrived back home, she had already planned her next trip to Britain.

There were many silks in the web that connected mum with her Welsh roots. How was it, I wondered, that she could still be so connected across the Atlantic, after fifty or more years? Why does she see her Canadian ties as so thin? How can the web of husband and children, parents and siblings, be weaker than that of distant cousins and aging aunts and uncles? I wondered if she would ever be satisfied with her life in this country or if she would continue to dream of life as it might have been in Wales.

MUM RETIRED FROM TEACHING in about 1978, although she continued to do some substitute work. And she continued volunteering with a host of local, provincial, and international associations – the Women's Institute, the Anglican Church Women, the Retired Teachers' Association, the Order of Eastern Star – to name just a few. None of these organizations allowed her to simply be a member – she held executive positions in all of them, and rose to become Worthy Matron in her Eastern Star chapter.

She continued to travel, sometimes alone with a tour group, sometimes with a neighbour as companion. She and Jimmy weren't good travel companions – he liked to be in bed at 9:00 p.m. and to get up at 5:30 or 6:00 a.m.; she didn't retire until midnight and liked to sleep until 8:30 a.m. and she snored – loudly! They only took one extensive trip together – to Australia, a three-week long journey during which they visited sheep farms, grain farms and cattle ranches, as well as a few tourist destinations. After that, mum travelled alone or with other female companions.

"Would you like to go to England, Jean?" Mum asked. "We could go in the spring, I'd take care of your airfare."

"Mum, I'd love to go but honestly, I'm really strapped for cash and for time. You'd have to make all the arrangements." The year was 1981, I'd ended my twenty-one-year-old marriage the previous year, I was working on a science degree part-time and working full-time. There was a surplus of stress and a deficit of cash in my life. I knew I'd better accept Mum's offer as it wasn't likely to be repeated.

We flew to Gatwick on the wonderful but now defunct Wardair, took the train into London, spent a few days on a bus tour north of the city, then caught a train to Reading. Mum's cousin JeanAnne and her husband Eric picked us up and took us to their home. JeanAnne drove us to Wales where we visited descendants of the relatives who had remained behind when mum and her family emigrated.

"Phyllis, you've brought your daughter. Come sit here now, have a cuppa. Mary's brought some cake, see, now have a biscuit and a bit o' cheese. You're going to Stonehenge, you say? You'll stop by Jack Pursey's place, then, won't you? [Another of mum's cousins.] And you're going to drive all that way to Land's End y'say? All by yerselves? You two ladies?" I could see the concern in their eyes. I assured them it would be alright. My only concern was driving on the other side of the road.

At the end of our week-long, sometimes hair-raising drive, we'd travelled just over 400 miles (645 km). I didn't have the heart to tell them that at home, I often drove 200 miles to attend a meeting, then returned home the same day.

These people were my mother's friends, and they welcomed me as one of them. The connections made during that trip developed into close relationships, connections that I, in turn, gave my own daughter and granddaughters twenty years later.

Mum returned to Wales every couple of years. She revisited the homes she'd lived in, trod the paths she'd walked to school and to church, found cousins who lived ten or twenty miles apart but who didn't know one another (probably a continued separation that began when grandpa's brothers quarrelled fifty years previously).

I CONTINUED TO DEVELOP my business from offices in my basement, as well as plodding through my studies.

Mum and Jimmy came to my graduation from the University of Alberta in November 1984, probably as relieved as I was to have finally (after nine years) completed a Bachelor of Science degree.

The clock they gave me bears a little plaque: "Congratulations JEAN E. CROZIER B.SC. Nov. 17, 1984". It hangs on the wall above my computer as I write.

❧

MUM AND JIM, as well as Colleen and Mike until they left home, poured huge effort into the farm. There were good and not-so-good years. They farmed several quarter sections, some seeded to grains, some kept as pasture for their cattle. Jim loved his cattle – his 'girls' as mum called them. He handled the calves as soon as they were born, they trusted his care and allowed him to administer inoculations or medicines even after they'd reached greater than thousand pound weights.

Phyllis and Jim weathered the years of flea beetles in the rapeseed (now called canola), Bertha army worm infestations, drought, early frosts, and irregular grain prices. They built fences and bought good tractors, built a machine shed, and drove decent vehicles. When a tornado hit their farm, they held blankets against the windows to keep them intact and wondered at the power of a wind that could lift their barn, implode the walls, and set the structure down again, right on its eaves. The insurance covered the cost of repainting the house but not replacement of the cedar siding, badly pitted by the huge hailstones.

My phone rang one summer day in 1985 or '86, that unique ring that seems to occur when there's trouble at the other end.

"It's Dad," said my brother, "he's had a heart attack. I don't know if we can reach Mum, or even if it would do any good. Dad's in Wainwright hospital, I don't think Mum can get home, she's in the Caribbean. I'll try to reach her."

Jim was still in hospital when mum arrived several days later, tension in her every fibre. Sleep had come only in snatches as the cruise ended and she flew home. Jim recovered and was soon back at the wheel of his tractor. He never lost his sense of connection with the nurse who literally shocked his heart back to life.

Jim recovered and returned to farming. He rented most of his land out to his nephews, but worked alongside them as they worked the land and harvested the crops. He and mum were free to socialize, to take long drives around the country, or to attend the auction sales where they bought everything from machinery to office equipment, fixed it up and returned it for resale a week or two later. Life went on.

"What do you want to do for Mum and Dad's 30th anniversary, Jeannie?"

"Gosh, I don't know. What do you think they'd like? A tea for the neighbours and relatives? Dinner at the Honey Pot? [At the time, Wainwright's one good restaurant.]"

"Yes, I think a tea would be nice. We should check with Mum and Dad, see what they want."

July 11th, 1989 dawned brilliantly clear, a blue sky, warm temperatures, a perfect day. We had an afternoon tea at the farm. Mike hung the photographs taken at mum and dad's wedding and the dance that had followed, at the North Irma hall. He had put the photos in plastic frames and made dialogue bubbles for each one...

Messages of congratulation came in from England and Wales, Australia and the United States and from across Canada. They came by mail, by fax, and even by telegram – email was still in its infancy and few people had access to the new communication method.

Colleen, by then divorced and living in Wainwright, baked, organized the event, invited the guests, and made sure everything flowed smoothly.

I found a recipe for Devonshire cream, that delicacy Mum spoke of so often. A huge quantity of milk produced a small bowl of the cream, which we enjoyed with tea biscuits and strawberry jam, and several cups of tea, after the crowd went home.

My sister Maureen and I drove to Irma together. She had moved from Calgary back to Edmonton in the late 1970's. Our sister Colleen lived in Wainwright with her children. Our brother Michael, his wife Donna, and their children also drove down from the city. It was a lovely day, a good celebration. We didn't know the gathering would be the last of its kind.

Mum and Dad cutting the cake on their 30th anniversary; behind them (l to r) are Colleen, Mike's wife Donna, Mike, me, Maureen. It was our last time together.

Maureen died just a month later, a victim of alcoholism and over-use of prescription and patent drugs. She had been my sister, the person I fought with and cared about, the woman I had defended and supported. Her death brought a rain of sadness and a thunder of confusion. Through it, and with supportive counselling, I came to better understand alcoholism, and my sister, as I'd never done before. My mother neither sought counselling nor discussed her loss.

No parent expects to live longer than his or her child. Mum suffered as only a mother can. Especially so since her eldest daughter had succumbed to a disease no-one talked about, whose existence was hidden, held close to the chest. My sister had been brilliant and artistic, a talented musician, a deft seamstress, a phenomenal cook, an excellent bookkeeper.

She was also difficult, troubled in her relationships with others. If she were alive today, I suspect her health problems, in addition to the severe sleep apnea she knew about, would include Attention Deficit Disorder and who knows what other neurological or hormonal disturbances.

My sister Maureen in about 1965, with her champion Lhasa Apso.

There is no name in the English language for a parent whose child has died, no equivalent to the term widow for a bereaved spouse, or orphan for a parentless child. Neither is there a name for the sibling whose brother or sister has died.

Phyllis's grief was intense and personal, suffering to be boxed up and stored, not discussed, not opened to share with others who also grieved.

MUM CONTINUED TO TRAVEL, especially in the spring and summer. Before leaving, she filled the freezer with casseroles for Jim, tuna and chicken and beef suppers, bread and buns and cake and cookies, enough to feed several people.

"Your mother always makes these casseroles for me," Jim said. "I don't know what to do with them. I really don't like casseroles. I'd rather just cook my own meat and potatoes, but she feels she has to do it."

"I know Dad, she really tries to take care of you doesn't she? And then all the neighbours invite you for dinner, and you don't get a chance to eat those casseroles even if you wanted to!" We chuckled at the enormity of it all.

One morning while mum was away, Jim got up at his usual hour, plugged in the tea kettle and made his tea, fixed some toast and, likely, a bowl of porridge. He didn't make it to the fields. We will never know exactly what happened.

A nephew, Bob Burton, came by the farm house that day around noon. He thought it odd that Jim wasn't out and about – his uncle was always up with the sun and outside immediately. When there was no answer to his knock, Bob looked through the window. Jim lay crumpled on the kitchen floor.

Bob called the ambulance. Jim had suffered a massive stroke. His entire right side was paralyzed, he couldn't speak, and who knows what his vision was like?

It was April 1st, 1990.

Mum got home as soon as she could.

"Stroke often happens after a heart attack," Colleen told me. I hadn't known of that connection. My sister has a whole storehouse of these information nuggets, which she passes on at will.

Dad was moved to the General Hospital in Edmonton, then back to Wainwright, to a room in the Auxiliary Hospital.

"Mum," we told her, "you can't go down there every day. They're taking good care of him. You're going to wear yourself out."

She was still on the farm. There were no cattle any more – dad had sold the last of his 'girls' in 1980, when he turned sixty-five and started to collect his Old Age Pension. The land was rented out to his nephews. We worried about our mother, a woman alone, her closest neighbour half a mile away.

"I'm fine, I'm going to stay here on the farm as long as I can. This is my home and I don't want to move."

A year or two passed. Mum bought a house in Wainwright and rented it until she was ready to move.

The farm auction sale – people came from miles around to buy Jim's restored farm machinery and Mum's antiques and collectibles, as well as the modern household and farm equipment.

Finally, she began to pack. She identified hundreds and hundreds of items for her farm auction sale. All the antiques she'd collected and stored in the old house were to be sold, the artifacts she'd wanted to preserve for the museum she'd dreamed of setting up. The aged John Deere™ and McCormick™ farm implements Jim had found and restored to like-new condition went on the auction block. Modern tractors and the combine, a mowing machine and a seed drill went to new owners, as did the tools and the nails and nuts and bolts and pieces of iron.

"Do you know what that woman paid for my old 25-gallon pail, Jean?" Mum said in astonishment after the sale was over and the auctioneer had gone away, along with all the people and their treasures. "She paid eighty-five dollars, eighty-five dollars, can you imagine that? It was just an old lard pail. I can remember when we used to buy all our lard in those things. And she paid eighty-five dollars for it. But other things, things that really had value, some of them went for a song. I should have kept them myself." Her dreams went down the road with the stuff, stacked in stranger's trucks or placed carefully in the trunk of a neighbour's car.

Many trips in cars and trucks, as well as the moving van, were needed to transfer the rest of our mother's goods to her Wainwright house.

"I want to move all that stuff, I'll get it sorted out after I'm in the house. I just don't feel up to doing all of it now."

We chuckled and shook our heads. There was good stuff in some of those boxes. There was also fabric Mum had bought to make dresses for Maureen and I when we were small girls, stuff she and dad had purchased at the Daysland auction for dad to fix up and resell, kitchen tools that we remembered seeing when we were children.

"Oh, well, it's her stuff," we consoled each other.

"THERE'S A GOVERNMENT GRANT available for handicapped people," Mum told us. "I'm going to get a ramp built on the house so I can bring Dad home to visit." And she did. Jim had learned to propel himself around the hospital in his wheelchair, regardless of his paralyzed right side and his inability to speak. Mum visited him several times a week, and brought him home when someone was available to help get him in and out of the car, up the ramp and into the house.

Jim lived at the auxiliary hospital for four and a half years after his stroke. One Sunday in the late fall of 1994, I felt oddly uneasy about him.

"Mum, how are you? Is Dad okay?" I asked her by phone.

"Yes, he's alright." My intuition told me otherwise.

Colleen and Mum sat with Jim that evening. By 9 or 10:00 p.m., his breathing exhibited the Cheyne-Stokes[12] characteristics unique to those who are near death.

Colleen sought the nurse: "What's going on? Is he dying?"

She phoned my brother, he phoned me: "I'm heading down there, Jeannie, I don't think we should wait," he said. He picked me up; it was 11:00 p.m.

We drove east in the dark, two hours and a half of talking and driving. Dad was unconscious when we arrived. My siblings and I sat vigil with our mother throughout the night until Jim died about 5 o'clock the next morning. It was November 21, 1994. Our mother was widowed again.

❧

JIM WAS BURIED in the Irma cemetery, in the plot he and Phyllis had purchased several years previously. Maureen's grave was nearby. His parents lay buried in the same graveyard, a fence-enclosed area on the north side of Highway 14, just east of Irma, a mile and a half south of the land where Jim had spent most of his life.

Mum wasn't ready to part with the farm for a few more years, but eventually she sold it to a young couple with children. They moved into the house and promised to take good care of it. They moved their equipment into the steel, quonset-style machine shed. They didn't use the old chicken-coop, or the barn that Pa Craig, Jim's father, had built and that still sat on its eaves just as the tornado had landed it. They planted a garden, painted the house, and added a porch around the west and south sides to keep their children out of the spring mud.

Mum settled into her new home in Wainwright. She threw herself into association and volunteer work. She joined the Wainwright Historical Society and donated a day or so a week to the Wainwright Museum. Her knowledge of the area is documented in the histories of the Irma village, the local school districts, the Wainwright Women's Institute, and St. Mary's Anglican Church in Irma. She still reads the Sunday morning Lesson at St. Thomas Anglican Church, and attends bible classes and church meetings. She and her friends play cards at least once a week.

Her curiosity about other places continued unabated. She continued travelling, went on several cruises including two with Colleen, to England and Wales with Mike and Donna. She took some of Colleen's and Michael's sons and daughters on cruises to Alaska. Other times she travelled with friends.

The rest of us lived our lives in our own way. I married again, on November 7, 1996, to a widower, a Chartered Accountant, recipient of both professional and volunteer accolades. He and I marvelled with the joy of our new relationship. We treasured every day until disaster struck with unmitigated force.

In August of 2002 he was diagnosed with cancer. Then a stroke felled him, left him paralysed but still able to speak. His energy and his ability to live were stripped away. The tumours had reached his brain.

I rented a hospital bed and arranged for palliative assistance. Ron was brought home in an ambulance. The neighbours and our friends rallied around, ran errands, made meals, and sat with him when another person was needed. My sister phoned and came to Edmonton, my brother cut short his vacation in the north.

Mum came to our house one afternoon. "Now you get better, I'll see you when I get back," she told Ron. Her cruise on the Russian waterways was scheduled to begin a day or two later.

Ron died while Mum was gone. She had told him once that he was "the only son-in-law she could be proud of".

BY THE TIME Mum reached her ninetieth birthday, she had outlived four of her siblings. Before the year was out, two more would die, followed by her favourite brother the following year. Only she and her youngest sister remained.

Mum's ninetieth birthday party in September 2003 was such an occasion. Over two hundred people came to wish her well – two hundred people who still remembered a woman of that age, who were themselves able to come to her party. She greeted them all from a big wooden chair – the throne borrowed from the Masonic Lodge and carried across the street by my brother and our cousins.

"How are you Phyllis, we haven't seen you for ages."

"My God, you're looking just like you did forty years ago."

"Well, Phyl, never thought we'd make it this far, did we?"

Phyllis on her ninetieth birthday – she greeted neighbours and friends, co-workers and relatives from across the country.

They laughed and they chuckled, reminisced over tea and goodies. I had spent weeks practicing a selection of piano pieces that I thought mum would enjoy. My sister organized the event with its yellow and blue tablecloths, its gay balloons and colourful lettering. My brother was Master of Ceremonies – several people answered his invitation to say a few words – co-workers from mum's Correspondence School Branch days, teachers from Avonmore School, members of mum's associations, local teachers and neighbours and relatives.

The following January, mum and I flew to Santiago, Chile, boarded a cruise ship at Valparaiso, sailed down the west coast of South America, around the Horn, spent five days cruising the Antarctic archipelago, then sailed northeast to the Falkland Islands.

"I always wanted to see the penguins, and now I have," she told me after we'd bounced across the island's tussocky terrain to an area where black and white penguins came to wait out their moulting season.

"Well, at least one of her life desires has been satisfied," I thought.

"I don't need your help," she told me repeatedly on the ship and as we went on day tours. She said the same thing to our tour director and his wife, other female members of our group, and strangers who noticed her occasional struggle to keep up. She enjoyed letting the busboys transport her tray to a table at mealtime.

We flew home the day after we'd sailed past Sugar Loaf Mountain into Rio de Janeiro's stunningly beautiful harbour one brilliantly clear morning.

"OH, YES, I have to tell you..." My siblings and I waited expectantly, amused by the excitement in our mother's voice. We'd gathered to celebrate her ninety-second birthday. "Do you know what? They renewed my driver's license for *two* years, two more years, that's what. Now I won't have to worry any more."

Our congratulations covered our concern, recollections of too fast approaches to some turns, lengthy turn signalling, and her own story of dropping off to sleep and putting her car in the ditch. Her big Cadillac would protect her from small incidents.

"DO YOU REMEMBER that reed-work cradle I made for Joanne?" Mum asked another day. She was starting to sort her stuff and dispose of the things she'd spent a lifetime collecting. The task would prove long and arduous.

"Sure I do, I saved it and took it out to her a while ago. She really treasures it," I replied.

"Well, do you think Beth's girls would like to learn to make one? I found some of that old reed, and a cradle I started and half-finished years ago. I could come up and teach them."

"I'm sure they'd like that Mum. I'll call Beth and get her to talk with you."

"She still wants to teach," I thought. "That dream doesn't die."

Our mother was aging, she'd had a heart Pacemaker implanted and arthritis was attacking her bones. "You can't stay here alone any longer, Mum," Michael told her.

The decision would not be easy. "I don't know if I should put my name in at the Lodge here in Wainwright, or if I should come up to the city where you and Michael are," she said.

It was mid-December, the darkest time of the year, short days and long black nights. Our mother went through this depression every year about this time.

"I've never felt this awful. No, I haven't, I've never been this down before."

We'd heard the same statement the year before about this time, and the year before and most years before that.

"I'll be glad when I can get to Victoria. I hope the hotel gives me the suite I asked for, the same one I had last year."

The March-long stay in Victoria, where the climate is much like that of Wales or south England – mild, moist, and cloudy – is a welcome change from Wainwright's snow and cold. Spring comes early to Victoria, the daffodils bloom, then the tulips, the almond and cherry trees burst into blossom, the grass is green and the leaves appear again on every tree branch. Mum returns home re-energized and with renewed vigour.

"I wish we could get the bulbs to bloom here, like they do in Victoria," she says. "It's so beautiful out there, the flowers are so pretty, all different colours. And it's so green, just like it was in Wales."

❧

PHYLLIS, my mother, the woman who always wanted more. The woman who constantly struggled, seldom found peace, selectively bestowed acceptance. A woman with intelligence, widely varied artistic skills, untapped musical ability, intrinsic curiosity, tremendous energy, and a highly developed sense of responsibility. A woman who resented being uprooted but never returned to live in the land of her birth. A woman who sought and gained respect, admiration, and status. Many envied her life.

CHAPTER 11

Ted

He bore few grudges that I ever saw, laughed at the slightest provocation,
enjoyed life, offered support quietly but clearly.
Ted was always there when we needed him.

FITTINGLY FOR AN ELDEST SON, he was named in accordance
with tradition: Edward for his maternal grandfather and George for
his father's father. But he was always called Ted.

Uncle Ted was tall, his body strong but not husky. He had thick
hair, dark at first, then snow white as the years passed. His smile
always lurked just below the surface, ready to jump up to his lips
at a moment's notice. Crinkly, mischievous eyes were set into his
smoothly-shaved face. He was a kind man, generous and warm, easy
to be with.

Ted wore overalls or cotton pants and a shirt, depending on the
weather and the task at hand; always loose-fitting, suspenders but-
toned into his waistband. His sleeves were always rolled up but he
never seemed to wear short-sleeved shirts or T-shirts. Dress-up was a
suit – not particularly well-tailored, bought off the rack for comfort
and a good price – with a shirt and tie.

He stood in as father at my wedding, picked up my siblings and I at the train station when we were on summer holidays, laughed at our antics but never made us feel bad, offered financial and family support when crises arose in my life.

"Ain't that right, Maw?" he'd say to his mother after he'd told her a slightly risqué story, generally beyond his father's hearing, always with a huge grin.

He was a man who led his family in partnership with his wife, seldom travelled far, accepted what couldn't be changed, dug his heels in when he chose to. He spent his days doing what he wanted to do – raise grain and cattle. He had the love and support of his family, and enjoyed the respect of his neighbours. His life had a sense of balance, a reasonable perspective.

MY SISTER MAUREEN AND I saw Uncle Ted frequently during our summer holidays. He and Molly, his wife, lived a few miles north and east of our grandparents. They never passed gran and grandpa's driveway without coming up to the house. The kids were usually with them: Donny, closest to my age; Marjorie with her brilliant red hair, sturdy Gordie and then Aletha, the baby born at home while the doctor tried to get his car out of the ditch beside the road a few miles away. Ted would park his truck close to the house, and everyone would tumble out, he and Molly and the two younger kids from the front seat, the two older kids from the back. They didn't knock on the door, just walked right into gran and grandpa's house.

"Hi there, Maw, how're things looking today?" Ted called out, as the whole family tromped through the back kitchen and into the house. "Got the kettle on? Well, who's this? I heard you kids were comin' down. How are ya? Bring the eggs in yet?"

Maureen and I watched quietly, glad to see Uncle Ted and his family, but mindful of the social differences between the farm and our home in the city. There, we always kept the door latched.

"You keep the screen door locked, now, and don't open it for any-body," taught our mother.

And we never, ever simply walked into someone else's home. But it seemed okay here. Gran didn't mind that they just walked in, and of course, she knew from the sound of the truck's engine that it was Ted and Molly coming up the driveway.

Ted settled into Ivor's chair at the end of the table, never into grandpa's chair at the other end. Molly perched on the green wooden chair outside gran and grandpa's bedroom doorway. Donny claimed the chair that sat beside the cupboard on the south side of the kitchen, just inside the doorway. Marjorie and the other kids found places on the floor or hung around their parents looking for a lift up onto a lap.

"The kettle's just boiling," said Gran, "you'll have a little tea, won't you?" She spooned loose leaves into the Brown Betty teapot and filled it with boiling water, then set it on a trivet, and covered it with a knitted tea cosy.

"You get the cookies, Maureen. Yes, you can get the cups and sau-cers, Jeannie," directed our grandmother, glad as always to see her eldest son.

Grandpa was in the garden when he heard Ted's truck coming up the driveway. He set aside his hoe and headed for the house. It was time for his morning tea, anyway. Smut, the black cocker spaniel, tried to come in the back door with his master. "You stay out here, now," Grandpa said gruffly and the dog retreated to its own house.

Grandpa hung his hat on the hook beside the washstand, carefully cleaned his square-fingered, calloused hands, then stumped toward his chair. Without looking, his practiced right hand found the bat-tered old pipe in the rack on the wall. He tamped it full of Old Chum tobacco and struck a match on the kitchen stove. Clouds of smoke bil-lowed from the bowl. Sometimes, he used to smoke cigarettes, before he'd developed chronic bronchitis and a heart condition. Then, he would take a single paper from the yellow Chanteclair™ package, carefully place it in his palm, and pull some tobacco from the blue

Player's™ tin squeezed between his knees. He offered the paper and tobacco to Ted, then the two of them rolled their cigarettes tightly, licked the gummed part, and twisted the ends. Their talk was of weather, the crops, and the neighbours.

I don't remember much conversation between gran and Aunt Molly, mostly it was the men who seemed to talk. Gran was quiet but still the chatelaine of her domestic domain. She poured the tea and passed the cookies, then perched on her old green kitchen stool. Sometimes she and Molly compared notes on the quarts of fruit and vegetables canned, the state of the saskatoon berries ("Are they ripe yet in that bluff behind the house?"), or the availability of peaches.

"Come on, Ted, we'd better get going," said Molly as soon as she'd finished her tea. "Gotta get those groceries so we can get home and do the peas before supper." Molly had a huge garden, and the peas all ripened at once. Molly's perpetual energy was contained inside a frame that might have reached five feet high on a tall day.

"You kids want to come along?" Ted asked us. "How are you at shelling peas?"

"We're pretty good. We do them for Mom," we said shyly, looking at gran for permission. She nodded her assent and we joined the parade of cousins heading outside.

"Anything you need in town, Ma? No, well then, thanks for the tea. We'll bring these kids back after supper."

Maureen, Marjorie and I tagged along behind Auntie Molly as she went to the Co-op for groceries, carrying Aletha on her hip. Uncle Ted took the boys, collected the mail at the Post Office, bought veterinary liniment from the drugstore and picked up a part for the tractor at Carl Anquist's John Deere dealership.

"You want to ride in the back with Donny and Marj?" he asked when we'd returned to the truck. "Up you get, then. And you keep your head down, now, hear?"

Riding in the back of the truck was a treat beyond words. We sat on old blankets or straw bales or upended milk pails and grabbed the side of the truck-box when we hit the bigger bumps. We faced the front so the wind could blow our hair. We revelled in the scent of fresh-cut hay or the sweet clover growing in the ditches and loved the sinking feeling as the truck travelled over the road's dips and rises. This was freedom, real and simple. A child's heaven.

Uncle Ted home drove along the gravel highway, five miles north, one mile east, and another half mile north. Neither the house nor the barn had seen paint for years, but the fences were strong and straight, the animals content. Molly's carefully tended flowers cuddled close to the weather-beaten house, displaying their brilliant blooms against the nondescript backdrop.

Ted and the boys helped unpack the truck, then went off down the yard. We girls picked peas, a job we hated at home. "You kids keep on picking. I've got to go in and get dinner on," said Molly. "I'll come back and help you after I've got the potatoes and meat in the oven."

The pea pods hung thick and lush on the vines. Molly hauled water to her garden whenever she could. Each of us filled two milk pails with the sweet green pods. We filled our mouths too, when Molly wasn't looking.

In those days before plastic pails, shiny steel milk pails were used for many things. They were big enough but not too big, strong but light, and easy to clean. They carried vegetables from the garden, lunch to the men in the field, then they were washed and scalded and placed under the cow to catch the day's warm milk.

After dinner, we put our chairs in the shade of the caragana hedge. "Here, you take this bowl, I'll take the big one," said Molly, as she showed us how to hold the bowl on our lap, fill it with pea pods, shuck the peas into the bowl, and toss the pods into the 15-gallon slop pail. "Pigs'll love those," Molly commented, "they'll have a good supper tonight."

It was a hot July day, the sun beat down on the dusty earth, and the grass was already dry and crackly underfoot. "Want to fill the washtub and cool your feet?" asked Molly – another treat for the city kids as well as her own offspring. The peas were shelled and in the house, the slop bucket was full of pods, ready for the pigs.

Marj raced for the square galvanized washtub in the back porch and hauled it close to the well. We took turns pumping water and dumping it into the washtub. It was cold, straight up out of the earth. We dabbled our feet, shivered with goose-bumps till we were used to the coldness.

"A-a-a-a-h!" shrieked Marj as Maureen threw a can of cold water at her. The fight was on --we used old cans and cups to splash one another till we'd had enough and the tub was almost empty.

In the meantime, Molly filled fourteen quart sealers with peas, added a pinch of salt, poured boiling water to within an inch of the top, placed the wet sterilized rubber rings onto the lids, and loosely tightened the metal rings. The quart jars went into two canners on the stove, where they stayed for the three hours needed to process them. We kids hauled wood, Molly kept the fire going in the stove, the canners boiled rapidly, and the kitchen temperature rose higher than the hot July day outside.

"Okay, you guys, get that tub back in here and clean up. Time for supper." Molly kept things in order.

After supper, Uncle Ted took us back to Gran and Grandpa Thurston's.

"Did you get those peas all done?" asked grandpa in his gruff voice, his eyes twinkling just a bit.

"Yes, we did. There were fourteen quarts," we responded, proud of the help we thought we'd given.

Soon, we made our final trip to the outhouse, said goodnight, and crawled into our bed in the middle bedroom.

Sometimes Uncle Ted would stay and visit with gran and grandpa for a while. They sat around the dining table in the room outside our bedroom, or on the big, wide-armed chair or chesterfield, or occasionally on very hot evenings they took chairs out to the veranda that ran along the west side of the house. The adults' talk was of family.

"Heard from Mary lately, Maw?" Ted would ask, and gran would give him the news as Mary had written it in her weekly letter home from Ontario. Or Ted and grandpa would discuss crop prices, or when the crops would be ready to cut or how the garden was producing. The adults' murmuring voices were a lullaby for our tired selves.

Many years later, I sat with Uncle Ted and Aunt Molly and reminisced about those days when Maureen and I were children, when we knew that a vacation with our mother's family at Irma meant being enveloped in love and warmth. "We have such wonderful memories of those days, you know, the four of us. We figure we're the luckiest people in the world to have had all these relatives who loved us, and who took the time, every summer, to shelter these kids from the city," I said, hoping they had always understood our feelings even though we'd never actually said the words.

"I remember you and Maureen coming down to stay," Ted recalled, "and you came to stay, by yourself, too, I remember."

"Thank you for taking us in the way you did," I said, urgently wanting them to understand.

"We-e-e-ll, we were glad to have you. Now, can I pass you some more of that meat, Jeannie?" said Ted.

❧

I'D TALKED with my brother, Mike, about summers at Irma when we were kids, before we knew about money, or that wooden buildings needed paint, or that success could be defined in a million ways; when all we needed to know was that we were loved by our relatives. We were given lots of food and space and tasks. What more could fatherless city kids need to know?

"Mike, did you ever drive the tractors at Uncle Ted's place?" I asked.

"Oh sure. Uncle Ted always took us for rides, remember, he'd put one of us on the seat and then stand up to drive. By the time I was eight or nine, Gordie was probably about six or seven, we'd be out driving tractors and doing work that a man might do. I remember at that time, Ted bought or borrowed grandpa's old Ford tractor - it was kind of an oversized garden tractor - and Gordie was a pretty competent driver by then. He drove half-ton trucks when we were seven-or eight- or nine-years-old. We'd drive the truck mainly along the roads, out to the fields, and we did a lot of chores like hauling wood or hay, or whatever around the farm.

"But there was lots of time to play. They had a pinto pony called Kit, we used to ride him bareback, never put a saddle on him. He was pretty hard on us, though, always reaching back to bite me or Colleen!"

"Riding those horses was great, wasn't it, even if they didn't always do what we wanted them to. There always seemed to be cattle roaming around in the yard, weren't there? And the pigs – lots of them, in that field on the north side of the road. Remember feeding them, and how they used to squeal at one another, and push and shove and climb over each other to get at the trough? But none of the animals were vicious, remember? Some of them seemed really big, but none of them were scary, were they?" I recalled, knowing that Ted and Molly wouldn't have kept mean animals on their farm when Mike and Colleen were kids, just as they hadn't when I was a young visitor.

The eight years between my brother and I gave us quite different perspectives on farming, as did our opposite genders. Then too, I was away working in the summer by the time Mike and our sister Colleen were old enough to ride tractors and horses at Ted and Molly's place. By then, horse-drawn implements had essentially been replaced by tractor-pulled or self-propelled equipment, and the farms were becoming increasingly mechanized and electrified. But still, to be a city kid with relatives on the farm – where else could a young boy play out his dreams of driving trucks and tractors, herding cattle, building fences, being enfolded in the fraternity of men?

"What else did you do, Mike, how did you spend your time in Irma?" I queried my brother.

"Well, I think that the things kids might consider work, a lot of things that we did, were work but they were play. You know, if you take a kid that's eight years old and he's supposed to be sixteen to drive, and you let him drive a half ton [truck] to take fence posts out to build a fence, or you let him drive a tractor that he shouldn't be driving – is that play or is it work?

Top: Ted's eldest children, Don and Marjorie, with their dog. Behind them is a wagonload of bundles, the thresher is ahead of it. The belt from the tractor powers the thresher, the grain is blown directly into the granary where it will stay until prices and time are right for selling it.

Bottom: Ted brought his children and his horses together early on; he has two-year-old Donny on the horse, c1946.

"We always played ball – baseball. Gordie's a very good baseball player. It was a close community up there around Irma, and around Ted and Molly's place, so there were always sports days and baseball tournaments, at Irma or the North Hall [just north of Ted and Molly's home]. You walked across the field to get there, walked home after the games were over. It was a very social community. On Saturday night everybody went to town, even if you were seven years old, and you'd sit around the pool hall and listen to the stories, and get your hair cut.

"The barber's name was Barber – Harold Barber. Ted would drop Gordie and I off. He'd go and do what he had to do then come back and chew the fat for a while with the guys, and then we'd all go over to Jim Pond's Irma Café for ice cream, and then we'd go home.

"There were a couple of pool tables at the back of the hall. I don't think we very often played one on one, we more often played four to a game, kids or men. I don't remember very many girls in the pool hall in those days: the girls didn't play. The men and the boys had a very social atmosphere. Everybody – all the males at least – were there."

"So typical of that time," I thought to myself. "The boys and men go off to do a few errands, then gossip and play pool. The women buy the groceries, take care of the small children, go to McFarland's General Store for pots and pans, to the drugstore for medicine, and the post office for the mail. And chat with one another if they get done in time, before the men finish their game and want to go home. Ah, the social structure of small towns. Life is full of similarities and differences." But at some point I also came to realize that the women developed multilayered relationships, and were generally satisfied with their role in their families and in the community.

I reflected, another day, on a different social gulf – the one between the Wales that Ted had known as a boy and the one at Irma. He and I were chatting in his living room.

"Ted, do you remember going to school in Wales, before you came to Canada? I think you were eleven-years-old when you came here, weren't you, in 1927? What was life like for you over there, in the old country?" I sought to comprehend the decision to emigrate from a country which my mother described as so beautiful, to a land of often harsh realities.

"Well, I can remember quite a bit, actually. We went to Romilly Road school, right in Barry. There was school for boys and girls, but they kept us separate, you know, boys in one school and girls in another. We had uniforms, short pants, dark blue, and a little hat. We walked to school together..."

"No mischief?" I interrupted.

"Oh, I wouldn't say that! But at least we didn't get caught, put it that way!" chuckled Ted. "We had men teachers, women teachers on the girls' side. And we had geography, history, just about the same as over here. Paper and pencils. We had our own desks.

"We went to school pretty well right up until we left for Canada. I remember, the teacher gave a reading on Alberta, Edmonton, and the kids were interested, but they didn't ask too many questions. We hadn't studied Alberta at all, in school, before that. I didn't know anything about the country before we came here. I don't know what dad knew. There were those caravans[13] that went around the country, you know, drumming up immigrants for Canada, but I never knew much about them."

"Ted, did you work with your dad on the farm in Wales? You were pretty young, but I expect that all kids had chores to do didn't they?"

"Oh, sure, sure we all did. Dad used to deliver milk in town, and I went with him until time for school. We had about 25 or 30 cows. He had one of the biggest farms over there, it was 172 acres[14], you know.

"I don't remember doing any milking. You should ask your mother about that. I kind of remember that she used to do some milking. Maybe dad had some hired help too – we sure didn't have any milking machines the way people do now!

"Dad used to bottle all the milk and sell it that way, not in bulk the way other dairy farmers did. He had a route, with regular customers. I don't recall just how they used to do it. The customers would leave the empty bottle on the front step, with so many coupons in the empty bottle and that would be to pay for what milk they wanted that day, I guess. That's how you knew how many quarts, or whatever it was, to leave there. We'd pick up the empties and leave full ones. I helped him with the customers around the school, and then I'd go off to classes, and then dad would tend to the farther away customers."

"It would take all morning to do the rounds. Dad had 30, 40, 50 customers, I guess. We'd start at half past 6, or 7 o'clock, cause we had to go two and a half mile into town to start with, just the one horse, a pony actually, on a two-wheeled cart. I think he had three work horses, quite a bit of Clydesdale in those work horses. And then this mare that he used to deliver milk, Dolly her name was."

"What kind of cows did you raise, Ted? Were they Jerseys or Guernseys or...?"

"No, no, they were Holsteins. I imagine they'd be purebred, or pretty close. Cause they were strictly for milk, and that was all. There was quite a bit of dairying in the area. Dad sold whole milk, we didn't separate it.

"Dad always had good stock, you know, he didn't bother with what we'd call here 'range cows', he must have started out with some good cows and a bull, and he bred them for production."

"Yes, I'm sure that's right. He always did things well, didn't he? I don't remember grandpa ever being satisfied with poor anything – cattle, or the garden, or any kind of a job.

"Mom said that grandpa's dairy was the first one in the Barry area to sell bottled milk, do you remember him talking about that?"

"Well-l-l, that could be now, I don't really know. But if your mom said it, then it's probably true."

"You know, Uncle Ted, growing up here in Canada, we don't really know much about the class system that used to be so evident in Britain. I guess it's still there to some degree or another. But I read somewhere that the agricultural labourer was the lowest of the low on the social scale, around the time when you left there. Grandpa wasn't a labourer, but still...how did that class structure affect you?"

"When we were there, there was a lot of class, class in everything, let's put it that way. And I hated it so – I wouldn't say anything good about it. We weren't at the bottom, you know, that was a pretty big farm that grandpa was running, but maybe half-way up the social scale." Ted's antipathy toward the class system was evident, his voice hard as he remembered the injustices to which he'd been subjected. "You'd get snubbed a lot of times for different things, if they thought you weren't quite as good as they were, you know. By the grownups, not the kids in school.

"The year or so before we came out here, they had these pheasant hunts in the fall, like. And they'd expect the farm kids to go out with a stick, and beat the bushes to make the pheasants fly out, so these big 'nobs'[15] could walk out in the grass and shoot the birds. That went over just like a ton of brick. I did it once, never went back again. Never got paid, of course. The landlord ran the whole show. I suppose if we hadn't come to Canada, I think we would have got in trouble for not going back to do it again. 'Cause if they tell you to go, you're supposed to go. At that time, like."

"How did grandpa feel about that? Was he supposed to flush the birds too?" I asked, curious about a way of life so different from the relative classlessness of early 20th century Canadian prairie customs.

"No, just the kids flushed the birds. Your grandpa, he felt the same way I did," Ted responded. "I remember one time, he went out, he needed some little bushes to stick in the garden, and we went out one night, we had to go out after supper, cause you're not supposed to cut anything down. And Dad had a kind of a scythe affair there, and he was cutting something off in the hedge, and he cut his foot. And he was scared to go to the doctor, 'cause he figured somebody would find out that we'd been out there cutting these blessed little things down to put in the garden for peas, and he'd be run up and in trouble. That's just the way it was over there, too." Seventy-year-old resentments lurked in Ted's eyes and voice.

"The landlords' kids didn't go to our school either, you know. The other kids at Romilly were other farmers' kids. There were two or three landlords around there. Pretty big holdings, maybe eight or ten farms each. And they had a castle down the bottom to live in, and I think that's all they ever done," Ted recalled.

"Hmm, no wonder the offer of assisted passage and the chance to buy your own land in Canada was so attractive," I said. "You'd never have owned land over there, would you?"

"Well, you couldn't, you know. Rents were pretty steep, and there was no way to get enough money together. Even if land ever came up for sale, probably some other big landowner would have bought it," Ted explained.

OUR CONVERSATION CONTINUED another day, as my husband Ron and I sat in Ted and Molly's living room, a few miles north of Irma, not far from where Gran and Grandpa Thurston had settled in 1927. Ron loved to chat with these relatives of mine and to talk with them about their lives as newly settled farmers. My husband had been born in Winnipeg, and he had had little contact with farms and farmers. Marrying into a family as large as mine took more than a bit of getting used to. Ron soon developed a special love and respect for my Uncle Ted.

"You have some good memories of Wales, don't you?" I asked Ted, remembering my own trips to Wales, where lush green fields were surrounded by ivy-covered stone walls, and both grasses and cereal crops were thick and heavy. Over there, cattle can be supported with only a few acres per head, a fraction of the ten to fifteen acres needed for each steer or cow on the prairies.

"I'll bet you remember your trip over here, Uncle Ted? That must have been some trip across the Atlantic at that time of year," asked Ron.

"It was quite a trip. We left Liverpool the day I was eleven-years-old, 25th of March 1927. We arrived in Irma on the 7th of April. I was only sick one day, when we were half or three-quarters of the way over. It was a rough day, that was. They covered up all the hatches, and they shoved us all downstairs, because there was a thunderstorm up, but as a rule it was pretty nice weather. Mum was an awful poor sailor; she was sick all the time," Ted shook his head as he remembered the journey's impact on his mother.

"We had two staterooms, I think, and we all stayed in there. Bunk beds. They had a big dining room. Everybody ate together, and the food, well it was good too. First time I ever tasted frozen milk, that's how they kept it fresh. They opened a barrel one night and run it off, and gave us kids a sample. It was a good trip."

I could see Ron's thoughts turn to photography as he asked, "This country must have looked pretty brown to you that April, probably still some snow on the ground? South Wales would have been all green, and then with the spring flowers beginning to bloom."

"Well, yes, it was, but you know, I think we were pretty happy to get to where we were supposed to get to. You travel around for two weeks, on the boat and the train, and you're glad to get home. And mum, when she seen it from the road, she just thought the world of it. That made a lot of difference," Ted recalled.

"We got back into school right away, too. Mum, she took us to school right away, I think.

"See, before we left the old country, they'd told dad that he should work for somebody else, the first year, get the way of the country, and that's what he did, that first summer. Worked for Cal Goodale, breaking land with an eight-horse outfit. That's all Goodale did, you know, break up the prairie land."

"Had grandpa had much experience with horses, Uncle Ted? I hear he liked to hunt foxes, on horseback of course, but workhorses and land breaking – that's a whole different story, isn't it?" I asked.

"Yeah, it is. He brought his own saddle out, an English saddle, he had that out here. That's all he ever used there and here. And of course, the farm in Wales, they'd used horses, heavy horses, for all that work. He was good with horses."

"Gosh, I wonder what ever happened to that saddle, Uncle Ted. Do you suppose it's still around?" I'd never heard of the saddle – it must have been both precious and expensive to have been included in the family's transported baggage.

"Ah, I haven't seen it in years, Jean. Must be long gone now, I'd think," Ted replied. "Stuff disappears, you don't use it, you know.

"Anyway, in the winter, dad went to work for Tom Shaw. He had cattle and sheep, so dad used to come up here every day and feed them. Shaw, he lived in town in the winter time, in the hotel with his wife, like. Different people did that, you know, maybe have a job in town and a farm in the country. The land was open and their horses or cows used to run out on the prairie in the daytime. No fences when we first came here. A lot of raw land out in this country then. Virgin land. The CPR [Canadian Pacific Railway] owned some of it, every other quarter I think it was. During the better years they sold a lot of their land. Then during the Depression they got a lot of it back, too, when people couldn't meet their payments! There was a lot more brush on the land then, in the 1920's and '30's, a lot of land's been cleared since then."

My stepfather, Jim Craig, had told me about the countryside too: the way it had been in the early days. He found arrowheads, and even some pemmican[16], as he worked his farm. Jim was born in 1915, on a farm twelve miles north of Uncle Ted's place. He spoke of the prairie fires that raged across the land in earlier days, the scourges of grasshoppers in dry years, and the cycles of tent caterpillar and flea beetle infestations, plagues that the Thurstons would soon experience.

"When grandpa was away working, you kids must have had to carry on with the chores at home, I guess?" I asked, aware of the enormous adjustments my grandparents and the entire family must have had to accommodate in their new Canadian home.

"We had to haul wood," Ted responded, "haul water, and when dad was away working, we had to look after the cow. I think we had two cows then. But you had to haul wood every day, cut wood and haul it, you know, every night that was the first job we had.

Top: A youthful Ted, pictured on the farm about 1934, his cap and his suit like his father's.

Bottom: All dressed up, 1935 – apparently Ted didn't spend all his time farming.

"The horses never gave me too much trouble," Ted maintained; beside the barn, c1935.

"When we first came, the well wasn't working, so we had to haul water from town, in cream cans[17]. And then for washing and laundry, we'd get water from the slough in the summer and then in the winter, we'd melt snow."

"Wow, that's a huge job, to melt snow for drinking and washing and bathing in. How much snow to make a pail of water?" I asked, thinking that it took a lot of our dry prairie snow to make a pail of water.

"Oh gosh, I don't know, probably a pail of snow, packed down pretty good, would give you less than a quarter of a pail of water. We used to do it," Ted recalled.

"You know, I've searched out some microfilmed copies of the *Irma Times*, Ted, your name appears on the front page many times," I teased.

"No, I don't think so. What for?" responded my uncle, his curiosity sparked.

"Well, the newspaper used to print the students' names, and their grades, every month. Can you imagine that? And there you were, all you Thurston kids, while you were in school. You pretty well all got good marks, too."

"No, well I didn't know the old *Times* did that. Haven't done it for a long time, that's for sure. Course, there's no *Irma Times*[18] any more, either!"

"You didn't stay in school for very long after you got here, did you, Uncle Ted?" Ron inquired, curious about the educational needs of farmers, especially in earlier days when farming was less technical than it is today.

"I went to school here for four years. It was a big change from Wales. Boys and girls were all mixed together in one class. I passed out of school in Grade 8 – started in Grade 5. Money was short, Dad needed help at home, and that was one of the reasons why I had to quit school. I got into farming right away."

(Canadian law kept kids in school until they were fifteen, or had completed Grade 8, whichever came first.)

"That house must have been pretty full in those days, Ted. I guess Mary went out to work right away after you got here, and my mum was only there for three or four years before she went to Normal School in Camrose. But still, that's a lot of mouths to feed."

"It was a pretty big family. Len and I, we rented this land up here, and I guess it was just agreed that we'd move some of the cattle up here, and we'd stay up here along with them – a few of Dad's cattle, mostly our own. We'd usually buy calves and let them grow into cows, we'd have four or five, six maybe. Bought them with money we'd got for threshing, couple of bucks a day. You could buy a calf then for three bucks! But that was a day and a half's work too.

"And we worked out in the winter, I worked for Arthur Charter one year, and for Mac MacMillan another year. And Abe Fisher. Made $10.00 a month and board. They had a lot of cattle. They were the only people who could afford to hire help. Len worked for another guy by the name of McLean most of the time. You probably wouldn't remember them, Jeannie. Charters came here the year before we did – they started a dairy farm just west of here. Fisher's and MacMillan's

The older boys, Ted and Len, slept in this bunkhouse during their first summers in Canada.

were here early – they homesteaded about 1907 and ran mixed farms, side by side, there weren't even any fences between the two farms. They worked together a lot, threshing and such, you know, and there was always need for another hand.

"So Len and I stayed in that old house for a few years, one working out and one staying home to help dad. The place was so cold, it was a terrible place – a lot colder than mum and dad's, and of course there was no woman there to keep the fires burning! The house had two storeys, but not a bit of insulation. We rented it from a lady in Edmonton, and after a while we bought it.

"That was some time," Ted shook his head. "Mum used to bring us some food and we cooked for ourselves too. We had a bowlful of porridge every morning, I know that. We'd cook meat and potatoes, all that kind of stuff. We'd eat good enough. Prunes were the...the damned things!" Ted chuckled. "Seemed as though we always had dried apples or dried prunes."

"We worked at home too, took turns working on our own place and at home, at dad's. Even when we rented this place, we still farmed together. We farmed dad's land, and we farmed this land with the same

Eight- or ten-horse teams were needed to pull the big breaking plows.

equipment, whatever had to be done. We always farmed together, never had any problems. Time never meant nothing, we never kept track of any labour. If we had to work down home, we worked down home. If we worked up here, we worked up here. But we never kept track of any time. We never had a bit of trouble."

"How much of the land was broken then, Uncle Ted?" I asked. "There's not a lot of brush out there now, less than when I was a kid. Remember how we used to bring lunch to you in the fields, and before we went home we'd scour the brush patches for saskatoons? It looks as if most of the brush has been taken out now. Even the brush along the fence lines is gone. Actually, there's not even a lot of fences any more, is there, except where cattle are pastured?"

"Ah, that's right. I dunno, the municipality's done that, you know, taken out all the brush. And the young guys that are farming now... they think they need to get every bit of land for their crops."

"But we always used to believe that you needed the brush to catch the snow for moisture – has that philosophy gone out the window now too?"

A field of wheat being cut, bound, and stooked; 1936.

"We-e-ell, I guess it has! Them young fellers, you know..." Ted chuckled with the knowledge that the young always have the answers.

"Brushing, clearing must have been hard work in those early days when you were first farming. What percentage of your land would actually have been cleared and available for seeding?"

"Oh, not that much, you know, Jean. Dad had three quarter-sections, Len and I rented another couple of quarters. Only about 80 or 100 acres each on Dad's quarters would have been broke, [out of the 160 acres in a quarter-section]. This place here had a little more broke on it, and 40 acres broke on the other quarter."

"And you did it all with horses? Didn't you tell me you had twenty-three head of horses then? How did you get all those horses, and get them trained to pull the equipment?" I asked, overwhelmed with the thought of managing such a huge herd.

"Well, you know, they weren't all our horses. We had some, of course, but there was lots of horses in the area, and always some that needed breaking. So we'd take the ones that were a year or two old,

Every fall at least 75 bags full of potatoes were dug, dried in the field for a day or two, then bagged and hauled down to the basement.

The tractor made short work of tasks that had required lengthy days with horses. Fred drives as Leo and Ron look on; Leo became the principal tractor operator.

keep them for the summer, break them in, use them, then give them back to their owners in the fall.

"I always liked the horses. Ron too was okay with them. Leo, well, he just couldn't seem to work with them too well. Len either.

"And then dad bought his first tractor in '39, a John Deere™ AR. Leo drove the tractor most of the time. I just stayed with the horses."

"How many horses did the tractor replace?"

" A team of eight. And the spares, you know, we'd have to have two or three teams, keep spelling them off on those long days, keep them fresh."

I remember the teams that pulled farm equipment when I was a child; four or six horses, two or three abreast, to pull the spike harrows through the black soil; eight horse teams, four abreast, for the breaking plows. Dust rose up in the dry years, and engulfed the person sitting on the iron seat, holding the reins, steering the horses, keeping it all under control; slow-moving but not lazy; long days under the unrelenting sun; thirsty work, hard work for men and horses. But it was honest, a day's toil clearly visible; satisfying for those who loved the soil and the sky and the horses, the men and women whose kinship with the land was their reason for being.

ANOTHER DAY, another year, I sat alone with Ted and Molly in their front room. It was a cozy room, full of children's and grandchildren's photographs, a couple of paintings, a piano; comfortable furniture, covered with knitted afghans; a table that could be pulled into the middle and extended for family gatherings. Home. But now, as I continued my conversations about Ted and Molly's earlier days, it was without my Ron. Several months had passed since we started the process of gathering family stories. Ron had succumbed to cancer only a month after he'd been diagnosed. I struggled to pick up the threads of my life, and of my family's story.

"You're not keeping quite the same pace now as you did in those early days, are you, Uncle Ted? What would a day have been like, when you and Len were batching?" I asked, curious about the activities that filled the early farmers' days. "Did you both like farming?"

"Oh, no, Len wasn't so good with the horses, you know, and he just didn't care for farming. Me, I'd always intended to farm, always wanted to farm. It was right in my blood, I wanted to do it, and I was lucky enough to have the chance.

"When we were working together, well, you started good and early in the morning, Dad always said we should have the horses all hooked up and going at 7:00 o'clock. So we would have had breakfast, and then we'd get going out to the fields right away.

"If a bad storm came up in the afternoon when you were out there with eight horses, it could turn out to be quite a shemozzle. They wouldn't face into the rain or wind. Thunder didn't seem to bother them, unless it was really close. Lots of times you couldn't hardly get them to turn around and back into a storm, if it was windy. We had a lot of wind and a lot of dust storms. Sometimes you'd drive them into the brush," Ted remembered with a chortle, "only way you could stop 'em. Long as they were going, the storm was in their back, didn't bother them so bad. But it was to bring them around again and bring them back so's they'd have to face down the other end of the field."

"The farmers don't do much plowing or even harrowing any more, now, do they? It's all 'zero tillage' around here now, isn't it, the way they farm? No more disturbance than what you absolutely have to do, right? Quite a change from the way you used to do things," I said.

"That's right. We used to plow every year in those days. Everything. We could get out there earlier in the spring than you can with a tractor, you know. The horses didn't pack the ground down like a tractor does. And usually you'd pick rocks first, and then you'd get on with the plowing. Sometimes we'd sow the fields that'd been summer-fallowed the year before, first, then get on with the other fields."

"How long to plow an eighty-acre field? And how did you ever learn to plow a straight furrow, the entire length of the field?"

"We just targeted right onto a tree down on the fence line, and headed straight for it! Tried to make it straight, anyhow! We did weeks of it. And then we seeded, mostly wheat and oats, 'Triple Two' wheat mostly," Ted remembered. "Had to be in the ground by the tenth of May, at least between the 10th and the 24th, that was the limit, or it'd be frosted before it ripened."

"What does 'Triple Two' mean, Ted? I don't recall ever hearing of a wheat species by that name."

"Well now, I don't really know, Jeannie. We just called it 'Triple Two', that's all, everybody did, and we all grew it."

THE 'TRIPLE TWO' NAME piqued my curiosity. What on earth was it? I'd heard of durum wheat, been told that Marquis wheat was the primary strain, as well as Saunders and sometimes Red Fife. But 'Triple Two'? An Internet search proved fruitless. I contacted the new librarian at the Canadian Wheat Board in Winnipeg – my old friend Ruth, who had run the library there for many years had retired, so I couldn't tap into her storehouse of knowledge. Nothing. "I can't find any reference to a 'Triple Two' variety," replied the librarian.

The Canadian Encyclopedia (p. 2298) notes that wheat is properly called 'Triticum', and that T. aestivum and T. turgidum are the most common modern cultivars. The encyclopedia follows along with a discussion of stem rust, a fungus that attacks wheat – and the rust-resistant 'Thatcher' cultivar that was developed in Minnesota in 1935, licensed for use in Canada, and that became the most widely-grown wheat species on the prairies.

Uncle Ted's 'Triple Two' may have been a 'triple T': Triticum turgidum Thatcher. At least that's my guess.

"I helped you pick lots of rocks, in those days," said Molly, joining the conversation.

I remembered seeing Molly out in the fields, when I was a small girl. There she would be, a petite woman, maybe five feet tall, her blond hair awry, her body covered with overalls and a shirt, her feet in red-soled rubber boots. With dust-covered face, dirt in the folds of her clothing and her skin. She would pick rocks from the tilled fields, or rocks and roots from freshly-broken land.

"Would you ever pick rocks and roots like that, Jeannie?" asked my sister Maureen, years later as we talked about our summers at the farm.

"You bet I would, if that was what we had to do to make a living," I had replied. But neither of us envied Ted and Molly or their children that back-breaking, tedious chore.

"What a never-ending job that was. But once you'd got the rocks picked and the soil plowed, and the seeds into the ground, what happened next? Summer comes along, let's pretend you've had a good summer, enough rain and sun, no hail. When could you start to harvest?" I asked, remembering that I'd always wanted to be around to see the fabled threshing crews in action, but I'd had to return home to school in Edmonton long before harvesting began.

"Oh, it'd be September before you'd start to cut it. We'd have four horses on a binder, and we'd cut it, and the binder tied it into bundles so we could stook it. Seven or eight bundles to a stook. We could do twenty acres in a big day then.

"Just one binder, but you'd change the horses three or four times a day, keep them fresh, so they'd go a little faster. Four horses on the binder, another four in the barn, somebody'd bring them out to you at 11 o'clock. Keep them spelled off." Ted discussed each of these steps as clearly as if he were still working that way. Memories ingrained, countless hours and days and weeks spent raising grain crops.

"What did a bundle weigh?" I asked.

"They were pretty darned heavy when I lifted them," laughed Molly. "Thirty pounds or so, I guess, eh, Ted"?

"Yeah, that'd be about right. And you'd stook them, stand them up in a circle, heads up, to dry.

"Sometimes the stooks stood outside all winter, you know, if the weather got bad and you couldn't get at it. Lot of wet weather some years, snow came early.

"And then when it would be dry enough, you'd move in there with a threshing machine and thresh it. The outfit I used to work on had six teams that made up the crew, like. You'd have six men on the teams, and two engineers on the machines all the time. One year I worked on a machine that had eight teams, and a field pitcher, and a spike pitcher. Our threshing machine was a 'Red River Special'; lots of companies made threshing machines.

"Longest time I was ever out on the crews was thirty days, we never stopped. One year, we started and put in two or three days, had a lot of wet weather, and then it dried out and we started again, and that time we put in the 30-day stretch and never quit once. That's when I was working for Archibald."

"Went out in the buggy, pretty often, taking lunch to you," interjected Molly, smiling with the memory.

"That never-ending supply of food again," I laughed, knowing that a successful threshing depended on sufficient food for men and horses, as well as cooperation from the weather. The farm women worked from sunup till sundown during threshing days, just as the men did.

"Molly, you went to school at Alma Mater, didn't you? To Grade 8 only? And then what, did you stay home, or go out to work? What was the norm for girls then? "

"Oh we all had to work. Worked at home, there were nine of us. My father was here before the railway, 1909 I think it was. Before Ted and I were married, I worked for George and Marjory Fisher, and for a school teacher. I remember I worked for six months, and got paid $72.00 plus my board. Bought all my wedding clothes, and blankets for the bed with that!" Molly easily recalled the details of her youth.

"In those days it was all so straight-forward," I thought. "You were a girl, you grew up on a farm; you went to school. Maybe you worked for a while, then you got married and had your own life, farming. In the years prior to the 1960's, that was so much the norm. Too bad for you if you didn't want that life."

"Ted, you worked on the threshing crews both when you and Len were batching, as well as after you and Molly had married?"

"Yes, that's right."

Ted and Molly were married on November 2, 1940. Molly was late for the ceremony but Ted waited; they honeymooned in Edmonton for a few days.

"You were married in 1940, November 2, after Len had gone east to Ontario, weren't you? But you two didn't have babies right away, like so many young couples did. And you had a different place, not this house that we're sitting in – where was that, I know I've been there, but I've forgotten? Did you get married in the Anglican church?" I tried to sort out the sequence of events.

"We sure did. He talked me into it," said Molly. "My people were United Church. I was late too, the ceremony was supposed to start at 11:00 o'clock but Chris [Molly's brother] couldn't get the car started! Ted waited for me up there in his three-piece suit. I got there eventually!"

"What did you wear, Molly? Did you have a white dress with a veil like brides wear now?"

"No I sure didn't. Couldn't afford something that I'd never wear afterwards. I wore a navy-blue suit and I had a hat that swooped way over." With the hat on her head, Molly almost reached Ted's shoulder.

Ted and Molly worked, played, and danced together for four years before they had any children.

Ted with their first child, Donald, wearing the christening robes originally made for his Aunt Mary; 1944.

Grandpa brought Ted to Edmonton for major surgery sometime in the early 1940's; he recuperated at Phyllis and Max's home.

The reception – Molly isn't exactly clear on the menu but she thinks they had a chicken dinner – was at the Burton's home – Molly's parents. Then she and Ted took the train into Edmonton, and stayed at the upscale Royal George Hotel. They remember visiting with my parents – I would have been just a few months old then, my sister not quite two. They saw some shows and did a little sightseeing. And Molly lost her beautiful hat as the wind caught it and tossed it along Jasper Avenue, the city's main thoroughfare.

They moved into an old house on land Ted bought from Tom Shaw. The Shaw's had homesteaded the place, improved it and got title. They farmed for a few years and ran the hotel in town at the same time. The house was old and drafty, not much more than a shack. Ted and Molly built onto it and made it habitable.

"We lived in that old house for ten years, all the children were born while we lived there," remembered Molly.

"Now, I think all the kids but Aletha were born at the Wainwright Hospital, weren't they?" I asked. "But I've heard stories about Aletha's birth...didn't the doctor go off the road and get stuck? And finally got here after the big farmer man here had had to catch his new baby daughter?"

"Ah, I'm not talking about that story," laughed Ted. "No, I think we'd better just go on with what we were talking about." And he did. Apparently, talking about birthing a calf wasn't a big deal, but a human baby was something else!

"That was a cold house when the wind blew. It was just a mile east and a mile north of this house. But there was no water at first: the well was a quarter of a mile away," Ted explained, as Molly shivered, her thoughts replaying the hours spent hauling water.

"I'd bundle up the kids, and load them onto the stoneboat, along with the barrel for water, and drive the horse down to meet you, remember? And we'd pump the water, and fill up the barrel, then you'd drive it back up to the house." Molly watched Ted as they dredged up the old memories, and the challenges they'd coped with in earlier years.

"What did you two do for fun in those years, Molly? Did you work all the time, or was there time to enjoy life and each other?" I asked.

"You know, we had more time for fun then than we do now!" Ted exclaimed. "We went to town once in a while, not very often. We just went to the school houses. Alma Mater school was just a mile east from where we lived. Straight across the field, like. Sometimes we'd walk, sometimes take the wagon, or a horse and put him in the barn when we got there. There was always a barn at the schools, you know, in the country, for the kids' horses."

"We didn't go to many dances in the summer time, just the winter," said Molly.

"We had a club, the Merry Makers, and we'd put on dances at the school every two weeks. Ten cents a head for the men, and the women got in free if they brought a cake for lunch. For a couple of years, Joe [Burton, Molly's brother] and I, we put on dances up there for two or three years. We'd buy a half dozen loaves of bread for sandwiches, make some coffee, and that would be midnight lunch. We paid the orchestra a dollar and a half apiece to play all night. Evelyn Pyle played the piano, and Harry played the violin. Old Ivan Archibald would be there, banging away on his banjo. They'd start at 9 o'clock, and then we'd break for lunch at 12, and then we'd go on till 2." Ted and Molly laughed together, remembering the dances where people came from miles around. Babies were plunked down on the coat tables. Little children danced as long as they could, then they dropped off to sleep in a corner.

"There was a guy by the name of Fisher, and Russell Lim, remember him, Molly, they used to call the square dances, and Cal Goodale, too."

"Is that the Cal Goodale whose son travelled east with Len?" I asked, trying to piece things together.

"Yes, that's right. He and Len went east together," Ted said.

"Whole families went to those dances," said Molly. "We'd have fifty, sixty, a hundred maybe! That old floor at Alma Mater used to just go up and down! You'd go down the basement, and the floor would be jiggling. They were good days.

"Most of the people were older than us, old men, no women, they used to just get up there and dance every dance. I dunno where the women were, maybe they just stayed home to get some sleep."

Occasionally, Molly's dad went to the dances – to look after his girls, he told Molly, before she and Ted were married. Her mother didn't go to the dances, and neither did Gran and Grandpa Thurston, which I wondered about.

"What about the summer time? You didn't hold dances then, so what did you youngsters do for fun?" I asked. "You didn't have babies for four years, and you chased around with one another for a couple of years at least before you were married – I know you did, the rest of them have told me the stories about playing hide-and-seek and never being able to find you two! Seems there were some pretty handy haystacks and hills, yes, I see you can still blush a little bit there, Auntie Molly, and so you should, according to what I've been told." It was fun to tease this pair, turn the tables a bit from when I was a kid, when my uncles delighted in pestering their nieces and nephews, as well as their own kids.

"We skated in the winter time, too, on the sloughs down there. One time we'd make a skating rink, next year Burton's would make one, next year Craig's. Light a fire, have some coffee and lunch.

"Played ball in the summer. They'd make ball diamonds just anywhere out on the prairies. Everybody who could throw a ball played. Little kids too, just one big ballgame, that's all," Ted said.

"Tell me about the Merry Makers, Molly." I'd talked with Molly before about the Merry Makers and had read several descriptions of their parties and plays in old issues of the *Irma Times*.

"We'd get a truck sometimes, and go down to Clear Lake [ten miles east of Wainwright, a trip of about thirty or thirty-five miles from Ted and Molly's place]. We all shoved in the back of the truck, 25 of us, went down to the lake. There's a picture of us in that Irma history book.[19]

"I remember once, we were all going to a dance somewhere, we was all loaded into a sleigh, and it tipped over, dumped us all out!

"And we put on two plays – *Wild Oats* and *Little Clodhopper*. Remember, Ted, you and my brother Joe were in the *Little Clodhopper*? We took them plays to three or four places, too, remember?"

"Did you write the plays, Molly? And who would have directed them?" I asked.

"Oh, no, we didn't write no plays, we bought them. And little Harry Ryley, remember, he bought up the *Irma Times* later on, well he and Ted Orton directed us. We just wore our own clothes, didn't need no costumes," Molly explained.

There were other high points for these homey farmers, too. Shortly after George VI and Queen Elizabeth ascended to the British throne, the year before World War II broke out, the new monarchs crossed Canada by train. It was the first ever cross-country tour by a reigning monarch. At that time, British immigrants and their descendants made up about 50% of Alberta's population; they turned out by the thousands to see their new King and Queen.

"We had a holiday that day, to see them," said Molly. "They stopped the train down there in Wainwright, and got out at the station."

"That's right, isn't it, Ma, and you know, at that time, I think monarchy meant quite a bit more to everybody, and they were just a young couple and they were quite smart-lookin'," Ted recalled. "He was a little taller, but it was a big deal anyway, and lots of times they said they'd stop at some siding on the railway, if there was a lot of people waiting for them, and they'd get out on the platform and wave to them.

"The train had slowed down in Irma, that's where gran and grandpa went to see them, but it stopped and they got right out onto the platform in Wainwright," remembered Ted. "It was a good thing to do. War started not too long after that. People rallied around.

"And then, after we saw them, we went to the show – *The Merry Widow*, in Wainwright. At the Alma Theatre."

I listened in amazement as Ted and Molly talked about that day. Most of us have difficulty remembering what film we saw last week or last month, let alone sixty years previously.

"That was quite a time, wasn't it?" I said. "The Depression was just ending, ten years of the worst drought on record, plagues of grasshoppers, banks that couldn't or wouldn't extend agricultural loans, farmers who lost their land. And then World War II broke out, just a few months later.

"You were married the year after the war started. You moved into this house after a few years, yes?" I looked around at their home, remembering that they'd bought an old school house and remodelled it for their own use.

"That's right, we bought the old Battle Heights school – that was about the time when the little rural school districts were being consolidated. The schoolhouse used to sit two or three miles north and a mile east of Fabyan [a village about 15 miles east of Irma]. We hired a moving company, Nick's from Vermilion, to haul the building onto its new site. We set it up on blocks for the winter. Next spring, we had

Mickleson come and dig us a cellar with his cat, then we built a foundation and had Nick come back to set it on the foundation.

"We built onto it, and we've been living here ever since," Ted explained, as he looked around their cosy home. "The house was built in 1918, the main part. And we built onto it, a piece on this end and a piece on the other end, in 1960."

The kitchen window faces south. They can see the main north-south road as well as the east-west road from that window. It's a homey kitchen, with a wooden table big enough for four, or seven in a pinch, a stove and cupboards. The refrigerator is over against the north wall, beside the basement doorway. The freezer sits in the back porch, beside the washer and dryer. A living room. Three bedrooms, and a bathroom.

"We heated it with coal and wood, a stove in the kitchen kept that end warm, and we had a little heater in here to keep this end warm." Ted looked so comfortable on his chesterfield, at ease in the home he'd lived in for half his life. "We put power in here in 1952, when we moved into this house. And then we got the gas in, natural gas, when we built the addition on.

"And the barn was the same. First it belonged to my dad, on the quarter north of here. I bought it off my dad. A neighbour said it came from eastern Canada on a flat car, it was dismantled down there and brought here in pieces, and rebuilt. It's a very old structure, has morticed beams in it, cut with an axe, morticed rather than nailed together. Very little maintenance. It's lasted very well. Stood well through storms and hail. Those old barns in Ontario, the siding was placed up and down, like most of the barns down there. We changed it around – the boards shrunk up, and it got pretty drafty, so then we put plywood on the outside. Nick moved it for us, too."

"You don't have many animals around here now. I remember lots of creatures when I was a kid. Pigs, and cattle, milk cows and beef cattle too, I think. And cats and dogs. I remember when Marjorie was a little girl, she's younger than me, maybe six years. I was always astounded, being a city girl, to see her get a drink of milk. When she got thirsty, and she was probably only seven or eight years old, she'd just catch one of the cows here in the yard, put her head under a teat, and squeeze some milk into her mouth!" I was still amazed that a little girl could manage a huge cow so easily.

"Oh, yeah, she did, didn't she? Those cows were pretty gentle, you know, we couldn't have animals around here that weren't okay with the kids," responded Ted.

"Did you always have cattle, Ted?"

"Oh yeah, we did. About a hundred head of cattle. We haven't milked for six or ten years, now. And we don't have any cattle anymore, either."

"What about the equipment? Did you always share equipment with your dad, or your brothers, or did you buy your own?" Farm equipment is a huge expense, the four-wheel drive tractors of today have a price tag of close to a quarter of a million dollars.

"Well, we did share a lot of things. Then we each bought some of our own equipment. I bought my first tractor in 1947 or '48. Then in 1952 I bought a new little John Deere™ – the only new tractor I've ever had!

"It's a sad thing, you know, but after we all started using tractors, most of those horses went for meat. Gord, he still drives horses in the winter time, takes feed to the cattle with a team and wagon," Ted reminisced. "Courted Molly here with horses too, a horse and a closed-in cutter."

This last comment brought forth laughter from both Ted and Molly, as they remembered the little shelter on skis, pulled by one or two horses that had been their winter-time transportation. But they refused to provide further details...

"We had six horses and four cows when we started out. Herefords, Hereford crosses [cross-breeds]. Then in later years, we went into Charolais. By the time I quit raising cattle, I had all purebred cows. The money from the cream, it bought groceries, put gas in the car, took us to the odd show, put shoes on the kids' feet. Molly, she always raised chickens. Turkeys too."

"And I always had a big garden too," Molly interjected. "Canned quarts and quarts of vegetables for winter, before we had the deep freeze. Pickles, and jam too, saskatoons from the bushes over there on the fence line just north of here. Canned the chickens too, and beef. Handy to have, all you had to do was open up a quart jar, and you could make up supper real quick. The freezer's good, but you have to remember to take the meat out ahead of time."

"I remember having such good food here at your house. Mike told me that he remembers mealtimes here too, lots of laughter and good talk. And that you, Ted, always had time to stop and tell a story or a joke. Stories around the dinner table, or out in the field when Molly and the little kids brought lunch to you. Sealers full of hot tea or cold tea with lemons, and sandwiches or cold chicken, pies and cakes."

"And we shared the workload between us, you know," Molly said. "We'd both drive the tractors, or the truck. Pick roots and rocks." There was no men's work or women's work on this farm.

"Molly, you've got an automatic washing machine now, and a dryer. Some change from the old days, eh?" I asked, remembering the huge chore of laundry, every Monday, rain or shine.

"That's for sure. First I used a washboard, then we got a washing machine with a handle to swish the dolly around inside it, after Donny was born. Then we got a gas one, didn't get an electric machine till after we got the power in. Bought it from Carl Anquist, same guy that sold John Deere™ tractors! Wringers to squeeze the water out. And those big square washtubs, remember them? Two of them, galvanized, sat on a wooden stand I got from the Co-op, and we'd wash the clothes and wring them out, rinse them twice, and hang them out to dry. They sure smelled good though. I still like to hang things out 'less it's raining."

"Remember all those diapers, Ma, when the kids were little? Cloth diapers, they were. Molly'd wash them, and in the winter time we'd hang them on lines all over the house, to dry." Ted chuckled at the memory of ducking through the hanging diapers.

"Remember when Marjory got lost, Ted, when she came up to the field where you were working? She would have been five or six maybe then, not in school yet," queried Molly.

"That was quite a time, wasn't it? She sat right down in the furrow, the horses veered around her, wouldn't hurt her a bit," Ted marvelled.

"What happened?"

"Well, I'd gone to town with Lillian Glover, we'd stopped to talk with Ted on the way home, then after we got here, Marjory wanted to go back, so she just walked out the door and back to the field. Sat right down when she got tired and waited for him to get to her," remembered Molly.

"How did you find her?" I asked.

"Followed her tracks. It hadn't rained for quite a few days, pretty dusty out there, so I just followed her tracks. Found her about the same time Ted and the horses had got to her," Molly replied. "She didn't do that again!"

"There must have been some tough times, too, for you folks?"

"Well, there were, but not too bad. Hail was the worst, we had quite a few hailstorms over the years. It just takes a few minutes, and you've lost your whole year's work. That was the worst. With frost, you always get feed, but with hail you've got nothing left.

"In the start, we didn't insure for hail damage. Afterwards, we had to take out insurance every year. We still do that."

[All risk crop insurance is available to farmers through the federal and provincial authorities. The insurance is intended to stabilize farm incomes by indemnifying farmers whose crops have been destroyed through natural disasters such as hail.]

"There have been a lot of organizations in this community, Ted, according to the Irma history book. Were you active in any of them, or were you mostly focussed on the farm and your family?" I asked.

"No, not too many of them. Oh, I sat on the Co-op Board for a long time – fifteen years, I think. Your grandpa was one of the main people

Ted and Molly took their family to church every Sunday, regardless of the weather. Here's grandpa minding Don outside the church, probably waiting for Ted to get the car warmed up, c1949.

who started that Co-op, you know. He wasn't ever on the Board, but he got things started. And then I sat on it, and it's been a pretty successful operation. But I never got involved in the Elks or the Masons, you know. We made sure the kids were involved with 4-H[20], too I don't think I ever acted as leader, you know, but I always set them up with a good calf. Gordie, now, I think he spent some time leading the 4-H, you'd have to ask him about that. And Ron too, I think he was a leader when his kids were raising calves.

"I put in a little time on church things, over the years. Sat on the Vestry, got roped in to be treasurer sometimes, stuff like that. Ron and I promised mum and dad that we'd keep that church going, you know, for as long as they lived. And we did, too. Kept it open even after dad died, till mom went in 1981. Then we shut it down. People don't go to church like they used to. Or they go to Wainwright. We tried going there, but it didn't work out very well," Ted explained.

"We tried going to the church there," Molly interjected. "But they were all divided about the minister, and we didn't want to get involved in that. He seemed fine to us. So we just don't go any more."

*Top: Ted and Molly all
dressed up, likely for their
daughter Marjorie's wedding
in August 1967. The cars
were decorated with Kleenex
flowers.*

*Bottom: Len and Ted at the
family reunion in 1985; they
seldom stopped laughing.*

Not even religious congregations escape the vicissitudes of life, it seems.

"Ted, if you had your life to live over, would you choose to do things differently?" I'd always wondered whether this very contented-seeming uncle had had a yen to do something other than farm.

"No, I wouldn't. I'd still go the way we went. Things have gone well," he replied.

What a wonderful response, I thought to myself. Neither my Uncle Ted or his wife Molly craved the city's lights or its comforts, or a different way of life. They were content in their comfortable home, its feeling similar to that of my grandparents' home. A team. Not world travellers, they don't even go to the city [a distance of 125 miles, 200 km] unless they have to. Like when Ted's health became poor. That time, the Edmonton oncologist prescribed drugs to keep his prostate cancer at bay.

Uncle Ted had quietly offered financial assistance, as well as stability, when my life went into crisis – when my first marriage ended in 1980, and again when my husband Ron died in 2002. Ted had offered assistance when I'd headed up the family reunion committee in 1996. He was strong and stable, quiet and kind. Always fair. A gem that needed no polish.

Sometime in the 1990s, Gordie and his wife Leone organized the first old-fashioned threshing bee. A few acres, perhaps twenty, of barley or oats were cut and bound the old way, and the bundles placed in stooks. Gordie harnessed his handsome black team to the hay rick and gave visiting children and adults a ride as he went off to pick up the stooks and haul them to the threshing machine. The uncles forked the bundles into the thresher, ran the equipment, made sure the grain went into the hopper and then the truck, watched as the straw blew into its pile, and generally kept everything running. The women visited, watched with amusement as their men harvested just like the old days, and were glad they no longer had to prepare meals and provide accommodation for the fifteen- or twenty-man threshing crews.

Just like the old days: the long belt from the tractor powers the thresher, bundles are tossed from the hayrick into the hopper, grain kernels blow into the grain wagon. Everyone had a turn picking up the stooked bundles from the field and riding the loaded hayrick back to the thresher.

Bundled up and sheltered by the big bales: Ted, Phyllis, Leo, Olive with her granddaughter Rebecca, Ron. Family and friends came out to watch, then gathered at Gordie and Leone's for food and drink, laughter and talk. c1995.

Top: Ted was seldom happier than when he was handling horses; here he is with one of Gordie's handsome black work horses. c2000

Bottom: Ted and Molly surrounded by their family (l to r) Aletha, Gord, Don and Marjorie, c2004.

SUNDAY, APRIL 24, 2005. Just home from Disneyland late last night, with my daughter Kate and her husband Mark, their sons Tylor and Jadyn. Colleen phoned today to say that Uncle Ted had been taken to the palliative care ward in the hospital. His catheter had fallen out. He had to have a bit of anaesthetic so the doctors could replace it – the tumour had filled the bladder, and the fluids were not draining. Ted told the doctor not to do any life-saving procedures. He didn't want any more treatments or surgery.

I think he's tired of it all. Molly and he were admitted to the Auxiliary hospital in late January, in a double room so they could stay together. Molly's forgetfulness is becoming more pronounced.

Molly had become so frail, able to take only a few steps at a time. Her family held an eighty-ninth birthday party for her on April 10th, at the hospital. Then she and Ted went upstairs, to the active treatment side of the hospital, to visit their youngest daughter, Aletha, who was too sick to come down to the party.

Aletha had been diagnosed earlier that month with cancerous tumours on her liver, one grapefruit-sized, the other orange-sized. Diagnosis was only about two weeks ago.

Aletha's funeral was April 17th, Sunday, from the Irma school gym, filled to capacity. Ted and Molly attended the funeral in wheelchairs. That day, an aura of intense sadness surrounded my aunt and uncle. Molly knew that Aletha was gone. Ted was waxen-faced.

I went down to Wainwright to see Ted on Monday afternoon. By that time, he no longer knew me. Molly gathered him up in her arms, and gave him a big smacking kiss – "There, now you know who I am, don't you? Your bed-partner." He still didn't really know her.

She and I sat on the chesterfield in the family room. "I'm glad he opened his eyes," she said, "That means he'll live and he'll be able to get up out of that bed and come home with me."

Ted slipped away in his sleep, about 1:30 a.m., Tuesday April 26th. His grandson Allan Crawford, Allan's wife Cindy, and their son were with him.

They told Molly the next day. She was fully lucid.

The funeral was held Saturday, April 30th at St. Thomas Anglican Church, Wainwright, at 1:30 p.m. Lunch followed at the New Horizons Seniors' Centre in Irma. Burial was in the Irma cemetery, where Ted had bought plots for himself and Molly.

Ted's family sat close together as they drank their tea or coffee, nibbled at sandwiches and cookies and fruit. Red-haired Marjorie, her husband Allan and their eight children – all with their mother's hair colour – took up an entire table. They laughed as they remembered their time with Ted, the wrestling matches between Ted and one or two or more grandchildren at once, with Molly calling "Ted, you leave those kids alone," and Ted continuing to tickle the children's ribs as they all laughed crazily.

Or the times when Ted and Molly went to Marj and Allan's to check on the progress of the kids' 4-H cattle. Ted usually started the kids with a calf from his own registered Charolais herd, and watched as the youngsters learned to feed and groom the calf in preparation for the spring 4-H Calf Club show.

The kids laughed about Ted's gambling days – when he and his brother-in-law, Roy Burton, bet 25¢ on the pony chuckwagon races at the Vermilion Fair. As the kids got older, Ted allowed them to pick the winner. He'd hoot and holler and cheer on the chosen team, then win or lose he'd squeeze the youngster's knee and promise that "We'll get 'em next time".

Precious memories.

CHAPTER 12

Len

When did Len go east, and why? Who was this multi-faceted man,

this intense perfectionist, nervous entrepreneur, captivating beau,

authoritarian but loving father, devoted but absent son?

THE THURSTON FAMILY's embarkation photo shows Len in front of his father, dressed in short pants and long socks, a beanie cap, and a warm woollen coat belted at the waist. He was a sturdy nine-year-old with large, wide-open eyes, a strong high forehead, and white teeth. He was a boy full of enthusiasm, apparently eager for the adventure ahead.

Len grew to be a tall man, dark-haired, strong, with an energy field that brought people to him like a magnet. Perhaps it was his smile and the glint of his eyes; although he was not good at small talk, his laughter could fill a room. He was adored by his granddaughters, respected and perhaps feared by his children, loved by his wife, honoured by his customers. Len was honest, hard-working, impervious to cold weather and adverse conditions. He gave his all and expected others to do the same.

He was also conscious that he'd never gone beyond high school – perhaps didn't even finish Grade 12. As an entrepreneur, he was in his shop seven days a week, and propelled the initially one-man operation into a business with many employees and highly special-ized equipment. But his hands-on management style got in the way of long-range business planning, and his fear of debt eliminated the opportunity to make judicial use of borrowed funds.

Len was impulsive. He could suddenly appear at his parents' home – 2500 miles (4000 km) from his own home – with little or no notice. He thought a family vacation meant phoning his wife at 3:00 p.m. to tell her he'd be home in an hour or two and to pack up the kids.

Len lived his whole life eagerly. He searched for challenges, over-came obstacles, and hid his fears from all but a select few. Overtly low-keyed, he covered his anger with his smile. He was a dynamic individual with a huge need to succeed. And an even larger need to love and be loved. I saw him as simultaneously enigmatic and caring, aloof and connected. I wish I'd had the chance to know him better.

ALTHOUGH UNCLE LEN popped into and out of my life at widely disparate intervals, I always felt a connection with him, a bond that gave us freedom to talk, a sense that we mattered to another. Len had moved to Ontario before I was born. His visits to Western Canada were infrequent, always brief, and only occasionally included his wife or children. But as my own career and business necessitated trips to Toronto, I called or visited with Uncle Len and Aunt Jean in Brampton whenever I could. Those few visits remain treasured memories. Uncle Len died before this narrative was conceived. The stories told here are true to Len's character; only the dialogue is creative.

LEN'S BRITISH SCHOOL-BOY ATTIRE was soon discarded in favour of the local uniform – denim overalls, cotton shirts, and boots with heavy socks – men's wear in a micro-version. Hand-me-downs were the norm, or made-overs created from the good parts of a bigger person's worn-out pants or overalls.

With his four brothers and sisters, he walked the three miles (5 km) to school and back. The route angled southwest from the house, across Barber's field, past Milburn's slough, across the road and through the field that now is the Irma golf course, into the village and over to the school.

"There's no houses, Phyl," Len may have said on one of their early journeys, "none at all. Nobody lives between us and the school."

"It's not like home, is it?" responded his sister, as she picked her way along the higher ground. "Nothing's the same, not the school, or the town, or the houses. Not even the roads."

They were used to walking a fair distance to school – it was almost five miles from Welford Farm to the Romilly School in Barry. But in Wales there were houses, farms, green fields, people, and proper roads, not these muddy, ungravelled routes. But the prairie anemones, crocuses, didn't bloom in Barry as they did on the prairies. The children were intrigued with the carpet of furry, light-purple flowers that bloomed in the pastures and sprang up everywhere in still-unbroken land

Everything here was different, including the school. Not all the Thurston siblings enjoyed learning as much as Phyllis and Len, although they all obtained good marks. Len excelled in math and geometry. In those days, long before privacy issues were raised, the *Irma Times* published the students' marks every month. The March 8th, 1929 issue of the newspaper showed that Frederick Thurston, as he was known in school – his full name was Frederick Leonard – was at the top of his Grade IV class with an average of 86%.

"He sure hated that name, by golly," Ted told me once. "As soon as he was out of school, he dropped the Frederick part, never used it again that I know of."

"Well I guess that's right. I didn't even know his name was anything but Len, I'll bet none of the cousins ever heard that either."

The boys made play out of work sometimes, just as these two are doing, c1936.

Len in summer, c1936, wearing a woollen cap like his father's.

Len and his siblings settled into their new routine – chores, breakfast, school, more chores, homework, supper, bed during the school year. As they grew older, they were given increasing responsibilities for crop production and livestock care. Spring, summer, and fall were busy times. There was always land to be harrowed or plowed, animals to be fed, horses to be trained, water wells to be tended, a million chores to do. The family's garden had to be tended; it was their lifeline to food during the Depression years when produce prices were so low it was hardly worth selling their grain or beef, cream or eggs, even if they could find buyers.

As a young man, farming wasn't Len's choice of vocation. He had a hard time with the horses, disliked the dust and grasshoppers, and was impatient with the monotonous back and forth, back and forth plowing, tilling, and seeding operations. He especially disliked his father's demands.

"A-a-a-a-a-and we'll be working up on 9 today, Len," his father's stutter always seemed worse in the morning, or when he started a sentence. "Y-y-y-you get that black team up to me before noon, now, and mind you don't leave the mare's foal behind."

With that, Fred grasped the reins of the six-horse team that stood waiting, harnessed and impatient. They were heavy draft horses with huge hoofs, gentle eyes, and stoic manner, four of them well-broken to work the fields, the other two youngsters in their first year of harness. Fred Thurston and his sons were used to working with these big creatures. The family had developed a reputation with the neighbours for treating the horses well, and for training them with firmness, not cruelty.

"Ron, can you get those other two black horses rounded up for me?" asked Len in exasperation. Ron was putting up new fencing around the sheep pasture, but he was better at horse-handling than his brother.

Len had already spent most of an hour trying to catch the two young horses. Sensing his dislike, the pair raced from one end of the field to the other, let Len almost catch them, then charged off again just as he was about to get the halter on the darker one. It was past 10 o'clock already, and it would take an hour to get up to [Section] 9 where his dad was working. He had to be there with the team and his father's lunch before noon, and he'd had unending trouble as he had tried to round up all eight horses and the mare's rambunctious young foal.

The bandaged fingers on his left hand were bothering him too, and he hated what he knew he'd see when the bandages came off. There'd be a blank space there where the ring finger should be, the one that had been amputated to stop the infection that had set in after the doctor had cut apart his last two fingers, the ones that had always been joined. Nellie blamed herself for the unseparated fingers, explained them with a that tale about having squeezed her own fingers in fear as she was almost struck by a runaway team while she was pregnant with him …"There couldn't be any truth in it, could there?" he wondered as he shielded the aching hand.

"Alright, I'll catch them for you, Len," replied Ron, glad of an excuse to leave the box-wire and fence posts for a while. "Where did you leave the oats pail?"

"Look Ron, don't tell dad, but I dropped it in the field and old Joe here stomped on it, I'll straighten it out before dad sees it," said Len, by now hot both from the sun and from his own frustration.

Before long Ron was back, leading the two young Clydesdales. Soon Len had them harnessed. He picked up the pail of dinner for his father and himself, and headed down the hill to the main road. The horses' hooves stirred the dust and the slight northwesterly breeze blew it back into Len's face. By the time he reached his father, Len's face and hands and clothes were covered with fine brown silty dust.

"C-c-c-caught them, did you?" commented Fred as he steered his team toward Len and the fresh horses. "Look sharp now, you should have been here an hour ago. These horses can't go much longer." He unhooked his team from the plow and watched as they headed for the grassy shade outside the bluff.

The two men also headed toward the poplar bluff, found a bit of shelter from the noonday sun, and sat down to eat their dinner of cold chicken, potato salad, thick pieces of home-baked bread and butter, cool tea, and some saskatoon-and-rhubarb pastries. Then Len hitched the fresh team to the plow. His father loosened his boot laces, pulled his tweed hat over his face to keep the flies away, and instantly fell into a sound sleep. Fifteen minutes later he woke up, cleared his throat, lit his pipe, visited the poplar bluff briefly, and was ready to take the first team back home.

Len plowed until late afternoon, when Ron arrived with the day's third team and some supper. The two young men repeated the earlier meal break.

"Got some tea there, Ron?" asked Len. "Thought for a while we were going to get some rain, but it's blown off again."

"Yeah, there's tea here in the bucket," said his brother, as he pulled the big two-quart sealer of tea from the milk pail. "And a cup to go with it!" he said with a laugh. "Sure is dry up here, ain't it? Even the weeds don't grow worth a darn."

"Naw," Len replied, "there's hardly even any moisture down there at the bottom of the furrow."

It was the mid-thirties, and the Depression's drought had hit the Irma area with a vengeance. No rain had fallen for weeks on end and the sun beat down so hard even the earthworms and grubs couldn't stand to inhabit the top few inches of parched earth.

❧

"LEN, I BEEN THINKIN'," Ted said to his brother as they replaced the weathered shingles on the barn. "This house is pretty small, them kids are all getting bigger, and you're done with school now. See this ad in the *Irma Times*, this here Chamberlain woman in Edmonton has that half-section just north of dad's, not the next quarter section but the one past that, and she wants to rent it. There's a house, I think it was one of those old Hudson's Bay[21] houses, and a barn. I haven't been

Looks like Winnie up on the broad back of the horse, with her brothers Ted and Len watching out for her.

in there, been past it every day though, what do you say we go take a look tomorrow, see if the house could be lived in? We could rent it, take our steers and heifers up there, set ourselves up in housekeeping. Mum could spare a few dishes and things maybe. We'd be alright, you and I. What about it?"

"Say, that's a good idea. We could batch, give them a break here, and we'd be on our own," replied Len. "Let's go see the place."

As soon as their day's chores were done, before the sun had set on the long, hot prairie summer day, Ted and Len were on their saddle horses, headed up the road to the old Chamberlain place. They found the house barely livable, but it would do for the two young men who were itching to get out on their own. It was a two-storey, wood frame place[22] with no insulation, doors that almost fit their frames, windows in every room, a stove with a chimney-pipe that went through the upstairs hallway to provide a modicum of warmth before its exit out the roof. The barn wasn't very big, but it was sound enough to provide shelter for the horses and cattle during the bitterest of winter weather. The young men moved in with a few dishes and kitchen tools from home, a couple of beds from the hardware store, blankets their mother had pieced together from worn-out melton cloth coats, quilts made with woollen batts from their own sheep. Within a few months the alkaline well-water had eaten holes in the aluminum saucepans, but the young men's stomachs seemed to suffer no ill effects.

"Quiet without Ted and Len, isn't it, Mam?" growled Fred. "Mary's gone, Phyllis is at Normal School. Won't be long until there's just you and me again."

"The boys will be home for supper tomorrow, Dad," responded Gran, "Len was in today looking for some bread. That's a cold house they're in."

Only five youngsters were left at home by 1935. Mary came and went, sometimes boarding with the farm families for whom she worked, sometimes at home between jobs. Winnie, the youngest, felt especially bereft when her older brothers moved out.

"HEY LEN, you going to the dance tonight?" called Earl Goodale from the back of his saddle-horse as he rode into the yard one fall afternoon. The horse's hooves crackled against the poplar leaves covering the ground where they'd been blown just the day before. "There's going to be a couple of new girls there, I hear, just moved in up the way," he said with a chuckle.

Earl, or Slim as most people called him, his twin brother Irwin, and their brother Ellsworth, all tall and good-looking, lived with their parents on a farm north of the Thurston farm. The Goodale family had its share of trouble. They moved from Hamilton, Ontario to Irma in 1918, but had insufficient land broken to make a living. Calvin (the father) bought a Van Slyke plow and did custom breaking for other farmers. It was Cal Goodale who hired Fred that first year the Thurston family lived in Irma. In the late 1920's, Cal sold his horses in exchange for a Rumley tractor, but the tractor wasn't intended for such heavy work and in the 1930's, Cal reverted to horses for pulling the breaking plow. Disaster struck the family in 1934 when Mrs. Goodale died suddenly.

"Those boys took it real hard when their mother died," Ted told me. "They sure did. They grieved so hard, I don't know if they ever got over it."

Although Cal tried, he couldn't convince any of his sons to find and marry a woman who would keep house for all of them. The Goodale and Thurston boys went to the local dances, picnics, and parades when they weren't tied up with their fathers' farms.

The two eldest Thurston boys lived in their rented house for three years. They'd driven their own and some of their dad's cattle up to their place, and kept them close to the barn where the hay was stored in the loft and in carefully built stacks. They took turns working for other farmers, but always made sure one of them was available to work with their dad. Income was excruciatingly low. The *Irma Times* listed buyers' prices each week: on April 14, 1933, choice heavy steers were selling in Edmonton at $3.25, a full $2.00 less than on May 8th, 1931. Upland hay was selling at $7.00, loaded onto cars at shipping point; compared to the $9.00 price in 1931. Similarly, buyers paid only 8¢ a dozen for extras (that is, the best and biggest eggs) in 1933, down from the 12¢ paid in 1931. Prices continued their downward spiral until the late 1930's. It wasn't until the outbreak of World War II that prices fully stabilized, then rose to profitable levels. By then, there were major changes on the Thurston horizon.

Nobody was surprised when Ted announced his engagement to Molly Burton, the diminutive blonde who lived a few miles northeast of the Thurstons. His brother's wedding on November 2, 1940 brought Len to a crossroad. He didn't really want to batch it alone, but neither was he anxious to live somewhere else. Still, there was an itchiness in his feet. He had a little money, crop prices were on the rise, so were cattle prices. Maybe a vacation in Ontario...perhaps to see his friend Slim Goodale.

There are conflicting stories about when and how Len went to Ontario, and with whom. The family legends range from one in which Len and his friend Slim took a load of cattle to Ontario, with a contract to keep the animals fed and watered until they reached their

Top: Len in winter, perhaps the last one he spent in Irma, c1939 or 1940.

Right: In front of someone's house, perhaps the Goodales's, in Ontario, probably summer 1940.

destination. (In those days, Alberta beef was shipped live to Ontario for slaughtering and butchering.) Some siblings believed Len went to Ontario for a holiday and just didn't return. Both versions of the 'off to Ontario' story have Len and Slim travelling together.

The Irma history book, however, tells a different story. The Goodale entries, prepared by Earl Goodale himself, say that Earl and Ellsworth went to Hamilton in 1939, intending to get work in a Hamilton steel mill or factory. Eventually, they joined the army. In Irma, Cal married Helen Prosser, then in 1941 they also moved to Hamilton, the centre of Canadian steel production.

By 1940, most Ontario factories were converting to war supplies production – gas masks, bombs, armaments, airplanes. Len got a job at the Bridge and Tank Ltd. steel plant in Hamilton, Ontario. Again, family legend says that Ellsworth Goodale worked at the plant as a watchman, but the Irma history entry says that Ellsworth had a "security job with Westinghouse". Regardless of the location or the connection, the job had an irreversible impact on Len.

The plant in which Len worked manufactured steel beams, which were moved through the plant suspended from overhead cranes. Inside the plant, the light was low, acrid fumes emanated from the iron-smelting furnaces, and heat from the molten metal dissipated throughout the work area.

The work was hard and hot, but didn't involve horses and it paid regularly. Within a few months Len was promoted to foreman. Never able to stand by and watch, he continued to work with the men he supervised. Just as they moved a partially completed beam, the steel supporting chain broke. The beam that fell on Len crushed his leg, broke the bones in too many places to count, and severely injured his back.

Len set the record for the shortest time ever as a foreman – he'd been promoted at 3 o'clock and the steel beams ended his career two hours later. Len was rushed to hospital.

The doctors that surrounded Len's bed were the best in Hamilton.

"Mr. Thurston, we have to take that leg off," announced the senior surgeon. "You'll never use it again, the bones are shattered beyond repair. We can't fix them."

"Not my leg," Len retorted. "I've only got two legs, and I'm going to keep them both."

"Mr. Thurston, if those wounds get infected, gangrene is likely to set in and you'll lose not only your leg, but your life." The doctors were intense and urgent. Their only defense for infection was sulfa drugs. Len already knew about infections – he'd battled that when his fingers had been separated. He lost a finger in that battle. He intended to win this fight. Who knew that penicillin[23] would be available within a few short years, the miracle cure for the infectious bacilli that had killed so many?

The discussion between Len and his doctors went on for some time. Len won. The victory meant months in hospital, a year and a half out of a young man's life, while the bones healed with the steel plates and screws inside them. He endured months of agonizing pain from a wound that scarred him forever, but he did recover. And he learned to walk again. On both legs.

❦

DURING THOSE EIGHTEEN MONTHS in hospital, Len had plenty of time to think. He couldn't do much else.

"I remember the rain, Jeannie," Len told me many years later, "drop after drop falling against the window, running down. Lying there in bed, with the leg all bunged up. Lets you figure out what's important in life."

The pain lines deepened in Uncle Len's weathered face, visualized in his memory as a young man lying in his hospital bed, seeing the rain, searing pain in his back and legs. It was a movie that must have played on the inside of his eyelids time after time.

For sure Len would never farm again, at least not with horses. He would never be able to manage that backbreaking manual labour. How would he support himself, and what kind of life could he build, this handsome, virile young man with the inquiring mind, the intense energy, and the battered body?

As soon as he was able to get around on crutches, Len enrolled in a tool-and-die maker program at a Toronto trade school; Workers' Compensation provided financial support. On the weekends, he took the streetcar to Brampton where his sister Mary and her husband Bert lived.

After lunch with his sister and her family, Len suggested ice cream. "Come on Teddie, let's go get some dessert," he said, grasping the child's chubby hand. Off they went, Len on crutches with his little nephew close beside him, the boy's stubby legs churning to keep up.

A sparkling-eyed young woman worked behind the counter. Len had noticed her riding the trolley out from Toronto, but they hadn't spoken.

"Hi," she said, "what can I get for you today? Some ice cream maybe? We have chocolate, neopolitan, strawberry, vanilla – well, the names are all up there on the board, you can read them yourself."

Was it really accidental that Len and this feisty ice cream lady, Jean Rudd, arrived at the bus stop in time to ride back to the city together? Jean looked forward to seeing the young man with the bad leg. He was intrigued by her laughing view of life. They were married on June 12, 1943 at Christ Church in Jean's home town of Brampton, Ontario, not far from the café and store where Len and Teddie had eaten an inordinate amount of ice cream.

Soon Len completed his trades program and was ready to find work.

"Len, would you like me to put in a word for you at Victory Aircraft?" asked Bert. "The plant is running 24 hours a day. There just aren't enough men to do all the work. We're turning out Lancasters as fast as we can. I'm sure there'd be a place for you."

Len stayed at the plant until the war was almost over and the production lines slowed. The men's talk turned to the new challenge of finding jobs.

Top: Len and Jean's
wedding, Slim Goodale on
the left; Winnie Allen was
bridesmaid, 1943.

Right:Len and Slim on Len's
wedding day. Who wouldn't
have fallen for either of these
handsome, mischievous
men?

Jean's first trip to Irma, 1945; playing with her son Johnny in front of the house. Len's brothers told Jean all sorts of wild stories about life on a western farm.

"Well, what now, Bert? Got any plans? It's easy to see the plant will be laying men off pretty soon."

Len and Bert lay on the lawn behind the garage at Cooksville as their wives prepared supper. The children played with their dump trucks and earth-movers on the vacant lot.

Len and Jean and their eldest son, John, as well as Bert and his eldest son, Ted, had just returned from Alberta. They had considered a return to farming, had looked at available land, discussed farming methods and incomes with the neighbours, and visited with the Thurston family. As usual, Len's sister Mary had instigated the trip – she wanted to be close to her parents, and she'd encouraged her husband and brother to seek work in Alberta.

But Len's wife was a city gal – although it was fun for her to visit the farm, Len knew she wouldn't be amused should she get lost on a trip to the outhouse on a dark night. Nor would she be happy if she had to wait another eight or ten years for electricity and the conveniences it powered.

❧

I TALKED WITH AUNT JEAN about that trip. She recalled stories of gran being frightened of Indians who camped beside the driveway to the farmhouse, and of tramps and wild animals.

"Good heavens," I thought, "I've never heard those stories, I wonder if those guys were pulling Jean's leg again."

I checked with my uncles and saw that funny little look men get when they've been caught out at some mischief. And to think Aunt Jean had believed them, had actually believed the Indians on the warpath stories, tales that might have looked good in Hollywood westerns, but certainly had no element of truth in Western Canada – especially in the prairies of the 1940's!

Bert and Len looked at land (prices had increased exponentially since pre-war days), and checked out the job market. Edmonton was still the province's agricultural centre. Oil had not yet been discovered at Leduc; there were no major manufacturing concerns in the province.

"There's nothing here for us. There's not much manufacturing, not even much construction except houses. We don't know anything about carpentry, and besides – that sort of thing shuts right down in the winter."

The two families returned to Ontario.

Now, as they watched the little boys move dirt with their toy trucks, ideas began to form.

"You know, those kids just might have something there. See how they're moving that dirt all around, loading it and dumping it, making holes and hills? I'll bet there's work to be done for all these greenhouse operators. Jean, where does your father get the soil and manure for his greenhouse?" asked Len.

"Oh, I don't know, Len, he never tells me where he gets his stuff from. Why would I want to know anyhow?" responded Jean as she accepted a cigarette and light from her husband.

"You could be right, Len. There's a lot of greenhouses in Brampton. And you know, those boys are all going to be coming home soon from overseas. There's going to be a huge building boom I'll bet," Bert commented, again reviewing the economic predictions he'd read about in the *Toronto Star*.

The nursery business was a major player in the Brampton economy. The town is only a few miles northwest of Toronto, on fertile soil beside the Etobicoke River.

A new industry had emerged in Brampton by the mid Victorian era. In 1860 Edward Dale established a flower nursery. Within a few short years Brampton became known as the "Flowertown of Canada" and soon Dale's Nursery was Brampton's largest employer. By the turn of the century hundreds of acres of land were filled with greenhouses growing prize orchids, hybrid roses and many other quality flowers. Most of these flowers were grown for export around the world...notes the City of Brampton website (www.city.brampton.on.ca).

"And they'll all be buying flowers for their wives, and their mothers, and their girlfriends. Those greenhouses are going to make a killing. Well, I don't want any part of running a greenhouse, but we could sure supply them with soil and manure and sand," Len warmed to the subject. "We could get a couple of trucks, I know a guy that's got a couple of Reo's for sale, they won't cost all that much, one for you and one for me. We could hire students in the summer if we need to. We'd do okay, I'll bet we would. What do you think, Bert?"

And so the next venture began. Oddly enough, Len became involved with the nursery business about the same time as did his Great-Uncle Bill Thurston in Dinas Powys, South Wales, although Len's activities were from the soil-supply end rather than Bill's grow-and-produce end of the business. In his own way, each man worked equally diligently at his vocation.

Sweat poured from their bodies as Len and Bert hand-shovelled manure into the old Reo trucks. They were always on the lookout for manure piles. There were numerous dairy farms in the area; the farmers were glad to sell the manure and have it hauled away. Len

Len with his pipe-smoking brother Leo, summer 1947. Leo's theological studies were funded by his summer work in Len's construction company.

Len and his equipment, 1948.

and Bert loaded topsoil and sand from land they'd leased. They delivered their loads to the greenhouses, created piles wherever they were directed to dump their loads. In the summer, Len's brother Leo, an Anglican theological student in Winnipeg, came to them. He'd always liked driving trucks, knew how to do it, and wasn't afraid of working long hours.

It was a good relationship, with no more than a normal share of difficulties. Except the day when Leo drove a loaded truck onto an old wooden bridge, a bridge that may not have been designed to support such a heavy load. The truck broke through the decking.

"Well, what the…! My Gawd, what a mess this is. What am I supposed to do here? Don't you fellas know how to build bridges in this gawd-awful neck of the woods? For Pete's sake…Will one of you call me a tow truck?" and Leo went on with a string of un-priestly oaths and epithets.

Then he got out the shovels, emptied the truck of its gravel, shovelled the load into the replacement truck Len brought in, and supervised the tow truck driver as he fastened chains around the truck and hauled it to a more secure spot. Leo spent the next few hours fixing the bridge deck.

Leo wasn't the only hired hand in Len and Bert's operation that summer. The business was growing, and even though Len worked from dawn until dusk, he was forced to hire additional workers to keep the business operating effectively. Len was also happy when his four-year-old son tagged along.

"Hey there, John, going to shovel cow manure with your dad today?" teased Len's hired man. John was always welcome on the job site – the men watched out for him while Len's attention was elsewhere.

Young John waited eagerly for his father's invitation: "Want to come along with me today?" A day with dad, in the truck, was a special treat.

John's little round face shone as he rode in the truck's cab, wedged in between his father and his Uncle Leo, often with Bert squeezed into

Top: Sitting on the truck's running board with sons John and Bob, c1947.

Bottom: If Jean didn't go to Len while he was working, she seldom saw him; John in the shovel, c1948.

the front seat too. The pitchforks rattled against the truck racks in the back. John's miniature pitchfork was with the others, a fork Len had bought him so he could pitch manure just like dad.

But one day, while John helped pitch manure, a dog ran past chasing a cat, and John looked up just as his hands shoved the fork down. The tines punctured his boot, the points stuck right into his toe.

Len reacted instantly. He picked up his son and raced to the farmer's house. Off came John's boot and bloody sock. Len washed the foot clean and checked to make sure no serious damage had been done. The housewife applied a bandage. John was left in her care, eating cookies and drinking fresh milk, until the truck was loaded.

Patience was not Len's forte, either with things that interfered with his work, or things that made the work even harder or less efficient.

"Bert," he said, a couple of months after the incident with young John, "this hand work is just too hard, it takes too much time, we'll never make any money at it. We've got to get a tractor with a front-end loader. I think I can get one from a guy that I know, good price, used but not in bad shape, I know we could keep it running most of the time. What do you think?"

Both Len and Bert were exhausted. They worked from dawn till dark six days a week, from early spring until late fall.

"Ah, I'm not so sure of that, Len. That's an awful lot of money, you know. It'd take us years to get the investment back, and what would we do if the tractor broke down? We sure can't afford a new one, and that used one you mentioned…. I dunno, Len, I don't think I could do that," responded Bert gloomily, too tired to consider spending any more money. After all, they'd just got their trucks paid off. Bert didn't want to go back into debt.

A few days later, Bert watched as Len operated his front-end loader, filled a truck with manure in minutes and with little manual effort. Len's idea had, in fact, been a good one. Bert wondered at his brother-in-law's ability to see the operations so clearly, and to be able to calculate the cost and cost-recovery time in his head. They didn't have a

Finally a daughter – Jean is holding Barb, John and Bob looking on, c1950.

business plan. Len had simply purchased the loader himself, repaired the broken parts, and set it to work.

"Come on Jean, Johnnie: we've only got a few minutes before the stores close. We'd better get some groceries in here," called Len to his wife and son. Only his Thurston preoccupation with food could drive him to stop working on a sunny Saturday afternoon. The shops in Brampton were only open till 6 o'clock and never on Sunday. They climbed into the only vehicle they had – the old Reo that had just dumped another load of manure at Dale's greenhouse.

"LEN AND I HAD LOTS OF ROWS," Jean told me years later. "He thought I should just keep house and look after the kids. I found all that kind of boring. He'd be gone all day and half the night, he'd come home for supper – all he wanted was meat and potatoes and lots of pies – and then he'd go back to the shop or sometimes he'd just fall asleep in his chair.

"And he never used to give me any money," she laughed. "He figured only he should have money, I shouldn't need any 'cause he'd buy the groceries and what else would I need money for? I had to get my dad to talk to him, and eventually he started giving me some money of my own. But that was just how he'd been raised, you know. He was a good man."

❦

WHEN LEN AND JEAN were first married, they lived in a garage on the back of the Rudd property, behind Jean's father's greenhouses. They were comfortable there, Jean hung curtains on the windows, they fixed up a small kitchen and sitting area, and there was space for Len to park his trucks. He usually worked from dawn till dark, sometimes even later.

"Len, how can you work out there so long, you haven't eaten a proper meal or slept in your own bed for three days," cried Jean as Len opened the door to their garage-home.

There had been an immense snowfall just days earlier, and Len's contract to clear the heavy white stuff from Brampton's roads and parking lots was lucrative – but time-dependent. The front-end loader that Bert had been so skeptical of had paid for itself within weeks. Len's revenues far exceeded his expenses.

"Let me get you some stew, I made it yesterday thinking that you'd be home for supper, it'll just take a minute to heat up. And I've got some fresh buns too, the whole wheat ones you like, do you want some of those?"

She bustled about the kitchen, taking care of this man who could work like no other she'd ever known, seemingly impervious to the cold. He was tired though, she could see that right away, the drag of his injured leg most pronounced with fatigue. Len ate his meal and fell into bed.

The timing was right for Len and Bert's contracting endeavors. Brampton was booming, manufacturing plants were being built on the town's outskirts as well as in all the neighbouring communities.

Len and Jean bought a lot on the corner of Woodward and Sophia Avenues on Brampton's outskirts. They built a garage and lived in it until the early 1950's when they completed construction on their red-brick bungalow.

Len and Bert ran their contracting business together for only a few years, until Bert had sufficient money to open a garage in Cooksville. Len continued the business. He hired men to run his three trucks, the excavator and the backhoe. He continued to run the equipment himself, as well as taking on the tasks of fixing it, seeking business, and dealing with his nemesis – administration.

MY ELDEST COUSIN, Ted Russell, was especially close to our Uncle Len. Long before he was old enough to drive a car, he rode his bike the ten miles or so from Cooksville to Brampton to see his Uncle Len and Aunt Jean. There he sought advice and companionship from Len, roast beef and pie from Jean.

Ted worked with Uncle Len frequently over the two or three years it took to build the new red-brick house. His skin bore the brunt of fibreglass insulation, sawdust, and the wood, metal, brick, and other materials used in the house. The hazards of house construction were a small price to pay for his Uncle Len's companionship.

"MARY'S DETERMINED to go back west this time, Len. I don't know how we can make a go of it," said Bert as he and his brother-in-law sat on the front step of the garage at Cooksville, late in the fall of 1953. "She just has never been able to settle here. She always wants to go back to Irma. I don't know. Here we have power, running water, paved roads, neighbours close by. Out there, it'd be like starting all over again, no power or water or even a decent house to live in. And what would I do with this business? It's taken years to build it up. It's making us some money now. I just don't know."

"Well, you know, Bert, I'm beginning to find this construction business is getting tough. It's this damn leg, gives me the dickens sometimes, especially when it's cold. If you folks go west, I'll have a shot at the garage. We could do it on a lease basis, then if you had to return you'd have someplace to come back to." The deal was struck. Bert, Mary, and their family went west in the spring of 1954 and Len took over the garage business.

Jean wasn't as happy with the deal as was her husband. "Oh, sure, you want me to move down there to that little village of Cooksville? Now why would I want to do that? I've got my family here, and the church, and the kids' schools, and my friends. Why would you want to take me away from this and go all the way down there?" Jean had grown up in Brampton, her family and friends were all there. Len persuaded. Jean agreed to move.

They packed up their goods, the children and their toys, and moved into the house Mary and Bert had lived in with their children, the house that was attached to the garage.

Within a month they were back in Brampton. Every day for the next two years, Len drove back and forth between Brampton and Cooksville.

❧

WHEN LEN TOOK OVER the garage at Cooksville, his son was a young teenager, just starting to recognize that girls could have a place in his life – but he needed money to make that happen.

"My dad was a little tight in those days," remembered John. "And I think there was a lot of stress – it was a big operation. There was the Morris™ dealership, the Rambler™ dealership, three mechanics, and he pumped gas besides. He was pretty happy down there, though."

If John wanted money, he was going to have to work for it.

"I can pay you $1.00 a day to pump gas, check oil, and wash windshields," Len offered his eldest son. "Every Saturday, and I don't care how late you're out on Friday night, you'll have to be at the garage by 8 o'clock. I'll close the place at 7; you can come home with me then."

The deal was struck. Len was usually long gone by the time John got up on Saturday mornings. John caught a ride with a friend, and was never late, regardless of his social activities. One Saturday, Len was nowhere around when John got to the station.

"Where's Dad?" John asked one of the three mechanics. The garage was busy that day, one of the new Ramblers was out on the lot. It looked as if the clean-up boy was getting it ready for delivery. There was a bright blue Morris Minor scheduled for delivery also.

"He's got another of his headaches, John," said the mechanic. "He's sure been getting a lot of them lately, sick to his stomach too, till he's able to sleep it off. He's lying down on the cot in the office."

John peeked in. His dad was asleep, pain lines etched into his face. The migraine headache was clearly in control. Len's huge hands with their long fingers, strong and calloused, lay flung out beside his body. Funny about that left hand, one finger was missing and the little finger curled in, but it didn't seem to stop him.

"Hmmm, wonder if he'll ever tell me the real story about those fingers, instead of that cock-and-bull thing he does, telling the kids he got it caught in a screen door. But this is the third migraine he's had this week," John thought to himself, "I don't know how he can manage like this."

Len, however, was not destined to stay in the garage business for long.

"Jean, they're coming back, Mary and Bert and the kids, they've been hailed out and they're moving back here. Well, I'm going to have to hold him to that lease. It's got another year to go. He'll have to find a job for a while," said Len, hanging up the telephone after speaking with his mother and father. "Tough for them, they should never have gone back out there, but we've got a business deal and we're going to stick with it."

The lease agreement continued for a year, then the business again became Russell's Garage Ltd. Len went to work for Strip-It-Tool Ltd. as a tool-maker, then moved to Moore Dry Kiln Ltd. on Rosedale Avenue in Brampton.

YEARS LATER, my cousin John and I sat in the home he shared with his partner Barb, a condo in the old section of Brampton. Fifty years had passed since John had accompanied his dad and forked manure into the old truck. John remembered his father's work habits, the long hours, his adaptability and his skill with machinery.

I was curious about the kiln business. The greenhouses of the Brampton area were surrounded by manufacturing plants, light and heavy industries, businesses that supplied manufacturers just as, in Western Canada, there is a whole variety of oilfield supply businesses.

"John, do you remember when your dad worked for Moore Dry Kiln? What was that like? What exactly does a kiln business do?" I asked my cousin.

"Well, they made kilns for drying lumber, and lumber-handling equipment. All the kilns were built to specifications and designs from the parent company in the United States, so there wasn't a lot of figuring out to be done with the standard designs.

"Anyhow, at some point, the guy who was foreman quit to start his own business, and dad just marched into the office and applied for the job, and they gave it to him. Shocked the socks off a lot of people who had been at Moore's for a long time," chuckled John. "He stayed there for years. And see, when Moore's wasn't building a kiln, they'd take in other jobs – railings for bridges and highways, small machine jobs, repair jobs for businesses or farmers."

"I was in high school then, and he'd bring drawings home with him. He and I would work on those things...you know, there was a certain amount of trigonometry needed to arrive at angles and do fabrication. So we'd work on them, he'd take them back in the morning, and be all set to roll for the day. He did a really good job there.

"But I think dad kind of pushed Moore's to take some of those little jobs, and some of them just didn't really pay. So that's when dad started doing stuff himself, after he'd finished work for the day at Moore's."

I thought about my uncle and his drive to succeed, his ability to know when he needed to learn some new skill, and the way he'd always find someone who could help him. Ontario was industrializing heavily then, in the post-war decades, and there was a great need for people with trades skills and a desire to get ahead.

Len couldn't afford to put new equipment into his fledgling shop. Rather, he sought and found used equipment here and there, machines that perhaps needed a little attention, a replacement part or maybe just a thorough cleaning.

One fall day, John and his dad went looking at some old machining equipment in a barn in Cookstown, not far from Brampton. They came away with an engine lathe, an old welder and a hacksaw, bought for $1,000.00 from a guy who'd run a small machine shop out of his barn. Then Len bought an old mill for about $250.00 from Grosse Machine Co., all covered in grease but Len figured he could get it to work again. He began machining small jobs for farmers and plant owners, working during his off hours, evenings and weekends. He talked Ontario Hydro into giving him 600 volt power – in a residential district, where 110 volts was the norm, 220 volts for running stoves.

"I remember seeing trucks delivering 40-foot pieces of steel to the garage, the engines and winches roared as the steel was placed on the driveway right at the end of a quiet, residential street of family homes – there wasn't another plant around for miles," laughed John.

JEAN CONTINUED to run her household, and to look after her husband – when he let her.

"Hey there, Len, don't you think it's time you stopped for tea?" asked Jean late one night, long after dark. The street lights threw long shadows on the fresh snow. "I've just made your favourite peanut butter cookies, come on in and have some."

"Can't, Jean, I've got to get Jack's repair job done before morning or the day shift won't be able to work," he said, rubbing his fatigued leg for a moment.

"Well, will you drink it if I bring it out to you?" she asked.

"Ah, yes, would you, I could sure use a cup of tea and some cookies," Len responded with a winsome smile.

Soon he'd finished his first cupful, along with several cookies. "More tea, Putsy," he said with a laugh, and Jean reached for the pot.

Many evenings were spent like that. Jean helped in the only way she could.

Eventually Len quit Moore's to run his own business. He worked out of his garage, then moved into a one-third portion of his friend's 4,000 square foot building. The auto industry was booming in Ontario – those were the days when cars were big, heavy, vehicles with fins and chrome and lots of shine. Many of the auto parts were manufactured by small plants throughout Southern Ontario. The mining industry was also expanding. The time was ripe for Len and his talents.

The 1,200 square foot space Len rented from his friend Walter Mullin at Peel Industrial Supplies only suited his needs for a couple of years. The next move was to a place three times bigger, at 111 Orenda Road, still in Brampton. He filled that space with the twenty millwrights he'd hired to work on the new contracts with the Ontario Seed Co., Hudson Bay Diecasting, and other such clients.

In Ontario's manufacturing heartland, large companies and small ones sought Len's skill, his expertise, his common-sense approach, and his absolute honesty. Len's company installed and repaired manufacturing plant machines, and moved the huge equipment and the production lines in other plants. He bought a couple of lathes and a mill, as he needed them, but he continued to use his old original welder.

The expanding business didn't make life easier or more relaxed. Len was hesitant to schedule time off for vacations. What if a client needed him, or if his absence meant a missed opportunity?

Jean was alternately exasperated and persuasive. "Len, summer's coming, d'you think you'll be able to take some time off? The kids would really like to go to a lake or something," she said after dinner one Sunday evening, the one day she could entertain her sister Nell and brother Fred or other family members.

"I dunno when I'll be able to get away, you know, looks like it could be a busy summer," said Len, not ready to commit to a time or place. "I'll think about it."

A few days later Len arrived home to announce that: "We can leave tomorrow if you like, take a few days up north around the lakes."

The family scrambled to find their swimming gear and summer shorts, then watched as their mother scurried about, packing clothes and food, and muttering with both happiness and exasperation. "I wish he'd just tell me sooner," she thought, "but maybe he can't. Oh well, we'll find a place."

They all piled into the car the next morning, got off onto Highway 9 or 400 or 107, stopped for lunch beside the road, sandwiches Jean had packed, pop, and oranges, then climbed back into the car. They drove and drove, past all the No Vacancy signs until finally, at 9:30 p.m., they found a funny little cottage cluster where the 'No' in No Vacancy was dark – and there they stayed for ten days. They swam, dived off the swimming platform, built sand castles, and played 500 or euchre on rainy days. The kids caught frogs while their dad slept on his chair, in the shade on the porch. Jean watched over John, his brothers Bob and Ken, and their sister Barbara. It was a good holiday.

LEN WAS BUSIER THAN EVER after they returned. Not too busy, though, to bring his truck to a screeching stop one day when he saw his fifteen-year-old daughter Barbara walking across the field just down the block. The boy she was with had his arm around her, holding her close. Clearly he was up to what any father would interpret as no good. Len was beside the young couple in seconds.

"Get into the truck, young lady, and don't you ever let me see you with this guy again. And you," Len snarled, pointing directly at the sloppily-dressed sixteen-year-old boy, "get outta here. Stay away from my daughter. You're not welcome in her life."

Len and Barb were home in minutes, although it seemed like hours to Barb. Every second was taken up with a father-daughter monologue.

Barb did live down the embarrassment, and in 1968 married with her parents' approval – but not to the unkempt sixteen-year-old who had caused her father so much distress.

LEN CONTINUED TO STRUGGLE with the intricate machining and design details he'd never had a chance to formally learn. John had much of his father's natural aptitude for things mechanical, as well as the benefit of having learned more advanced mathematics in school.

"Okay Dad, let's see if we can do something with those drawings," said John as his father unrolled the plans left by his clients.

Although Len Thurston Ltd. had become an important player in the Brampton area, Len's Grade 11 education left him feeling inadequate with detailed design or complicated fabrication work. John's perspective helped, although his adolescent attitude was sometimes a challenge.

My cousin John was a product of the 1960's revolution – photos of him then show a lanky young man with long hair. He attended the University of Waterloo, then sat on the Board of Directors of Rochdale College, the institution which the rest of us in Canada considered Ontario's hippie college. That was when student bodies across North America protested everything from food to academic authority, a decade when drugs were readily accessible and widely experimented with, a time when young men and women bandied the slogan 'make love not war'. Len and John crossed swords frequently.

This particular night, the two men worked well together as they planned Len's next big project – the complete installation at the new

Argo Plastics plant. The following year there was the machining and millwright work for the Morgan Adhesives production lines, then an even bigger installation for General Latex and Chemicals, and so many other Brampton area industrial plants. There was always work to be done, the shop was never without work; the clipboard hanging on the wall always held new work orders.

Len spent days, evenings, sometimes all night in his shop.

"How do you ever get to see your Dad, John?" asked the teenage boy as he trudged down the street beside John, "I've never seen him any place except the shop."

"Yeah, he's always at that shop. But you know, I never have to worry about my father because when I need him, he'll be there, but you know, I can't talk to him," responded John, his hair a bit longer than his friend's, both of them dressed in bell-bottom pants and tight shirts. "I always know when he needs me in the morning. You know what he does? He shouts at us down the stairs 'Come on you guys, there's daylight in the bush.' And man, we'd better get ourselves up the stairs like we'd been shot out of a cannon,"

John laughed with typical teenage amusement, shaking his head and rolling his eyes.

Just as his wife and children never knew when to expect Len home, neither did Len's parents know when he might call – or appear. He made time to talk with his parents by phone every week or two.

"Who has time to write letters?" he'd say.

At least once a year, Len arrived at his parents' farm home, often unannounced, after jumping on a plane in Toronto for the 4-hour flight and then a two-hour drive from Edmonton to Irma.

Nellie watched in surprise as Len's vehicle wound its way up the driveway, then stopped outside the picket fence that surrounded the tiny flower bed and the back entrance. She clasped her hands with joy and exclaimed, "Oh Len, here you are. 'Ark, Dad, look who's here, come in now and take off your coat. We've just got some fresh tea made. I must have known you were coming, there's Welsh cakes baked this morning."

How many hours did it take to snare this gopher? c1958.

He brought the whole family to the west in 1958; l to r: John, Bob, Jean, Len, Barb and Ken in front.

John on horseback at George and Olive's farm, 1958.

Len's ready to get on his way again; leaving the Pugh's, 1964.

His mother smiled with the special warmth she reserved for her absentee son.

Within a couple of days Len reversed his journey, drove to Edmonton and returned the rental car, flew back to Toronto, picked up his own vehicle from the parkade and drove home to Brampton. He usually made the trip west in the summer or fall, seldom in the winter. Not only was the Western Canadian weather colder than he chose to experience, he often had complicated projects underway during the winter months.

Occasionally he trusted one of his experienced foremen to supervise a complex installation or plant changeover. Len stayed close to the action and to his workmen.

"How are you doing?" asked Len as his crew arrived back in the shop after midnight in the dead of winter, the roads icy and snow still falling. "Able to get it all into place, or are we going to have to get back there early tomorrow?"

"Nope, boss, we done 'er. She's all installed, every bit's working, it's all tested out. Ran a line of fluid through the whole thing, it'll be fine. The day shift can get started at 8 o'clock," replied the foreman, his face lined with fatigue.

He'd been at this installation for weeks, had tried hard to get it finished before the month-end deadline, and was proud of himself and his team for having accomplished an almost impossible task. The client would be pleased, maybe there'd even be a bonus. And to have the boss still here, waiting for them to come in, hot coffee and donuts ready, eased the discomfort and soothed the men's tired crankiness.

"Take the day off tomorrow, guys, there'll be a bit extra in your pay packets this week," said Len, grinning, knowing that these men deserved a pat on the back and then some.

Throughout his career, Len was a fine craftsman, and an exceptionally straightforward human being. He worked hard, paid reasonable wages, treated his staff well at the right times, and became good friends with most of his clients.

His nemesis, though, was administration and financial planning. The term business plan was not part of his lexicon.

"Damn," he said to himself one day. "It's the 29th, tomorrow is payday, I don't think we've got enough damn money in the bank to cover the payroll. Guess I'll have to see who owes us."

He riffled through the work orders on his desk, and the invoices his bookkeeper had sent out earlier that month and the month before. After a few phone calls, and a quick "I'll be back before lunch," to his receptionist, he was out the door to collect some debts and get the money into the bank before the paychecks hit it.

Thoughts of the next big machining job ran through Len's head, intrigued and exhilarated him as he worked out the complex mechanics, only half concentrating on his driving as he headed around town.

While Len often turned to John for assistance with the drawings and engineering specifications, he was less able to accept the advice or organizational skill developed by his second son, Bob.

One summer while Bob was attending the University of Guelph, Len offered his son a job at the shop, ostensibly to clean up and organize the business's administration. Bob had watched his father agonize over the business end of his shop. He'd visited the office frequently, and had watched as Len shuffled through the piles of invoices, statements, accountant's letters, and cheques piled helter-skelter on every flat surface.

Before the end of Bob's first week in the office, he'd sorted through the piles, separated invoices to be paid from those completed, and developed a system for maintaining a semblance of order. Len had given little direction and had stayed out of his office. Bob called his father in to see the new order.

"Okay Dad," he said proudly. "I've got your office all sorted out, there's clipboards for your work orders, separate ones for work in progress and jobs not started yet. Over here I put some file baskets for invoices and accounts payable are over there for your book-keeper.

"You've got a stack of phone calls waiting for you, so I made a 'Do

Not Disturb' sign for your office door, no-one will interrupt you till you've got those calls taken care of." Bob was astonished to see his father's face flush. Angry words spilled from Len's mouth as he yanked the sign down and threw it into the garbage.

"Never mind your school-book tricks in here," he stormed. "You'd better take the rest of the day off."

Bob's summer job didn't go quite as he'd anticipated. He found work elsewhere the next and all the following summers until he graduated.

In the meantime, his father's business continued to expand.

Moving plants from one place to another, installing new and already-used equipment into the new space – and getting it working – had become a major part of Len's business. He'd added a tilting apparatus onto flat-bed trucks, to carry machines needing repair over to his shop, return and lower them back into place on site. Len hired machinists, millwrights, and welders and kept them busy and satisfied. He expected a lot of himself and of his tradesmen, more of his supervisors...even the experienced foremen found it a challenge to work at Len Thurston Ltd.

"We have to move the shop again, Jean," Len said one night as they drank their after-supper tea.

"What? You just moved a couple of years ago." Jean was proud of her husband's success but surprised that he again needed more space. "Where do you think you'll go?"

"Well, there's a place over on Hansen Road South, you know where we moved the Emco plant out of? It's got 12,000 square feet, and with those other contracts coming in, we're going to need to hire more people," said Len, wonder in his voice. He'd never planned for this size of business, hadn't considered a need for this much space.

There were fewer and fewer moments of rest for Len, greater and greater stress in balancing expenses against revenue, cash inflow correlated with cash demands. Len's bad leg bothered him, as it always had when he was under stress. Jean became increasingly worried about her husband.

"John, go talk to your Dad," she said one evening when John and his wife, Liz, were home for Sunday supper.

Len was having a little 'eye-rest' in his easy chair in the front room.

"He's had so many headaches lately, bad ones, every week, he's in that darned shop until midnight just about every night. You know, he's just running himself right into the ground, John. He can't take it anymore, he's closer to sixty than fifty years old. His leg's bothering him. He never complains but I can tell what it's like, he drags the foot along, he even uses his cane during the day sometimes.

"You said a while ago that you're about finished that job you were doing for Rochdale College. You studied mechanical engineering for a while till you tossed that all in, and you've been around the shop enough, you know what's going on. I'll bet he'd jump at the chance to have you working over there."

John did as his mother suggested. After much discussion with his wife Liz, and even more with Len, the father and son worked out an agreement.

John went to work for Len, agreeing to take over the inside work, the machining and design, administration and operation of the shop. Len was freed to do the work he enjoyed, installations and testing, getting plants moved from one location to another, make sure all the pieces fitted together and worked properly, that there were no down times for any of the clients' shifts.

The two men's management styles were as different as were their haircuts – Len's brush cut never changed, while John's hair just got longer.

No longer did Len have to do everything from promote the business to authorize the cheques. With John on board, Len was able to cut back on his work hours. There was even time to relax occasionally. Sunday dinners again became occasions for family to gather, for the siblings to assemble with their spouses, and for both Jean and Len to laugh and enjoy their offspring.

Always at Sunday dinners, special occasions, even regular family meals, Len's place was at the head of the table. He sharpened the knife

There was time for other things after John bought the business; Len with Jean, probably at one of the family functions he so enjoyed, c1970.

on the steel just as his father had done, and carefully sliced the roast beef, the crispy-brown turkey or chicken, or the pineapple-and-brown-sugar encrusted ham. He chuckled as his grandchildren sneaked the first bits of meat from the platter. He brandished the carving knife like a sword as he pretended to protect the meat slices from all oncomers, a game to see who could quietly get their fingers in under grandpa's knife. No-one ever received so much as a touch or a scratch from that oh-so-sharp blade.

John and Liz, who had married in 1966, brought their two daughters to Sunday dinner, to visit with their grandparents, their aunts and uncles. The little girls had exclusive rights to their Grandpa Len's head – only they were allowed to run their hands over his brush-cut, giggling as the hair tickled their gentle palms.

"Get out of there," he'd say, batting Lisa or Sarah's hand away but smiling the whole time.

The girls weren't very old when they figured out that their grandfather, this man with the sometimes stern exterior, was really a big marshmallow inside.

"I loved his great physical presence, the safe solid feeling when he held me on his lap, his worn old plaid shirt and farmer pants...his craggy fingers, he had such big hands and fingers.

"Grandpa always wanted to be a farmer...he leased some property north of Brampton, and grew wheat and a vegetable garden. I'm sure this is where I found my passion for fresh vegetables," Lisa told me. "I particularly remember eating peas fresh off the vine and digging up little new potatoes with a pitchfork. I think he was very proud of and felt connected with what he grew. He wanted to share it with us – we always came home from grandpa's lot with a 6-quart basket of fresh vegetables.

"Without a doubt, he was the patriarch in our family. I'm sure it was much easier to be his grandchild than his child."

Being Len's granddaughter was undoubtedly easier than being his eldest son. Although there was no humour at the time, John can laugh now about his father's reaction to the news that he, John, and his girl-friend, Liz, were going to move in together.

"You can't do that and live in my house," were his words as he tossed John's belongings onto the lawn.

The next day Len stormed over to Liz's parents' house, asking them what they intended to do about the situation.

John and Liz were married within a few months.

❧

TWO YEARS LATER, in October 1968, both John's brother Bob and their sister Barb were married.

Bob's marriage to Sylvia was a relatively short-lived union, fraught with difficulties. Bob graduated from the University of Guelph and set up a veterinary practice in Drayton, a few miles northwest of Guelph. He and Sylvia had a son, Rick.

Barb moved to Hamilton with her husband, Harry, and raised two sons, Tim and Michael.

Ken, the youngest of Len and Jean's children, remained single until 1981. Then he married Carol Sherwood; they and their two sons, Colin and Ian, remained in Brampton, close to Len and Jean. Ken visited or phoned his mother every couple of days.

❧

By the mid-1970's Len Thurston Ltd. was a well-equipped business. In the shop were two lathes, a turret mill, a couple of Bridgeport mills, a couple of other mills built to the company's own specifications, a tilt-load truck, a couple of lift trucks. There were fifteen or twenty staff, depending on upcoming contracts.

The shop was busy, in spite of Ontario's down-turned economy. Len continued to arrive at the shop by 8 a.m., went home for dinner and a power nap at noon, back to work till 5:30 p.m. when he went home for supper. Sometimes he went back to the shop in the evening. Saturday was a bit more relaxed, and so was Len. Sunday meant work only until noon. Len was tired. He and John had worked out a mostly-satisfactory arrangement, although it was difficult for Len to let go. He and John had a few shouting matches. Len did the shouting and stomped out. John stood his ground and eventually managed to hold his father in one place until they came to an agreement. John would buy the business, and Len would continue to have the run of the shop.

The sale transaction was completed in 1977. John bought out the business and changed its name to John Thurston Machine Ltd. He had no intention of working the hours his dad had. He was ready to put his own stamp on the business, plan and operate it differently, build on the solid foundation his dad had created.

Soon John moved the business into an even bigger space – 30,000 square feet. The staff and the equipment were unbelievably busy, even through the downturn of 1980, and the 19 to 20% interest rates charged on bank loans. Len came and went in the shop, appearing as he wished to do bits of his own work or to give John advice or information. Better for him to be away from the shop, allow John to take it over. Len was no longer in control of the business that he'd spent untold hours and energy building up.

Len's days still contained 24 hours, though, just like everyone else's. He continued to exude energy and had to find a way to expend it. When I went to Ontario on business and was able to visit with him and Aunt Jean, they were both available to chat, or simply to hang out with. Jean continued to look after their home. Len continued to amaze me with his drive. Like his mother, he never seemed to be in a hurry, but he always accomplished a lot in a short time.

"Uncle Len, what are you doing – farming?" I asked, chuckling as we rode together into the country. He wanted to show me the land he'd bought, a few acres, two bits of ground where he could plant some corn or oats, ride around on the tractor he'd bought after he left the machine shop. Touch the soil. "Do you drive out here every day, from the house? Would you like to live here on this little farm?"

"Well, yeah, I would you know, but Jean, she's a city girl. I couldn't get her to leave Brampton, come out here where there's no neighbours right next door," Len replied with a rueful grin.

"He'd really like to be out here, I guess. It's beautiful to see how much respect he has for his wife, to know that he won't pressure her into doing something she doesn't want to do," I thought. I'd recently extricated myself from a marriage that had been fraught with just those kinds of pressures.

"It was sure good of you to come and pick me up, all the way to downtown Toronto. I'm glad you folks were home this weekend, so we could visit after I got finished exhibiting at the library conference."

"Well, that's okay. I wanted to drop in and see Bill anyway, his office is close to where your conference was."

"I would have enjoyed being a fly on the wall when you dropped in to see your friend Bill Davis [then premier of Ontario]," I chuckled.

"Oh, sure, Jeannie, he always has time to listen to me. I've known him since he was in school," Len said. He was dressed in his work clothes, overalls and plaid shirt, heavy boots with thick woollen socks.

After Len's parents died, he seldom travelled west. His siblings occasionally made the trip to Ontario, sometimes to attend the agricultural shows, sometimes just to visit.

Ron flew to Ontario every couple of years, accompanied by his wife Florence until her multiple sclerosis prevented long trips by car or even by air. Then Ron travelled alone. The two men visited Len's farm, sat on upturned logs in the sunshine smoking cigarettes and talking about farming and family. They visited the shop and made a game of repairing broken bits of machinery.

"It was great to see him there with Ron, you know, Jean," John told me, years later. "It was as if there was a real bond between the two of them. They'd laugh at one another's jokes, tell stories about when they were growing up. You never saw them without a smile on their faces. Some of the guys in the shop, the ones that had been with Dad for years, they really enjoyed seeing Dad and Ron together."

Sometimes Len took his brother out to Drayton to visit Bob, although they never knew whether Bob would be in his clinic or not by the time they arrived. If Bob was available, he'd talk animal health with his dad and his uncle. They compared conditions and issues and discussed the differences between Alberta beef cattle and Ontario beef and dairy herds.

"I used to like seeing Ron, you know, I remembered him from when I spent my summer out there in Irma when I was fifteen," Bob said. "That was a great summer. I don't know if I was really a help to them, or if they just tolerated me because I was their brother's boy, but I sure had a good time.

"But at the clinic, I never knew whether I'd still be in when they got out there or not. Most of my practice was large animals, and the only schedule the cows stuck to, especially during calving time, was in delivering their calves during the coldest, stormiest January days. Especially those cows that needed the vet's help in birthing their babies."

Bob returned in 1961 and spent the summer working with his aunts and uncles; here he is on horseback at George and Olive's or perhaps Ted and Molly's.

Like his dad, though, Bob always had good staff. Unlike his dad, Bob's marriage did not survive. Bob continued to live and work in the Drayton area.

One day in late 1984, Bob's secretary issued an invitation: "Bob, come on over and have dinner with us on Saturday."

"Well, that'd be nice," replied Bob, later thinking the invitation was a bit odd, she'd never done that before in their entire five-year working relationship. The other guest that evening was Nancy Gibb, whose warm, engaging laugh immediately caught Bob's attention.

They were married on July 23, 1985 in Drayton. Their household soon included both Nancy's daughter Dena and Bob's son Rick. Francesca was born a year later, Ivor appeared in 1988 and young John in 1990.

"How's it going, Dad?" asked Bob one day not long after he and Nancy were married.

"How do you think it's going?" snapped his father, his voice clearly conveying exasperation, his normally smooth brow deeply furrowed, lines showing around his eyes. "You get married, and the next day John gets separated."

Poor Len struggled mightily with the concepts and expectations of the younger generation. He wondered how young people could renege on their marriage vows as they seemed to do so easily, and railed against the apparent expectations and individualities. Life seemed to hold few constants.

Len did regain his sense of humour. He came to accept that life and marriage in the late 20th century were not what had been the norm fifty or more years earlier.

"I think it was hard for him, Jeannie," said John's partner, Barb Dodwell. She readily remembered the day in the late 1980's when she and John told Len of their new relationship. "Len really seemed to accept me, he was always friendly and he appeared to enjoy having John and I around."

Perhaps Len's acquiescence with the status quo reflected his inherent practicality. Perhaps it was also a reflection of Barb's own personality – "Barb just sees strangers as friends she hasn't met yet," laughed John.

One of the things Len could count on was the intense beauty of the Ontario autumn. The maple leaves had turned red in the fall of 1990. The colours even more intense than usual as the temperatures dropped very slowly, easing into autumn, giving the trees time to approach winter gently. Len spent most of his time outside.

Bob and Nancy bought a farm close to Arthur, an hour's drive north-west of Brampton. There was feeling of warmth at this place, although the almost two-hundred-year-old house was in great need of repair. Bob had been alone for years after his first marriage ended, every second weekend spent with his son Rick.

Len often visited Bob and Nancy's farm. He'd arrive at 10 or 10:30 in the morning, and come into the house asking "Is the coffee on?" The

Top: 'Seventy, Seasoned, and Saucy' shouts his apron – that's the Len I remember! 1988

Bottom: More seventieth birthday celebrations, here at the machine shop, where the staff laughed and teased, then presented him with gifts.

grandchildren's eyes lit up whenever they heard their grandpa's truck in the driveway. On one such day, Len had a special cargo.

"Come on, Ivor, I've got something for you," said Len. Off they went, hand in hand, the little boy who had suffered some oxygen starvation at birth, his slight limp matching that of his grandfather.

As they neared the truck, Ivor's eyes grew large, his mouth curled up into a grin, "For me Grandpa?" he asked, hopefully, spying the small-boy-sized wheelbarrow hidden in the truck's shadow, surrounded by the fallen red maple leaves. What a wheelbarrow it was, with a metal frame and wheel, carefully molded body, painted bright red and brown. It was the expression of a grandfather's love for a boy who needed help in learning to use his hands, a grandpa who knew that a wheelbarrow would be the best therapy possible.

Len lived long enough to see his grandson master the art of wheelbarrow transport. He was in his Brampton kitchen when disaster struck.

"Len, Len, oh my God," cried Jean, as her powerful husband fell to the floor, collapsed under his own weight, this tower of energy who had been her rock for 48 years.

"What's happening, what is it? I'm calling the ambulance, be quiet, I don't care if you don't want it, you're going to have it," she said, frantically dialling 911, disregarding Len's protests. Within seconds she could hear the sirens screaming, louder and louder as the ambulance neared their house, red lights flashing against the windows.

"How are you doing, Mr. Thurston," asked the attendant. "Let's get you up onto this stretcher, and we'll have you in the hospital in just a couple of minutes."

"No you won't," said Len, clenching his teeth, talking through the terrible pain in his abdomen. "I'll go if you make me, but I'm going to get there on my own feet."

He slowly made his way out the door and along the sidewalk, climbed into the waiting ambulance and eased himself onto the gurney, the attendants at his side.

John was at his father's side a few days later when Len briefly opened his eyes. "You did a good job, Dad," he assured his father. It was his parent's forty-eighth wedding anniversary – June 12, 1991

THE TABLE at the front of the Brampton church held Len's ashes, the urn surrounded by flowers and a photograph of this man who was, as his son described, "Easy to hurt, easy to anger, a big marshmallow inside."

Five years passed before his children went west to Irma for a family reunion. They carried their father's ashes with them. On Sunday afternoon, as the sun shone and the breeze gently riffled the maturing grain, the family gathered on the home place. Uncle Leo officiated and pronounced the blessing as he threw his brother's ashes over the land where they would become part of the soil and the family Len had loved. He was back home.

CHAPTER 13

Ron

His siblings said he was their father's 'best boy',

but he was angry anyway.

He wouldn't talk about his years in the army.

His laughter was infectious, hearty and frequent.

DARK-HAIRED, smooth-faced, smiling Ron. The handsome middle child. He was a hard-working, energetic man, sometimes gentle, sometimes angry. Remembered by some of his siblings as their father's 'best boy'. Remembered by my siblings and I for the hospitality he and Aunt Florence offered when we were children, for his resounding laughter, and the infectious cheer of his greeting. I also recall his aggressiveness, his sharp tongue, his disregard for peoples' feelings and his apparent disinterest in resolving disagreements.

Ron was a smart but minimally-educated man who loved his farm and worked it carefully. He loved his family but was far from gentle with them; he valued friendships but had little time to cultivate them. He was a man who made rice pudding for his beloved granddaughter, who invited her ministrations and those of his adopted daughter, but often rejected those of his own kin.

Ron and his brother Ted with their mother, c1940.

"I REMEMBER HIM SAYING 'You betcha', " said the Rev. Doug Coubrough at Ron's funeral in St. Thomas Anglican Church, Wainwright on February 11, 2002, four days after his death in the Viking Health Centre. "Ask him if he was going to be the Parade Marshall again for Irma Daze and he said 'You-u-u-u betcha'. Was he going to join all the rest of you at the family reunion? – 'you betcha' he laughed. And did he figure on looking at the daisies from above for a while longer, even after he'd lost his bladder and his colon and his prostate to cancer? 'You betcha' he told me, 'I ain't goin' anywhere for a while yet' ".

Both Coubrough, the United Church minister, and Pastor Bart Eriksson from the Lutheran church assisted Anglican Father Will Drake at the funeral service. Leo, Ron's minister brother, was the fourth cleric at the altar.

Dark-haired Tanya eulogized the grandfather she and her siblings and cousins loved.

"Grampa always said to me 'If you have someone to love you, you are truly blessed.' And he also said 'Do not cry for me when I am gone, for I have lived a good life and I have no regrets.' So, if you see tears in

God saw you getting tired
And a cure was not to be
So he wrapped you in his loving arms
And whispered "Come to me"
You suffered much in silence
Your spirit did not bend
You faced your pain with courage
Until the very end.
Our hearts were all most broken
You fought so hard to stay
But when we saw you sleeping
So peaceful, free from pain,
We could not wish you back
To suffer that again.
God, put your arms around him
And give him loving care,
Make up for all he suffered
And all that seems unfair.

Farming was Ron's joy, his vocation, his way of living; he drove his tractor until just a few weeks before his death. A final photograph.

our eyes, they are not tears of sadness, they are tears of joy and love for the greatest man we have ever had the honour to know and love. He has left us a wonderful legacy – may his legacy live on through us."

A long cortege of vehicles accompanied the remains for burial in the Irma cemetery, just a half mile from Ron's home, in the plot where his wife Florence and their infant son lay.

He'd lived his entire life in Canada within sight of the graveyard, with the exception of the time he'd been forced to serve in the army. He'd never really wanted to go elsewhere.

RON WAS ONLY SEVEN when he began his daily walk to the Irma school with his brothers and sisters, almost three miles (5 kms) each way, morning and night. In the winter, Fred sometimes allowed his sons to hitch a horse to the cutter, build a fire in the metal heater with the chimney that went through the cutter's roof, and drive to school over the frozen fields and roads. They carried some hay in the cutter, enough to feed the horse as it stood sheltered in the school's barn until late afternoon.

Long before he reached adolescence, Ron knew he wanted to farm. He shunned school whenever he could, preferring to seed the grain, harrow the summer fallow, or harvest the ripened crop on a brilliant fall day. Ron turned fifteen on March 3, 1935, when the Depression was in full swing: grain and cattle prices were close to the bottom of the cycle. But he was old enough to leave school. He'd completed Grade 8. What more could he possibly need?

Ron provided one more pair of full-time hands, and he could contribute a little cash income when he worked out for other farmers. Besides, with his exit from classes, there was one less student in the Thurston household who needed money for books and pencils. Ron worked with his father and his brothers Ted and Len while Leo and Ivor continued in school.

The young men and their father picked rocks for days and days. The rocks never ceased working their way up through the soil. Left in the field, they would break every plowshare, every harrow tooth, every seed drill. Odd, though, that in Wales the farmers marked out each field with a stone fence. In Western Canada, the fields were only fenced if cattle were to be turned loose – and then the fields were fenced with barbed wire. Field stones were simply dumped along the edge or at the corner of the quarter section, where they inadvertently provided shelter for bees and wasps, chipmunks and the occasional fox or coyote or badger.

As soon as the rock-picking was finished, the fields were harrowed and seeds drilled into the ground. Then, while the seeds germinated and sprang through the warming soil, the brothers cleared brush from a few more acres. It was back-breaking work: cutting and hauling trees, pulling stumps, and plowing the virgin sod. Eventually most of the acreage on each field was cleared, although that took years of labour. A strip of trees and shrubs was usually left along the property line to provide a buffer from the winds. Wherever the field had a low spot, a ring of willows grew to encircle the rainwater or spring snow-melt. In other places, often where there was a poorer patch of soil, or an area that was low but not low enough for a slough to develop, Fred and his sons left a patch of native brush. It was cool inside the bluff, as we called it. Aspen or black poplars were left growing, as well as saskatoon bushes, wild roses, and sometimes high-bush cranberries or hazelnuts. Grasses and wild flowers, weeds and sedges covered the ground. The bluffs provided shelter for the cattle and the horses, as well as the wild creatures – partridge and grouse, migratory song-birds and resident chickadees and nuthatches, coyotes and deer. As land settlement and clearing progressed, fewer and fewer prairie fires raced across the landscape – and the bluffs became increasingly per-manent homes for wildlife, both flora and fauna.

Every field operation needed manpower and horsepower. There was a resident population of ten or twelve horses on the Thurston farm, bought at auction sales or directly from other farmers. Every summer, several young horses were added to the herd, trainees loaned to the Thurstons at no cost in exchange for training them to work in harness with other horses. Fred expected his sons to learn horse-handling by example. He seldom gave direct instructions, such as "Catch that mare like this..." or "When that young colt tries to get away..." It didn't take long for the horses to figure out that Fred meant business, that Ted would be good to them but he expected them to cooperate, Len was okay but he didn't have much patience, and that Ron simply didn't like them. The horses reacted to Ron's lack of empathy.

"Git over here," Ron barked at Bess, the big Clydesdale cross and her four-legged partner. Leo had already left the yard with the new tractor. Ron struggled to get the last pair of horses into their traces, a six-horse team hitched to the disc harrows.

"Feeling their oats today, are they?" Fred chuckled, his pipe clamped between his teeth, as his son got the last buckles fastened. "They'll be quiet after they've done a few rounds in that field."

He took the leather traces from his son and snapped them against the lead horses' flanks. Another day of field work had begun. Ron and his brothers Ted and Len had plenty of chores on the home place that day – the barn roof needed repair, the south fence needed fixing, and they were almost out of chop[24] for the pigs.

The western sky was dark with a gathering storm when Fred returned for dinner. Ron released the horses into the field, and readied a second team before he also went in. He washed in the same murky water his father had used and slid into his chair. Ted grinned – his brother was just in time to escape a late-comer's glower from their father.

"For what we are about to receive, may the Lord make us truly thankful," intoned Fred.

Silence prevailed as the perpetually ravenous young men dished potatoes, vegetables, meat and gravy onto their plates. As their appetites were appeased, conversation began.

"Y-y-y-y-you tie those horses up?" Fred directed his query at Ron. "That looks like some wind that's coming in." They turned to watch the storm roll in over the Craig fields across the road.

"You put Pet in that team? That'll be a go, he sure don't like wind in his face. You watch now or he'll run that whole team off," Fred grumped as he untied his boots and prepared for his after-dinner snooze, the fifteen minute nap he needed each day.

Ron skipped a second helping of saskatoon pie and cream. The screen door slammed behind him as he headed toward the horses. The impending storm riffled the horses' manes and played with their sensibilities. Nervous, they shuffled their huge hooves and tossed their heads. Pet rolled his eyes and tried to get his back end to the rising wind.

"Get over here, you damned things. It's just wind." Ron led the harnessed team to the lee of the granary down the yard. "Settle down, now," he barked as he fastened the traces to a fence-post.

The team stayed put until Fred collected them. They didn't dare disobey this master. Ron was glad his father had taken charge. He wouldn't soon forget the trouble he'd had just a few days earlier, when another storm had blown in from the west, just as he'd started the team on a west-facing track down the middle of the field. He'd seen the storm coming. So had Pet. The young horse, new to team-work, always caused a big shemozzle when the wind blew sharp-edged grit in his eyes and against his ears. With a great whinny, Pet panicked and charged off down the field toward the poplar bluff, dragging the rest of the team with him. Ron was unceremoniously dumped from the harrow's cast-iron seat. Two hours passed before the storm abated and the horses again stood calmly in their harness.

"I'm not going to deal with these fools much longer," Ron muttered to himself. "We should have another tractor, not these ornery damned things."

In mid-summer, around the end of June, when the air was dry and no rain threatened to fall, Ron harnessed the team to the mower and cut the hay up on the north quarter. Around and around the field he drove the team, the sickle mower's blade moving back and forth, back and forth. The timothy and brome grass fell, perhaps some sweet clover and fescue and the few remaining native grasses. The scent filled the air, wrapped itself around Ron and the horses, hung across the entire quarter section until a breeze came along to blow it away. Even the horses didn't seem to mind this work; it was steady and clean, without rough patches or heavy loads to haul through mud or over stumps. Ron's thoughts turned to his plans for buying his own land, building a house, and finding a wife. But that wouldn't happen for a few years yet – there were hurdles to conquer and challenges to overcome before Ron would be able to settle down.

That summer, as usual, Ron cut the hay and left it lying in the field to cure under the sixteen or seventeen hours of sunshine that poured down every day in midsummer. Then he or one of his brothers hitched a two-horse pair to the rake and pulled the fragrant stalks into piles. The young men forked their hay into the haywagon, hauled the load close to the barn or into the middle of the pasture where they built a haystack, two men forking the stalks off the wagon while the other two stomped it down. A firm stack, nicely rounded on top, would be built to let the snow and rain slide off and keep the inside fresh and mould-free.

In the fall they cut wheat, oats, and barley, the crops that represented most of their year's income. One of the boys drove the team

Harvesting the old way, behind a team of four or more horses. The team worked a few hours then was replaced with a fresh team; the men continued on.

In winter, Ron or his brothers hitched the horses to the wagon to haul hay or straw or oats, or to bring groceries or equipment home from town.c1940.

hitched to the binder, the others walked behind and picked up the bundles, each bound with one circle of twine as it dropped from the conveyer. Each bundle weighed perhaps thirty pounds (14 kg). The brothers set seven bundles upright with the tops leaning against one another, a field full of golden stooks waiting to be threshed. Twenty acres could be completed on a good day.

The only time off in summer, apart from Sunday, was for special events – the Orangeman's Parade, church socials, ball games (although none of the Thurston boys played much ball), and, later on, the annual Irma Daze. Ron looked forward to the festivities, and joined whatever organization invited him in.

"Yeah, I'll try that out," Ron replied when Tommy Averil asked him to join the Orangeman's Band sometime in the early 1930's.

"I'll show you," Tommy said as he handed Ron a flute. This new challenge was met with Ron's normal approach – listen intently and learn quickly.

Ron continued to practice his recorder, occasionally in the winter, more frequently in the early spring. On July 11th, twenty-five or thirty Orangemen and their white-gowned counterparts of the Women's Orange Benevolent Association formed up at Bandmaster Watson's place, north of the Thurston's. The flautists played to the drummer's beat and the participants marched out the gate and down the road. Their music carried for miles across the silent fields and into Irma. A large Union Jack, the British Empire flag flown as Canada's own until 1965, was held aloft to unfurl in the breeze.

The onset of World War II ended Irma's Orange Parade – most of the men volunteered or were called up to serve in the armed forces.

I wonder if Ron supported the Grand Orange Lodge and its purpose, or if he joined to simply be included in an organization of neighbours. The Orange Lodge dates back to 1688, when William of Orange was invited to leave his home in Holland and assist the Protestant English in resisting the efforts of James II in re-establishing Roman Catholicism in that country. Ron could have joined any one of the numerous lodges and fraternal societies in Irma during the 20th century – the Masonic Lodge was active, as were the Independent Order of Oddfellows, the Elks Lodge, and the Kinsmen, as well as their female counterparts.

Perhaps Ron felt membership in the Lodge to be important; perhaps he wanted to be included in the group, perhaps he was influenced by the framed Orange Lodge poster that hung on his parents' wall.

Meanwhile, life on the farm continued in its normal day-to-day routines.

"Geez, Ron, ain't you done that barn yet? You've been at it all day," teased one of his brothers. Barn-cleaning wasn't one of Ron's favourite jobs.

"You-u-u better watch out," came the response, and a pitchfork-full of straw and manure catapulted toward the teaser, who easily ducked out of the way.

It was mid-October, the golden sun shone warmly in the brilliantly blue sky. It would take two more days of this sun to remove last week's snow from the stooks. Soon the cows would shelter in the barn all night. Even the horses were allowed inside on the coldest winter nights. Barn-cleaning would be a frequent chore in the months ahead.

The half section just north of the village was up for sale, and Ron wanted it. The land belonged to the CPR – one of the many parcels awarded to the Canadian Pacific Railway Co. in exchange for building the rail line across the country in the late 1800's. Specifically, the land Ron wanted was known as the N 1/2 – 35 – 45 – 9 – W4 or the North ½ of Section 35, Range 45, Township 9, West of the 4th Meridian.

"Dad, that's a good piece of land. I've got some money and he's only asking $20.00 an acre. There's a war coming on. We're going to be getting decent prices for everything pretty soon, crops, meat, even eggs I'll bet."

"Well, you're going to have to find the money somewhere else. I can't give you it," Fred turned his back and marched into the house for supper.

"I'll be damned to see that land go to somebody else," Ron muttered as he slammed the pitchforks into place. "I've been working my ass off here. I'm going to get that piece of land myself."

A neighbour loaned Ron the three or four hundred dollars he needed as a down payment. Then his life changed, and he was thrown into a fray not of his own making but from which he had no choice but to become involved.

❧

MY HUSBAND AND I sat in Uncle Ron's home, chatting with the one-time soldier over half a century after the end of World War II. The tape recorder ran as my husband queried Ron about his life, and I made notes on my laptop computer. Ron was relaxed, seemingly glad of the chance to share his memories.

"You never know with Ron," I'd previously warned my husband. "He can be cheerful and laughing one minute, and the next he's like an ugly, aggressive bull. He doesn't give a person any warning, either."

Uncle Ron had willingly talked to us about his parents and his siblings, his own family life, his hopes and dreams. We hadn't yet asked about his army life.

"Ron, could you tell us a bit about your wartime experience?" my husband asked.

"No, I will not." The man who had been jovial and relaxed suddenly became abrasive. His forefinger stabbed its emphasis through the air and smashed down onto the table.

"Well, could you tell us even a little about the time you spent in the army, or at the POW camps in Lethbridge? You must have had some pretty interesting times," wheedled my persuasive husband.

"Dammit, I told you no. And I meant it. Now you turn that damned thing off. I ain't telling you anything else."

My husband, the man of a thousand puns and the sharpest wit in the west, soon had Ron's good humour restored. But nothing would induce my uncle to talk about the four years he'd spent in the Canadian army.

Later, long after my uncle died, I asked his daughter Eva if she knew anything of her father's army experience. "Did he talk about that time? I don't remember him ever telling any stories about it."

"Never," she said. "He'd never tell us, never talked about it."

We wondered what on earth could have caused Ron such anxiety and reticence. It was unlikely he'd been in trouble – our grand-parents had instilled their own values of right and wrong, honour and honesty, in every one of their children. We knew Ron had spent all his military service time in Canada. He hadn't gone overseas, hadn't spent any time in the front lines, hadn't been sent to Britain for more training or to Russia, Germany, North Africa, Hong Kong or Burma. Why, then, was he so reticent? Why had he never shared his thoughts or his knowledge with us or with his children?

"Maybe we could get his service record, Jeannie," suggested Eva. "I wonder how we could do that?"

"That's a great idea, I'll ask Colleen if she knows how to get it. She has lots of friends in the military there in Wainwright."

Within a few weeks, Eva was on the telephone. "I've got Pap's record, it came in the mail today. Would you like me to send it to you?"

"Well, send me a copy, Eva, would you, I don't really want to have the original. You're his daughter, you should keep that. But a copy would be great. Thanks so much."

A few days later, a long brown envelope was deposited in my mail box. Inside were several pages of the most amazing set of acronyms I'd ever seen – whatever was the meaning of 'SOS to A.20 RCASC T.C.' or 'Cease att. to #3 Wks Coy. RCE for R&Q 15-2-43 & att to IC Leth. FAP but P&A&D & Disc.'? There were two full pages of what appeared to be postings, complete with rank, date, unit, place, and authority.

"Eva, what does all this mean?" I wailed to my cousin.

Her laugh was simultaneously humorous and puzzled. "I don't know," she said. "I've never seen the thing before. Somebody must know what it means, but I'm not the one."

I turned to my sister, who lives not far from the Canadian Forces' Camp Wainwright. "Colleen, help! This stuff is beyond me, I haven't got any experience with military jargon at all, and I sure can't figure this thing out. Do you know anyone who could decipher the acronyms and abbreviations? This entire record might as well be written in Swahili for all the good it does me."

"Sure, Jeannie, I have a friend in the army. Can you fax me a copy?"
I did. And she did.

Initially, I'd wondered if Ron had volunteered for the army, or if he'd been conscripted. I'd asked everyone I could think of, and received an entire range of responses.

"Did Ron join up, or was he drafted?" I queried his siblings.

"Oh, he must have joined up. He wouldn't have waited to be drafted," said one of them.

"No, I think he must have been drafted," said another. "I don't think he liked the army, so I wouldn't think he'd join voluntarily."

"Well," I thought, "it looks like that's the first question to address."

The Second World War was declared on September 2, 1939. Canada was ill-prepared at the time. Her armed forces were at an all-time low; military equipment was aged and poorly maintained. The entire country was just emerging from the Depression. Britain's war declaration didn't automatically extend to Canadian involvement as it had in the First World War. But still, the ties between Canada and the mother country were strong. If England was at war, it was natural for her Commonwealth partners to support her.

Prime Minister William Lyon Mackenzie King, Canada's wartime prime minister, recognized that Canada would need vastly strengthened armed forces, but he also remembered French Canada's opposition to World War I. 'Why should French Canadian men die in an English war?' they had reasoned. Conscription – compulsory military service – had been such a big issue in that war that the nation's electoral process was irrevocably changed because of it. In 1917, women were allowed to vote for the first time, but only if they had sons or husbands in the services. Prime Minister King had no desire to replicate the conscription issue. He did, however, need to uphold the country's commitments for men and equipment.

On June 21, 1940, the Canadian Parliament passed the *National Resources Mobilization Act*. That piece of legislation enabled the government to requisition the property and services of Canadian men and women for home defense. Every Canadian age 16 or over was required to appear at a Post Office on August 20, 1940. The post offices remained open from 8:00 a.m. until 10:00 p.m. to accept registrations.

All the Thurston brothers registered. Most were exempted from future service – Ted and Leo as essential farm labour, Len may have registered in Irma or perhaps he'd already left for Ontario. Ivor was just fifteen, too young to register.

Ron was called up for service. He enrolled at Camrose on December 4, 1941.

Within a couple of months, on February 4, 1942, Ron reported to sick bay. Two weeks later, on February 17, he was admitted to hospital with scarlet fever. He remained in the Red Deer Hospital for 32 days, according to his service record, but was on sick leave until April 1st. Much of that time was spent at home on the farm, where he passed on the contagious streptococcus bacilli to his sister Olive.

"You'll soon get better, now, Ron," said his mother, as she prepared meals of meat and potatoes, fresh vegetables from the garden, pie and cream and fresh bread with home-made butter. "Home will do you good."

The army allocated Ron $1.00 a day subsistence allowance from March 19th until April 1st – he likely reported for light duty then, but wasn't re-categorized as fit until May 1st.

In June he was assigned, as a Home Defence soldier, to the 6th Division Supply, Royal Canadian Army Service Corps (RCASC) and sent to Valcartier, Quebec for training – perhaps that's where he received his motor transport training. It appears to have been a short training session, for on June 10th, he was attached to the 6th Division Supply Company, RCASC First Aid Post. Was he injured during the training? There's no record of injury, although his record does show that he had

Ready to return to the Army, boots polished, uniform pressed, hair slicked down. He was drafted under the National Resources Mobilization Act and signed up at Camrose on December 4, 1941.

With his sisters Winnie and Olive, c1944. Ron was often able to get harvest leave; this photo may have been taken in the late fall, just before he returned to Lethbridge.

a 'lump on back of head'? Why was he granted 'Compassionate Leave' on July 24th, hospitalized, then granted leave without pay and allowances from July 24th to October 31st, the leave then extended until November 15th? What happened to him?

I wonder if Ron might have run afoul of some regular soldiers during this period. Canadian service personnel were under huge pressure – casualties at Dieppe on August 19th of that year were immense, as had been the casualties and imprisonments at Hong Kong in December of 1940. The regular servicemen had little respect for healthy, able-bodied individuals who restricted their service to Home Defense. Or perhaps Ron was involved in a motor vehicle accident.

Ron spent most of his first year of army service in hospital or on compassionate leave. We will likely never know the details. He never spoke about this period to his siblings or to his children.

On December 27th of 1942, he was sent from Calgary to Lethbridge to work on a construction project, attached to 3 Works Company, Royal Canadian Engineers. Perhaps he hauled supplies, drove trucks, or did some other kind of construction work for the army. Or was the project, in fact, the prisoner of war camp at Lethbridge?

One half of the 34,000 German prisoners of war (POW's) brought to Canada were sent to Lethbridge[25]. Internment Camp 133 was opened in November of 1942 – about the same time Ron's compassionate leave ended and shortly before he was reassigned to Lethbridge. The camp had a capacity of 13,000 inmates although its population eventually peaked at 17,000 – 2,000 more than the entire population of Lethbridge itself. The POW's included *Wehrmacht* soldiers from the North African campaign and El Alamein, as well *Luftwaffe* aircrew and *Kriegsmarine* U-boat sailors. The POW's were responsible for their own organization and internal discipline; they were fed the same rations as were Canadian troops.

I was astonished to discover the facts of the Lethbridge POW camp, and to learn that a second camp was built just outside Medicine Hat, perhaps a hundred miles away. That camp was almost the same size as was the Lethbridge camp. Both camps have long since been destroyed; this significant bit of Canadian history almost disappeared before a few writers documented the events and existence of the camps[26, 27].

Thirteen thousand prisoners of war had to have been guarded – but by whom? Surely we didn't divert men from active duty to act as prison guards? Might Ron have been assigned to the POW camp? Ron's service record notes that he was taken to the 'IC Leth. FAP' on February 16, 1943 – the Lethbridge Internment Camp First Aid Post. Had he been injured again? The record includes no description, no explanation.

A national plebiscite in April 1942 released the federal government from its commitment to use Home Defense personnel for exclusively domestic use and authorized the government to send NRMA soldiers into active duty. Perhaps Ron was one of those men identified for future mobilization to active duty.

> Between 1940 and 1944 close to 60,000 NRMA soldiers [some-times referred to as zombies] volunteered for general service and several thousand more were sent to the front after the use of conscripts for overseas service actually began late in 1944[28].

The press often contrasted zombies to 'real Canadians' – the men who were doing the fighting. The zombies, on the other hand, main-tained that

> they do not owe the country anything, that during the 'Depression Years' the country didn't care whether they were alive or not, but now it is at war they are wanted. When it is pointed out that there are plenty of men overseas who were just as badly off as they were, they merely state, 'If they want to be suckers, we aren't'.[29]

What did our Ron believe? Did he truly not support the war effort? Did he dispute Canada's involvement? It's difficult to imagine strong-willed Ron obeying as an army private must. Perhaps that's why he hated the army so. Or perhaps he simply was determined to not become cannon fodder as he was heard to call the active servicemen.

Whatever his beliefs, it appears Ron spent most of 1943 and 1944 at Lethbridge. Was he driving trucks, hauling supplies, doing construction or maintenance work? Or was he guarding the POW's?

Guard duties at the POW camps were carried out by the unarmed Veteran Guards of Canada (the VGC); by 1941 over 10,000 veterans had volunteered for the VGC. There was also a whole contingent of regular army personnel attached to the Calgary command – including some who had been injured at the front and temporarily returned home for light duty, others who were NRMA soldiers assigned to domestic duties. Ron appears to have been part of the latter group for most of his service.

My cousin Eva believes her father spent much of this time at the POW camp. I can only imagine the internal conflict he would have experienced if he were assigned to guard the soldiers. They were men who had killed allied personnel – clearly a reprehensible action – but Ron had chosen to not be one of those fighting men. Where did he stand? And how did he feel about the intimidation the captured Gestapo[30] imposed on those who did not share their beliefs?

I chatted with Eva several times. "You know, Jeannie, Pap just couldn't stand even the sight of macaroni," she laughed. "He said he'd seen so much of that stuff when he was down there at the POW camps. Pap told us they fed 2,500 people at every meal in the camp he was stationed at, and a lot of times it was macaroni. They'd put it on the table in a big vat."

It's curious to hear these snippets of stories, eyewitness accounts of life in the camps, for we know that POW Camp 133 held many more than 2,500 inmates, and we also know the meals were the same as those served Canadian servicemen. There must have been some basis for Ron's hatred of macaroni, though.

By 1943, the Canadian armed forces needed reinforcements. The war in Europe continued, as did action in the Pacific theatre. Men such as Ron who had joined up for Home Defense, in accordance with the *National Resources Mobilization Act*, were increasingly being called up for active service.

Ron's service record shows a series of assignments that would culminate in his deployment for overseas duty although some of the entries are confusing. On February 15, 1943, he was removed from #3 Works Company of the Royal Canadian Engineers (RCE) and assigned to the Lethbridge Internment Camp (IC). On December 1, 1943, he 'ceases to be HD on becoming NRMA soldier'. He appears to have spent the remainder of 1943 and all of 1944 in Lethbridge. His duties aren't shown on the service record, although clearly he was assigned to the POW camp. On February 4, 1945 he was assigned to the Veteran Guards of Canada and appears in a photo taken in early February. That transfer may have been one of the army's administrative assignments, for a few days later he was on his way to Calgary, 'SOS to #13 District Depot'.

After a brief, four-day leave – did he go home to bid his parents good-bye, I wonder? – he was reassigned to No. 1 Training Brigade Group at Debert, Nova Scotia, the place from which Canadian army personnel boarded their ships for transport to the front.

"Appears to be very straighforward, well balanced soldier. His conduct has been good, and he has no doubt conducted himself efficiently. As noted this soldier has completed Basic and Corps Training and states he had a course in Supply duties and is qualified Driver I/C Class III," notes his Personnel Selection Record, on February 20, 1945.

The record goes on to describe Ron's military background as: "Enrolled at Camrose 4 Dec. '41 and completed Basic; Advanced at Red Deer, short time with 6th Div. at Valcartier. Harvest leave 3 mos. 1942, Supply and M.T. [Motor Transport] Duties at #133 Lethbridge Nov. '42 to date."

The selection record recommendation was that "...because of age and profile is suitable for C.I.C. Operational Duties (XAG 33 withdrawal)."

In plain English, that statement meant "we're sending him to the front".

Top: Ron with a friend – a photograph with no date, no caption, no location, likely taken around Lethbridge where he was stationed most of the time between 1941 and 1945.

Bottom: The Veteran Guards of Canada, men responsible for guarding the 10 to 15,000 prisoners of war in each of the two camps in southern Alberta. Ron is third from the right in the middle row.

The vision of my mother's reaction to the news of her brother's assignment for overseas duty remains as an indelible, early childhood memory. We had an old Winnipeg lounge that sat against the west wall of our living room then, a sofa by day and a spare bed when we needed it for visitors.

A letter from gran was in the mail. My mother retrieved it from the black box on the wall outside our front door early that afternoon. She opened the letter right away, as she always did.

"Oh no," she said, "oh no, not Ron. What will we do? Oh no..." Tears ran down her cheeks.

I'd never seen my mother cry before and would probably not witness her tears more than another half dozen times in her entire life.

"Eva, how did your dad feel about going overseas?" I asked.

"He said that all those guys they sent overseas were just cannon fodder. The only story I remember him telling was about the time he was almost shipped out for Europe. They'd sent him to Debert, and the men were all lined up at the harbour to get on board the troop carrier. Pap said they were lined up by rank, the most senior men first. Pap was just a private so he was way down the line. You know the army; they couldn't even seem to count – there were a lot more men lined up than there were places on the ship. The cut-off was just a few men before Pap, so he didn't get on, and that was the last ship sent before the end of the war.

"I've got a couple of pictures here, of Pap and some of the other guys in the army, I don't know who they are and he never talked about them, and never seemed to have anything to do with any of them after he got out." Eva spread the black-and-white snapshots on the table in front of us. It was easy to find Ron's handsome face in the group of smartly uniformed soldiers.

Nine days after V-E (Victory in Europe) Day, on May 17, 1945, Ron was reassigned to the Central Maintenance Depot in London, Ontario, then in August was granted three month's leave without pay, at his own request, to November 4, 1945. When November came around, he was granted an extension of his payless leave, to February 5, 1946. It took a long time to demobilize the thousands of men and women in the Canadian armed forces, after the war ended. Ron was finally discharged on January 9, 1946. He received a hundred dollars with which to buy civilian clothing and to seek rehabilitation services.

Ron's discharge record was formally completed and submitted to the Veterans' Land Authority (VLA):

> Total service 49 months, in Canada, driver and supply man R.C.A.S.C. 8 months farm leave...Age 25 years. A clean-cut, alert young man of neat appearance and friendly, co-operative manner. Thurston has been operating his own farm while on compassionate leave, from which he has been called in for discharge, and where he is returning immediately. He plans on applying to V.L.A. for a mortgage loan[31] on his equity in the farm for the purpose of effecting improvements and the purchase of additional equipment.

Ron returned home to his farm. He used his veteran's grant money to upgrade his farming equipment.

Canadian farms and farmers had been called upon throughout the war to produce, produce, produce. There was a lucrative market for all the wheat, oats and barley, the beef, pork and chickens they could grow. There were sugar beets in southern Alberta, honey in the Peace River country. Every bit of food was needed. Ron's father and brothers farmed their own and their brother's land throughout the war years.

Ron returned to a farm where the weeds had been kept down, where crops had been rotated and the land summer-fallowed according to the practices of the day, and to a family ready to welcome him back to take his share of the workload.

Back at home; c1945.

Ron returned readily to farm life, driving equipment, seeding and harvesting, feeding and managing the cattle and pigs; Rosie the dog was his constant companion. c1947

They produced grain both as a cash crop and to feed their animals; here Ron throws oats or barley into the chopper to be ground into pig feed.

Within a few months, his brother Leo was accepted at St. John's Theological College, Winnipeg. The Thurston farming pattern became the father and his three sons working together. Two married men, two bachelors. Most of the young women Ivor and Ron had known at school had either married or moved away. Although there had been rumours of Ron and a woman in Lethbridge, nothing appeared to have developed from that liaison. Now, with all the men returning home, there would be intense competition for female companionship. For Ron, life would soon present an interesting option.

Over supper one day in mid-August, 1947, Nellie announced that: "Olive's been offered a job at Giles. The school superintendent sent her a letter today. He said she could board with a family named Pugh."

Olive flushed with anticipation. Her brothers looked up, impressed and pleased for their sister, although they couldn't pass up the opportunity to tease her.

"How're you getting there? Shank's mare? That'll take you a long time. Giles is way up north of Edgerton ain't it?"

"Well, I was hoping you might drive me up in the truck, Ive," wheedled Olive. "Could you take me?"

"Oh sure, I guess we could do that. When do you want to go?" Ron and Ivor agreed to take their sister to her new place the following weekend. It would be a significant event both for Olive and for her brother Ron.

Harry and Violet Pugh's farm was close to the Battle River, 18 miles (29 km) north of Edgerton. One of the quarter-sections was Harry's original homestead, the land he'd worked and gained title to during the pre-World War I land rush. He and Violet had four sons and two daughters. Eileen, the elder daughter, was slim and quick-moving. Her sister Florence was a bit taller, slower-moving, a soft patient woman.

She was at home when the Thurston boys arrived with their sister and her belongings. Was it Florence's blue eyes, the softness of her smooth skin, or her curly blonde hair that attracted Ron? Whatever it was, the young farmer from Irma responded immediately. Ron readily agreed to return Olive to the Pugh's after a weekend at home – any time.

"Your brother bringing you back on Sunday, Olive?" asked Florence. "I could make something for him, does he like cake or pie better? Make sure he has time to stop for a while now."

It wasn't long before Florence was not only baking cakes and pies, but skillfully creating a new dress.

She and Ron were married at St. Thomas Anglican Church, Wainwright on October 14, 1948. Her dress was fashioned from soft white silk, with a beautifully shirred bodice. Ivor stood up for his brother, Eileen was maid of honour.

The young couple moved into the house Ron built on his land just south of Millburn's slough on the road between Irma and the Thurston's hilltop farmstead. Florence turned the little three-roomed house with the asphalt siding into a home. She cooked and sewed,

Top: Ron and Florence were married after the harvest in 1948. Ron's brother Ivor and Florence's sister Eileen stood up for them.

Bottom: Florence with Darrell, bundled up against the prairie cold, c1952.

produced embroidered linens and innumerable jars of canned fruits and vegetables, pickles and jams. Within a year or so she was pregnant but the result was heart-breaking.

"It's God's will," Nellie said sadly as she listened to the tale of the baby's difficult birth and the forceps-inflicted damage. Harry Thomas Thurston died on June 11, 1950, just one week after his birth. He was buried in the Irma cemetery, the first Thurston to die in Canada.

Ron and Florence comforted one another. Ron buried his grief in the land. Florence recovered physically and yearned for a baby.

"Geez, woman, are you sure you want another one so soon?" Ron was incredulous. It was early fall 1950. "We've only just buried that little guy."

"I do, Ron, we need to have a nice family. Look, we've got all these baby clothes and things wanting to be used." Florence was persuasive. Darrell Ronald was born on July 31, 1951, followed by his sister Eva just fifteen months later.

Ron continued to work with his father and brothers. "Never had a lick of trouble working together," Uncle Ted told me more than once. "We bought some equipment together, swathers, threshers. And we just worked on everybody's place till the work all got done."

Florence worked at home – she became a typical farm wife. She and Ron invited my sister Maureen and me to come and stay with them at the farm during our summer vacations. The little house was crowded, but it was yet another welcoming home for us city kids.

"Did you ever see one of these?" Florence asked us one day, pointing to a wooden box with a golden clasp. We'd had dinner and washed the dishes, Uncle Ron had gone back out to the field and we three had had a short nap. We'd spent much of the hot summer afternoon sitting in the square galvanized wash tub set out on the prairie grass on the east side of the house, filled with sun-warmed water. The black clouds and crashing thunder of a late-afternoon storm sent us scurrying inside.

"No, not really. We don't have anything like that at home," Maureen replied. "What does it do?"

Occasionally there was enough moisture in the air to form hoar frost, sparkling crystals that clung to every branch, every fence line; Darrell and Eva, c1960.

"I'll show you." Florence cranked the handle on the side of the box, then she lifted the lid and placed a round black disk on the turntable, lowered an arm with a heavy head, and flipped the switch.

"Yodel-o-del-eeie-ee, yodel-ee" came the mellow voice of Wilf Carter, the singing cowboy who had left his Nova Scotia home to work in the woods around Rocky Mountain House in central Alberta, then became a cowboy. His first songs hit the airwaves from a Calgary radio station in 1930.

We stood, enthralled, fascinated by the melodious voice and the electricity-less record player. Eventually, Florence got tired of Wilf Carter and Johnny Cash and all the other cowboy singers whose voices were pressed into the black, 78 rpm records.

"I think that's enough now," she said. "We'd better give those guys a rest."

My sister and I went back to other amusements, helping Florence shell peas or tip and tail green beans, or watching Uncle Ron milk the cows or chop oats for his pigs.

Within a short time, Florence's life became both that of a farm wife and a mother of two for Eva was born on October 21, 1952. My sister and I grew into adolescence, old enough to find summer jobs. Our visits to the farm were restricted to weekend jaunts.

I remember one visit when I was about seventeen, working part-time and going to high school. I'd gone down to see my grandparents. It was Saturday night, the go-to-town-and-visit evening.

"Come on, then, I'll bring the car up," Grandpa said gruffly. He had changed into clean pants and shirt, put on a jacket and picked up his tweed cap. Gran had finalized the grocery and errand lists. We were on the step ready for grandpa as he brought the car up to the gate.

Milt Fonert, manager of the Irma Co-op store, greeted gran and I as we gathered the week's groceries. "How are you tonight, Mrs. Thurston?" Milt never called my grandparents by their first name. "I see Florence is here with that new baby of hers. Isn't she a beauty?"

We found Florence a couple of aisles over, chatting with a neighbour. Eva waited patiently, holding her mother's skirt with one hand while she ran the other hand over the tinned vegetables on the shelf. Eva's adopted sister, Joan, lay against Florence's shoulder. Her brown eyes watched and understood everything within eyesight. She was less than a year old. I'd never seen such a beautiful child, or one with such an expressive face. Neither had I ever experienced an adoption. Although Florence had borne three children, the latter two were delivered by Caesarean section; in those days, not more than two C-sections were allowed. Adoption was the only answer for couples who wanted more children.

"How did you feel about your new baby sister, Darrell?" I asked one day, long after that initial encounter. "You were about six when Joan came to your house. Do you remember her?"

"Oh sure I do, Jeannie," my cousin responded. "But you know, I never knew she was comin'. One day, she was just there, that's all there was to it. But I was never in the house, you know, I spent all the time outside with dad. Eva now, she might'a' known but she was pretty small too, wasn't she? All of a sudden this kid shows up. But we all thought it was cool. Seemed pretty normal, too, y'know."

There were lots of babies available for adoption in the Canada of the 1950's. Unmarried women who became pregnant out of wedlock, as we used to say, generally were sent away, ostensibly to stay with an aunt or a relative in some other town. In fact, they lived in one of the several 'homes for unwed mothers' described by broadcaster Anne Petrie[32]. Most often, the young women weren't allowed to see, hold, or touch their babies. The women gave birth, recovered physically, and were sent back out into the world. Their secret – considered so shameful – was covered up, papered over, kept quiet – and their grief was seldom recognized, never condoned, and often used against them. Alberta was the first Canadian province to extend welfare benefits to single mothers who couldn't prove their children had a legal father – but that move didn't take place until about 1951. Immediate adoption of the babies was the norm.

Eva has vivid memories of her baby sister.

"I remember going to Edmonton to get her," my cousin recalled. "I went up with mum and dad, and we went over to your mom's house and got her, and then we went to some other place, I don't know where it was. But there was a big room with cribs all around the walls, lots and lots of them. Mum and dad picked out a baby, and it turned out to be Joannie!"

They returned home in the 1952 Chev Ron had bought from his father. Typically, family farms in those years included cattle and pigs and poultry to be fed, a dog at the door, an immense garden, but no electricity or running water.

Ron helped Florence take the baby in, along with the clothes and diapers, bottles and milk they'd purchased on the way home. Within minutes he'd changed into his overalls and boots and was out the door.

"Got to get that hay picked up before it gets too wet," Ron tossed over his shoulder as he headed for the truck; his father and brothers were haying up on section 14 north of the home place. He'd have time to put in a couple of hours before Florence had supper ready at 7 o'clock.

They took Joannie to church on Sunday, then up home to Fred and Nellie's. Ted and Molly and their four children were waiting. Nellie put her arms out to receive the new child.

" 'Ark, now, look at those big brown eyes," crooned Nellie, "isn't she precious? Just hand me that towel, dad, she's spitting a bit. She'll be alright. Does she sleep well, Florence?" The talk turned to babies and formulae and lack of sleep. The older children lost interest in the baby after a while, and went outside to play with each other and the dog.

The following Sunday, they went 'down the Valley', 50 miles (80 km) away, to show off the new baby to Florence's parents. It was a trip they made every two or three weeks for many years.

"That's what we did on Sunday, Jeannie," Darrell told me. "We visited the relatives, family, didn't really visit other people a whole lot. There wasn't time, you know, dad was outside by seven o'clock every day, stayed out there except for meals until seven o'clock at night. Every day except Sunday. That's what he did - work. As kids we didn't know where were going to go on a Sunday, we just knew we'd go somewhere. We spent probably half the time down with Mum's side and half the time up here with dad's side.

"After gran and gramps bought that cabin at Clear Lake, why then sometimes we'd go down there on Sunday. And in the summer we always took some vacation. We'd go to Saskatchewan different times. Do things down there like the Pioneer Museum or the Diefenbaker Dam. Generally went with George and Olive [Ron's sister Olive had married Florence's brother George] or Ted and Molly and their kids. We'd stay in a motel, all packed into one room, that's all they could afford."

Darrell was just a little guy when he started riding the tractor with his dad. By the time he was six or seven, Darrell could drive the tractor himself.

"It wasn't much bigger than a lawn tractor, Jeannie," he laughed. "We learned out in the hay field. You couldn't get into much trouble

Joan and her dog on the back step with her uncle Walter watching from behind the screen door. c1968

out there, and then threshing too, we had to drive the rack, and the men pitched the bundles. Me and Gordie and Donnie and a couple of other kids drove the tractors."

Until 1960 or 1962, all the Thurston men and some of their neighbours worked together at harvest time, using equipment that was hauled to the field and remained stationary while the grain was hauled to it. The men brought in one or two threshing machines and took turns operating them. Several men harnessed their teams to wagons, loaded on the bundles and hauled them to the threshers. Other men tossed the bundles into the thresher. The boys or younger men hauled water to the horses and drove the threshed grain to the granary.

While the field work was underway, the women cooked. They prepared huge meals for the ten, fifteen, or twenty hungry men who worked from dawn until dusk. There was no refrigeration or running water, no way to cool the kitchens heated by scorching hot cookstoves. And the regular chores still had to be done. Chickens had to be fed

Florence and Eva took tea, sandwiches, and cookies to the men in the field. Ivor and Ron sit here in the shade of the granary with Eva and Darrell, c1968.

Ron and Ivor worked the farms, sometimes bought equipment together; shared laughter as well as work. c1955.

and eggs collected. Cows had to be milked and the cream separated. Clothes had to be washed and dried. The need to wash dishes, haul water and cut wood was never-ending.

My cousins' help was essential during threshing time, Eva in the kitchen and Darrell in the fields. Even Joan had a few duties, although she was only five when her father finally converted to combining, rather than threshing, his crop. They remember the food – Eva recalls preparing it, her brother remembers eating it.

"It was the only time we had potatoes for breakfast," remembered Darrell.

"We threshed right up until the early 1960's," he said. "They didn't see how a combine could hold the grain inside, bouncing up and down the field the way they do. They just thought that you had to keep threshing, you know, hauling the bundles to the equipment and trucking the grain away. It's kind of funny now, but the Thurstons and a lot of their neighbours just didn't think a combine could work. Seems pretty funny now, but that's what they thought."

"Your dad didn't do change very easily, did he?" I laughed. "He and your mom weren't the first to get power into the house either, as I recall."

"Gosh, no, Jeannie, they didn't put power in here until the sixties, 1964 I think it was. Didn't make a whole lot of difference to me, just meant we didn't have to haul water no more. Before they put power in, we pumped from the two wells. We had a gas engine on one of them, and we hauled it up to the house in cream cans. Made an awful difference for mother and the girls in the house. Didn't make a lot of difference to me, I was hardly ever in the house. Started to get noticeable when we got electric tools, drill and saw and stuff like that."

"Did you put lights in the henhouse and the barn, Darrell?"

"Oh yeah, a few. Enough to see by. Dark so early in the winter, you know, before we'd take a Coleman lamp down there to the barn in the morning, at night, for milking. We had three or four cows to milk usually, my job most of the time. Mother did the separating. She was the boss of the chickens, too," Darrell remembered with a chuckle. "I

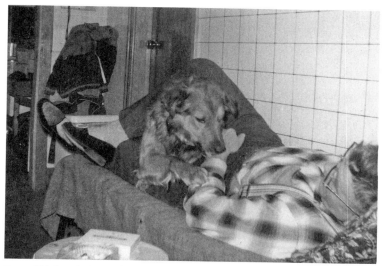

Ron and his dog relaxing on the cot in the kitchen. It must have been Sunday, for there was seldom time to relax any other day.

mostly fed them but she was the boss of them. Dad and I would clean out the henhouse. Turkeys too. And pigs, I used to feed them."

"Did you get a share of the proceeds from the pigs, then, Darrell, and the chickens?"

"No, you never got paid then, but he put the money in the bank and saved it for us. Till he died...We got two bits a week for allowance; that was all. When you turned fourteen it was a buck. We'd spend it on a game of pool and a bottle of pop. Gordie and I played a lot of pool on Saturday nights. And then at 9 o'clock, you were back home. Town closed up."

My cousin's gentle voice hardened a little as his boyhood memories burbled from buried storage. "He was army trained, Jeannie, and it showed all through his life. You're no good to the army dead, just do what you need to stay alive. Just work, every day, 'cause slack time got you into trouble so you just stayed workin' and you didn't have time for trouble.

"We worked from seven in the morning till seven at night, every day but Sunday. Sat down for coffee and dinner and afternoon lunch

Eva joined the 4H Beef Club with a calf from her father's herd. The year's prize calf was purchased by the local packing plant, often to the dismay of its owner. "If you have livestock, you have to have dead stock," was Grandpa Thurston's quote.

and that was it. It wasn't until he got cancer that he quit the seven o'clock thing. He was out there working by seven in the morning, had breakfast over and done with by then, and he didn't come in for supper until seven at night. All his life."

"And you worked alongside him, then, from the time you were a kid?"

"Yep."

"Did you talk? I always found your dad kind of hard to talk with. Or did you just work?"

"Just work. It was probably different before you had machines to work. When you were doing stuff by hand, you maybe talked, but once you got a machine, it was making a big racket, and so you couldn't talk anyway. There wasn't much conversing, really, on how things were done 'cause he was the boss. I had no investment in anything so I couldn't make any decisions till I started farming on my own."

Uncle Ron, it seems, ruled his world. It was his right. He brooked few questions, accepted no challengers.

"Darrell, I know there's other farm kids who worked alongside their dad, but I've heard stories about kids being given a car or a truck as a graduation present, or else they'd get a calf to raise for themselves and they'd keep the money when it was sold. It sounds like you just worked. If you had a chance to do it all again, would growing up like that on the farm and working all the time with you dad, would that be your first choice?" I was curious to see what changes time and maturity had wrought. Stories of conflict between Ron and his son Darrell were familiar and plentiful.

"Oh, I think so. Now, lookin' back on it, yeah, not at the time, it sure wasn't my first choice, but lookin' back on it, oh yeah. Now, I don't have to keep working cause I've worked hard every day. Any of my friends, they didn't work every day, and that was pretty tough for me to see them but the way it is now, they're still workin' but I'm not."

"Hmmmm," I thought, "living fifty-plus years has gentled the sharp edges."

"I didn't always listen to him, you know, and that probably didn't go down too good. They were just tryin' to keep you out of trouble. You know, it was probably a good thing, if they hadn't, you'd 'a been in a lot more trouble. The English come out in him, them English get pretty ornery."

Ornery or not, Ron was always active in the community. He was a volunteer fire fighter for several years, his home and land close enough to town that he could hear the horn used to call the firemen. He belonged to the Chamber of Commerce and sat on the Irma Co-op's Board of Directors. He led the Cubs and Scouts when Darrell belonged to those organizations, and was on the Vestry for St. Mary's Church for many years. For years and years – perhaps thirty-five of them – Ron marshalled the annual Irma Daze parade, organized the merchants' floats and the cars, trucks, tractors and other equipment decorated by individuals and associations, as well as the marching bands from the Irma and other district high schools. It was a task he enjoyed. He always made sure his wife's entry had a good spot, for Florence spent

Ron was Parade Marshall for the annual Irma Daze parade. Here's the 4H Club entry, c1965.

hours every year decorating her car with Kleenex™ flowers, streamers, and other fancy items.

My Aunt Florence had her own way of coping with life on the farm. She laughed easily, joined the local women's groups, taught her daughters to help with the housework, and didn't take life as seriously as her husband did. We used to tease her about listening in on the party line before individual telephone lines were installed, spending more time embroidering than mending, and going to town whenever there was a good excuse to do so. She just laughed, her blue eyes sparkled and she never seemed to get upset.

Florence was still laughing, but glad of company, the day I picked her up from the hospital in Edmonton.

"They said I had an oat hull in my ear," she giggled, "that's what they think has caused my trouble." She had spent several days at the University Hospital, referred there when her own doctor in Wainwright was unable to identify the cause of her poor balance, vague ill health, double vision and unresponsive digits.

"An oat hull? An oat hull would cause all those problems? Well, I guess it's good they found it, and that that's all it is!"

I took Florence home to our house for dinner. Ron came to pick her up the next day. Within a few weeks there were more tests – the oat hull find hadn't cured Florence's problems. She was diagnosed with multiple sclerosis – MS – the dreaded, incurable disease. The year was 1970.

"It's not too bad," Florence maintained as she eased her large, soft body out of the pew at St. Mary's Church a few years later. "I can still get Ron's dinner, and mend his overalls. Ron has to help me can the peaches now. I can't tighten down them lids anymore. Eva helps when she comes home, and Joan too. Darrell picks up the mail and brings things from the Co-op for me. The doctor said I shouldn't be driving any more."

Florence was admitted to the Wainwright Auxiliary Hospital in 1985. Ron had kept her at home until he could no longer handle her needs. He continued to take her home most weekends, at least for a day if not overnight.

"You ready there, Maw? Taxi's waitin', let's go." Ron propelled Florence's wheelchair out the automatic doors, across the concrete sidewalk. He stopped beside the car at the curb, its motor running and the heater on. Last night's snow glistened brilliant-white against the clear prairie sky, hoar frost covered every branch and twig. "Kids'll be home for dinner. I've put a chicken in the oven, and I made a big lot of rice puddin' yesterday. They won't go 'way hungry, that's for sure."

Eventually the MS made their weekend visits impossible. "I can't lift you up any more, Maw. You're pretty heavy and those arms of yours can't help a bit." Ron's voice was harsh with frustration, the lines around his eyes and mouth deep. "I'll be down here every couple of days." His shoulders stooped as he left the hospital, head down, weariness written in every step.

I sat with four or five cousins at Florence's funeral tea in the New Horizons Centre that winter of 1991. There was snow on the ground,

Ron decorated his house and yard with figures, lights, and signs – it became a beacon of Christmas decorations; c1990.

cold in the air; Florence had died on January 31. Her daughters Joan and Eva were there, and Olive's daughters Ellen and MaryAnn and Linda, and my sister Colleen.

"We've got to get together at times other than funerals, Jeannie," Joan blurted, her grief clearly visible. "It's so good to have everyone here, we have to arrange a reunion or something for a happy occasion."

After Florence's death, Ron went back to his farm, his fields of grain and his purebred Hereford cattle. He collected old threshing machines and lined them up along his west fence line, south of the house where Poverty Acres was emblazoned in big letters across the sign at the gate. The grass in his house-yard was trimmed neatly; flowers grew in the beds around the house. The two-car garage and the house were painted regularly.

At Christmas-time, Santa Claus rode over Ron's rooftop, and brightly outlined reindeer pawed the night air. There were bells and ribbons, lights strung around trees and shrubs, a cacophony of colour. Friends and relatives, strangers and neighbours stopped to examine the display, discover the current year's additions and exclaim over their favourite light set. Ron's scene led the community's Christmas-decoration display.

Every fall, beginning some time in the 1990's, Ron, Ivor and Ted, together with Ted's son Gordie, organized an old-fashioned threshing bee. Gordie and his son Wade harnessed a team of Percherons or Clydesdales to the haywagon and, along with several young boys and girls, hauled stooks from the field to the threshing machine. Ron had pulled in one of the many threshers he collected. He'd positioned the long canvas belt between the thresher and the tractor, around a circular drum at each end, to power the thresher. George parked a grain truck under the thresher's funnel to catch the plump kernels.

While the men were setting up and running the threshing equipment, Phyllis and Olive and their sisters-in-law, sometimes their brother Leo, and various other friends and relatives, huddled behind stacks of bales. They talked of the old days and present times, of people they knew and, occasionally, world affairs.

Leone, Gordie's wife, kept them supplied with coffee and cakes, a prelude to the feast waiting at home, meat pies and cold roast, potato salad and coleslaw, fresh buns, cookies and cakes and pies. It was even better than the old days, when threshing crews worked hard and ate ravenously.

This threshing was vastly different from the harvesting they'd done in the time before combines. This was fun: they weren't dependent on the equipment or the crop for their year's income. This was pure nostalgia.

Several years passed. Ron continued to farm. His grandchildren grew into adulthood, married and began their own families.

My sister phoned one evening, as she often did. "Jeannie, guess what? I think Uncle Ron and Auntie Muriel are seeing one another. I was up at Irma last week and there they were, the two of them glowing like thousand-watt bulbs! Isn't that cool?"

Excitement and happiness poured across the telephone lines. The life of a bachelor farmer is unenviable, as is the life of a small-town widow – Muriel was our Uncle Ivor's widow. As I would discover a few

Ron with his children and grandchildren, and Muriel, August 1996.

years later, finding a late-in-life companion is an unbelievable gift. My sister and I felt only happiness for our aging aunt and uncle.

Ron's daughters reminded me of our mutual commitment for another family reunion every time I saw them. Our Aunt Olive had organized the first reunion at the Paschendale Hall in the summer of 1985.

"It's your turn now, you younger ones, I've done my share," Olive chuckled.

We organized a family reunion for the summer of 1996. I assembled a committee, we sent out letters, marshalled energies, planned activities. The committee arranged an unending supply of food, with catering for one dinner. We rented the campground, assembled spare trailers and RVs. We cooked and baked and organized activities and games for the adults and the kids.

Uncle Ted offered to donate money: "Don't you run out of money now...you let me know if you need anything."

On the August long weekend we gathered at the Riverdale campground north of Wainwright. There was enough food to feed twice the two hundred or so Thurston descendants and their spouses and children. Most of the western Thurstons were there, and some of Len's and Mary's families came from Ontario. We had T-shirts made, colour-coded to the nine original siblings and adorned with a sketch of our grandparents' farm home. We ate and drank and played games and talked forever – all the things people do at family reunions.

On the last afternoon, there were a few short speeches of thanks, pleasure expressed at being together, friendships made or renewed. My brother Mike caught much of it on videotape, including Ron's fiery message.

"You lot, what a thing to do, charge everyone ten dollars for this... that ain't right. You had no business..."

His words were missiles, fired helter-skelter into the crowd of family, adults and adolescents, children and babies. I could hardly believe my ears.

"Jeannie, don't worry, that's just Ron. It's the way he is."

Ron's abrasive words smarted. Why hadn't he spoken up some time sooner, any time during the two years of planning for this shindig, I wondered?

"That's just the way he is," my cousins said, "I could tell you stories..."

I'm sure they could.

Three or four years later, my husband and I parked in the University Hospital's underground lot and rode the glass-walled elevator to the surgical floor. Ron Thurston. One of four patients in the large room. A nurse sat at a console in the middle of the room, surrounded by displays that monitored every heartbeat, every breath, every measurable vital sign for each patient.

"Hi there guy, how are you? Doing okay?" we asked.

"You-u-u betcha," he replied with a groggy laugh, "I ain't looking at those daisies from the wrong side yet. These young doctors, you know, they look like they ought'a still be in school but they're smart, boy they're smart."

He was in the Edmonton hospital for a few days before being ambulanced to the Viking hospital for several more days. Then he was released to fend for himself at home. His cancerous bladder had been removed, discarded along with the pieces of bowel he'd previously lost.

Ron lived with his colostomy and bladder bags for several years. He farmed his land, hauled his grain to the elevator, played cards with family and friends, kept company with Muriel, baked the best rice pudding in the world, and loved being a great-grandfather.

Ron's granddaughter Tanya, Eva and her husband Jim's eldest, was the only one who could help Ron with his colostomy and bladder bags. She stopped in to see him most days on her way home from work. Sometimes he had a rice pudding ready for her.

"I don't know what grandpa does, Jeannie, but I can't make rice pudding like his no matter what I do. And I just love his rice pudding."

Eventually he had to stop making rice pudding.

"Left it too long," his brother Ted told us. "I told him about the problems I'd had with my plumbing. He had the same problem but he didn't want to take time to see about it. Now look at him, the darned stuff's spread all over inside him. So much of it in this family, Ivor, me, now Ron." He shook his head.

Ron, the middle brother, died on February 7, 2002. My husband and I flew home from Arizona for his funeral. The family was together for yet another goodbye.

CHAPTER 14

Leo

He smoked a pipe, could swear a blue streak and
his shirt was forever falling out of his pants.
He always wore his backwards collar, he was an abysmal speaker
but he was known across the diocese as a kind and caring minister.

TALL, SKINNY LEO. He had dark hair, a round hairline, high cheek-bones beneath deep-set eyes, and a sharp nose. His wire-rimmed glasses coordinated with his backwards collar and black shirt. He carried himself casually, always a bit hunched over. In later years, a tummy developed – the 'Thurston baggage'. He had a smile that kept us guessing – lips curled up at the corners, slightly pursed in the centre – was he laughing with you or at you? He was as ambiguous in his behaviour as in his smile. Leo spent hours with parishioners in need; he accepted his role as my godfather but didn't exercise his duties; he espoused love but offered no counsel when I most needed it until late in both our lives.

His son Lorne nicknamed him Kotch, after the teacher in a tele-vision sit-com of the 1970's. He adored his wife but had little patience with her sometimes severe health problems. He expected her to be his

Leo was a frequent visitor at our house in Edmonton, here with Maureen and I; c1944.

right-hand woman: to lead the church choir and to play the organ or the piano, to serve tea and work with the women in every parish he took on.

I came to know him best as a solitary widower, a person in need of support and friendship, father of my cousins, friend and human being.

Leo, my minister uncle.

I REMEMBER LEO'S VISITS to our house on 77th Avenue, when I was a child, especially after our father died. He came for a meal (was he ever not hungry?) on his way to or from the farm at Irma.

"How are ya?" he'd ask, often with a semi-gentle poke at a child's tummy, or a punch to an upper arm. Sometimes he listened to the answer.

Leo's visits to our home in those years were brief, but they always included at least one real meal as well as a mini-meal of tea and biscuits or cookies. We kids knew Leo was mother's special brother. A cocoon closed the two adults off, whenever they were together, an invisible barrier between them and us. The bond became even greater after our father died and mum was left with four kids.

Occasionally, if my mother needed help with a big project, Leo stayed over for a day or two.

It was one such day, perhaps mid-1951, when Leo and Mum dove into their work immediately after breakfast. Leo placed 1" x 10" boards on a pair of sawhorses, Mum covered up the blueberry and white canisters on the cupboard, turned off the stove and covered it with sheets. She collected scissors, a ruler, pencils, and a huge paint brush. The icky, cloying scent of flour and water paste soon filled the kitchen as Mum mixed a bucketful of the sticky white substance. She and Leo measured the wall above the sink, cut a length of brown and orange and yellow wallpaper to fit, laid the paper onto the sawhorse-table, and applied a liberal coat of paste to its entire length. Quickly, while paste dribbled from the bottom of the length, Leo climbed onto the cupboard and pressed the top edge tightly against the wall. Mother handed him a wet cloth. Leo's first stroke ran the length of the paper, then he sent little strokes outwards to each edge, careful to push out the bubbles and stick the paper completely to the wall. Leo measured for the next section, Mother cut and pasted the paper, and handed it up. By day's end, the kitchen walls were freshly covered. Mother and Uncle Leo stood back and admired their handiwork.

The day had been punctuated with sibling banter: "No, that's not the way" or "Leo, don't you dare paste my ear" or "Give me that paper, Phyl, before you rip it up, by golly, it's upside down, what are you doing woman?" There was laughter too, as long as we kids stayed out of the way.

"Well, that's not so bad, Looly," my mother said. "We've got time to put the border up, before supper."

"Let's get at it then. Is this what you want?" Leo pulled out the small roll of border print. "We'll cover up those bumps, nobody'll see what we did to the edges, will they?"

The next morning, Uncle Leo caught the train for Edson, where he had been assigned as one of four ministers and deacons, ministers-in-training, to work at the Anglican mission. It was 1949, Leo's last summer before his graduation from St. John's Anglican Theological College in Winnipeg.

One summer evening in 1949 or perhaps 1950, the phone rang. It was Leo on the line, from the farm, we could hear his voice from the receiver. "Phyl, is that you? Are you going to be home tomorrow? Well, yes, I thought I'd have dinner with you. At noon. Will you be home?"

"I'll be here, Leo, you'll be up on the train in the morning? You remember where to catch the bus don't you? …Yes, I know you've been here before, you dolt, do you remember how to find us? …That's right, you get the Number 8, right across from the train station. You stay on it till it gets to the turn-around on 89th Street and 76th Avenue, then you know how to find us. We'll see you then." Quickly, they rang off. Long distance telephone calls, even after 6:00 p.m. and over the short distance between Edmonton and Irma, were considered costly, not an opportunity to chat.

The next day, Mother put a rare treat of beef roast, potatoes, onions and carrots into the Dutch oven, the big cast-iron pot with the glass lid. As our dinner cooked, the aroma wafted through the house, hurled itself at us as we set the table, and sent us to repeatedly look out the window. Where was he? By one o'clock, the roast smelled over-done, Mum worried that something had happened to her brother, and we kids were cranky with hunger and anxiety.

The phone rang. "Leo, for heaven's sake. Where are you? Your dinner was ready hours ago." My mother's anxiety showed as she spoke into the heavy black receiver.

"Well, Phyl, you know what happened? I'm back down here at the station, dammit, I rode that bus all the way over to your house, and then it turned around and brought me back up here. I must have fallen asleep, for gawd's sake. And now I have to catch this next train. I'll have to visit with you next time. Is that okay?"

MOTHER ASKED LEO to be godfather when my sisters and brother and I were baptized. The ceremony was held after the regular morning service at Holy Trinity Church in Edmonton, in late 1951 or 1952, not long after our father died. Leo didn't attend, of course, for by then he'd been appointed rector at Ashmont, 150 miles (240 km) northeast of Edmonton. He was named godfather anyway. He was likely godfather to many of us cousins, and who knows how many other parents assigned him to that role for their children. He could have spent a lot of his time overseeing the religious education of his godchildren.

"Well, you been to church lately?" he asked every time I saw him, during the days when I actually did attend church regularly.

"You bet," I'd say, the answer easier then than in later years, after my view of regularized religion had become skeptical, and I wondered how he could so fervently recite the words in the Anglican communion service " '...unworthy so much as to gather up the crumbs under Thy table...' " But that was a discussion we didn't ever have.

"What, and take part in those pagan rites?" my brother would chuckle, in response to Leo's question, as he bopped his uncle on the bicep. "Nah, I'll let you take care of that for me."

MY VISITS WITH LEO were infrequent after I married in 1959. Mum remarried in July of that same year; then she and my brother and sister moved to Irma with Jim Craig, their new husband and stepfather. After Leo transferred from the Edmonton to the Calgary Diocese in the 1960's, he attended Synod and other church meetings in Calgary rather than Edmonton, so visiting was no longer simple. He and I were seldom in the same place.

But there was always an enthusiastic Christmas letter, typed by Leo's wife, Joyce. We saw one another at family gatherings, occasional 'Irma Daze' or other local celebrations. They were purely social visits, not the sort of place for confidences. There were no invitations of spiritual help, no in depth inquiries, no apparent recognition that all was not well.

It wasn't until after I'd remarried in 1996, then closed my business two and a half years later, that Leo and I formed a different kind of relationship. Aunt Joyce had died in 1997, and soon I also would understand the profound sadness of the widowed.

Leo came to stay with my husband Ron and I in Edmonton. He enjoyed watching the ducks on the lake outside our window, listening to the wrens and American goldfinches singing, the sights and sounds of the city. He would take the Greyhound bus from Stettler, or have someone drive him to Red Deer so he could catch the express from Calgary. Ron and I picked him up from the bus depot downtown, he with his backwards collar, a fraying suit and well-worn shoes. His suitcase showed every one of the many miles it had travelled.

We took Leo home for tea and Welsh cakes, made especially for him although both Ron and I also loved the funny little tea dainties. As Leo drank his tea, he considered how to best present his plan for the coming days. There was always a plan, but we only became privy to it after he was settled into our spare bedroom.

"You know, I can't see the damn writing in my Bible any more, Jean. The darned letters, you know, they must have got smaller, I don't know what's the matter. Do you think you could take me to a place where I could get a new Bible?"

"Oh sure, what are you looking for?" I checked the Yellow Pages for stores that would likely sell large-print King James' versions of the Bible. "We could go right now, if you like."

"Al-l-l-l-right, let's go then. Where's your car? In the garage? I can't get into that thing. I'll go out the front door and meet you outside." And he did, retrieving his hat as he passed the closet.

"Where's the one I need?" he barked, as we entered the Canadian Bible Society store on 109th Street. Startled, the clerk asked if she could help.

"Well, yes, maybe you can," responded Leo. "You got any Bibles here?"

The astonished clerk gestured toward the shelves of Bibles. There were big Bibles, little Bibles, King James' versions, New Testaments, New English Bibles, leather-bound Bibles, paper-backed Bibles, Bibles on CD and on paper, illustrated or not, tiny print or huge letters, a stock to satisfy customers from anywhere. But not necessarily Leo, who surveyed the entire array, fingered a few samples, then turned to me with grumpiness written all over his face. There was a Bible in his right hand.

"Look, how much is that? Is that the price? Is that for one book or a whole carton? I'm not paying that much, Jean, what do you think I am? I can't afford that much money. Come on, let's get out of here." And he stomped from the store, muttering loudly all the way. Ron and I threw unspoken apologies to the clerk as we exited in Leo's wake.

"Leo, what's the matter with you? Those looked like perfectly good Bibles to me," I said as we climbed back into our vehicle.

"Well, I can't see the damn print, you know. And they want more than fifty bucks for something I can't read. What do they think I am?"

"Well, maybe what you need is new glasses, have you thought of that? Can you see the other things you read?"

"No, I can't see nothin'. Maybe you're right, I'll get Lorne to take me to the eye doctor, maybe he can do something. I'm not paying that much money for a book that I can't see, for gawd's sake."

Ron sat in the back seat, his expression confused – for sure, he'd never before met a minister like this one!

LATER THAT SUMMER, one day in July 2002, Ron and I sat in Leo's little holiday trailer, chatting about Leo's life and his work in God's ministry.

Leo had pulled his travel trailer out to White Sands, not far from Stettler in central Alberta, and set it up on his son and daughter-in-law's property beside Buffalo Lake.

"Oh yeah, he loves it out here, Jean," Leo's second son, Lorne, said when I had called the night before. "We're at work all day and half the night sometimes, but he visits with the neighbours, and takes little walks up the road. Come on down any time you want to, Kotch would love to see you."

"Kotch? What do you mean, Kotch?"

"Don't you remember that film, Jeannie, about the old guy that ran away so he wouldn't be put into a nursing home? I think it was Walter Matthau. Dad's just so much like that guy it isn't even funny."

"Well, I don't know the film, but I can sure see your dad as a Matthau-type guy." We agreed on a time, and Lorne gave me directions. Little did I know that in two months time, my husband would be dead, and that Leo would follow him just a year later.

The next day, Ron and I drove through fertile farm country, past small rolling hills and duck-inhabited sloughs. Leo was waiting for us when we arrived. "Alright, let's have some tea," he said, "I've got a propane stove here in the trailer." He set out cups and saucers, store-bought biscuits and Cathy's Welsh cakes.

We looked at Leo's photo albums, the pictures that Joyce had so neatly fastened in and labelled, a record of their family life, the parishes they'd served, their trips with Gran and Grandpa Thurston, and the family visits Leo had enjoyed so much. I recalled Joyce complaining that Leo always wanted to spend his four-week summer vacation at the farm: "And then he'd do nothing but work, and we'd get back home and he'd still be tired. What a guy."

LEO'S FIRST CHOICE after graduating from the Irma High School in 1940, had been to join the Royal Canadian Mounted Police (R.C.M.P.). They wouldn't have him – he failed the physical examination.

"They told me I had flat feet and poor eyesight, so that was the end of that idea," Leo told me. "Guess the good Lord had other plans for me."

The Thurston family had survived the Depression years intact, but they'd struggled to meet the immigration scheme's loan payments to the Soldier Settlement Board (SSB), two hundred and fifty-eight dollars and ten cents annually for twenty-five years. Leo remembered the inspections, his parents' anxiety, and the strain of maintaining the loan payments.

"That damn SSB, those inspectors, they were sure tough to deal with. Dad had a hard time with them."

The 1930's drought ended, war was declared, and the farmers of Western Canada were needed to produce food, food, and more food for Canada and for Britain. The people had to be fed, and tons of meat and dairy products had to be preserved for distribution to the front lines. Leo was needed at home, to drive the tractor through the fields, to help produce the grains, the beef and the pork for domestic and overseas consumption.

Then, in the early 1940's, after thousands of Canadians had lost their lives fighting in Europe and southeast Asia, Leo was called up for the armed forces. His first thought was to join the Royal Canadian Air Force, but no, they wouldn't have him – his eyesight was too poor. Then he was labelled an essential worker, his labour on the family farm necessary for the country's food production commitments. There would be no aircraft training for him... Leo stayed home and farmed while his brother Ron upheld the family's armed forces commitment.

The Thurston men worked hard, and worked together. They bought more land, and successfully farmed six quarter-sections (960 acres) throughout the war years. They tilled and seeded and harvested with six- and eight-horse teams, and the John Deere AR™ that Fred had purchased in 1939. It was the company's first rubber-tired tractor, small by today's standards, only 35 or 36 horsepower. Grandpa Thurston bought it from Carl Anquist, Irma's John Deere dealer.

"Cost twelve hundred dollars, I remember that too. First payment was a cow, didn't have any money, the dealer took a cow for the first payment," Leo said as he recollected his father's march down the road with the cow. They were both a little tired by the time they got to the village, but a deal was a deal, and Fred drove the tractor home.

Leo's father and brothers Ted and Ivor worked well with horses and were less anxious than Ron and Leo to mechanize the farm. Leo

The years of Depression and the family's hard work didn't impede Leo's growth. "He just grew too fast, he was never very strong," his sister said.

simply didn't have his brothers' horse-handling skill, or their strong healthy bodies.

"He just grew too fast," my mother once told me. Photos of the time show him as a gangly, bespectacled youth.

The tractor became Leo's to drive. He had plenty of time to think as he steered the new John Deere AR™ up and down the fields, eyes fixed on the trees or the fence line at the end of the field, plowing and harrowing the black soil in long straight rows or using the seed drill to start the new year's crop. He drove for fifteen to eighteen hours a day in the summer when the sun shone from 4:00 a.m. until almost 10:00 p.m. Leo had plenty of time to talk with his Lord Jesus.

When the war ended in 1945, it was Leo's turn to follow his own path. The Lord called, and Leo was determined to answer. He had a little money, perhaps $1,000 in profit from the beef cattle he'd raised during the war years. That would be enough to keep him for his first year of the mandatory university arts program. He'd find a way to support himself for his second year, then the three years at St. John's Theological College.

Leo did become a minister. It was a curiosity to me, his ministerial vocation. There had been no other clerics in the family, as far as I knew. He was born on Easter Sunday in 1922. Had the coincidence of that birthdate had any impact on his eventual calling, I wondered later on? By then it was too late to ask.

TODAY, I had other queries for him.

"Leo, why did you go into the ministry?" I asked, struggling to understand this man whose parishioners showed him immense love and respect, but who had seldom been available to me when I needed him.

"Well, I had a calling, you know. I felt I'd heard the Lord, and I had to answer Him. A-a-a-a-MEN," in a voice that reflected his firm conviction.

"Why did you go to St. John's College in Winnipeg? That's a long way from Irma, I think there was a theological college in Saskatoon or maybe Regina, either city was closer than Winnipeg. Why not one of the other theological colleges?"

"We-e-e-ll, you know, the bishop, Barfoot, he used to be the principal of St. John's, so he had a connection there. Used to send all his students to St. John's, you know. He was our bishop, we got to know him pretty well. He'd come down to Irma to do the confirmations and he'd visit with us. He helped me get into college. It wasn't easy, you know." Leo was emphatic.

"I had a difficult time settling down to study. It was five years since I'd left high school. In fact Bishop Barfoot thought I wasn't getting high enough marks in college and didn't know if I should continue or not. I told him I was determined to enter the ministry, and if he didn't want me, I would go to another diocese and to another bishop.

"When I graduated in 1950 he sent me a letter of apology for his remarks. What a great friend and bishop he was." Leo's irritation at the bishop's affront was still evident, although he chuckled at the concept of his bishop's apology.

Leo's parents supported his decision to enter theological college, but they had no spare cash. Leo was on his own. There were few if any bursaries or scholarships. He worked part-time during the school year, hired by a hardware and lumber supply company to haul its goods between the railway and the storage yard with an old truck. In the summer, he trucked soil and manure for his brother Len in Brampton, Ontario.

"Oh gawd," he remembered, "there was a place down there you used to get the dirt, we used to get the dirt from individuals, you know. Topsoil, black stuff. Then we'd go out to the farms, you know, in eastern Ontario, and ask them what they wanted for 'that great big pile of manure out there'. Oh, gawd. Dairy farms, there were lots of them out there.

"We'd deliver the stuff to the nurseries, they'd take all kinds of manure. Brampton was just a small town then about 6,000 people when I was down there. 'Bout the same size that Wainwright is now, where your mother is."

"Did you work all the time down there, Leo, all summer long? Or did Len give you some time off?" I asked, knowing my Uncle Len's drive to work unceasingly.

"Oh, sure, we had some time off. Boy, we worked hard too. Long days. Lots of trips. Those old trucks, you know, it was a wonder they stayed on the road."

"You must have taken a little time off, Leo. Do you remember the story my mother tells about you going to Niagara Falls on one of your days off? The time you drove down to Niagara, bought a ticket and got on the Maid of the Mist to go under the Falls – then woke up in time to climb back off the boat?"

This story invariably brought a chuckle, for Leo's ability to sleep through anything and everything was legendary.

Leo worked part-time for a hardware store in Winnipeg, picking up and delivering the store's orders from the railway in a rattle-trap old truck, while he attended St. John's Theological College.

Summers between college sessions were spent in Brampton working for his brother Len. Leo often had Len's son John with him in the truck or on the loader. c1948.

Joyce rode the bus from Winnipeg to Edson during Leo's summer there as a minister-in-training, 1949.

"Did I do that? Who told you that? Your mother wasn't there, now, was she? Well, maybe I did, but I'm not so sure it was just like that," Leo slithered about but ended up laughing at himself.

"Leo, look at this picture in your photo album. It's Joyce – what's the story here?" I asked.

"Oh, look at that will you? Ye-e-e-s, Joyce came to visit me that summer in Edson, and I took her out to Jasper. We stayed at this hotel, the Astoria I think, or maybe the Athabasca, I can't remember. It was the main hotel then, is it still standing?"

"Yes, they're both still there, Leo. Upgraded from those days, that's for sure," I said, as I waited to see if he'd comment on the perceived propriety of a single woman travelling alone with a minister-in-training in 1949. He never did explain, and I chose not to ask.

"That was the summer I was in Edson, at the mission. What a place that was. There were four of us, the others were all high church, didn't speak at all in the mornings until 10:00 o'clock. I just had to get up and go for a walk. I don't think the other boys were from St. John's, you know, but they were great guys, great boys. I can't remember their names, for gawd's sake.

The tiny church at Mountain Park, a coal-mining town south of Edson, Alberta; the town disappeared after the mine closed in the early 1950's.

Leo held Sunday services in this hotel in Hinton; the caged budgie birds sang along with the parishioners – then flew around the room to Leo's utter distraction and dismay.

"We had at least thirty points to serve, from that mission. Evansburg, Entwistle, then down south to Drayton Valley and another town in there, Alder Flats, another place I can't remember. I stayed there for about a week, one of the parishioners lent me an old Plymouth car to run around in, I remember that. Cadomin, and Mountain Park, there were lots of men living there, miners from all over the place. Everybody came to the services."

"That was a really interesting area, wasn't it? We had a cabin up there at Robb for fifteen years or so. The entire countryside is spectacular, there on the eastern slopes of the Rocky Mountains. We met a lot of real characters – I'll bet you did too, probably more than we did."

"I met some great people up there. They'd all come to services on Sunday, with the kids and everything. What a great time that was."

"I was reading about the Coal Branch not long ago, Leo. Did you know that area opened up in 1912, to supply coal for the railways? The miners came from Ukraine and Poland, Germany, Galicia, Italy. By the early 1920's, there were mines strung out for 50 or 75 miles south of Edson, with people living at Cadomin, Sterco, Robb, Mercoal, Luscar, and Coal Valley.[33] "

"That right? Well-l-l-l, I wouldn't know anything about that. They never brought any of that stuff to the services, I can tell you that. There were some great guys up there."

I noticed that Leo seldom ever mentioned great women but clearly remembered the 'great guys'. He'd mentioned a lot of miners living in the Coal Branch, but seemed to completely disregard the women and children – without whom few miners could have endured the isolation and extreme winter cold. One more piece of the puzzle that was my uncle.

"Hinton, you know, the old town, that old hotel was where we held services. They had those damn birds in a cage, they kept flying around during the service. Budgies or something like that. Maybe they opened the door for services, I don't know!

Leo drove Joyce to Hope Valley in his father's old truck – good thing it was summer time, as winter driving wasn't a lot of fun.

Feeding the chickens – another new experience for the city girl, c1948.

"And then we had Vacation Bible School. I lived in a tent you know, taught the kids in the old church at the Macleod Valley. What a summer that was.

"Guess I did okay there, too, 'cause then I went back to Winnipeg, you know, for my final year. Joyce was there. Her mother thought I could do no wrong 'cause her maiden name was Thurston! What do you think of that?" Leo clearly enjoyed the memory of his unblemished status with his mother-in-law.

"Leo, Joyce was a wonderful woman, wasn't she? You must miss her dreadfully." I remembered Leo's partner in life, the woman whose laughter had bubbled forth, whose eyes reflected their owner's vitality.

"Ah, you know, I met her in Winnipeg. What a great wife she was, right up until she died in January 1997. She was a great help to me in my ministry, and a great singer, led choirs. She was a wonderful typist. A great person, you know. To cope with her death is the most difficult task of my whole life.

"We were married in 1950, August 19th, in Winnipeg, the year of the great flood. Joyce kept some of those newspaper pictures for a long time: what a flood that was. They said almost a quarter of the city was covered in water[34], a lot of people were homeless, maybe 10,000 or so. Lot more than that evacuated. The Navy was called in to put sandbags around some of the major buildings. They were starting to get the city cleaned up before our wedding, but there were still lots of buildings falling down, bridges were out. It was a mess. But we went ahead. Nothin' was going to get in the way of our wedding.

"We had the ceremony in the Winnipeg cathedral, Joyce's home parish church wasn't big enough, because some of my professors were there from the college, a lot of people were there."

"How about gran and grandpa, Leo, were they at your wedding?" I asked.

"No, no of course they couldn't come. Money, I guess. Not enough. No, they weren't there at the wedding. None of my family was there. Winnie was there – she was bridesmaid, you know.

Leo and Joyce's wedding, at the Anglican cathedral in Winnipeg – it was a long way from St. Mary's, Irma!

The wedding party – Joyce's brothers Jim and Steve at the far left, Leo's sister Winnie second from the right.

"We were going to have our reception in the hotel, but it had been flooded – we had to have our reception up two or three floors. What a time that was. We'd filled sandbags at the college, to help keep out the floodwaters."

"And the railways were on strike too, I remember that 'cause we were supposed to go to our honeymoon at our friends' place near Winnipeg Beach, and there were no roads into it. The only way we could get in there was by train. But we couldn't go there because the trains were on strike, so Joyce's brother Steve lent us his car, a 1934 Chev, and Joyce's aunt had a nice cottage on Winnipeg Beach, so we went there. 1950 was quite a year."

"We had so many good friends there in Winnipeg. One of them, I remember, a great lady, she made me a cassock, can you imagine that? Made me my own cassock, all by hand."

"I'd been ordained a priest already on June 4th that year, in Holy Trinity Church in Edmonton. Bishop Barfoot was there, and Canon Nainby, mum and dad.

 And they sent me up to Ashmont [about 120 miles, 193 km northeast of Edmonton], yeah, Ashmont was my first parish. The bishop said to me 'Before you move in there, you'd better get that house insulated, because if you don't you'll freeze in bed!'"

"So I remember we got a fellow, and we drilled a hole between each stud, there were several small lumber yards around there, Ashmont, lots of wood chips, so we blew them into the house for insulation. No electricity of course. One bedroom, wood stove, front room and a kitchen, and we had another room, cause that's where we kept the piano."

"What piano?" I asked.

"Well, yeah, you know. After we were married, they shipped Joyce's piano out. It was a real old piano. I don't know where it came from, Ontario or someplace. And they shipped it out by train, right to Ashmont." Leo laughed and shook his head as he recalled the beautiful piano in the tiny rectory. "I gave it to this place, Paragon Place,

Top: With Bishop Barfoot at Leo's ordination, Holy Trinity Church, Edmonton.

Bottom: Leo's first parish, Ashmont, Alberta: the church and the rectory, in front is the 1932 Durant which Leo bought from Joyce's father.

when I moved in here. They've got it in the big room downstairs. They'll use it for sing-alongs and stuff."

"Leo, whatever did Joyce think of your place in Ashmont? I mean, really, she'd grown up in Winnipeg, the most civilized city on the prairies in those days. Stone houses, big trees, power, running water. I'll bet she'd never even been on a farm before!" I wondered at the adjustment Joyce must have faced.

"I can't remember, Jean, but she never complained about nothin'. She never used to complain, whenever we went to a new parish, she just came, never complained. I don't know how she ever did it, going to Ashmont, no power, no running water. Muddy roads."

It seemed to me that the Anglican church really did get two for one when they hired Leo – Joyce probably spent as many hours doing church work as Leo had done. She taught Sunday School, played the piano and the organ for all the church activities, led and sang in the choir, and made friends with everyone. And always, a smile that lit up her whole face. She had an aura of joy.

There were tough times for her too, surgery after surgery – fifteen operations. "You should see my belly, Jeannie," she laughed one day, as we stood watching the Irma Days parade sometime in the 1980's. "Leo and the boys could play tic-tac-toe on it!"

Joyce's future held even more medical issues, problems that compounded other problems, drug reactions and responses, intense pain and unending discomfort. Through it all, she tried to take care of Leo.

Herding cats might have been easier than was Joyce's self-imposed task of keeping her husband well-groomed. Leo cared about his parishioners, but his appearance was another matter. He could be ready to conduct a service, baptize a baby, or marry a loving couple – on time and in the right place, but with his hair askew, or his shoelaces undone, or his shirt falling out of his pants.

"Leo, do up your shoes," Joyce often commanded with a merry laugh. "You'll be falling over them at the altar."

"Leo, the ministers all had to serve several churches in those days, didn't they? Did you go to other churches besides the one at Ashmont? How did you get there?" I asked.

The roads in Alberta in the early 1950's were pretty awful – lots of clay, not much gravel. Oil had just been discovered at Leduc in 1947, but it took a few years before the oil royalties transformed Alberta into the wealthy province it is today. The Edmonton-Calgary highway was one of the province's few fully-paved roads the year Leo was ordained. Most of Highway 28 from Edmonton to St. Paul and Ashmont was gravel only.

The district roads were far worse than the highways. The local authorities were responsible for maintaining the roads that crisscrossed each county, the north-south roads one mile apart, the east-west roads two miles apart in most areas. Every county in the province had miles and miles of roads to build, maintain, and plow in the winter. The farmers needed the roads to provide access to their homes, fields, and cattle; likewise, Leo needed access to his churches and his parishioners.

"Oh yes, I had about five churches," Leo remembered. "Cold Lake, Grand Centre, they treated us great there. The Saddle Lake Reserve, we'd hold services in a lady's house, you know, I remember that. Quite a big house, it had a dirt floor, she used to clean that place up before services on Sundays.

"I had a 1932 Durant, I brought it from Winnipeg. It had been Joyce's dad's car. It was a great car, that old Durant. The only thing was I had to carry an extra axle with me; it used to break axles, so several times I changed the axle on the road. I remember one time, I went out to a parishioner's, one of my points, churches, for a kids' Christmas party. We drove out there, Joyce and I, on the road to Lac La Biche actually, and we got the kids to the party, and it was about 12 o'clock, and out there in the yard, there were drifts. I went to turn around in the yard, and I broke the axle! So anyway, the guy had a tractor there, and he pushed my car into the garage, I don't know why because the windows in the garage were half open and the door wouldn't shut. It was cold anyway.

"I used to be able to change an axle in about half an hour, but this particular time – the axle usually broke off about half-way, and I used to carry rabbit wire, you know, because we used to catch rabbits in the bush, to snare the axle out, you know.

"But this time, the dog-gone axle broke off right at the crown gear, the back of the car. There was a half an inch, no about two inches of the axle was in the crown gear and we couldn't get that darn piece out of there, and so we had to take the rear end out of the car that night, I remember that. Then I held the crown gear up like this, you know, and that little piece just fell out like that! Anyhow, we got that fixed and we got back to Ashmont. It was about 4 o'clock that morning. But I changed axles two or three times in a row in that old car."

Leo's Durant was an historic vehicle, probably built in the Canadian plant in 1932, after the U.S. parent plants had gone into bankruptcy. The car was constructed on the 1931 design, using 1931 parts, but completed in 1932 – hence, it was a 1932 vehicle.

The Durant Motor Co. production was small in comparison to the Model A and Model T Fords being produced at about the same time. Less than 10,000 Durants were made in 1931 and 1932[35]. The cars were flashy – not at all like the utilitarian Model A's. The price tag matched the flash – in 1929, when a Model A sold for $485, the audaciously ornamented Durant, with its steel and chrome carriage, sold for $1,045.

Leo's salary in 1951 was $150.00 a month, plus the little house in Ashmont. He and his fishing rod were frequent visitors to Mann Lake. Snared rabbits graced their table in winter. The young couple picked saskatoons and raspberries, low-bush cranberries and blueberries. Joyce canned the berries, made jam and jelly, and canned or pickled the vegetables given to them by their parishioners.

Kenneth, their eldest son, was born on September 9, 1952 at Elk Point, the nearest hospital to Ashmont. Joyce's mother came from Winnipeg to help her daughter through the first, difficult days of motherhood.

The Mayerthorpe rectory, with a backyard full of potatoes.

Leo and Joyce stayed at the parish until 1953, when the bishop sent them to Mayerthorpe.

"Tell me about the parish at Mayerthorpe, Leo. Did you have a bigger house, were the parishioners active church-goers, or did you have lots of challenges?"

"Oh gosh, yes, we had some struggles there. It was a good parish, but there was a lot of work to do. Lorne was born in Mayerthorpe, July 11, 1955. And you know, that house was so cold, when Joyce got up to change the baby's diapers at night, if she threw the old one on the floor, it'd be frozen to the floor by morning.

"The furnace was a 40-gallon drum, that's what it was, and they burned wood in the damn thing. Eventually, of course, they took that old drum out of there and they brought in a furnace. We burned coal for a while, then gas came along. But it was cold.

"The guy before me was a bachelor, and he collected all of his damn cans, and he piled all of them up on the shelf. I remember going down the basement, they were just piled up. Empty cans. And I remember the kitchen, there was no cupboards in that damn kitchen, you know that? There was a what-you-call-'er-counter, but there was no cupboards. And so we took some apple boxes on their end, on top of the counter, with a board across, to make cupboards. I had a saw in those days, a what-you-call-'er saw, electrical saw, so I built cupboards in that kitchen. It was crazy, that kitchen."

We laughed together, remembering the make-do years, the availability of wooden fruit boxes and their myriad uses, the necessary inventiveness of a country minister.

"Did you travel a lot in that parish too, Leo? To other churches?"

"Oh, sure. The church held about 100 people; we had a parish hall there too, I remember that now. We had a Sunday school. There were some good people there. People who appreciate you visiting them, talking to them, that kind of thing, that's what I like to do."

"And I went to Peavine, out in the country, roads were really bad up there too. I went to Sangudo, three or four places." Leo's voice – and his eyelids–dropped. It was time for another nap. Remembering life is tiring work.

SEVERAL TIMES THAT SUMMER, Ron and I visited Leo in his travel trailer at Lorne and Cathy's home a few miles northeast of Stettler, Alberta. Each time we went to see him, he told us a little more about his ministry, his life, and his family.

"Alright, Leo, we want to hear some more about the life of a small-town minister. I think you've got a lot of stuff to tell me about yet," I teased. "It looks like you're all settled in here for the summer."

We'd finished our afternoon tea, served with the inevitable Welsh cakes. Joyce had used Gran Thurston's recipe for this family delicacy and passed it down to Cathy. Joyce, however, had made some improvements in the recipe. She cut the sweet griddle cakes with a serrated edged cutter (rather than the cup gran used), and then she sugared them while they were still hot from the stove (our gran hadn't added a sugar coating).

"They're better that way, aren't they? Otherwise, you just have those dull little things, hardly any flavour. We like to put butter on them too," Joyce had shown me one day, ages ago it seemed, in some rectory where I visited them.

Today, Leo seemed relaxed and well. "I like it here, you know, Jean. Lorne and Cathy let me put the trailer here, and I can visit with the neighbours, great people here, Lorne's a pretty important guy too. He's mayor of White Sands, this area around here. And Cathy's managing the Legion in Stettler. I don't know how they do it. They go into Red Deer and buy the groceries for the place, and he helps her out sometimes too. She works so hard."

"Leo, I want to hear some more stories about when you were still working and about Joyce and the boys. Okay? Have you got that?" I laughed, knowing that Leo would tell what he wanted to, as he pleased, and in the way he wanted me to hear it.

"Al-l-l-l-right, I'll do it. But we have to have some more tea pretty soon, you know. Do you remember how to make tea? Warm the pot first, by gawd, keep it hot. Alright, what do you want to know?" Leo settled in to talk about his other parishes.

"Leo, where did you go after you left Mayerthorpe and the rectory with the tin cans?"

"Well we went to Barrhead of course, in 1956, and we stayed there for three years. I liked Barrhead. It was a good town, good country. I used to go west of Barrhead too, what's that town west of Barrhead, it's quite a town now. Used to go south of Barrhead, to Belvedere, a church in the country there, and another church, I can't think of its name. It was a good time. I had a good Scout troop in town too. David was born there, in Barrhead hospital. May 9, 1958. He was the last one."

"You and Joyce had your hands full, didn't you? You must have had running water and electricity in the rectory, I guess, eh? A six-year-old, a three-year-old, and a new baby. And I'll bet Joyce kept on playing the piano and leading the choir, right?"

"Well, I guess she did. I don't remember exactly."

"What did a day look like for you, then, Leo? How did you spend your time? Did you work on the parishioners' farms, or study the

Scriptures, or...?" I'd never had a chance to talk with Leo like this before, to ask questions and explore the things he'd done, the place he'd been, the people he'd met, and cared for and about.

"Well, I used to spend the mornings in my study, studying and preparing for the sermon. But after that, most of my afternoons were out, pastoral work, visiting people. I used to stook for some of these farmers, you know. In fact, I guess it was Barrhead or Mayerthorpe, I bought my first radio. I went out and stooked for the farmer, and then bought a radio. I used to work, most fellows used to go out and help them."

"So they paid you to help with the farms? Probably not much, right? But that's not a bad way to spend a sunny fall day! And you knew how to do it, too, not like some guy who'd grown up in the city," I prompted.

"Oh, yeah, I sure did know how to work those farms. Knew how to cook and work inside too, you know. I remember lots of days, at home, when your Gran had one of her bilious attacks, at harvest-time, you know, and I'd stay home from school and cook the meals for the men and stuff. My gawd, I don't know how she managed, those bilious attacks, she'd be in bed for days."

"I didn't ever know, as a child, that gran had such attacks, Leo. I think that what we used to call bilious attacks we now know as migraine headaches. There are lots and lots of people in this family who have migraines. I can't imagine how she managed to run the household with such headaches."

"She was such a good woman. I remember, she walked with me all the way to school, my first day. Three miles to town. Right across that field, where the golf course is now. Boy, what she didn't do for us. None of us went hungry. But it was nothing for her to put down 100 quarts of berries every fall. And she never complained, you never heard her say '...at Welford Farm, we had...'.

"We used to have some great talks," Leo said, as he recalled the woman whom we all treasured.

"Leo, where did you go after you left Barrhead? Was that when you went to Rocky Mountain House? You transferred out of the Edmonton Diocese and went to Calgary Diocese then, didn't you?"

"We went to Rocky in 1959, and you know, we stayed there until 1965. Maybe it was Tommy Teape that had recommended me for that place. I went out to Rocky for an interview, and they had a new house there, you know," he said. "But I liked the place, the people were good people out there, kind people.

"The town was small, only about 3,500 people. I had to go to Caroline, and the prisoners' work camp at Nordegg once a month, and another church south of Rocky, I can't remember the name now. The house was a Nelson home, one of those packages that you buy from the plant in Lloydminster. You know, with the pieces all cut to the right length and partly put together, all the plumbing and wiring and everything comes in the package. The parishioners put it together, I think they paid $3,500 for it and then they put it up. The nicest house we ever had.

"I had to do all the landscaping, I remember. Winter time, we had a skating rink in our back yard for the boys. And I used to run the Boy Scout troop, and Helen Hunley [later appointed Alberta's first female Lieutenant-Governor] ran the Girl Guides, we did a lot of work together.

"There weren't many aboriginal people in the church, but they were always calling me for funerals and stuff. There were three reserves out there, close to Rocky. The roads were pretty mucky around there. But I never got stuck.

"We were there for six years, good years. There was a nice church, an old church but solid, you know, and it was big enough to hold a hundred and fifty people or so. Nice altar in there and coloured windows in the east end, good solid pews. The parish hall was a wreck; we built a new parish hall there. I got a company in Calgary to come up and put the frame up. All the rest was volunteer, and the hall was still there when I left. They called it Thurston Hall, can you imagine that?"

Framing and trussing the new parish hall at Rocky Mountain House – that's not Leo up top! c1962.

When Leo and Joyce and their boys left Rocky Mountain House, the parishioners presented them with gifts and money, and a scroll that read:

To Rev. and Mrs. Thurston:

Many long hours you have laboured as a carpenter, organized work bees and encouraged workers to erect a Parish Hall to the greater glory of God and the closer brotherhood of man. In recognition of your efforts, the vestry requested permission of his lordship, the Bishop of Calgary that they might change the name of this hall.

Permission was granted and we, the faithful vestry and parishioners of Holy Trinity Church, Rocky Mountain House, are pleased to announce that from henceforth the name of this building shall be: 'Thurston Hall' in recognition of your valiant services and guidance.

Dated at Rocky Mountain House, Alberta,
this 26th day of March in the year of our Lord 1965.

Burning the mortgage on the church at Lacombe – a big occasion.

It was a permanent tribute in a church brotherhood that seldom allowed a cleric's name to be used on a structure.

"Then the bishop called me. He wanted me to go to Lacombe. There'd been some problem with money. He wanted me to sort of clean it up. He'd made me a canon too, so I had duties associated with the cathedral in Calgary. So anyway, I went to Lacombe, packed up Joyce and the boys and away we went.

"Was that a good church, Leo? Active parishioners? And you likely had other churches to attend to, also. How would you do that, keep in touch with the people in more than one church?" I asked, wondering how these small town ministers managed the load of their far-flung parishes.

"Well, yes, it was a good church. I'd go out to Rimbey. They'd let me know when they needed me to visit, if there was some sort of trouble."

"They raised my stipend one year at the annual meeting. I went out for a while like you always do when they're going to talk about your salary, and when I came back in, they said 'We've raised your stipend $800'. And I said 'That's crazy, you can't afford that.' That's what they did, you know. We needed the cash, the boys were in school, Joyce worked at the federal government's Lacombe Experimental Farm. She was such a great typist, worked for Lou Peding over there. And I liked to get out and help the farmers too.

"We stayed there till 1971, then we went to Banff. What a parish that was, lots of young people there. They needed a lot of counselling: they were away from home, and homesick. They'd come to church, and I'd have to sit down with them and talk to them and get them back on track as much as I could again. People used to come there from all over. Lots of Americans used to come to church in the summer time, but we'd go down to maybe twenty-five people in the winter.

"It's a pretty little church, St. George's in the Pines. Built well, a stone church, coloured windows, people donated all that stuff. And I had to go to Canmore for 9:00 o'clock service, then back to Banff for 11:00 o'clock."

"How did the family like Banff, Leo?" I asked, thinking about the difficulties of raising a family in a resort town.

"Oh, they liked it. Lorne went to work in the Post Office there, after he finished high school. He met Cathy there, and they got married, and lived in a basement suite till they moved to Stettler. Been here ever since, too." Leo's voice reflected the deeply-caring relationship he had with his son and daughter-in-law.

The family's need for space again placed demands on Leo's carpentry skills. He and David, his youngest son, built two bedrooms and a huge family room in the rectory basement. "We use them still," said Bob Purdy, the St. George's in the Pines' rector in 2003.

"Wasn't it in Banff that Joyce hurt herself so badly, Leo? Her leg..." I questioned, remembering the months and months Joyce had been laid up after severely damaging her leg.

"Oh, yes, it was. She fell down those stairs, broke her knee-cap. She'd just finished playing the piano for the students at the Banff School of Fine Arts, and she was carrying her music in a big bag. There were eight or ten stairs down into the basement. She tripped on the carpet or something, and down she went, missed a stair or something, and

Top: Banff is a wonderland of snow in the wintertime.

Bottom: Icicles hanging from the parish hall at Banff's St. George's in the Pines Anglican church.

The perpetual snoozer – this time on Tunnel Mountain in Banff, c1978.

she just rolled down the bloody stairs, smacked herself up good. They had to remove her kneecap, the guy in Banff, then they referred us to Edmonton, he was a good guy. She had osteoporosis too, you know.

"Yeah, well, Joyce wanted me to get out of Banff, too much work, too much counselling she thought. So I went to Taber – remember when you came to visit us? Remember that?"

And I did remember, both the good parts and the painful ones. My first marriage had been failing for several years, and had almost reached the breaking point in the late 1970's when I went to visit Leo and Joyce in Taber. I'd spent a couple of days in my employer's Lethbridge office, so it was just a little scoot over to Taber, a nice opportunity to visit overnight.

After dinner, Leo asked a question that wasn't a question, "Well, aren't you going to phone Clyde?"

"Oh, I dunno, Leo, he likely won't be home anyway. I don't often call him when I'm away, he'd just complain about something and yell at me for phoning," I replied.

"Now, you get over there and call him," Leo insisted, and I dutifully headed for the study and placed the call.

A few minutes later, I rejoined them in the living room. "He wasn't there. The kids said he's gone to the bar in Morinville." Leo's look could have shrivelled a bishop.

I didn't hear from Leo during the excruciating divorce period that followed.

Taber is in the far southern section of Alberta, close to the border with Montana. The land is flat, flat, flat. The only trees are those that have been planted. The area is renowned for its sweet corn as well as sugar beets. If you're lucky, you may catch sight of a herd of antelope racing across the grassy fields and sailing over fences in unison.

"That sure is flat country down there around Taber, isn't it Leo? Good place for sweet corn and sugar beets, though."

"Yeah, that's right. My gawd, there'd be huge piles of beets sitting out there in the fields. I don't care about that corn, don't know how a guy could eat that stuff. Some people do, I guess, but..." his voice trailed off as he brushed his hand across his face to erase the memory of field after field full of sweet – and highly sought-after – Taber corn.

"It wasn't an easy parish, you know, the guy who'd been minister there before me for ten years retired, but he couldn't let it go. So he lived right there, and there was another retired minister there too, so I had two of them! We didn't always see things eye-to-eye. Like the Vestry meetings, the other guy had had those meetings at various homes around the parish, and there was a lady who was his friend, and she nailed me one day and said 'Why don't you have the Vestry meetings at people's homes?' Well, I just told her 'I have Vestry meetings in the church, because I think that's where they should be...' She wasn't very happy. But that's where they should be, in the church, not in people's houses. Lots of things like that.

"Every fall they used to have a church corn party. A couple who lived just outside the town grew corn, and we used to go out there every fall, the parishioners did. We'd have a corn party. We used to pick corn, three-ton truck load, and they used to bring it in to St. Peter's church in Calgary. We used to do this on a Friday evening, then leave about 5 o'clock in the morning, and we sold all the corn. We used to make quite a bit of money on it too. After we'd picked all those damn ears of corn and filled the truck up, we used to build a bonfire and cook the damn corn over the bonfire and have a corn party. I probably ate a bit of corn, I don't know, just to be social, I guess. Joyce used to like corn. And the boys."

"How long did you stay in Taber, Leo?"

"Well, we had to stay there for seven years. It was a long time. Pretty windy down there, but the bishop wanted me to stay. He'd offered me to go to Edgerton, but I didn't think that would be good, not with the family all around there. Doesn't work, you can't counsel people, get them to talk about their problems, when it's family. Too close.

"And Drumheller, but there were a lot of stairs there, and Joyce couldn't have managed those stairs, not in her condition. Then the guy from Strathmore called me up, and told me he was retiring, and wouldn't I like to go to Strathmore? So I did.

"The old house was a wreck but I got it fixed up. It was a comfortable old place. I liked the fireplace; it was a great old fireplace. Wood. The basement was no damn good, though, it was steam heated, so you had to know how to run the furnace, that's for sure. And the plumbing wasn't very good. The town or somebody had to fix up the sewer line. After that they had no trouble.

"I had Gleichen church too. We had our one hundredth anniversary of the church in Gleichen when I was there. Helen Hunley came down, the Lieutenant-Governor. I'd known her in Rocky of course, and I thought it would be nice to have her down, and she came down for the service. Read the lesson. Joyce and I lived in our trailer in the churchyard for the weekend, and we had the service outside. Bishop Ford was there. He was one of the first rectors of Strathmore, years ago. I know him well, nice guy."

"Leo, help me get the time sorted out on this church, will you. If it had its one hundreth anniversary when you were in Strathmore, sometime between 1981 and 1986, then the church must have been built shortly after the railway came through here, is that right?" I

Leo's last service at Strathmore, August 30, 1986.

asked, trying to nail him down to a date. Leo tended to brush off the need for detail with a wave of his hand and a broad-brush statement.

"Oh, you know, Jean, something like that...!" he'd say, as if the date were totally unimportant. After all, the event and the fellowship were what mattered to him...

Leo and Joyce were in still in Strathmore when Leo's sister Olive organized the first Thurston family reunion, in 1985. We rented the Paschendale community hall northeast of Irma for the August long weekend, and family came from Irma and Wainwright, Strathmore and Edmonton. Mary was the only one who came from the Ontario families. There were games and races, laughter and some tears, a variety show on Saturday afternoon, and, of course, a Sunday morning church service.

"You going to be here for church tomorrow?" I asked one of the cousins.

"Ah, I dunno, probably not," was the common answer. I wondered about Leo's influence on the family's religious practices.

"You coming to church tomorrow, Jeannie?" my sister asked.

"Last place I want to be," I responded. "You know how I feel about that stuff."

"Well, you don't have to believe it all, you know," she chuckled.

We were all in our places the next morning as Leo droned through the morning service. Prayers were said and responses given: the Lord's Prayer and the Apostle's Creed recited in unison, a few familiar hymns sung.

Colleen leaned over to me, her laughter barely concealed, "You're doing well," she marvelled, "I haven't even heard you snort." Her sense of humour re-balanced my post-divorce anger and anti-church sentiments. Together, we got through the service and exchanged mirthful glances with our other cousins, whose church-going practices also no longer toed a uniform line.

Leo's faith, however, never seemed to waver. He served the church for thirty-seven years, always in smaller communities. Neither did his wife's faith falter, or her support for her husband and his calling. Joyce told me about Leo's parish ministrations.

"Leo spent all day Friday at the hospital with our pal. His wife is dying of cancer, and they've got three young kids. He doesn't know what he's doing. You'd never think that Leo would be good at times like that, would you? And to hear him in church, he's so awful sometimes," she laughed. "But when somebody's sick, or in trouble, they always call him. He spends days and days visiting people."

Joyce and I stood together, as the younger parents encouraged their children in the three-legged and spoon races. "He walks around with his shirt hanging out, and half the time he forgets where he put his car keys." We chuckled together over Leo's idiosyncrasies, and marvelled at his ability to keep his flock together.

We ate and drank at that family reunion, non-alcoholic drinks only, of course, although I suspect my male cousins had a few bottles stashed in their trucks. There was food enough for an army, as there is at every Thurston family gathering.

FOOD FIGURED PROMINENTLY in Leo's recollections of his parish life, too. Picnics and outings, church suppers and teas, the fabric of parish life.

"We liked Strathmore. We always used to have our parish picnics down there, down at the Wyndham Provincial Park on the river south of Strathmore. We'd have our open air service down there, and then we'd have our dinner, and we'd have games for the kids in the afternoon. You know, I can remember I used to play that game with these kids, what do you call it with one leg?"

"Three-legged race?" I guessed.

"Yeah, that's it. Three-legged race. They put together a scrapbook for us, when we left Strathmore. All kinds of things in it. Great people, wonderful friends. Never forget them. They had a party for us, out at Larson's place just north of Strathmore. I remember they made a money tree for us, that big crowd, that's when they gave me the book." The memory was clearly playing itself out inside Leo's head as he talked about his last parish.

"You and Joyce had bought a house in Stettler to retire to, hadn't you? So that you'd have a place to live once you no longer had a rectory?" I asked, considering the change in lifestyle for Anglican ministers and their spouses, upon retirement. "Why did you come to Stettler? It must have been pretty tough to finance a house, wasn't it, on a minister's salary?"

"Well, Lorne and Cathy were here, you know, and I always liked Stettler anyway. I took over the mortgage on that house and then rented it out. And I borrowed some money from Len, and that was the year mum died, 1981. Each of us got about $12,000, between eleven and twelve thousand dollars, eight of us you know, Ivor was already gone."

"And how has your retirement been, Leo? It's a huge transition, isn't it? Did you and Joyce have some quality time together after you got here?" My own memories of Joyce are so strong, this woman who was able to laugh her way through almost anything.

"We sure did. Joyce was pretty healthy then, in 1986, she had a good ten years. We went to Disneyland one year, and we went to Hawaii for our fortieth anniversary. Then the last four or five years she got, I don't know, this damn trigeminal neuralgia, and her osteoporosis bunged her up. She was really sick then."

"Ah, Leo, remember when I came to visit, and poor Joyce could only sit in her Lazy-Boy™ chair? You cooked and did the housework, and took care of her. She lived in that chair, didn't she, for quite a while?"

"She sure did, couldn't sleep in bed, you know, and if she turned over or tried to get up, she'd break a bone. Then I had to put her in the Auxiliary Hospital, she was there for nine months or so, cause I couldn't handle her at home anymore. She was a great woman, never complained, even with all that sickness. A great help to me in my ministry."

"You were lucky she saw her purpose in life as being your aide, Leo, rather than having a career or a life of her own," my own viewpoint blurted forth. Leo's look said it all. There were no questions. Life had been as it was meant to be.

"Your brother and his wife, what's her name, Donna? They have an ideal marriage. That's what I think." Leo was emphatic. My brother, a lawyer, and his wife, a clever and well-educated woman, lived in a very traditional marriage, Donna as a stay-at-home wife and mother with four children, a fine home in a good location, my brother the breadwinner.

Later, as I discussed Leo's life and his priorities with Lorne, he told me that: " Kotch loved his family. My mother used to get so annoyed sometimes, you know, dad always had to spend a lot of his vacation time in Irma and all they did was work! He just loved it when his brothers or sisters came to visit – never happier. I remember when gran and grandpa used to visit, when we were in Rocky Mountain House. Dad would take them into the mountains on the old trail. It's the David Thompson Highway now but then it was just an old corduroy road. They'd get stuck, and somebody had to haul them out. He loved it."

But that conversation took place much later, a few months after our visits with Leo in Lorne and Cathy's back yard.

❧

AFTER JOYCE'S DEATH in January, 1997, Leo sold their little retirement house. He moved into Paragon Place, the seniors' retirement apartments in Stettler, but spent most of his summer days living in his trailer at Lorne and Cathy's White Sands home.

"We persuaded him to buy Paragon Place's meal service, but then he refused to eat in the dining room," Cathy said.

"No, I'm going to cook my own meals," his words were emphatic. "They'd probably try to give me corn or something. I'll do it myself."

Cathy and Lorne kept him supplied with microwaveable dinners.

In April of 2002, Cathy and Lorne organized an eightieth birthday party for Leo. Friends and former parishioners came from Lacombe and Taber, Strathmore and Rocky Mountain House, Edmonton and Calgary and points in between. Three of Leo's four remaining siblings were there, as well as several nieces and nephews and all three of his sons.

❧

LEO WAS AWAY in Pennsylvania with his son Ken, daughter-in-law Jane, and their son Jonathan when my husband was diagnosed with cancer in August 2002. Both Leo and Ken phoned frequently, offering their love and support.

"Jean, give Ron our love. God bless you both. You're in our prayers every day."

Leo's eightieth birthday party, sons David, Ken and Lorne (l to r); April 16th, 2002.

With his siblings: Phyllis, Olive, and Ted, Ted's wife Molly and Olive's husband George Pugh.

WE CALLED EACH OTHER often after my husband's death, connected through our personalized understanding of grief. And he came to visit.

"Jean, I was thinking, did you know Kathy Teape?" Leo was on the phone to me one evening.

"No, I don't think I know her, Leo, but I remember the name. She must be Canon Tommy Teape's widow? Why do you ask?"

"Well, she's having a birthday, her ninetieth. And they've sent me an invitation, can you imagine that, remembering me after all these years? I dunno, I might come up on the bus if you think you could pick me up." We made the necessary arrangements, and Leo stayed in Edmonton for a few days.

We attended Mrs. Teape's birthday party, and sat with Leo's friend Donald, the man with whom Leo had been ordained in 1951.

I searched for other entertainments to keep Leo busy during his visit to Edmonton.

"Leo, I have tickets for the symphony, with four other friends. Would you like to come along?" I asked, knowing he'd enjoy the music. "We'll have dinner first, downtown, then go over to the Winspear Concert Hall."

"You think I'd like the music? Yeah? Well, okay, that'd be nice. You're sure are you? Alright, amen."

We dined at Sorrentino's downtown, where we were assured of good food and fine service, with an easy walk to the Winspear. "You boil the water, now, okay? That's for sure, you can't make tea without boiling the water. And warm the pot first, too." Customers at the neighbouring tables glanced over in amusement, as Leo instructed the server in a loud voice. An evening out with my uncle Leo left me amused but a bit unnerved.

I TOOK HIM HOME to Stettler the next day. "Leo, was going into the ministry the right choice for you? It can't have been an easy life, but was it good?" I asked, seeking to keep the conversation alive and interesting as we embarked on our two and a half hour drive.

"Oh sure, I had a calling, you know, Jean. I couldn't have ignored it. Well, I suppose I could have, but I didn't think I could. It's been a good life, serving the Lord."

"There's a lot of change, dissention, in the Anglican church now, isn't there?" I wondered how Leo felt about some of the more controversial decisions and changing philosophies within the church.

"Damn fool stuff, the lot of it. Do you know, there's a woman teaches out at Sorrento, she teaches a class about women in the Bible, women's right to be ordained and all that stuff. Things that aren't in the Bible at all, women's history in the church. Trying to change what's in the Scriptures, for gawd's sake.

"Other stuff too, you know, seems like the bishops are being carried along, they're not paying attention to the Scriptures, are they? Homosexuals, some of them want to get married, for gawd's sake. And I know they can change, you know. I've seen them do it. What are they trying to do, anyhow, make the Scriptures change for them? What they're doing is wrong, it's just absolutely wrong, against God's teaching." Leo warmed to his topic, made sure I heard what he believed. His increasingly loud voice filled my car.

LEO HADN'T FELT WELL during that last visit at my house. Within weeks, he was hospitalized and tested for colon cancer. Some polyps were removed. He returned home, but continued to complain of discomfort.

Then he broke his leg in a fall from a recreational vehicle. The biopsy showed bone cancer. He was admitted to Stettler hospital.

"Jean, I don't know what to do with him. He's so rude to the staff, you know, and then he gets mad when they don't treat him 'right'." Cathy's love for her father-in-law was mixed with sadness and frustration. "He won't eat the food. He asks the staff why they're trying to feed him that stuff. He's not in a lot of pain right now, but he's just so grumpy."

Leo's eldest son, Ken, together with his wife Jane and their son Jonathon flew home. David and his sons came from Calgary. Lorne and Cathy and their son Charlie seldom left the hospital.

Leo Sidney Thurston died, angry and indignant with the process of dying, on September 25, 2003. His grandson, Charlie, was with him. His body was laid to rest beside that of his wife, in the Stettler cemetery.

I can almost hear Leo saying "A-a-a-a-MEN", in his loud and resounding voice.

CHAPTER 15

Ivor

*What went on inside the head of our bachelor uncle, he who remained
alone and aloof as his brothers and sisters married and had children?
Did he have any private life at all?*

IVOR, youngest of the five Thurston brothers. The silent, observant
one. His forehead was topped by a rounded hairline, inherited from his
father's father according to the photograph above the sideboard. He
had thick auburn hair which he carefully groomed before going anywhere. His face and neck were weather-roughened, his arms tanned.
He was always clean, even in the days when water had to be hauled
into the house by the bucketful. Ivor exuded energy: he attracted children and animals and perhaps women although none of his family
ever would have known if that were true or not. He was gentle with
his mother, kind with children, firm with his animals, and quiet with
most human beings. He was a man whose life ended too soon, a few
years after he had finally found happiness.

IVOR WAS FIFTEEN YEARS OLD when I was born, the only uncle still at home after all his brothers and most of his sisters had left. I was ten or twelve when my youngest two aunts married and created their own homes. In my childhood's memory, Ivor was a strapping young man.

Ivor's teeth fascinated all us kids. Each tooth was a whiter-than-white tile, large and gleaming in a face ruddy from the weather or covered with dust from the fields. His teeth were perfect, without a cavity or a crown, even though he hardly ever brushed them, maybe once a day after supper or before breakfast. He used tooth powder, not paste, a little poured into his palm then scooped onto the wet brush. As he worked the brush, he watched himself in the little mirror above the washstand. His parents', siblings' and neighbours' teeth were yellowed or crooked, with gaps where teeth had been. Few were able to afford store-bought dentures.

Ivor was such a handsome guy. His clear blue eyes were thickly framed by sun-bleached eyebrows and eyelashes. He was of average height or a little more. He wore fitted jeans, not the loose ones with suspenders his brothers wore. His shirts were cotton, Western-style, open at the neck with his chest hairs showing. His muscles strained to pop the snap fasteners, and the sleeves were rolled up above his elbows. A cap kept the dirt from his always neatly-trimmed hair. He wore lace-up leather boots for field work, shiny cowboy boots for riding or going to town.

Ivor trod alone, enclosed in a bubble of intense energy. Inside, a verbal dam restrained his words and restricted conversation. He was a man whom everyone liked but few were close to, a man who exuded sexual energy but seldom was seen with a woman. No-one knew what Ivor did in his spare time. No-one dared ask.

My sister and I used to watch, silently, as Ivor came in from the fields. That was long before tractors had cabs or air-conditioning, or protection from sun or rain, wind or grasshoppers. Dust would cover him completely, settling into every crease of clothes and skin, into pockets

Spring 1927: Ivor's first encounter with a Richardson's ground squirrel – the common gopher.

What is Ivor doing in the box? Summer 1930, with Olive, beside the house; behind them is the round tub the whole family used for bathing.

Top: 1933. Ivor is on the left beside Leo; 3-year-old Winnie is in front, Olive on the right.

Bottom: Here's Ivor with a new lamb, 1935.

Ivor and Leo take Olive sledding down the hill west of the house. c1929.

Winter on the farm, c1935; Ivor and the dog on the left, Olive and Leo.

Top: 1933. Summer, mid-
1930's – Ivor with a cap like
his father and brothers wear;
Olive and Winnie with their
dolls.

Right: By 1943 he's a young
man. The milk can on the left
was used to ship fresh milk
to the dairy by train. Cream
cans were the same shape but
smaller.

and inside the top of his boots. When he came home from the fields he headed straight for the reservoir on the kitchen stove. He lifted out a dipper of warm water and carried it to the wash-basin, sudsed his hands and face and arms with red Lifebuoy soap, then grabbed the threadbare towel from the rack above the wash-stand.

He smiled at us in the mirror as he washed. Pale little creases appeared in the tanned skin around his eyes and mouth. When he smiled, we knew our summertime world was as it should be.

"How are ya?" he'd ask my sister and I, his eldest nieces. "Find the light switch yet?"

Lights and light switches were an ongoing source of amusement among Ivor, our other uncles, and us. "Turn on the lights," they'd say, or "Run a jug of cold water," or "How about some cream from the refrigerator?" Then they'd laugh, "Can't you find it? I thought you were going to bring it down with you?!" Eventually other things would take their attention, or our grandmother would tell them to stop teasing the little ones.

THERE WAS NO POWER on the farm when we were kids. Most farms on the Canadian and U.S. prairies weren't electrified until the mid 1950's, although the towns and villages were supplied with power much earlier, in the 1920's and '30's. Power distribution was a favoured employment tool for governments when the boys came home from World War II and needed work. That's when power dams were built in Alberta: the Brazeau on the North Saskatchewan, Rundle and Spray west of Calgary, the Mica Dam in British Columbia, dozens of others across the nation.

Electricity didn't matter to my siblings and I. We were only at the farm in the summertime, when the prairie days were long. The sunset and its afterglow lasted until 11:00 p.m. or later, long after we'd gone to sleep. The birds awoke with the sunrise at 3 or 4 o'clock, long before we got up. We didn't know what it was like to have only kerosene lamps to read by during the long, dark winters.

Ivor and his friend Jim Paul on Jasper Avenue, c1949.

❧

"You guys got dinner ready yet?" Ivor asked after he'd washed. He held out his left arm, the elbow bent, forearm parallel to the floor. "Grab on there and I'll take you in."

Quickly, my sister and I grabbed his forearm and he lifted us with no apparent effort. We clung like monkeys, knees bent and our feet well above the floor as Ivor marched through the green doorway and into the kitchen.

"You're not so heavy. We'd better get you to the table and fatten you up a bit before your mother comes back." He chuckled as he carried us, still gripping his forearm, into the front room. "Okay now, go and help gran get dinner on," he said as he dropped us off.

Ivor's chair was on the long side of the dinner table, to grandpa's right, across from gran, close to the radio so he could turn it on to hear the noon grain and cattle reports. We knew better than to talk as he and grandpa listened to the male voice sing-song the daily market prices of beef and pork in hundred-weights, and wheat, oats, and barley in bushels.

After dinner, grandpa pushed back for his afternoon snooze, a few minutes in his chair with an occasional snore to break the afternoon quiet. We helped gran clear the table. Ivor stalked away through the kitchen and the back kitchen, the blunt end of a toothpick sticking from his mouth. The screen door slammed behind him as he headed toward the barn or the pig pens or the truck. We didn't really wonder what he did – he farmed like most of our relatives. Girl children weren't invited to accompany him – they worked inside with gran, or picked berries with the aunts, or took lunch out to the fields for the men. Granddaughters didn't drive the tractor or stook the bundles of oats or wheat or even feed the pigs. They fed the chickens, gathered eggs, chopped wood, washed clothes, separated the milk from the cream, made butter, and hauled water. Those chores were secondary to their real work – the never-ending continuum of food preparation.

Late one hot afternoon, we heard Ivor's deep voice, sudden and loud. "Hey, what the.... I'll catch you..." My sister and I ran to the screen door and watched, open-mouthed, as Ivor chased his youngest sister down the yard. His shirt was soaking wet, and water dripped from his hair and nose. Winnie had hidden behind the old Chev truck in the driveway, quietly awaited her opportunity to toss a dipper of cold water at her brother. Now she raced barefoot down the yard, dodging chicken manure and rocks and prickly foxtail weeds. Her laughter rang out across the yard, delightedly successful in having caught her brother unaware. Within seconds, he chased her down, lifted her up and tossed her into the water-filled horse trough, amidst shrieks of laughter.

"There, that's what you get," he stalked off, laughing, after he'd helped her out of the algae-lined trough.

Gran just shook her head at their antics, a smile playing about her lips.

MY GOLDEN CHILDHOOD SUMMERS ended too quickly. Soon I was sixteen, old enough to get a summer job. My visits to the farm became abbreviated, weekend jaunts. I married less than a year after high school graduation. My beautiful, dark-haired baby Jennifer was born sixteen months later. My grandparents were anxious to see their first great-grandchild, and we looked forward to showing her off. A few weeks after her birth on October 4, 1960, her father and I took her to Irma.

" 'Ack, that little mouth, just a wee rosebud," crooned gran as she cuddled her new great-granddaughter. "Won't Canon Crawley be pleased with her."

Gran retrieved the family christening robes for Jennifer's baptism, scheduled for the afternoon service at tiny St. Mary's church. Canon Crawley, a gentle, portly man who had spent his early years ministering to the Anglican flocks in the Peace River country of northern Alberta, would officiate.

"I'll fix her a little Pablum™, Gran, before church." I did not want my baby daughter to disturb the service. She wouldn't take a bottle, and breast-feeding was such a private matter then. The concept of nursing a baby during a church service was beyond comprehension in those pre-feminist days; a return to normalcy in breast-feeding practices would take another thirty or forty years.

Ivor watched as I mixed the baby cereal with milk. He picked up the Pablum™ box, read the label and started to smile, then laughed out loud.

"That's just the same as pig-starter!" he chuckled.

I REMEMBER THE WAY Ivor was with children – quiet, powerful, commanding, with eyes that saw everything. Little ones were usually cautious around him at first. Then, they clambered up onto his wide-armed chair and soon found that he would do almost anything for them in his shy, bachelor way.

Ivor always found time to give us rides on the work horses, but not on the strikingly handsome stallion that was his saddle pony. "No, not the pony, he's too wild for you guys," he used to tell us. He took us with him to town, or when he had to see one of his brothers, and let us ride beside him in the half-ton with the windows rolled all the way down so we could rest our arm on the window frame like he did.

"Too bad he doesn't have his own kids, isn't it?" I remember hearing my aunts say to gran. She always replied, "When God wills it," or words to that effect.

Ivor was the youngest, the only one in the family who hadn't married as a twenty- or even thirty-year old. Many of the young Irma women left town right after high school, hurrying to the city to work or attend college. There they met young men, married, and raised their children as city kids, just as my mother had done. Only a few returned to their parents' farms. A whole group of bachelors was left in Irma – Don McKay, Jack McKay, Jim Craig, Ivor Thurston, a few others. How could Ivor have a woman in his life, I wondered, while living at home with his parents? But what options were there? Besides, if Ivor lived somewhere alone, he would have had to take care of all his own meals and housekeeping, as well as the farm work. It wasn't that gran and grandpa stood in his way. They seemed to want him to lead a normal life, but somehow Ivor just didn't meet the right woman, not till much later. I often wondered at his loneliness.

"I'M GOING OUT TO EDSON [about 100 miles west of Edmonton] for a while, Mum," Ivor announced one late fall day in the 1950's. "Some of the guys are going to work for the mill. We'll be back for Christmas."

Farm boys often worked in the woods during the winter, cutting timber for the mills such as the one at Hinton[36], whose timber

The family's cattle herd increased in size and quality; they were moved closer to home for the winter, where it was easier to provide feed and water.

Ivor's brother Leo brought Joyce, his Winnipeg-born fiancée, to visit; she's on the tractor with Fred. That may be Ivor behind, cutting and binding the ripe oats.

leases were scattered over a wide area, south down the Coal Branch, east towards Edson. Lumbering was a way to earn hard cash, money for cattle and equipment, cars or trucks. Later, as Alberta's oil and gas industry developed, the young farmers worked as roughnecks on the well sites, jobs that were dirtier and even more dangerous than lumbering, but also more lucrative.

In the spring, Ivor returned to his farm. My grandmother continued to take care of her youngest son. She did his laundry, prepared his meals, baked his favourite pies, washed his dishes. In return, he watched over her and his father, mindful of their needs and their health, quiet if when he came in at night after they'd gone to bed, tidy with himself and his surroundings.

Ivor had the north bedroom, the one right off the living room where the family ate dinner, played cards, and wrote letters. A maroon brocade curtain, suspended from a brass rod, separated his room from the rest of the house. He had a small bed, maybe three-quarter width. On it lay a quilt gran made, heavy melton cloth squares sewn to a flannel back, a woollen batt in between, all fastened together with red yarn. Grey flannelette sheets, winter and summer. A large wooden bureau and a chair stood against the north wall. He hung his clothes on wallhooks, placed his hats on the shelf above the hooks. Ivor's tiny private domain. We only went in there to return his laundry, which we placed on his bed so he could put it away in the right drawers. We never stayed long, never poked into his bureau or explored his belongings.

THE THURSTON MEN each owned two or more quarter sections of 160 acres (64 ha). They bought their own tractors, purchased some equipment individually, jointly purchased other machinery.

"We all worked together," my Uncle Ted told me.

Working together included the boy children, who began to drive tractors and trucks when they were not more than seven or eight. Ivor had four nephews close by – Ted's sons Don and Gordie, Ron's son Darrell, Winnie and Bill's son Will.

Will's home was a half mile north of our grandparents' farm, on the quarter section aunt Mary and Uncle Bert had lived on during their disastrous return in 1955. Thurston Row the road was called, five miles of the old Mannville highway, where Thurston families owned all the land from town right out to Ted and Molly's place. The Askin's – Bill and Winnie and their children Bobby, Will, and Anne – lived there until Will was a teenager.

Of all the cousins, Will is the most like his Uncle Ivor. Will has the same high forehead, distinctly rounded hairline, even teeth, and tall strong body. Another quiet guy, strong and handsome, with the same intense energy as his uncle.

"Did you like being surrounded by Thurstons like that, Will?" I asked one day, long after we'd grown into adulthood. I'd always felt envious of my country cousins who lived close to our aunts and uncles, cousins and grandparents, surrounded by their love, immersed in the family's community.

"Oh, I was proud of it. Grandpa and grandma, everybody was right there," Will said. "The people I met in town, anywhere, they always wanted to know how grandma and grandpa were, were they well, how were the crops, all those things that really mattered."

"Yes, everyone did ask, didn't they? Maureen and I were always surprised that people remembered us – your mom would introduce us as Phyllis's daughters and the neighbours always said, 'Of course, you come down to your grandparents every summer don't you? Say hello to them for us.' And we always tried to remember who they were, but usually couldn't!

"Ivor took us to town with him sometimes too, in that robin's egg blue car he had – remember the steer hide he always threw over the back of the front seat? He was so proud of that car. Remember how we'd all go to town on Saturday night? Ivor always went first, in his own truck, before gran and grandpa and us kids. Then, after he bought the blue Chev, he'd take it. If Maureen and I were lucky, he'd offer to take us with him – but that didn't happen often. He usually had other fish to fry with his gorgeous, deep-throated car. I guess he took a rib-bing from his friends over that colour!"

"Yeah, he sure did, Jeannie. It just seemed so out of character, you know, him with a car that colour. But he liked it," responded Will.

It was a big car, with its rumbling V-8 engine – probably 350 or maybe 420 horsepower – like a big cat, its power all curled up, waiting for the signal to perform. There was chrome around the windows, the doors, and the wheel wells. Ivor kept his car so clean, dust hardly dared touch it.

What kind of statement was that car? I wonder now. Did Ivor see himself like the car – powerful, ready to win any race, cocksure of himself, ready for attention? Did he race the engine just a bit when a pretty woman was around? I can see him still, sitting in the driver's seat, grinning with the pleasure of power, his own laugh matching the engine's throaty growl.

The robin's egg blue car had long since disappeared the day Will and I reminisced about it and its owner. "Will, did Ivor ever hold you up on his arm, the way he did Maureen and I?" I asked.

"Oh sure. You know. I was happy to be around him, that's all. Some people say I'm a lot like him." The words to describe Will's special relationship with his uncle didn't come easily. How could he explain that it was Ivor who taught him to drive the tractor, handle cattle and pigs, read the weather, and crop the fields, Ivor who made time for him in the way that only uncles can.

"M-m-m, I'd say they're right, too," I responded. "But you're a pretty gentle guy. Ivor wasn't really gentle, was he? I always thought he was a no-nonsense, get on with it, I don't have time to fool around kind of a guy. You ever see his gentle side, Will?"

"Well, not too often. But guys don't let other guys see that side, Jeannie. You know that. At least not the guys in our family, or the ones that I work with. There's always lots of bantering, you know, remember how all our uncles used to tease us? And the guys I work with now, in the oilfield, they're the same. They probably save gentle for their women!" Will smiled.

"Ah, you're so right, Will. You spent a lot of time down there, at the farm, didn't you?"

"Yeah, I did. If I rode my bike down to grandma and grandpa's place, after breakfast in the summer, Ivor would already be gone, so then I'd have to ride out to him, or sometimes grandpa would take me in the car. Ivor always got up early in the morning, and he made his own breakfast. Instant coffee, and two eggs, fried with the yolks squashed, and toast, one piece with jam that gran had made, maybe rhubarb and saskatoon.

"And he'd take his thermos out to the field, full of coffee, an old tin thermos, red with drawings on it. Glass inside, of course, not the steel ones we use now."

I'd always assumed, without knowing why, that Ivor was a good farmer. He seemed so focussed, and he was never able to sit still for long. While the others took breaks from their work, Ivor continued on, whether he was driving a tractor or handling cattle. He never seemed to get tired. But still, I had to ask...

"What about his machinery, Will? He must have had good equipment. I can't imagine Ivor having the patience to put up with equipment that didn't perform well, or that broke down during seeding or harvest!"

"Oh, no, that's for sure," Will responded. "He and Uncle Ron shared the spike and disc harrows, and the haying equipment. Ivor had his own tractor and combine. And there weren't many breakdowns!

"My first job driving for Uncle Ivor was on his Fordson™ 8N or maybe it was a 9N tractor, the little grey tractor that grandpa had when he quit farming in 1953. I was only about eleven when they let me start driving it, you know — it was a pretty big deal for a kid. I didn't really drive any equipment at home, so to do it for Uncle Ivor, well...

"See, Ivor always used a pull-type mower, not a self-propelled one. And the mower was attached to the Fordson, so Ivor would cut the hay, and leave it lying in the field to dry for two or three days, depending on the weather. And then I got to rake it, we'd take the mower off and put the rake on behind the Fordson. Uncle Ron did the baling, and Uncle Ivor had a bale wagon. It could take sixty bales at a time; he'd use his John Deere 4020™ to pull the bale wagon. Slick.

"An hour after the hay was picked up loose, it was baled and loaded into the barn. Sixty or seventy pound bales. They didn't handle those bales much, you know, those guys," Will explained.

"Gosh, that sure beats the way they did it when I was little. I remember taking lunch to them, out in the field where they cut the hay. They'd let it dry for a couple of days, and next time we took their tea out, we'd watch as they dragged the hay into windrows with a horse-drawn rake. And then they pitched it onto the hayrick, Ivor and Ron and Uncle Ted, each with a big pitchfork. Once the hayrick was full, one of them climbed on, clucked at the team, drove to where the haystack was being built, and forked the hay off. Remember, the haystack had to be built just right, so the rain would run off, not get inside and make the hay mold or rot. A lot more work than now, those big round bales need a lot of equipment, don't they, but not a lot of manual labour."

"Yeah, haying still smells good though, sweet, kind of dusty but a good, clean smell."

"Did you like working with Ivor and Ron?" I asked, thinking that boys never talk about the things they like. They just yell about the things they don't like.

"Oh sure, Jeannie. I worked for them every summer, you know, from when I was ten- or eleven-years-old. I was with the men, they loved me and I loved them back. I dunno, learning is a big experience for that age. You're proud to be half boy and half man and you're proud to be out there, and it's ..." Will's voice trailed off as he remembered the years of his childhood, and the days spent in the fields with his uncles.

"Uncle Ron and Uncle Ivor and Uncle Ted, they were always good to me. I wasn't very old when Uncle Ivor started to let me drive his big tractor, too. Guess I would have been about thirteen. I'd come home from school and get off the bus at gran and grandpa's, and go out to the field. I remember driving his grain truck behind him, behind the combine, when I was twelve."

"Lucky guy," I said. "The uncles used to give us rides on the tractor, they'd let us sit on the seat and steer. They'd stand right beside us, protectively, and keep the throttle in place, make sure we kept the tractor out of the ditch. But they never left us alone on it. Girls, especially city girls, just didn't drive tractors."

"I think it was 1967," Will said. "I remember sitting out in the field with them, Ivor and Ron, just after school started, so that would be the first week in September. I can still hear Uncle Ivor saying that that was the earliest he ever remembered getting the crop off. Wheat, it must have been, to be so early. You know that barley takes about 80 days from seeding to harvest, oats a little longer, and wheat takes the longest time, maybe 120 days – they used to say that if you don't have the wheat seeded by May 11th, you wouldn't get a crop. The farmers didn't spray the crops in those days, like they do now, with Round-Up™, to stop the growth so it ripens when they want it to. They only sprayed with herbicides in the early spring to keep the weeds down, and then a bit of fertilizer. None of these growth-killers like what's used now."

I REMEMBERED the farmers talking, as they always did, over our girl-child heads. "Grasshoppers get to your place yet?" one of them would ask.

"No, but I seen them comin'. They're up by Burton's today, they'll be at my place in another two days, I'll betcha. Them damned things, there's so many of them, the road's all slimy up there. You can almost hear them munching up the crop. Nothin' we can do, either. Crop was going to be a bumper one this year, too, god-dammit."

Or, as the trucks plied the road in front of gran and grandpa's house, hauling grain into town, grandpa would comment, "There goes Charlie Archibald again, that's the sixth time I've seen him pass today. He must have had a big crop of oats on that quarter he broke last year."

"They had some good crops back then, didn't they?""

Yes," said Will, "they did. If the hail didn't get it, or the army worms, or the grasshoppers in the dry years.

"That was how I made my spending money, you know. They'd pay me $5.00 for a full day's work on a Saturday. They never worked Sunday, of course.

"I remember Ivor riding his saddle horse, Sunday mornings when the rest of them went to church, checking the cattle in the coulee, you know, south of town. Or up north, if they were on Uncle Ted's place, fourteen[37] I think they called it. He rode a good-lookin' stallion, light brown, with a white blaze down the front and white socks.

"And he'd use his stallion when he was branding the cattle too, like a cutting horse. Or if he had to drive the cattle from one place to another, like from fourteen down to the coulee, he'd ride and I'd walk!" Will's eyes shone with the memory playing out behind his eyes.

"He was a pretty handsome guy, wasn't he, up there on that horse, wearing chaps and a Stetson hat, totally in charge," I remembered.

"Yeah, I guess he was. I didn't think much about that sort of thing then, but looking back, that's the way it was."

"Will, what kind of a cattle operation did he run? Did he keep a herd of cows and a bull all year 'round, or what did he do?" I certainly didn't know the details of Ivor's farming operation.

"Well, he and Uncle Ron used to work together lots on the cattle. I think they were partners on the cattle a lot of the time, then Uncle Ivor decided he wanted to get out of the cow-calf operation and go into feeder cattle. Buy calves in the summer, feed them up, and sell them again in the fall.

"It was always common knowledge that Ivor would make money at what he was doing. Everybody gave him a hard time about making so much money. He had a real knack for buying the feeders at the right time. He'd go to the auction marts and buy his cattle and get a fairly decent deal on them, and then he'd sell them again at just the right time in the fall." Will chuckled as he remembered the teasing Ivor got from his neighbours and brothers.

We chatted about the ease with which some people seemed to make money, while others struggled, seldom able to buy or sell cattle or property at the right time.

Alone, that's how I remember Ivor. Not that he disliked people, or that he didn't want companionship. Although he did have a pretty short fuse with people he didn't care for. He'd simply get up and leave the room, go and find something to do out in the yard or with his cattle. Such a loner.

Only two of Ivor's nephews stayed on the farm – Gordon, Uncle Ted's second son, and Darrell, Uncle Ron's son. Gordie grew up working beside his father and our uncles Ron and Ivor.

"So Gord," I said, one spring day in 2004 as we sat in the kitchen of the home my cousin shared with his wife Leone. Sun streamed in the windows and the birds chattered outside. "What was it like, when you were a kid, working with Ivor and the rest of them in the fields?"

"Oh, gawd, Jean, it was a time alright. I was probably ten- or twelve-years-old, you know, a kid. I used to be scared of them, for a while, but then I guess I just stopped being a-scared of them anymore.

"You don't want to hear what Ivor said when he got mad! He'd get out there with the farmhand, to pick up the hay. He and Ron would have cut it, and left it to cure out there in the field for three or four days. Then we'd rake it up in long windrows, and Ivor would go down the windrow picking up the hay with the farmhand, and he'd carry it to the haystack he was building in the middle of the field," Gord chewed on his toothpick, and chuckled as he recalled his youthful summers.

"You remember what a farmhand looks like, don't you? Mounted on the front of the tractor, with hydraulic arms on it, and big wooden teeth out in front. Twelve or fourteen-feet-long, those teeth, remember? Well," and Gord started to laugh, "everything would be fine till Ivor

Ivor loading the farmhand with bundles for the thresher, c1949.

Ted on the tractor, Ivor loading the wagon with bundles from the farmhand, c1949.

drove over some rough ground, and then the farmhand would start to rock and the teeth would stick into the ground and break off.

"You should have heard him then, used to make him madder than hell! He really went at it. For Ivor, there was no time to sit around or talk, so when those teeth broke...! He'd have to stop, and take the thing apart, go into town and buy new teeth, come back and put them in, fasten the whole thing together again. Wasted a whole afternoon, doing that. He'd be pretty hot."

"Such a difference between working with the men and with the women," I thought. I couldn't recall my grandmother ever losing her temper, or my aunts either. My mother did, at home, she used to yell at us sometimes, take the wooden spoon or a piece of hardwood flooring to our behinds. But there was no anger among the women on the farm, at least none that we kids ever saw. Perhaps we were simply shielded from all that. Heaven knows there must have been plenty of reasons for the women to lose patience, with little money and few conveniences, hard work that never seemed to end, and men who ruled the roost. But I never, ever heard my grandparents use bad language, never heard the uncles swear around the women or girl children.

"What did you use for hay, then, Gord? I don't remember ever hearing them talk about seeding a pasture," I questioned.

"Well, no, they really didn't. They used to cut some native hay, cut all the grass from the dried-up sloughs or wherever you could get it. Some brome grass, not near like what we have now. I mostly cut alfalfa and timothy and brome grass for my own use now.

"The equipment was pretty small then, too, compared to what we're using today. Back then, I must have started riding the tractor with dad when I was five or six. He'd put me on his lap, or else he'd let me sit on the seat to drive and he'd stand beside me. But the tractors were only about thirty or forty horsepower then, and six- or eight-foot cultivators. Heck, the tractor I'm using now is two hundred horsepower, pulls thirty-some feet of cultivator." My cousin Gord is a good farmer, prosperous, with pedigreed cattle and handsome black or tan horses, Clydesdales or Percherons or Belgians.

"Did you ride horses when you were a kid, Gord? I think Mike, my brother, said that you and he sometimes rode. That would have been before mom and Jim Craig got married, and they all moved back down here."

"Oh sure. Dad always had a horse or two, you know, he always liked to have horses around. But see, when we were working with Ivor, rounding up cattle, I'd be the one to ride the saddle horse and get the cattle chased into the corrals. Ivor had so many cattle. He had them all over the place, wherever he had some grass to put them onto. In the coulee a lot of the time, and on 10 there, north of dad. He probably had about 300 steers, he'd buy some as weaned calves in the fall, and he'd buy more in the spring, put them out on grass for summer, then fatten them in the winter, get them ready for market. Mostly all Hereford or Hereford-cross cattle.

"And you always have to check on them. One or the other of them always has pink eye, or hoof rot, or something. Ivor would go out in his Ford truck sometimes. He had an International truck later on, or else he'd ride his saddle horse. He sure used to like that saddle horse."

"Did you guys brand the cattle, Gord?" I asked.

Branding has always seemed barbaric to me. Maybe it's just the city kid side coming out, but I don't think so. I couldn't imagine subjecting cattle to an iron shaped in some unique form, heated in a fire and shoved onto the animal's side or its flank. I'm glad women didn't have to take part in that operation.

"Yeah, we did. Ivor's brand was like an SH with a bar at the end of it, put onto the steer's right rib.

"He'd have all his cattle in the yard, down home. He'd have kept them down there in the field close to the house all winter, so he could feed them and stuff. Then before he turned them out in the spring, onto the grass, he'd vaccinate them and brand them and dehorn them."

"Gawd, Gord, that must have been a terrible job. Branding, dehorning, I can't imagine doing that to a live creature," I shuddered.

"Well, that's the way it was done then. Now the cattle are mostly tagged, you know those yellow or red tags in their ears. Identify what

Fred and his sons branding cattle, c1943.

Ivor's cattle in the yard, c1958.

year and month they were born, we keep track of their lineage and everything now.

"But the dehorning was pretty bad. There was always one or two of them died. It was kind of a cruel process. That dehorner, it's just like a shear, kind of shaped so you could put the horns in between, and there was two long wooden handles, on it, and you'd just crush them. Had to be a strong guy to do it, so Ivor did it. On those big steers, there'd be two of them, Ivor and Ron or Darrell. The blood would spurt right up a foot or more when they chopped off the horn. Pretty cruel. And then branding them, besides. Always at least one of them died, bled to death, shock." Gord was quiet, the full-colour scenes again visible in his memory.

Neither of us wanted to continue this discussion. "Did Ivor do anything for fun, Gord? He always seemed to be working when I was around. He never seemed to sit and play cards or anything like that. I remember him getting all cleaned up and going into town on Saturday night. That guy, you know, gran or I would ask him if he'd had a good time and he'd just say 'yup' and smile and never tell us anything about what he did!" Gord joined in my laughter, recalling how impossible it had been to get Ivor to reveal anything about his personal life.

"Well, he never seemed to do anything just for the sake of doing it. He and I would go to the auction mart, not just to go there, but if he needed to buy something. Cattle or whatever. He was always good to me though, and he was a good farmer: there was no two ways about that. He worked his head off, you know. He'd got to what, about fifty-four-years-old, just started to enjoy himself a little, had enough money to do something, and then he was gone," Gordie shook his head.

Ivor did occasionally have time for fun. He used to watch the local boys play hockey or baseball, although he never played either of those games himself. He curled, as did almost all the farm men, women, and children during the wintertime when the fields were frozen, and there was time for recreation. "Whoa!" he'd yell at the rock as it flew toward the house, "Whoa!" as if the rock could hear and respond. He was a good curler, disciplined and intense.

Tossing bundles into the threshing machine, c1944; the Thurston family continued to thresh (rather than combine) until the early 1960's.

Ivor golfed, too, on the new course developed in 1960 on Emil Worth's place – SE 1/4- 34-45-9, just northeast of the village. The new golf course replaced the old 5-hole golf course that a group of Irma-ites had organized in 1922. The new group built a clubhouse, constructed tee-boxes and fairways, seeded and smoothed the greens. Ivor learned to play, as did his brother Ron.

I can picture Ivor with a club in his hand, his eyebrows white from the sun, his face tanned, a cap on his head. He would have been totally focussed on the ball, adrenaline pushing up into his back and arm muscles, his mind's eye picturing the place he wanted to land the ball. "Crack!" the sound would have startled the errant gophers or crows. I can see Ivor's grin as the ball hit the turf within a foot or two of its intended landing place.

He was invited to join the International Order of Elks Lodge No. 366, one of several service organizations in the area. The Irma Elks Lodge was chartered on October 15, 1952, with fifty-six community-minded men (membership was exclusively male). Children's ball clubs, 4-H clubs, hockey and curling benefitted from Elks' sponsorship. The members staffed the barbecues at the annual Irma Sports

Days, donated a wheelchair to the school, and provided financial assistance to the school band and to local sports teams. Elks members worked closely together.

Taciturn Ivor learned to square dance. He joined the club in Irma; dressed carefully each week in clean blue jeans, cotton plaid shirt, a bolo tie, polished boots on his feet. Single Ivor never had to look far for a partner.

I only danced with Ivor one evening, at the wedding dance held for my mother and her husband, Jim Craig. The dance was held in the North Hall, just past Ted and Molly's place. Neighbours came from all around, delighted that a favourite bachelor had finally bitten the dust. Jim had farmed in the area all his life, my mother had lived there as a teenager, before she moved to the city, and most of her family farmed close by. The community was in a festive mood that night in July of 1959. There was a live band, players who knew everybody's favourite music, as well as when to play fast sets and when to ease into waltzes. Everybody danced.

"Come on, Jeannie, you ever dance the Butterfly?" asked Ivor.

"No, but it looks like I'm going to learn how!" I answered, as Ivor took my right arm and his friend grabbed the left. Up we got, me in the middle, a tall strong man on either side. Slowly at first, almost a heel-and-toe polka. But then...the notes suddenly turned fast and furious. Ivor whirled me around, handed me over to our partner, then back to Ivor, whirling, twirling, till the world itself spun. Another change, slow music again, heel and toe.... and then, twirl again, and again. Somehow, these bachelors had become expert at the Butterfly, that most favourite of all country dances.

I DIDN'T SEE MUCH OF IVOR during the 1960's when I was busy raising my four baby girls and their stepbrother.

But one day, he telephoned. "Jean, are you going to be home on Friday?" he asked.

"Yes, sure, Ivor, you coming up?"

"Well, yes, I'm going to Toronto for a few days. Could you take me to the airport? Maybe I could leave my car at your place?"

I was more than astonished. Ivor never went anywhere. "Sure, Ivor, you can park in front of the house. The car'll be okay for a few days." We made the arrangements.

Ivor arrived at our house with lots of time to spare. He appeared at my front door, dressed in a western-style leisure suit and bolo tie, hat perched above his sun-bleached eyebrows and ruddy complexion. Nervous.

"Come on in, Ivor, would you like some coffee, we've got lots of time, it only takes about half an hour to get out to the airport."

I made coffee, found some cookies, pushed the toys off a chair and tried to put Ivor at ease. He didn't talk much, just drank his coffee and smiled at the antics of the little children at his feet.

"Time to go, isn't it?" he said. I'd seen him looking at his watch.

As I dropped him off at the airport departures level, he asked, "Aren't you coming in?" and I suddenly realized that he really needed company.

"No," I said. "Your plane will be taking off in just a few minutes, and I've got these little kids. You'll be okay, just go right up there to the Air Canada counter, see, you can see the line up over there. The lady at the desk will take your ticket, and show you where to go. And you have a great time. Give my love to Mary and Bert, and Len and Jean, and all of them in Ontario. Bye, now." I drove away.

A few days later, I returned to the airport and picked him up. "How was it, Ive?" I could see from his expression that he'd had a huge experience.

"That's quite a place, Toronto. You been there? You see those buildings? And that Highway 401? Cars and trucks never stop along there, hell-bent for leather, those cars. Sure couldn't take a tractor on that road," he laughed. He talked, non-stop, all the way home. I listened with pleasure as the words poured out.

A FEW YEARS LATER, I saw yet another facet of my quiet uncle. I'd moved with my family to an acreage ten miles north of Edmonton in 1970 but returned to full-time work in the city in 1974. Saturday morning was the time for housework, occasional soup- or bread-making, gardening and grass-cutting. It was early April, 1976 – the pussy-willows were almost ready to pick, the snow had melted every-where except the very shadiest places, and the kids were looking forward to spring break from school. We had just sat down for lunch when the doorbell rang.

I opened the front door to see Ivor, accompanied by a radiant woman, both completely enveloped in a rosy glow. The smile on each face left room only for a pair of joyful eyes. The tall, grey-haired woman wore a pastel suit with a beautiful corsage pinned to her lapel. The husky, barrel-chested man wore cowboy boots and a shirt with a bolo tie, pants and a casual jacket.

"You did it, you did it," I chortled. "Look who's here, it's Ivor and Muriel. Come on up, now, you're just in time for lunch." I ushered them up the half-flight of stairs to the main floor, and into the dining room.

"We-e-e-ell, well," said my husband. "Another one's bit the dust." And we all laughed with the new bride and groom.

"We'd heard a few rumours about you two, but nobody told us you were going to go and *do* it!" I bustled about, set two extra places and made sure there was enough food on the table.

"Well, they couldn't," Muriel giggled, "nobody knew!"

"What do you mean, nobody knew? Did you two just run off by yourselves?" I was incredulous.

"Yup, we did," Ivor could hardly speak through his Cheshire-cat grin. "Didn't need anybody else, now, did we?"

"Okay, you'd better tell me the whole story." I was totally delighted. Ivor looked happier than I'd ever seen him, clearly head-over-heels crazy about the woman he'd brought to our home. "Do they all know now?"

"Nope, nobody but Muriel's boys," responded Ivor. "At least, that's all we told, and we told them not to say anything to anybody else. Who knows what they've done now, though. Probably the whole town knows."

"Ah, and you'll be getting it when you get home. I can just imagine the teasing! And you deserve it too. Honestly, what a stunt you've pulled." I laughed at the pair.

We talked and laughed, heard the story of the wedding in Sedgewick the night before. "My son stood up for us," said Muriel, "then we went to Camrose for supper, and the boys went home to play hockey. And now, here we are!"

Big-eyed, our son and daughters watched their great-uncle and his new wife, the oldest "just married" people my kids had ever seen

Soon it was time for the newlyweds to leave. No, they wouldn't stay the night.

"Got cows to feed," they said, as they headed out the door and down to the driveway. By nightfall they were back in Irma, at Muriel's house, where they would live until their own new place had been completed, right beside Gran and Grandpa Thurston's home on the hill.

THE COUNTRYSIDE around Muriel's home south of Irma was quiet that night, only the occasional coyote sang in the distance, the birds had not yet returned, even the cattle in the corral were quiet.

BANG! BANG! CRASH! The sudden din shattered the night's silence. Ivor burst from sleep, wakened by the shotgun blasts. "What the hell's going on...?" he shouted as he leapt from bed and jumped into his pants.

He opened the front door, the dog escaped and people streamed in, laden with noise-makers, cakes, and coffee. It was a chivaree – neighbours and relatives from all around the area had come to celebrate this surprise marriage of the community's favourite bachelor.

"Phyllis was in our bedroom before we got turned around," chuckled Muriel as she recounted the events several years later. "They stayed almost till dawn!"

Sometime during the evening, Ivor's sister Phyllis read the poem she'd written to honour the new couple:

Dedicated to Muriel and Ivor Thurston

Oh, just north of Irma
Two and a half miles away
There lived a young farmer
Ivor Thurston's his name.

Oh, Wales was his birthplace
He came here when three
With his mother and father
And their big family.

He went to square dances,
His curling was good,
And on the golf course
He did what he could.

As Ivor grew older
The girls gave him chase
But he paid no attention
And they gave up the race.

Now down south of Irma
(Wrong side of the tracks)
There lived a young lady
And she wasn't lax.

She nursed all the sick folks
In Wainwright you see
And made them all happy
With her smile so cheery.

On a cold winter's evening
Ivor called on his dad
Who was Muriel's patient
The best one she had.

She dropped in to see him
When Ivor was there
Now what was her business –
"Monkey" I declare.

Her face was a long one
She looked very sad
Her car would not start
The battery was dead.

Now Ivor the bachelor
Offered to drive her home
Muriel was delighted
And so it began.

His car was well trained
So well you have seen
It turned south all winter
What results there have been.

And now they are married
We wish them all joy
In their brand new life,
With three bouncing boys!

The crowd of friends and relatives laughed and sang, ate and drank until just before sunrise. They left in time to get home for milking.

"And then we had more! The Sharon bunch [people from the Sharon Lutheran Church], just a few families, chivareed us a while later. Then

Ivor and Muriel at Niagara Falls, Ontario, c1977; they radiated happiness.

the ones north of town wouldn't let the ones south of town get ahead of them, so they had a chivaree the next week, and then the nursing staff had to have one too! But it sure was fun!"

The entire community was delighted with this new liaison.

MY HUSBAND, RON, and I sat in Muriel's living room several years later, long after Ivor's death. Muriel's eyes shone as she recalled the wedding and the chivarees, the happiness she and Ivor shared.

"Now I understand what that time must have been like for them," I thought, secure in the joy of my own second marriage. Muriel also had been married previously, then widowed in 1973, left with three boys to raise and a large farm to manage. "What a time she must have had. She deserved a second chance at happiness."

"Muriel, you and Ivor went together for just a short time before you were married, didn't you? Not a long time as I recall – it was the talk of the town, wasn't it?!" I laughed.

"Well, I guess it was. We went together for a little over a year. We'd always known each other, and we'd been in high school together. That first time we went to a show in Wainwright, though, it sure caused a sensation! Mary Ann [Ivor's niece, his sister Olive's daughter] and Jim Sparks were there, at the show, and she phoned her mom right away. 'Uncle Ivor was at the show with a lady!' she told her mom!" Muriel laughed, remembering the buzz of chatter – Ivor wasn't often seen with a woman!

"Ah, you must have had to make lots of adjustments, Muriel, you and Ivor. You had three teenage boys, and Ivor had never raised any kids," I said. "How did he make out? How did you both manage?"

"Well, we did have some adjustments, that's for sure. We'd talked that all through before we were married. The boys still missed their father, you know, he died in 1973 so that was only a couple of years before Ivor and I got together. We'd gone down to visit Leo [Ivor's brother] in Taber the August before, that's when Ivor asked me to marry him. I said 'yes, I think it would work', but I didn't think we should rush it. I wanted to give the boys, my three sons, a chance to get used to it. And Ivor, well, he said he still had his mom and dad on the farm to think about. He was really close to his mother. So we didn't get married till the next spring. We started building right away. We lived in my house south of town for a while, then we moved into our new house up on the home place on December 8, 1976. We put our house right north of where the Thurston house had been, and we left the old house there for a while, then we tore it down. There was no point in leaving it there, and the old folks were gone by then.

"Mom Thurston was glad Ivor was married, I think. So he'd have somebody to look after him when she wasn't there any more. She and dad had been thinking about moving into the Manor in Irma already, and they did that, they moved into the Manor the year after we got married."

Ivor drove to Hope Valley almost every Sunday to visit Nellie after Fred's death in 1978. Nellie was aging, her arthritis increasingly debilitating.

☙

I REMEMBERED the protective way Ivor had treated his mother, the air of gentleness between them. It was Ivor, not grandpa, who bought the easy chair that propelled gran to a standing position, when her arthritic legs and hands could no longer raise her body.

Gran always asked how Ivor's evening had been, when he'd gone to town on a Saturday night. He never gave her any details, just answered "fine" and went on to tell her the neighbourhood gossip, or to describe the weather or the crops he'd seen.

One late summer day when I was at the farm, Ivor came in with two cases of peaches. "Here's some fruit for you, Ma, I'll put it here on the stool," he said, placing the boxes carefully on the old rickety chair in the back kitchen.

"Thank you, Ive, they'll be nice for winter. Dad and I will do them up this afternoon, after we've had our nap," she responded.

After Ivor had gone out to the field, gran looked at me with a small grimace. "That was nice of him. He always does that. I thought we were finished putting down the fruit, but I guess I can find a bit more room in the freezer." She shook her head, anticipating the time she'd need to do two more cases of peaches, and thinking of her painfully arthritic hands. There was power on the farm now, and plumbing. And two big freezers in the back kitchen – two freezers full of food for herself and grandpa and Ivor. And all the children and grandchildren who came to visit.

It didn't take too much imagination to picture the rigours of the new life Muriel and Ivor led in the early days of their marriage. "Must have been a big change for the boys[38], Muriel. How did they adjust to a new father?"

"Well, the boys accepted him as a friend, not in the father role. They worked together. He was good for them. They needed someone to help them and direct them.

"I remember one day, they were haying and the weather forecast wasn't good, so Ivor said to Brian, 'You come and turn the hay, and I'll bale it.'

"So they went up to the field, but they were back pretty quick – there was no gas in the tractor Brian had! Ivor said 'I didn't think I had much patience, and I didn't say anything, but who would go up to the field with an empty tractor?' He was so proud of his patience that day!"

I thought that description of Ivor's reaction to his stepson's tractor management was pretty amazing. Even as a child, I'd felt Ivor had little patience. I'd never tested it, but always knew (as children generally do) Ivor had a short fuse, and little patience for ineptness. Nobody got in Ivor's way. And nobody even asked which way was Ivor's!

Spring 1978.
"Ivor has cancer. They operated but it's too late."

The news raced through the family, burned across phone lines in Alberta and to Ontario, among neighbours and friends in Irma and Wainwright. Shocking, stunning news. How could this be? Not our bachelor uncle, the one who had finally found a woman to cherish, this strong, handsome man who had never been sick a day in his life.

"Poor Muriel," we all muttered. "And poor gran." Gran, who had gone to live with Olive and George north of Edgerton after grandpa died the year before, April 28, 1978. Poor Mary too, Ivor's eldest sister – cancer had ended Bert's life a few months after grandpa's death. "It's not fair," we told one another, "it's just not fair."

I remember going to the University Hospital in Edmonton, being overwhelmed with nausea from anxiety, distress at my uncle's condition, the unfamiliar smells and sounds of the hospital.

I found his room. He was alone, momentarily I was sure, since the entire family was visiting.

Uncle Ivor. In bed. His face pale yellow under the ruddy exterior. His belly distended under the sheet, like a pregnant woman's. "I'm going to be sick," I thought. "I can't stand it. How can this be happening? This is my Uncle Ivor. The strong one, the one who hoisted Maureen and I on his arm. Who is that in the bed? It can't be him. No-one else is here, it's a private room, the sign on the door says Ivor Thurston. This can't be my uncle."

"Jean, can you get Muriel for me?" the man in the bed struggled to be heard. Ivor.

"Sure, right away, Ivor, where is she, in the lounge?" And I bolted out the door, escaped down the hall to find Muriel. Muriel, Ivor's wife. The nurse. He wanted her. I waited for a while before returning.

It was the last time I saw him alive.

The funeral was on Monday, July 30, 1979. Held in the high school gym, and still not enough chairs for everyone. People lined up against the back wall. Chairs in rows, people, people, people everywhere. The pallbearers, Ivor's nephews – Don Thurston, Daryl Thurston, Gordon Thurston, Michael Crozier, Will Askin, Jim Pugh. Strong, sad young men. Each one of them with his own memories.

My daughters, their stepbrother, their father and I in a row, together for the day. My family would be fractured in less than a year, but that day we shared our grief. Less than a year since grandpa died. No-one ever thought Ivor would go so soon, not now that he and Muriel were married and so happy together. "What is together?" my thoughts silently shrieked. "What is fair? Surely not this."

Poor, poor gran. Bent over with arthritis, burdened with a mother's unique grief. Ivor used to drive down and visit her most Sundays after she'd moved in with Olive and George. She'd wondered why he hadn't been around much that spring. The rest of the family dreaded telling her. When they did, she who seldom asked for anything pled with them to take her to Edmonton, to hold her son's hand one last time. But Ivor had said, "No, don't bring mum. I don't want her to see me like this." Poor gran.

His body was taken to the Irma cemetery, just east of the village. Grandpa was buried there, and Uncle Ron's baby Harry. The cars streamed in, first the hearse, then the family car, then the rest of us. The Reverend Jim Bennett, in his white surplice, Uncle Leo beside him. The coffin placed securely on the green straps between the brass rails, holding it until the service concluded and we all left the gravesite.

Silently, Ivor's brother Elks formed a single file at the graveside. Each man placed a small spruce branch on the coffin, symbol of the "far-reaching and o'er–sheltering branches of Brotherly Love that accompanies the member even to the far shore whither he journeys".[39]

Silence, except for the highway traffic, and a few birds in the poplars along the south side of the cemetery.

"Muriel, didn't anybody know he was sick?" I asked.

"I remember one day, we'd only been married a couple of years, he was standing by the kitchen sink, and I put my arms around him from behind. He said 'Don't do that, it hurts.' I didn't know what was going on, Ivor never got sick, even when we were kids in school."

Several years after Ivor's death, Muriel moved to a house in Irma. She was left with the grief and joy known by those who have been loved intensely, then widowed.

"He hadn't been feeling well for over a year. He did go to the doctor. They operated on Father's Day, June 1979. He was in the hospital just a little over three weeks before he died, July 26. Liver cancer. Inoperable.

"He told me to sell his horse, Tilley. He didn't want it getting onto the road, or into the grain," Muriel remembered. "Brian, my son, could handle Tilley better than anyone else, though, so I kept Tilley for him. After Brian died, then I sold the horse."

"Ivor was a pretty caring guy, wasn't he? And if he said he'd do something, he did it. No fooling around. He pretty much expected others to do the same, didn't he?" I remembered, and we both chuckled.

"He was so dependable. He loved the farm. And his horse.

"I told him once that I had a patient over eighty-years-old, when I was still nursing in Wainwright Hospital. That guy was still feeding cattle, even at his age. Ivor said 'I'll still be feeding cattle when I'm eighty if I can do it.'" Muriel laughed as she recounted the story. "He had some pretty strong ideas, too. Some jobs were his, some were mine.

"I remember one night, we'd moved into the new house, up there on the home place, and I was unpacking stuff in the bathroom. He asked if there was anything I wanted help with, and I said no. He and the boys were watching TV. But then, when he discovered that I'd put up a hook myself, he said 'You shouldn't have done that - it's my job.'"

Later, I would discover the mixed pain and joy of remembering a husband who brought joy, then died too soon. But that day, I watched as Muriel's eyes filled with tears, and we shared a sadness for this man who had occupied a space in each of our lives.

"It was his job to get the car out of the garage too, if we were going someplace together. The night of Brian's high school graduation, Ivor had had to finish the field he was working on, so he was a little late getting in to the house, and he had to have a bath, so I got the car out. He was quite put out! That was his job. I could get the car out if I was going by myself, but not if we were going together.

"He didn't play golf any more after we were married. I told him to, but he said 'No, we've got enough with watching the boys play ball and hockey. That's enough.' And he never golfed again. He stopped curling too. We watched all the boys' hockey games, though.

I wondered if the cancer had already set in by then and begun its task of draining its victim's energy.

"The boys brought him a Father's Day present that last year before he died. It was the first time they'd done that. I thought it showed they were accepting him in a different role," Muriel recalled the joys and challenges Ivor had experienced as stepfather to three teenaged boys.

❧

THE *WAINWRIGHT STAR CHRONICLE* listed those who had bought flowers, and those who had provided memorial donations – to St. Mary's Church, the Irma cemetery fund, the library, the heart fund, colleges and bible funds. Two columns of names and recipients.

Ivor's life ended, as it had been lived. Quietly. Alone as always within the circle of friends and family.

CHAPTER 16

Olive

She saw herself as rebellious but every nephew and niece loved her to bits.
She was the one who organized the first family reunion,
who took my siblings and I into her home,
and who cared for her aged mother after grandpa died.

OLIVE WAS THE ONE who kept in touch. She wrote letters and made telephone calls, invited people to visit and welcomed them with open arms when they did. There was never any question that she was pleased when a sibling, a child or grandchild, a niece or nephew came by, whether it was for an hour or for a week.

Olive was the eighth sibling in a family of nine. The fear she'd felt of her father, when she was a child, never dissipated, even as he and she aged. "Probably would have been better if I hadn't been so rebellious," she told me. None of her siblings had ever mentioned Olive's rebelliousness.

My Aunt Olive was neither tall or short, heavy or thin. She inherited her mother's long slender legs as well as her optimistic outlook.

Olive's hair was dark and shiny and only curled with the help of permanent waves and rollers. Her eyes were blue, her nose rather sharp, she had a lazy eye that didn't focus properly but who cared about it anyway? She walked a bit heavily, with slightly rounded shoulders, a gait not dissimilar to her father's although she might have denied that.

Olive ran her household without fuss or bother. She had her own way of managing the kitchen but she tolerated, even welcomed, her husband's help. She preferred to work outside, rather than in the house, and could drive a grain truck or a tractor or a combine if she had to. Her skin became brown in the summer, and the heels on her gardening shoes broke down.

She applied bandaids when they were needed, visited people who were sick or sad, helped her children with their homework and her husband with the farm. She taught school and Sunday School, took part in all sorts of community activities, raised her children, loved her husband, and generally got along with her in-laws as well as her brothers and sisters.

Right from the time she and her husband were married, they opened their home to my siblings and I. After grandpa died, they took gran home to live with them.

On the day of Olive's funeral, the Edgerton Agricultural Hall was filled to capacity. They came to bid her adieu, to share their sympathy and their grief, and then to bury her in the quiet cemetery where the crocuses bloom in the spring.

❧

OLIVE WAS THREE AND A HALF-MONTHS OLD the day her mother carried her onto the train at Dinas Powys, South Wales, headed for Cardiff then on to the coastal city of Liverpool, about 190 miles (300 km) north. Her eyes were red, her nose ran, and she coughed and wheezed with each breath. Soon she would be sicker: both Olive and her nursing mother suffered every day of the S. S. Cedric's Atlantic crossing. By the time they arrived at Halifax's Pier 21, both mother and baby were pale and exhausted. Their eyes were dark and sunken, and their lungs and noses mucous-filled. Nellie was afraid the immigration authorities would refuse the baby's entry.

"It's just a cold," she told the health officer, and he believed her.

The Red Cross ladies met the family at the Montreal train station. They presented Nellie with a layette, probably some flannelette nightgowns, undershirts, maybe a matched set of sweater and bonnet and bootees, flannelette diapers, and probably a blanket or two. By the time they reached Irma, Olive's cold was on the mend. Mrs. Shaw, owner of the Irma Hotel, told Nellie not to worry: "She'll soon get better in this lovely country air".

"Mary, you mind the baby while I walk Phyllis and the boys to school," Nellie said, a few days after their arrival. Perhaps that's when the lifelong big sister - little sister relationship was cemented. Silken strands held these two women together, even though the older sister spent most of her life half-a-country away.

I wonder how farm women managed their babies in those days of uninsulated houses, single pane windows, drafty doors and freezing floors. You can pile blankets and feather quilts on and under sleeping babies, but what do you do with them when they want to sit up, when they begin to crawl and to walk haltingly from chair to chair? How did the children learn to stay away from the hot stove, the trap door to the basement, the slop bucket and the pail of drinking water?

When Olive was a baby, there were no play pens, Jolly Jumpers™, baby swings, or Snugglies™. Nor were there electric washing machines, disposable diapers, stretch terry sleepers, or disposable Playtex™ baby bottles. Heinz™ baby food didn't appear until 1931. Baby raising meant constant vigilance and a lot of work.

Olive was three- or four-years-old when her father accepted a part Border Collie pup from one of the neighbours. Farm dogs, of course, were essential workers. They were used to herd cattle and to ward off coyotes, catch and kill mice and gophers, and sound the alarm if some-

Olive with her puppy, c1928.

thing went amiss – an animal out of its pen or pasture, an injured family member, a fire in the barn or in the long grass. Olive viewed the puppy as her pet.

"Skippy, catch," she called, tossing a small branch as far as she could.

The puppy raced for the stick, over-ran it, tumbled back and grasped it in his mouth. He growled and shook the stick as if it were a mouse or chipmunk.

A pointed finger and the words "Skip: gopher" sent the dog across the yard in a frenzy. He had much to learn about gopher hunting. Skip followed Olive everywhere – to the henhouse door but not inside, up to the garden, and out to the barn.

The dog quickly learned to chase creatures, but he couldn't get the hang of herding cattle only for morning or evening milking. He brought the cattle to the barn door, lathered up from running, at all hours of the day or night. The cows' milk production was not enhanced. Neither were the turkeys' lives calmed by Skip's barking and herding tactics.

Even as a small child, Olive understood that turkeys could and did die of fright. Skippy seemed unable to learn that lesson, regardless of his punishment.

"Come here," commanded Fred. Skip gambolled close to Fred's leg, wagging his tail in expectation of a treat. The dog and its master disappeared behind the barn. The dog did not return.

Olive's fear of her father became absolute.

Olive tagged along with her brothers as they went about their chores. She sat on a little stool in the barn and watched as they milked. Her eyes grew large with apprehension when one of the horses in a team became skittish. She listened to the pigs squeal as they were loaded into a wagon or onto the back of a truck. She watched her mother cook and clean, set the table, wash the dishes, mend the clothes. Gradually, Olive was given her own chores.

"Olive, go on out to Ivor and ask him to put a bit o' milk in here," said Nellie as she handed Olive a nippled bottle. "Take Winnie with you, she'll watch while you feed the lamb." Nellie's last child was three years younger than Olive.

After dinner, Nellie scraped leftover bits of fat or vegetables into a bowl or pot, then asked Olive to: "Take these scraps out to the dog's dish, Smutty [or Rover or Sam or whichever dog there was] needs his dinner."

Olive anxiously waited her turn to begin school. She trudged across the fields and along the road to school with her brothers Ron, Leo and Ivor. Undoubtedly, the children dawdled sometimes, perhaps to catch grasshoppers or dig frogs from the mud; surely they would have destroyed the pesky magpies' or crows' nests.

Phyllis was twenty-years-old and in her second year of teaching at Sunny Brae when Olive started school. Ted had already done as much school as he felt he needed. Len may have attended school for another year or two. No-one seems to remember just when he quit.

"Olive, did you like school?" I asked. "Do you remember what it was like, and how many kids were in your classes?"

Olive played while the pigs rooted about the bluff; logs waiting to be cut for firewood, c1929.

Olive bottle-feeding Sadie the lamb while Winnie watches, c1933.

"Oh, I sure do remember," she replied. "It was a long walk, but we did it every day no matter what. Mum and dad likely didn't even know how cold it was in the winter. I don't remember them having a thermometer. On the coldest days, when Ivor or Ron were still in school, dad let them harness up a team in the winter.

"The school had two rooms in those days – not like it is now, that whole big school with three or four hundred kids or more. The Grades 1 to 4 kids were in one room, Grades 5 to 9 in the other. The high school was separate, for Grades 10 to 12.

"I loved school, maybe that's why I decided later on to teach. We were little dickens, though, sometimes – we usually got to school on time, but sometimes we had to run as fast as we could to get there before the bell stopped ringing. We sure didn't want dad to hear we'd been late. He would have really given it to us."

I didn't want to ask what form of it they'd get from their father.

In the meantime, Olive's older siblings were forging their own lives, although they continued to contribute to the family's income. For the first time in her life, Phyllis had her own income.

"I remember a dress your mum bought for me, Jean. I guess I was nine or ten, and your mum took me to Edmonton for the weekend, on the train. We went shopping, I don't remember where, maybe to Eaton's or to Woodward's. I don't remember if Johnstone Walker's [these three stores were the city's major department stores] was operating then. She bought me a brown velvet dress: it was so soft and shiny. I loved the feel of it. I'd never had anything else like it." Olive's eyes glowed with pleasure as she remembered her sister's gift.

"How far did you go in school, Olive? I remember mum saying she'd completed Grade 11 because that was as far as the school went when she was there. Had it changed by the time you were in high school?" I asked.

"You know, I think Grade 12 was added not long after your mum graduated. I don't know exactly what year. I had to go to Grade 12 so I could get into university.

"After the boys finished school, Winnie and I used to walk by ourselves. Your grandpa would never hear of us taking a team to school like the boys.

"I didn't miss much school, except for when I caught scarlet fever, then I was home for weeks."

"That was a terrible disease wasn't it? I understand a lot of people died from it, and others were left with all sorts of ailments, especially heart problems. Is that what happened to you?"

"Well, I guess that's right. We didn't know it then: all we knew was that Ron caught it and was in hospital for quite a while and then they sent him home. I guess he was still contagious, and I caught it from him. I must have been about fifteen, I guess, when Ron brought it home. Nobody ever knew that it had done so much damage. Good thing those new valves had been invented by the time I needed one."

"That's right, isn't it? I believe Uncle Leo's son Ken was responsible for shepherding the St. Jude's aortic valve through the approval process in the United States. Thousands of them have been implanted now. But who knew all that would happen, back in the 1940's when you were still a kid? I'll bet you were glad to get back to school, after being sick."

"I sure was. I had a lot of fun in the earlier grades, but I really had to work in high school. It didn't come easy to me the way it had for your mother – I think her final marks in geometry and algebra were 98 and 99%. She was so clever in school, I don't think she ever had any trouble with anything. Me, though – well, I never did get physics, even though I had an excellent teacher. I don't remember her name, but I remember her – she was young, and so pretty. I finally got into university without physics – probably because they needed teachers so badly! And at first, they said I wouldn't be able to get a permanent certificate to teach until I'd passed physics but later on, I guess the rules changed, because they let me take a law course instead. I passed it, and then I could get the permanent certificate.

"But when we were in high school, we used to do our homework at the kitchen table. Remember that metal ring on the wall beside the window? Well, we'd put the kerosene lamp in there, with the wick as high as it could go without smoking. Your mum used to help me with my homework on the weekends. She was really good to me.

"Mum and dad both wanted us girls to go as far as we could in school," Olive said. "They didn't have the chance themselves, and I guess the boys wanted to get out and start farming as soon as they could. But your mum and Winnie and I all finished high school and then went on."

"M-m-m-m. It must have been hard studying by the light of the old kerosene lamps. How was your vision, Olive? Did that bad eye give you trouble?"

"Well, no I don't think so. It's been like this for as long as I can remember. Mum said she'd had flu when she was pregnant with me, and that's what made my eye go like this."

Silently, I wondered about the cause of Olive's lazy eye. My own daughter had been diagnosed with strabismus, as the ophthalmologist called it. He explained it was a genetic problem, and surgically corrected her eyes before she turned six. Olive's condition had gone on too long for surgery to be of any benefit.

My aunt coped with school, her vision problems, an easily upset father, unending chores, brothers who teased her, and the perennial lack of money. I wonder what a day might have looked like when she was in high school.

Perhaps her father woke her when he stoked the fire in the kitchen stove. She would have dressed quickly and made her morning trip to the outhouse. Perhaps she set the table as Nellie cooked the morning porridge. She would feed the chickens before she left for school, and carried in several armloads of wood while Winnie hauled three or more pails of water.

What was it, I wonder, that Olive rebelled against? Was it the chores? The lack of money? Did she dislike being tightly controlled, 'kept on a short leash' as we'd say now? It's hard for me to imagine my loving and cooperative aunt as an angry, rebellious young woman. It's too late to discuss Olive's other side with her.

"Mum, I've let the chickens out. I fed them and put water in their dish. The turkeys are out too, some of them went right up into those trees, they're so dumb," complained Olive as she and Winnie hurried to finish their chores. "Oh, you've put an apple pastry in our lunch, Mum, thanks."

The girls had to be out the door by 8 o'clock to get to school on time. They walked across the fields and down the road, past Milburn's slough and into the village. The Irma public school yard was full of kids, big and small. Forty or fifty teenagers (although they weren't labelled teenagers then) milled about the high school, waiting for the bell, finding reasons to talk with the boy or girl of their dreams, perhaps finishing off a bit of uncompleted homework. Several horses were in the barn, ridden to school by those who lived several miles away.

After school, Olive and Winnie walked the three miles back home, regardless of the weather, unless Jim Craig or some other neighbour came along and picked them up in a wagon or, later, a car or truck.

"There you are now. How was school today?" Nellie would ask as her daughters came in.

The girls gave their mother the news of the day as they changed into slacks or overalls – they each had only one blouse, one sweater, and a skirt for school.

There was little enough time to talk – the cows were bellowing at the barn door, waiting impatiently to have their heavy udders relieved. One of the boys was making chop for the pigs, two others could be seen in the distance repairing the south fence. Black smoke puffed from the blacksmith shop where Fred had the forge blazing to heat a broken tooth harrow. Nellie had supper in the oven. Everyone had his or her own list of chores. The girls' chores did not include animal breeding or birthing, castration or branding, killing or butchering.

"You know, I'd never even seen a kitten being born until after George and I were married," Olive told me. "Dad wouldn't let the girls in the yard when the cows were calving, or when the baby pigs were being born. Not even the dogs or cats. I don't know what he thought

Top: Olive and Winnie, perhaps dressed for church, c1938.

Bottom: Ivor with the angora goat, Winnie in the centre, Olive with the dog, 1936.

we'd see that we shouldn't. After all, we girls would eventually have our own babies, but dad didn't seem to see things that way."

The girls were responsible for helping Nellie with the housework, feeding the chickens and any orphaned or rejected lambs, keeping the woodbox full, and hauling water.

"We'll just need two buckets from the well tonight, Olive. I've brought some in earlier today so I could wash the fleeces from those sheep," Nellie said.

The reservoir on the side of the stove held two bucketsful, the kettle held almost half a pail full, and they always needed at least a bucket or two for drinking and washing up. Today the hauling job would be finished quickly, not like the days when water had to be hauled and heated for Monday's washing or Saturday bathing.

The one job that always fell to the women and girls was cleaning the separator. It had to be taken apart and washed with every use. No-one liked the job. Not only was it an every-day-without-fail task, but the milky odour permeated everything – the air and the floor, the shelves and the washcloths and even, it seemed, the steel milk pails themselves.

"I remember watching you stand at the separator. Ivor or Ron would pour a pail of milk into the bowl on top, and you'd get the handle going, you had to get it right up to speed didn't you, quickly, and then the handle got kind of its own momentum, and you turned on a switch. How did the separator work, Ollie? It was always a mystery to me, and I don't think anyone ever really explained it. What did that switch do?" I sought to dredge up forty- or fifty-year-old memories.

"Oh, my goodness, I hated the separator, Jeannie," Olive answered. "You'd pour the milk in the top, and start turning the handle... I know it worked on a basis of centrifugal force, and since the cream is lighter than milk, it gets separated off and comes out one spout and the skim milk comes out the other spout. You'd have to go to the encyclopedia[40] to get a better explanation than that."

"Okay, I'll do that, but what was it about the separator that was so detestable?" I could remember seeing my aunt take the separator apart, wash each piece, remove the thick scum from the crevices, scald the cones with boiling water brought from the house, then cover the equipment with a piece of clean cotton. The job had to be done every day. Cleaning the separator was no-one's favourite chore.

Short-circuiting the job resulted in trouble.

"O-O-O-O-Olive, smell this milk. The cream you put down the well will be just as bad," growled her father, his stutter pronounced as it always was when he was upset. "You've ruined this whole lot. There'll be no cream for mam. She'll have no butter to sell and no candies to buy this week."

Without waiting for Olive's response, Fred stomped out, leaving his daughter humiliated. She thought she'd done a good job on the separator. How could she have missed cleaning those cones? She knew that one little bit of leftover scum would turn the milk sour.

Now there wouldn't be any cream for the butter Nellie sold to the people in town on Saturdays. There would be no cash this week, no treats or even any fresh apples.

Scalding tears dribbled down Olive's cheeks. "I'm sorry, Mum. I didn't mean to do that." Nellie was torn between sympathizing with her daughter and supporting her husband. She would miss the week's cash.

ALTHOUGH PHYLLIS MOVED to the city when Olive was twelve, she returned to the farm every summer and took us kids with her. My sister Maureen and I could hardly wait to get out of our travelling clothes and into our farm gear. Shorts or slacks were the order of the day – the lesser, the better. To us, farm and freedom were synonymous. Splitting wood was our favourite job. Even hauling water was fun on a warm summer day.

"I am *so* old enough to chop wood. See, I can use the axe," said my six-year-old sister, with characteristic Thurston stubbornness. Her curly auburn hair was fastened into braids, her freckles had begun to pop out in the summer sun, and her skinny legs seemed even longer than usual. Our mother was not amused.

"No, you are not going to chop wood unless Auntie Olive helps you." Olive, only a few years older than Maureen, happily took her niece out to the woodpile to chop kindling with a hatchet, a much smaller and less lethal tool than the big axe.

Olive's teenage years were marked by huge social upheavals. She turned thirteen in December 1939, three months after the declaration of World War II. The Depression ended and prices for farm products surged, as did employment and manufacturing.

The period between 1939 and 1945 were years of economic optimism, tempered by domestic rationing of goods and apprehension for the fighting forces. The Thurston family became economically stable. Ted and Molly had a baby boy; Leo would soon enroll at Winnipeg's St. John's College. Ron would be released from the army. Olive finished high school and was accepted at the University of Alberta, albeit without conquering the dreaded physics. She visited my family in the city occasionally; the rest of her non-school time was spent helping on the farm.

"Dad, I could stay at Phyllis' this summer and get a job. I'd be able to pay my own fees," Olive said. It wasn't the first time she'd tried to persuade her father to let her go.

"You can go to Edmonton next month," Fred decreed from his desk beside the fireplace, "not before. You're not going to Max and Phyllis's house until she goes back home."

Olive accompanied my mother, my sisters and I (Colleen was born in early June, 1946) when we returned to the city, by train, in August. The third bedroom in our home became hers for the winter.

The city was a huge and scary place.

Perhaps mum suggested a walk to the campus – a distance of about four miles.

"Come on, Olive, we'll put Colleen in the carriage. It's a nice day. I'll walk you over to the university so you'll know where to go."

Top: Olive holding me, with my sister Maureen cuddled up closely, on the steps of our home in Edmonton, late summer 1940.

Bottom: Both Olive and Winnie learned to drive the tractor, pictured here in the field of ripe oats, c1943.

They would have walked north on 91st Street to Whyte Avenue, across the old wooden bridge above the Mill Creek ravine, then west towards the university. As they pushed the carriage up the slight incline to 99th Street, Corbett Hall[41] – where Olive's classes were scheduled – would become visible.

In 1945, the province transferred teacher training from the Normal Schools to the University of Alberta's Corbett Hall, a beautiful brick building at the west end of Whyte Avenue at 114th Street. Its windows, doors, and the crenellated roofline were framed with Tyndal limestone, quarried and shipped from Manitoba.

"There, see that brick building way over there?" Phyllis asked. "That's where you'll be going for all your classes. We'll time ourselves to see how long it takes to get there."

The two young women were used to walking, although they could have ridden one of the red and cream-coloured buses or dark maroon streetcars that traversed the city. The closest bus stop was across from the corner store at the end of our block, Whyte's Grocery and Confectionery, on the northwest corner of 89th Street and 77th Avenue. Bus fare was cheap but not free.

Olive walked to university every day unless she was late or the weather was bad. Her father paid her tuition fees, the $25.00 a month board to Phyllis and Max, and gave Olive $10.00 a month spending money.

"It sure was tough making that $10.00 last the month," Olive said.

"Olive, did you enjoy university? Were you able to join any of the social clubs? It must have been difficult, coming in from the farm and not knowing anyone but us. Were most of the education students from the city, or were they from rural areas?"

"Well, I didn't have much money, so I couldn't join in a lot of the things that the others did. But we had fun, and there were some really good students. Velma Hockenhall was my best friend. I forget where she came from but she taught at Carrot Creek.

"We wrote back and forth for a long time. Even after she got multiple sclerosis, her daughter wrote letters for her. We had a pretty good time..."

My sister and I loved having Olive stay with us. We could hardly wait for our aunt to get home. We'd hurry home from school, change our clothes, and if we were lucky, have our favourite snack – a piece of toast spread with butter, then sprinkled with brown sugar and cinnamon. We watched for Olive as we munched our toast.

"Jeannie, Maureen, I'm home," she called. She'd used the corn broom Mum kept at the back door to sweep the snow from her boots. Her glasses fogged up, as they always did when it was cold. We held her books as she took off her outside clothes.

"M-m-m-m, that stew smells so good, Phyl," she said. "And you've baked bread today too. You've been busy." We all loved those days when mum made beef stew and bread. The house was redolent with smells and we could hardly wait for our father to get home for supper.

Although we were all pretty healthy, my siblings and I did catch mumps, measles and chickenpox – some of them the year Olive spent with us. I remember her peering into our room as soon as she got home.

"Will you read to us, Auntie Olive, will you read *The Five Chinese Brothers* and *Snip, Snap, and Snur?*" I still recall the tale of the Chinese brothers, boys whose arms could reach the mountain tops, legs that could reach the ocean floor. Maureen and I loved the story. Olive may have become thoroughly tired of it, but if so, she never let on.

Once we were healthy again, Olive took us tobogganing down the hills of the Mill Creek ravine, just a block away. All three of us pulled on long underwear and slacks, heavy melton cloth snowpants and jackets with fur around the hood. We wore mittens mum had knit, and covered our shoes with thick socks and three-buckle overshoes.

When we got home, Olive brushed away the snow that stuck to our clothes and helped us out of them. "Let me hang those mittens on the line behind the stove, Maureen," she said. "Phyl, could I make some cocoa? These little girls are pretty cold." Occasionally, for a special treat, there might be a marshmallow or two on top.

After a year of studying, Olive qualified to begin her teaching career.

On the way to the Mill Creek Ravine hill, Olive pulling Maureen and I on the toboggan, our dog Cookie frolicking beside us.

That spring, a position at the Metropolitan school southwest of Irma, became vacant – the teacher had resigned for some long-forgotten reason. Olive applied and got the job.

The students, fourteen boys and girls, got to school by 'shank's mare'[42] – distances of one, two, up to four miles (6.5 km). Few children were allowed to ride horses during good weather – the horses were needed to work the farm.

"What did you do, Olive, when you first went to the school? The kids must have developed a routine with the other teacher. Did they pay attention, or did they take advantage of your inexperience?"

"Oh, most of them were pretty good. One of the older boys made a fire in the stove before school started on cold days. Another one filled the water bucket and made sure the dipper was there. Other ones took turns cleaning the board or sweeping the floor.

"The parents were so good to me, too. Every Wednesday, they brought a hot meal to school for all of us. And they never criticized in

Some of the students had long distances to travel; many rode their horses. 1946.

front of the children. They'd tell you what they thought about something, quietly, when the children weren't around."

One of the families boarded Olive during her three months at
Metropolitan. She paid them $25.00 from her $80.00 monthly salary.
"My entire month's pay in the 1940's was less than one day's pay as
a substitute teacher in the 1990's," she laughed as she recounted the
story.

Although Olive completed her university courses, she still hadn't
conquered physics.

"Ollie, there's a letter here for you from the Department of
Education," Nellie said as she handed over a brown envelope.

"Oh, Mum, they've changed the rules. It says here the university
has a new course, it's in law, and they'll let me take that instead of
physics. If I pass it, I can get my permanent certificate. They've even
sent an application form."

After her springtime stint at the Metropolitan school, Olive returned to Edmonton and summer school. She received her permanent certificate in due course.

Before the summer was out, Olive received a letter from the school superintendent offering her a job at Giles, fifteen miles (25 km) north of Edgerton.

"B-b-b-by golly," Fred stuttered, "that's a long way from town."

And he was right. The Giles school sat about half a mile (0.8 km) south of the Battle River valley. It was a small clapboard building, one room with a cloakroom and a wood-burning stove inside, a barn and an outhouse beyond the schoolhouse, similar to hundreds of other prairie schools. Twenty-one children attended the school, in Grades 1 to 8. Violet and Harry Pugh offered to board the teacher; little did they or she know how significant that arrangement would be.

"Will you drive me, Ive?" asked Olive.

"Yup, guess Ron and I could take you, soon as we get the oats cut," Ivor responded with his usual grin.

On the last Sunday in August, Ivor and Ron drove their sister to Hope Valley (the area in which the Giles school was located). They travelled east on the Highway 14, down the river hills at Fabyan and up the other side, past Wainwright and on for another ten miles. They turned off at Withnall's corner onto a slightly-gravelled road and travelled 10 miles (16 km) north, between fields of ripening wheat, barley and oats cut and waiting to be bound. The black poplar leaves were yellowing and the dogwood and wild roses in the bluffs were beginning to turn colour.

"Look, Ive, there's the school. That must be the Pugh's place, right over there. I can see the house from here."

Olive's contract for the Giles position was for one year...but there was a certain allure to the place...Although she returned to Irma and taught there for a year, she accepted a permanent position at Giles the following term. Once again, she boarded with the Pugh family, who by then had moved from their home beside the school to a larger house a couple of miles east and south.

Giles school – still standing, no longer used, an integral part of the community's history.

A wrought-iron sign and a rock with a plaque are permanent markers of the Giles school site.

Olive moved into one of the two slope-ceiling rooms on the second floor. From there, she could see the yard, the equipment sheds and the barns. The view extended for miles across fields where lush grain crops grew from the fertile soil in summer, and where snow kept its moisture locked in from November until March or April. The road petered out only a mile or so north, at the crest of the Battle River hills. Small poplars and shrubs grew along the fence lines. The coulee was just visible to the south, beyond the next farm, its road passable only when neither winter snow nor spring floods impeded travel through the lowest section.

She could also see George, the youngest son with the mischievous eyes and the infectious chuckle, as he went about his work on the farm. Perhaps he was the reason Olive applied for the teacher's job at Giles...

George was the youngest of six Pugh offspring, the one who stayed home to work the farm with his parents, as is often the norm in farm families. His brothers Walter and Stanley lived nearby; Alf was still at home. George had two sisters, Florence and Eileen. About the same time Olive moved back to the Giles school, Florence married Olive's brother Ron and moved to Irma. There would be a second Pugh – Thurston liaison within a short time...

"That George," Olive laughed and shook her head. "He used to play all sorts of tricks..."

"He was always up to something. I remember one time, something started to ring in the middle of the night, 3 or 4 o'clock, I couldn't figure out what it was but I didn't want George's mum and dad to wake up.

"He'd put an alarm clock under my bed, right in the middle of it, inside a tin pail. The whole thing shook when it went off. George's folks never said anything about it, but I'm sure they heard it."

My aunt and her husband alluded to other pranks – a word here, a chuckle there, exchanged glances – but with no further details.

"Hmmm," I thought, "I suspect they got into plenty of mischief, but they're not going to let the rest of us know about it. Who needs to know everything, anyway?

George Pugh, his hand
bandaged after severing part
of a finger, c1949.

As teacher, Olive was expected to join in the community's social life, much of which centred around the Rosedale Hall, a few miles south of the Pugh home. By the late 1940's every family had some form of automobile – half-ton trucks were common. When there was a dance, thirty or forty trucks sat outside the hall, regardless of the weather. George Harley came from Heath with his accordion and his guitar, and played all evening for a good plate of food and the $3 or $4 collected at the door.

George's older brothers were a little more aggressive than he was; one of them had beaten him to the punch in initially dating the new teacher. Although George was a handsome young man, he had some shyness to overcome...

"I remember you shaking so much, I thought you'd drop right down on the floor," Olive said describing George's timidity the first time they danced together.

"Well, now, I don't remember that," said George. "Are you sure you're not making that up?"

"Oh you... Remember those box socials we used to have? We'd have two or three over the winter, down at Rosedale. The women had to make a lunch and put it in a box, and make the box look nice – tie a ribbon around it or do something like that." Olive hesitated as I waited.

George took up the story. "One at a time, the women'd go up on the stage and stand behind a blanket. Somebody would rig up a light so only her legs would show, and the men would bid. The guy who bid the highest got the woman and her lunch. Those men had to be pretty good to guess who was behind the curtain! You always did have great legs, just like your mother." Olive's shy chuckles belied her seventy-plus years, while George's laughter told the story of fifty-year old images, youthful antics, yearnings and attractions. Most of their stories remain untold, images shared only by the players. No amount of wheedling could draw them out.

"Well alright, if you won't tell me any more of those stories, I'll just have to guess at the pranks you two got into...

"What about the Giles school, Olive, and your teaching experiences? How did you get to school? It was a long hike over those fields – or did you go around by the road? There's no shelter along there at all. The wind must have bitten right through your coat in the winter, with below zero temperatures and snow blowing around."

"Oh, it was pretty cold alright. I mostly walked along the road – the fields were pretty rough to walk through – and on the coldest days, sometimes George would hitch up a team and wagon and take me over to the school. Other times one of the parents would give me a ride if they came along while I was walking. We didn't have down-filled jackets and windbreakers in those days, but mum had made woollen mitts for me, and scarves and hats and things."

"What about discipline, Olive? There you were, in a one-room school with twenty or so kids, probably some of them were bigger than you. It's hard to imagine how they all learned. How could you keep them under control?" I had gone to school in the city, with thirty or so boys and girls all in one room, all in the same grade and found it hard to visualize the operation of those tiny country schools of pre-1950 Alberta.

"I never had to strap any of my pupils, Jeannie," Olive said. "Those kids were really good. They didn't give me much trouble. They were all different, none of them learned in exactly the same way, and I always felt I had to find the best way to help each of them.

"The parents were really supportive, too. It's different now, but then...well, if the parent heard about a problem a child had given the teacher at school, he'd get it again from his parents when he got home!

"Sometimes I had to give them lines to write, fifty or a hundred lines saying things like 'I must not shout in school', or 'I must always finish my homework', or 'I may not swear in school'. Other times, if they didn't finish their work, I'd have to keep them in at recess or at lunchtime, but that didn't happen too often.

"One time, one of the boys broke a window, so he had to replace it. He measured the window, and his parents got a new piece of glass, but it didn't fit – the boy had measured wrong, so he had to do it again and get another piece of glass. That was about the biggest bit of excitement we ever had!

Early in the spring of 1951, Olive gave notice she wouldn't return that fall. George Pugh, the man who had unerringly identified her long legs at the community box socials, had proposed. The ceremony was scheduled for August 1st. Olive returned home to Irma at the end of June to finish making her wedding gown and to complete the arrangements – as well as to help her mother with the summer work.

That summer, my mother did not accompany my siblings and I to Irma, for our father had died in the early spring and mum had had to find work. We kids did go to the farm, although the details of the arrangements escape me – the four of us were thirteen-, eleven-, five- and three-years-old. Perhaps that was the first summer we stayed for a few days at each of the relatives' homes, Gran and Grandpa's, Ted and Molly's, Ron and Florence's. I remember bits of the wedding ceremony, and the reception at the farm – but only bits, for I spent a good part of that time minding my little brother as he slept in the granary down in the yard, away from the festivities.

My wonderful aunt was being married – an unsettling event in itself – and I was relegated to child care...it's funny how past irritations become amusing memories. Maureen and I knew Olive would never again be ours and we couldn't create future mind-pictures of her or her place in our lives.

We didn't know she and George would welcome us into their home every summer for as long as we wished to be there.

August 1st, 1951 was a bright, sunny day, a good time for a wedding – after spring seeding, after all the calves were born, after the first hay crop was cut, and before harvesting could begin.

Olive's sister Winnie and George's brother Alf were the attendants, the Reverend Walters performed the service and Olive's recently-ordained brother Leo assisted. Olive was only the second Thurston married in St. Mary's Church. Ted and Molly were married there in 1940, and Winnie would be married in the little church three years later. Leo's own marriage was scheduled to take place in Winnipeg on August 19th.

"The church was full, about forty people, I guess. All of George's three brothers and two sisters and his mother and dad were there, as well as most of my brothers and sisters," Olive remembered. "The CGIT girls [Canadian Girls in Training, a United Church girls' group] formed an honour guard outside the church.

"Then we all went back to mum and dad's. I think you and Maureen helped put up those crepe paper streamers, didn't you? Remember the cake we had? Mum's friend Winnie Reeves made it, and then she decorated it – she used to do all the wedding cakes around Irma.

"We had sandwiches and some of mum's pickles, and we would have had tea and coffee. Cookies too, and I think mum made matrimonial cake – she used to make it for everything, and everybody loved it. Would you like the recipe? I can give it to you – it was so simple and you know, there were no instructions on it the way we do now, you just had to know how things went together. I had to add instructions when my girls started baking so they'd know what to do."

Matrimonial Cake
Mix together: 1 c brown sugar

                    1 ½ c. rolled oats

                    1 ½ c flour

                    1 tsp baking soda

                    ¾ c butter

Pat half of this mixture into an 8" x 14" baking pan
Boil and let cool:

                    2 c. chopped dates

                    ½ c. sugar

                    2 c water

Spread date mixture over rolled oats layer in pan. Cover with other half of rolled oats mixture.
Bake for 35 minutes at about 350°F

"Thanks Olive. I remember eating that matrimonial cake at your house too. Now, what about a honeymoon? What did you folks do for wedding trips in those days? I seem to recall some hijinks with that car you had…" I asked.

"You don't think I'd just take her home, do you?" George's eyes crinkled at the corners.

"Well, no, I could hardly think that of *you*. Are there tell-able parts of that story?" I didn't really want the intimate details!

The couple headed out for Ashmont, Leo's first parish, about 120 miles (195 km) northeast, driving George's Model A Ford[43] coupe. He'd bought the car from a neighbour, Alec Trefiak, for $300 in 1949. Olive's brothers, probably assisted by George's brothers, had done some decorating work of their own – tin cans tied to the axles, confetti inside the suitcases, words written all over the car body. At least they hadn't put a potato in the exhaust pipe…

Olive's brothers – probably with some help from George's brothers – decorated the car, complete with tin cans tied to the axle; ready to leave for their honeymoon at Mann Lake near Ashmont, August 1950.

"How did they get confetti inside the suitcase?" I asked.

"I'm not going to talk about that one! That Ted, yes, my brother the rascal, he thought it was funny but it wasn't!" said my aunt.

They turned north from the driveway, toward Mannville, across the Vermilion River, north again, through Myrnam and St. Paul, just a few more miles to Ashmont and Mann Lake. A sudden prairie storm had hit the area late the previous day. The steep approach to the ferry just north of Mannville was so bad they came close to sliding right into the river.

George got the car stopped in time and drove onto the cable ferry. "Must have been something wrong with the brakes." He smiled as he recounted the story although I suspect his palms left a little sweat on the steering wheel that day.

Their honeymoon cottage at Mann Lake was a small wooden structure set among the trees beside the lake. They didn't need much room.

They spent their two weeks fishing with Leo, picking wild strawberries and raspberries, walking the lake and driving around the country. They visited Leo in his tiny rectory and helped him saw a trap door in the kitchen floor – he wanted inside access to the dugout basement.

One night after the sun had finally set – it's usually light until at least 10:00 p.m. at that time of year – there was a sudden racket outside, thunks and bangs and crashings reverberating through the previously silent countryside.

"George, what is it, what's happening?" Olive quickly drew on her housecoat and slid her feet into a pair of slippers. George struggled to find a flashlight, then laughed out loud as he opened the door.

A whole gang of people stood outside. They surrounded the cottage, armed with noisemakers, whistles, pots and lids. They were Leo's parishioners, there to chivaree the young couple.

"Oh, you rascal," Olive shook her finger at her brother. "You did it to us again! And here we were, just asleep. I guess we'll be awake for a while now. Come on in, everybody."

The partygoers went home in time to catch a couple of hours' sleep before chores. The honeymooners slept in a little later than usual.

Olive and George returned to Hope Valley and amalgamated their belongings in one of the bedrooms. George continued to farm with his father and brothers, 1,280 acres (518 ha), two full sections, of fertile land. Olive kept house with her mother-in-law – a true test for any new bride, regardless of her own and her in-laws' dispositions.

The Pugh family had a mixed farm – acres and acres of grain, some of which was fed to their own pigs and cattle, as well as the chickens and turkeys. They kept a horse or two even though they didn't use work horses very often. The Pugh machine shed sheltered tractors, a combine, and all the other machinery needed to till the land, and to plant and harvest the crops.

The animals were tended with care, and responded predictably. "We couldn't have animals that were ornery, Jean, especially once we started having kids," George said.

There were always dogs and cats around for companionship and to do their own work guarding the property and keeping down the mice and other rodents.

The Pugh farm, house in the foreground, barn at the rear, close to the Battle River, north of Edgerton, Alberta; c1951.

Olive and her mother-in-law did the things farm women do – they gardened, picked berries, canned fruits and vegetables and meat. They made jars and jars of jams and jellies and pickles, raised chickens and turkeys, did the laundry for themselves and the bachelor brothers who had moved out, and prepared the meals. The work was endless. There was no electricity, although there was a pump in the kitchen so water was readily available.

The young couple needed their own house. In the spring, they hauled in a 12 ft. by 20 ft. (3.6 x 6 m) building from a neighbouring site. They poured a foundation and set the house on it. There were just two rooms, an 8 x 12 ft. (2.4 x 3.6 m) bedroom and a kitchen/dining/sitting area. The bathroom was out behind. They moved their belongings into their own house but continued to run the farm cooperatively with George's parents.

Our childhood fears of losing our aunt to George Pugh of course did not materialize. In fact, my siblings and I look back in amazement and appreciation at the way in which we were welcomed into their lives. They were a newly married couple, in love and deserving of time alone together. Instead, they invited us to stay with them every summer, even when Colleen and Mike were young enough to still need constant care. The Pugh farm became another golden home.

Neither did we know until many years later, that Olive and George had offered to take some or all four of us children, after our father died, to raise as they would their own. Our mother chose to keep us together but to accept her sister's offer to keep us for part (sometimes all) of the summer holidays. Whatever would have become of us in the summer, without the Pugh and the Thurston farms? How could our mother have held down a job and provided for our care?

Instead of leaving us to fend for ourselves, or in the care of some neighbour or stranger, she gave us the gift of enclosure, the experience of being welcomed and loved, shown and taught, the gift of being wrapped in a silken cocoon of family.

Neither she nor her sister could have given us a more precious gift.

We usually went to the Pugh's on the Greyhound bus. It was easier, and closer, for them to pick us up from the bus than from the train. Someone would instruct the driver to let us off at Withnall's corner.

We were always sure we'd be left standing, alone and abandoned, at Withnall's corner, beside the highway. We never were. Not once were George and Olive late.

"There you are, got a suitcase? Okay, we'll just throw it in the back, you'd better climb into the cab, it's quite a distance out to our place and it's cool tonight."

We would climb in the truck, squeezed between the two adults; perhaps the youngest of us would sit on an adult's lap. There were no seatbelts, no power windows, a truck box full of feed or equipment or groceries. The road was straight, gravelled, with grass growing along the side. As we neared the Rosedale Hall, just before the big slough, we came to the bumpety hills – three stretches of road with small hills that gave us a feeling of up and over, like a ride at the fair, when you go up, up, up, then fly over the crest and down the other side, feeling as if your stomach has been left behind suspended in mid-air.

Maureen and I at the Pugh's, c1951 or 1952; all dressed up, so we must have either just arrived or were ready to return home. Mum sewed and knitted most of our clothes.

We passed a few farms on the road north, turned east as the road climbed the hill at the James's farm, then north again. All along, we saw fields of ripening grain, a few pastures with beef cattle grazing, in later years a pig farm with its foul smell, hardly any other cars or trucks. In a few minutes, perhaps half an hour from the time we left the highway, we'd turn into the Pugh driveway. The dog – Shep or Bandit or Rover or whatever was the dog of the time – invariably barked his greeting and dashed forward for a pat as soon as the truck doors opened.

Olive and George lived in the little house when my siblings and I began spending our summers with them. I don't remember where we slept, although we likely spent our nights in one of the upstairs bedrooms at the big house, under the watchful eye of George's parents.

Violet and Harry Pugh were like a second set of grandparents. Violet was a short, chubby woman, not even five feet (150 cm) tall. She had almost-white hair and the most pointed chin we'd ever seen. To us, she was the quintessential grandmother, surrounded by an aura of love and laughter.

We knew nothing of Violet's history when we were kids. Later, we learned she was one of fifteen children born to a family in Athens, Ontario. Giles and Hettie James, a childless couple, neighbours, offered to take five-year-old Violet and to raise her as their own. They brought her west to the Hope Valley district.

Violet's own children were adults when they heard on the radio that the Layng family of Swan River, Manitoba was searching for the little sister who had been given away in Athens. It was the first time Violet had had any contact with her birth family.

Violet's adoptive parents were solid citizens, active in the community, leaders in education – the Giles school was named for Giles James himself. They had not, however, encouraged Violet to maintain any contact with her siblings. They raised her in the community, where she met and married Millard Harry Pugh.

Harry towered over Violet – he must have been 6 ft. 4 inches or so (193 cm) – at least, he seemed that tall to us. He smoked cigarettes, not a pipe as our grandfather did, and he used snuff too – the first person we'd ever seen put smokeless tobacco grains in his mouth. Most importantly, Violet and Harry welcomed us just as our own grandparents did. I can't remember ever calling them anything but Granny and Grampa Pugh.

Summer days in Alberta are so long that electric lighting isn't really missed in the summer, when there are only three or four hours of darkness. But the desire for other electrically-powered things, and the ease they would bring into the lives of farm families, grew rapidly in the 1940's and 1950's. Harry Pugh believed the provincial government ought to shoulder the cost of getting power to the farmers, as the Saskatchewan government was doing in the province next door. He was not prepared to buy a share in the local rural electrification cooperative or to pay for the power poles into the relatively isolated Pugh farm.

The Pugh family found another solution – a wind-powered generator. They bought and erected a tower beside the big house, assembled the windmill above it and put a row of glass-encased batteries in the basement to store the electricity. The 32-volt system brought light into their lives, both in the house and in the farmyard. It gave them a taste of what real power would be like. Then the very expensive batteries wore out. The family opted to install regular 110-volt power. As kids, we neither knew nor cared about those details – electricity wasn't something we needed.

We kids were happy with the novelty of manual tasks, especially the laundry.

"Are we going to do the washing tomorrow?" we might have asked, had we arrived on Sunday. Monday was always wash day. Granny Pugh and Olive heated water in the copper boiler on the stove and boiled first the white things, then the more heavily-soiled work clothes. They pulled the washing machine into the middle of the kitchen floor, filled it with hot water and just a bit of soap flakes – too many and the suds would billow out of the soft water and spill out onto the floor. They set up the two square tubs on a stand behind the washer, and shoved the exhaust pipe out the door. At least, that's what happened after George or Harry bought and installed a gas motor on the washer – before that, they'd had to use the long wooden handle to turn the dolly inside the washer.

My sister and I vied for the privilege of hanging the laundry on the line outside. The sun and the wind sucked the moisture from the laundry almost as soon as we had it suspended. Somehow, laundry day was always sunny. Olive generally helped take the clothes off the line – we likely helped her rather than the other way around, but she always asked us if we'd like her help.

"Mmmm, just smell those clothes," she said as she held the clothes against her body, plucked the clothes pins off and dropped them into the bucket, then put the clean dry laundry into a basket. Even later, after power had been brought to the farm, Olive continued to capture the outdoor scent in her laundry. She hung the clothes on a line or on a clothes horse on the front porch, then finished them off in the electric dryer.

I remember the crocuses that bloomed in the field between the two houses, where the clothes lines were. Prairie anemones, they're properly called, but we knew them as crocuses, hairy-leaved plants with purple flowers that poked their heads out above the soil but were sheltered by the taller grasses. "The fields here used to be covered with crocuses every spring," Olive told me once, several years ago. "I don't know what happened, but we sure don't see the crocuses now that we saw when you kids used to visit."

Not only were there crocuses and laundry to keep us interested and busy at the Pugh farm, there were all sorts of other things – young calves that licked our fingers, pigs that squealed shrilly and fought over their food even though there was always plenty to go around, chickens that laid eggs and occasionally bantam roosters that threatened to chase us, horses that pulled carts or stone boats and who tolerated city children for short rides. There was the garden with its molehills and gigantic earthworms, tractors that we were allowed to hitch a ride on, trucks with windows that rolled down so the wind could blow through our hair, grasshoppers that made clicking noises and sprang from the grass as we stepped through their territory, birds that sang in the trees and woodpeckers that beat insects from every dead or living trunk.

Most interesting of all, there was a baby – Florence Ellen, born May 6, 1952. She was named for George's mother (Violet Florence) and Olive's mother (Helen Maria Ada). That was before Gran Thurston wrote away for her birth certificate so she could collect her Old Age Pension, and discovered she'd been named Helen not Ellen, a surprising turn of events for a sixty-five-year-old person.

Baby Ellen had two cribs – one in the little house beside her parents' bed, and another crib up at the big house. She was only in the crib to sleep – her parents and grandparents played with her every chance they got, as did George's brothers and anyone who came to visit.

"Could we take the baby outside?" we'd ask, and Olive bundled her daughter up and put her in the carriage.

Curly-haired Ellen, always smiling, home on the farm, c1955.

"Be careful now. Don't take her down to the barn, there's quite a lot of flies there. You can push her around the yard. I think George is out by the tractor. You could take her over there to see him if you like." Nothing we asked for seemed too much trouble.

Olive and George ate most of their meals with George's parents. Each of us had our own places at the kitchen table. It was an arrangement that worked well, especially during the first three months of Ellen's life, when she screamed with colic every day from supper time until 8 or 9 p.m.

"I'll take her for a few minutes," said Grampa Pugh. His gigantic hands cradled the baby against his shoulder as he walked the house, his deep voice soft as he murmured quietly against her downy head.

"There, there, Punkin," he crooned. "Have a rest, no need to cry like that, you'll be fine."

No-one else could calm the baby's colicky cries.

Sometimes we'd take Ellen to the garden with us when we went to hoe between the plants or thin out the carrots so the remaining ones would grow to a decent size. We hated gardening at home, but on the farm, gardening was a wondrous task. Our garden at home was large by city standards, but tiny in comparison to the immense Pugh garden.

"Why do you have such a big garden?" we asked.

"Well, we have to grow all our vegetables to eat in the summer, and to can in quart jars so we'll have them in the winter. It's a long way to the store from here, not like your house where the store is right down the street.

"I have a neighbour who says she grows a garden for the bugs, a garden for the drought, and a garden for herself. If the bugs stay away and there's lots of rain, she has to give away a lot of her carrots and lettuce and things!"

The early 1950's were years of adequate rain and snow for soil moisture, reasonable prices for grain and meat production, significant developments in automotive power (both road vehicles and farm machinery), and population growth (post-war immigrants arrived in Canada by the thousands). Olive and George continued to farm, their lives impacted only slightly by external developments.

My siblings and I continued to spend part of our summers on the farm north of Edgerton. We thought we were there to help; in retrospect, we likely caused far more work than we accomplished but neither Olive or George, or his parents, ever made us feel as if we were in the way.

"Could you ice this cake for me, Jeannie, while I make supper? We're going to chivaree Doris and Howard Waddell[44] tonight, and I promised I'd take a cake." Olive bustled around the kitchen.

"Sure, I know how to do that." And I did know how to make icing – cream a little butter in the bowl, add some icing sugar, blend it together, add a little milk. "Where do you keep the other box of icing sugar, Olive?" I'd tossed in quite a bit of milk, more than enough to blend with the sugar from the now-empty box.

"That should have been enough, Jean. What happened?"

I could see my aunt was not happy, one of the few times she ever showed irritation with anything I'd done. There was no corner store from which to buy another box of icing sugar, which I would have done at home. "We'll have to fill it up with corn starch, I guess. I hope it doesn't taste too bad," she said as she handed me the small blue and white box of Canada Corn Starch™. "Be careful now, just put in as much as you have to, to thicken it up."

I've forgotten the chivaree – or perhaps we kids didn't go to it – but the memory of having disappointed my aunt remains, a slightly pain-tinged but now-humourous recollection.

By the summer of 1956, I joined the ranks of near-adult workers. I had had several summers with my grandparents, and a few spent partly in Irma and partly at the Pugh's. There would be no more idyllic farm summers for me, although their impact would last forever.

Intentionally or otherwise, Olive and George, as well as their siblings and parents, transferred so much knowledge, so many bits of wisdom, so much love, to each of us.

We saw that several adult people could work together harmoniously even when they didn't always agree. We learned that most people in the Hope Valley area drove Dodge trucks and cars, not the Chevrolets and Fords usually chosen by the Thurston families.

We saw that the Pugh's seldom went to church (although Olive did, and took the children with her) and that several of them professed to be atheists, but they treated one another with honesty and respect, supported their neighbours, and worked cooperatively within the family and the community. They didn't use bad language, and seemed to know a lot about love and harmony.

We listened as they discussed politics, and realized their views were far to the left of our grandparents'. We watched as our grandparents visited with Granny and Grampa Pugh, listened as they talked, understood their opinions were very different from one another – and felt the respect and affection between the two couples.

On the farm, George and Olive taught us to look the bantam rooster right in the eye and to never turn our back on him. That way, he couldn't ever attack our legs or feet. My younger siblings learned to pick eggs from under a hen, gently but surely, talking to the hen all the while so she wouldn't peck at their hand. I, of course, had already learned that skill from Olive at gran and grandpa's. "Take good care of them and they'll give you more eggs," Olive told us.

We learned that horses want to look at you, but they can't see anything close up right in front of them, you have to get over a bit to the side and then they can see you. And they only like to be mounted from one side, not the other, if you're going to ride them.

Cows, on the other hand, see directly in front but they don't like it if you pass too close behind them, and you have to be quiet while they're being milked or they're likely to knock over the milk pail or at least swish their dirty tail across the milker's face.

George taught us that coyotes are afraid of donkeys, so if there are coyotes in the area, a donkey in the pasture with the calves or the sheep or the pigs will keep the young animals safe.

We learned to read the telephone or electricity wires alongside the road – they reflected the lights of oncoming cars that you might not be able to see around a bend or at the bottom of a gully.

We learned that electricity can be made by a windmill and stored in batteries but that the fluid surrounding the batteries would eat the skin from your hands or make holes in your leather shoes. And we listened as they explained that windmill power was only 32-volt, not strong enough for normal, 110-volt toasters or irons or even light bulbs to work. The equipment all had to be designed for 32-volt systems.

We discovered that Olive and Granny Pugh canned vegetables and fruit just like Gran Thurston. The basement shelves were filled with jars of green peas, yellow beans and orange carrots, yellow peaches and golden apricots, blue plums and red rhubarb and purple saskatoons. There were jars of pickles – dilled cucumbers and carrots, sweet mixed pickles, and purple beet pickles. The women filled small jars with jam or jelly made from plums, rhubarb, saskatoons, crabapples, chokecherries, raspberries, and pincherries.

Olive told us she kept trying to salt beans the way her mother had always done, but she could never get it right. The two Pugh women canned chicken and beef in jars, and occasionally pork. If we got home late from town, or if we'd been too busy to prepare a supper with fresh meat, or if it was just too hot to cook, we could open a jar of chicken, make a potato salad, slice some fresh tomatoes from the garden and maybe some lettuce too, probably a few slices of homemade bread and butter. It was our favourite meal.

Olive showed us how to make salad dressing quickly – take some whole milk, add a little vinegar and some brown sugar, maybe a little salt and pepper, shake it up, and voila! dressing for fresh lettuce.

My brother learned that the sky is dark, even in the middle of the day, when viewed from the depths of a hole in the ground. He learned to drive a tractor without hitting a fence, and we all learned how to dig deep into the chop bin to fill a pail but not to fall in.

Most of all, we learned about unconditional love. At the Pugh's farm, all we had to do to be loved was to just be. There were no expectations, no standards to be met, no strivings for perfection. In return, my siblings and I poured our love into this relationship without question, without fear, and without limitation. None of us ever lost that connection, not even during the years when our own lives became so filled with day-to-day details that our visits were, for a few years, less frequent than we would have liked.

BY 1956, I began earning my own way, but my younger siblings continued to spend their summers, entirely or in part, with our aunt and uncle. They continued those summer sojourns until our mother remarried and moved back to Irma in 1959. After that, their visits to the farm at Hope Valley were limited to a few days at a time, or an evening or Sunday get-together.

Olive and her husband continued to build their own family. Olive became pregnant again and carried her baby throughout the winter of 1955/56, the winter of snow, snow, and more snow. The baby was

Top: Colleen and Mike continued to spend summers at the Pugh farm long after I started working; here's Colleen with MaryAnn, summer 1957.

Bottom: Colleen and Mike, Ellen and MaryAnn, 1957.

due in mid-March, the season of typically heavy wet snowfalls, the kind that sometimes required several days for the snowplows to clear all the district roads. The Pugh farm was one of the furthest from the road maintenance equipment centre.

The couple was worried. If labour were to start while the roads were blocked, they would have no hope of getting help. "What do you think, Olive, should we take you into town somewhere, or maybe to your mom and dad's? We haven't seen a snowplow out here very regularly," said George. "What would we do if the baby started to come. That road your mom and dad live on is always kept plowed, it never gets snowed in like these roads do back here."

It took an hour for Olive to get through on the old party line. "Mum, George is getting a bit worried. There's been so much snow this winter, and we're afraid we won't be able to get out of here to the hospital on time. Do you think I could come and stay with you for a few days? We'd leave Ellen here with George's mom. Oh, thanks, we'll come up as soon as the road is plowed, maybe tomorrow. I'll see you then."

Early the next day, the old snowplow laboured slowly along the road. Snow billowed out from the blade so heavily the driver could hardly see. The normally adequate road allowance had narrowed to one car-width in places, with snow heaped higher and higher on each side.

George brought the truck from the garage. Olive packed a few clothes for herself and a layette and blankets for the new baby.

"Granny will take care of you, Punkin, you be a good girl. Daddy will be back before supper." Olive kissed her daughter goodbye and headed out the door.

"It feels like we're driving through a tunnel," Olive said as George carefully guided the truck along the newly-plowed road. It took a long time to get to the highway.

Olive spent about three weeks with her parents in Irma. Ivor drove her to the hospital in Wainwright when labour started. Their second daughter was born safely. Within a few days, mom and baby returned home. A couple of weeks later, there were no more snow banks along the road, little snow left in the fields, the ice disappeared from the river, the dugouts[45] were full of melted snow, and the cars were likely to get mired in the low spots on the road.

"George, whatever are we going to do? There's just not enough room for us here." Olive struggled to prepare supper, keep toddler Ellen out of mischief and baby Mary Ann happy. "Do you think we could build an addition?"

Within a few weeks, a living room and another bedroom had been built.

And soon there was another child on the way. "George, I've tried and tried to find places to put all the children's clothes, and their toys, and all our things, the dishes and the pots and everything. But I just can't. There's no room for them to play in the winter, and we can't even let the old dog sleep in the porch on these cold nights, 'cause we don't have a porch. Do you think we should build more rooms onto this house, or start a whole new one, or what?" asked Olive, her brow furrowed in exasperation.

"Well, it has been getting cramped, hasn't it? I think I'll talk with mum and dad. Maybe they'd like to move down here and let us have the big house. There's just the two of them now," George replied. That evening his parents made the same suggestion.

"We'd be alright in the little house," his mother said. "We could move over after the spring work is finished, if you and Olive would like to."

So it was that the families exchanged houses. The girls had one of the upstairs bedrooms. The front bedroom on the main floor became a sewing room. Soon the other upstairs bedroom would have an occupant.

Jimmy was born on April 13, 1958. He had long dark eyelashes and a sunny disposition – and he knew without being told, right from birth, how to get his own way and keep everyone happy at the same time.

The last child in the family, Linda Olive, arrived on April 22, 1963. Of all the grandchildren, Linda looked most like her Gran Thurston, her eyes set deeply in her heart-shaped face. She had dark hair and long dark eyelashes.

Top: Jimmy's 3rd birthday; he had the longest, darkest eyelashes I'd ever seen – and he knew how to use them to get what he wanted.

Bottom: Olive and Linda, dressed to celebrate the 100th anniversary of Canada's nationhood, summer 1967.

The family was typical of good farm families in the 1950's and '60's. The kids learned to cook – even Jimmy learned some kitchen skills – and at harvest time, when every adult who could drive was in the fields operating swathers, combines, trucks, they were responsible for making supper. They'd get off their school bus at 5:00 o'clock, change their clothes and take a snack out to the field – they learned early on to drive the old truck.

They shared the day's experiences with their parents and grand-parents, along with the food. Then it was back to the house to make supper, Ellen in the lead, making sure the meal included potatoes and meat and vegetables, bread, and always dessert.

"Your dad's been working and he deserves a good meal," Olive told her daughters.

After supper, if the weather held during harvest time, Olive and George went back into the field till 10 or 11 p.m., to take advantage of the dry days and evenings, getting the grain safely into the bins. In the meantime, the kids tidied up the dishes and did their homework.

The Pugh kids were expected to do their homework and their chores as a matter of course. Their last chore during hectic fall days was to set out a late snack for their parents, to be eaten after the final load of the day had been emptied from the combine.

The kids knew better than to ignore their homework. Their mother continued to fill in for teachers who were absent, so she'd hear of any such misdemeanors. She rewarded each of them generously when they achieved academic success.

Everyone had his or her role, his or her chores. Division of labour was more along lines of choice and ability than gender. One of Olive's roles was that of disciplinarian. She used the wooden spoon on the kids' bottoms only when all other avenues failed.

"Mum was the one who kept us tuned in," Ellen told me. "Dad, he'd never spank us. He'd come in after mum had done her thing, and he'd try to reason with us. He wouldn't let us kids fight or talk roughly, not at all. Then he'd kind of oversee things when we needed to iron out our differences. Mom and dad both taught us not to go away mad or to pout and hold grudges.

"Mum was always fair, you always knew where she stood. It wasn't as if she ever just struck out in anger or without any real reason. And we gave her lots of reasons! Like the time I burned the grass beside the sheds. I almost set the woods on fire..."

"Ellen, whatever did you do? I don't remember hearing about you doing bad things when you were a kid!"

"Oh, I sure did, but that day was the worst. I remember running into the house, yelling for mom or dad. I was about ten. My heart was beating so fast I thought it would jump right out of my mouth.

"I remember yelling 'Mom, Mom, Granny Pugh set fire to the grass' – as if she'd believe me! But they believed the fire – I never saw them run so fast! And they got it out. And then I got it..."

A fire in the country, miles and miles from the closest fire department or fire hydrant, was enough to invoke terror in anyone's heart, especially when the fire was right beside a building and especially a building that housed thousands of dollars worth of equipment.

"Boy, I sure got a licking [spanking] for that. Actually, I got two lickings, one for setting the fire – I'd been playing with matches, something I was never allowed to do – and the other for saying Granny Pugh had done it."

It was the only time George ever said to her, sternly and without a hint of a smile: "Bed is a good place for you to be, and you'd better go there right now." She stayed there for the rest of the day.

Once Ellen's punishment was over, the incident was closed and life returned to normal. Ellen accompanied her father as he went about his daily chores.

One clear winter night as they walked through the snow towards the house, George stopped and pointed upwards. The dark sky, clear of clouds and pollutants, was full of twinkling lights, large and small, some seemingly arranged in patterns, others apparently tossed randomly into the velvet universe.

"See that star up there, Punkin, the one that's bigger than the rest?"

"That one or that one over there?"

"Well, the brighter one over there is the last one in the handle of the Big Dipper, see how the others follow it, right up to the bowl of the Dipper?" George guided Ellen as the two of them picked out the Little Dipper, the Big Bear, and the Warrior.

"We'd better get in now or your mother will think we've got lost." Father and daughter made their way to the back door, swept the snow from their boots, and hung their jackets in the back porch.

"I'll bring the dog's dish inside so it'll be ready for the scraps. Smells like mom has made a roast today and am I ever hungry."

"We actually had six parents – our own, plus two sets of grandparents," according to Mary Ann. "We were so lucky – well, we might not always have thought we were lucky. We sure couldn't get away with much, but now I think it was just the best for us. Anyone who has grown up in the same yard as their grandparents is very lucky – to have that extra special relationship with them being there continually."

The photographs in Olive's albums reflect the presence of grandparents at every family gathering, casual visits or special events. Christmas was spent with one set of grandparents, New Year's Day with the other set, and the next year the order would be reversed.

The family went to the Wainwright Stampede every year. "Are you ready there, Ma?" George brought the car or truck or, in later years, the van, from the garage.

"Just about, you'll have to hold on for a minute." Everyone lugged out boxes and coolers of food, jars of canned chicken, thermos jugs full of tea for the adults and lemonade for the kids, homemade bread and butter, tomatoes and cucumbers from the garden, cake with brown sugar icing, chocolate chip cookies.

They got to town in time for the parade, then followed the floats to the stampede grounds on the southeast corner of town. They watched the steer wrestling and calf roping competitions, visited with their neighbours, and got home in time to do evening chores.

Ellen's special treat was to stay with Gran and Grandpa Thurston at their Clear Lake cottage. "With some luck, once in a while, I would be invited along. Laying in the water close to the neighbour's dock for three or four hours at a stretch was great as there were no weeds in that part of the lake. Skin wrinkles meant nothing."

By 1970 or '71, Ellen had left home for the city. Mary Ann married Jim Sparks in 1974 even though she was still in high school. Within a few years, Jimmy Pugh married Linda Lacey – they lived in the little house for a few years, then moved a mile south into the house that had belonged to George's brother Walter. Linda, the youngest Pugh child, was at home for a few more years.

There were deaths. George's father died in 1970. Granny Pugh became less and less able to manage, moved into the seniors' lodge in Wainwright, then into the auxiliary hospital after she was diagnosed with dementia. She outlived her husband by twenty years.

In the meantime, Olive's parents also were aging. Fred was treated for chronic bronchitis and emphysema. Olive and George and the kids visited him in the Wainwright hospital after he was admitted in the late winter of 1978.

"Hi Grandpa, how're you doing? Do you need anything? We've brought you some grapes."

"No, no, I don't need anything. I'll have some of those grapes, though, ta." He dug around and found his pocket knife in the drawer. "I believe there's some paper towel in the bathroom, there now, we'll put some here so's I can put out the grapes."

"They're for you, Grandpa. We didn't bring them here to eat," protested Mary Ann.

"You'll have some, won't you, aaah, I thought so. 'Ere now, you pick out the bunch you want." Within a few minutes, the grapes had disappeared, the knife had been wiped off and put away, and the paper towel was in the garbage. Fred lay back on his pillows and listened to the chatter.

"Olive, what's going to become of your mother, when your father's gone?" asked George as they drove home. "Do you think he's going to get out of hospital?"

"I don't know, he seemed pretty good tonight. Mum's never talked with me about what she'd do if dad didn't come home. They've only been in the Manor for about a year. I don't know if they've ever made any other plans."

"Your mother's pretty easy to get along with. She always liked me, somehow," George said. "I'll bet she's worried about it, about your dad and about what she'll do after he's gone. Her arthritis is pretty bad some days. I don't think she should be alone, do you? Maybe she'd like to come and live with us?"

"We should talk with her, George. I think we could manage. We'd have to give her our bedroom. It's closest to the bathroom. We'd move into the front bedroom, I guess."

Olive's father died on April 28, 1978. Within a few days, Olive and Mary, who had come out from Ontario, packed their parents' belongings into boxes, distributed some to their siblings and took the rest back to Olive and George's. "Mum will want some of these things around her," they agreed.

Nellie spent the next three years with Olive and George.

"DO YOU NEED ANYTHING, Jean? How are you off for money? You let us know, now, if we can help."

The year was 1980. I had separated from my husband, bringing an end to a very unhappy liaison. All my cousins lived happily married lives, or so I thought. Divorce was uncharted territory, frightening, isolating and away outside the social rules I'd been raised to believe in.

Olive and George's words gave me support when it was most needed, encouragement in the midst of despair, love when my world was dark.

In the meantime, gran continued to live at the Pugh's.

"It was wonderful having Granny Thurston there," said Linda. "All the others had left home. Granny never complained, you know, even when the pain was so bad. She got so crippled up towards the end, she could hardly move even with her walker. It was really tough for mum and dad to have to put her in the auxiliary hospital for those last few weeks."

Nellie Thurston died on April 25th, 1981. Olive and George moved back into their own bedroom. Months went by before the vacancy left by Nellie's spirit dissipated.

"What will become of the family, now that gran's gone?" several cousins lamented at the funeral. "We'll have to keep on getting together somehow."

Get-togethers don't just happen. In 1985, Olive organized the first Thurston family reunion. She and her family rented the Paschendale Community hall, a few miles east of the original Thurston farm. Siblings and spouses and children from Ontario to the farthest reaches of Alberta, more than a hundred of them came; they brought their children, their food, their tents and their trailers.

And they brought their memories and their photos. They created skits and songs. Leo conducted a church service on Sunday morning and pretty well everyone was there even though many of them no longer shared Leo's Anglican beliefs.

"It's up to you young ones, now," Olive said after it was all over. "I've done my share – the next one's up to you."

Olive and George and their family were at the next reunion, the one in 1990 at the Riverside Campground just north of Wainwright. She was healthy then, as she organized the food, made coffee, and chatted with nephews and nieces and siblings.

We visited.

"What's been important to you over these years?" I asked.

"Oh, that's easy: teaching, marriage and family."

"If you had to do it all over again, Olive, today, when there are so many choices for women, not like those days when women could only become teachers or nurses or secretaries, would you do it again?"

Olive and George, at home, shortly before Olive developed lymphoma; 2001.

"Oh, yes I would," she answered without even a second thought. "It was wonderful, working with those children, and their parents were so good, kind, so good to me. I'd never want to do anything else."

That was after having taught for several years, married and raised children, and then filled in as a substitute teacher until she was sixty-five.

"How did you and George manage to stay together, Olive? You had a lot of tough times to live through, and so much hard work."

"Well, we worked it out, you know, we talked through our differences. We always work together, do things together," says Olive. "It's really important to do that And you just have to figure out what's important and let the other things slide by."

"I HAVEN'T BEEN SO PERKY LATELY," Olive told me on the telephone one evening a year or two later. "George thinks I should see the doctor."

There were tests. "The doctor says it's from the scarlet fever I had all those years ago. Remember, Ron came home from the army with it, they must have sent him home too soon, because he gave it to me. I didn't know it would cause all this trouble so long afterwards.

"I have to have the valve replaced, you know, with an artificial valve, the St. Jude's valve I think it's called. Leo's Ken had something to do with it."

She was sixty-eight-years-old when the surgery repaired her heart. I don't think she was ever the same.

❧

"WHAT'S THE MATTER with your mom?" I'd phoned Ellen one day after I'd visited her parents. Olive had not been her usual self.

"Gosh, I don't know, Jean, guess she's getting older. She sure forgets a lot of things, though, it's a good thing dad's still around. He remembers for her."

❧

OLIVE AND GEORGE came to stay with me in the fall of 2002, shortly after my husband Ron died.

"You let us know if we can help you, Jean. Come and stay with us whenever you want to."

❧

I WATCHED as George covered for Olive, helped her finish sentences and remember names and dates, places and people and things.

"Come on out with me to Joanne and Pete's place," I invited, the following spring. They'd been wanting to visit my daughter and son-in-law in British Columbia. I had a visit planned, and would take them with me.

My phone rang loudly on the sunny July morning we were scheduled to leave. It was George. "Jean, I'm sorry, but Olive's not very good. I've got to take her to the doctor. She has a lot of pain in her stomach."

There were more tests. Then there was surgery, two months in and out of hospital.

"No, she won't be able to get to your mom's birthday. You go on now, and wish your mom a happy birthday for us."

Olive, younger than Phyllis by thirteen years, unable to attend her sister's ninetieth birthday celebration. Inconceivable. The nephews and nieces who'd come from Ontario, the visiting English relatives, everyone dropped in to see Olive in the hospital.

Her daughters accepted the Lifetime Membership awarded by the Anglican Church Women, since their mother couldn't attend the ceremony. Olive struggled to recognize each person, to remember their names and their place in the family. She hugged us all.

Olive was admitted to the Cross Cancer Institute in Edmonton. "She has lymphoma. There is a treatment but it's very harsh. I don't think she could stand it. She won't suffer." The oncologist was kind. "The dementia will likely give her more trouble, day to day, than the lymphoma."

She was transferred to the hospital in Wainwright.

"I'm going to take her home," George said, and he did. They had a few days together before he had to take her back. She was admitted to the palliative care suite in the Wainwright hospital. Her room filled with flowers and cards. Children and grandchildren, siblings and their spouses, nieces and nephews came to visit.

Olive's children asked my siblings and I to give the eulogy. We could think of no greater honour. "She wrapped her love in cookies and pies, added a big spoonful of cream, and offered it to each of us...

"Auntie Olive was so in tune with her surroundings. She was always aware of people's moods, their cares, their joys. She noticed every little smile, every tear. She set us an example of unconditional love, a love that will last forever if we make it so...

"Olive and George provided a refuge when our world was a little uncertain and they were an enormous help to our mother when she needed them...She has left this world a far better place than it could ever have been had she not spent her life with us. We are all better for having known her."

We buried her at Rosedale, in the cemetery beside the church on the hill. In the heart of the community where she did the things that were most important to her. Where she made a difference.

> I am the sunlight on ripened grain
> I am the gentle autumn rain
> Do not stand at my grave and cry
> I am not there. I did not die.[46]

CHAPTER 17

Winnie

She's the most effervescent of the siblings, her laughter
rings out and pulls everyone close.
She has lived a life geographically distant from her children,
her parents, and her siblings.
How did she come to accept her realities, without the anger or
resentment of her siblings?

WINNIE OF THE SMILING EYES and curly hair. Winnie, whose laughter fills the nooks and crannies of her world. Winnie the people-magnet, enclosed in her own cocoon of tranquility. A wife and mother, daughter and sister, aunt, grandmother and great-grandmother. A woman who has raised pigs, grown grain, and trapped fur animals. A northern person, a bush person, a woman whose hand-hewn log home sits amidst young poplars and birch trees, without electricity or running water, almost thirty miles (48 km) from the nearest town.

Winnie adored her big brothers and loved her sisters. She kept in touch first by letters and later by phone; she still doesn't have email but she'd rather have a telephone conversation anyway. She is able

Dark-eyed Winnie, at home, c1948.

to only occasionally attend family wedding and funerals and other events. Yet, her siblings and their children are integral to her being. Winnie was the aunt who comforted my siblings and me the night our father died.

She remains a woman in tune with her own energies, her intuition, her sixth sense.

IN MY CHILDHOOD MEMORIES, Winnie is a dark-eyed girl with bare feet and almost black eyebrows. She was still at home when my sister Maureen and I went to the farm in the summertime for she was the youngest, only ten years older than me. Auntie Win worked with her mother in the house. She drove grandpa's rattletrap old truck long before she had a license. And she taught us how to chop wood and pump water, how to gather eggs from under churlish hens, shut the chickens in for the night, poison gophers, destroy magpie nests, and other essential farm skills. It never occurred to us to question anything she said or did, not when we were kids.

❧

Slam! Winnie looked up to see if anyone had heard the noise – she hadn't meant to let the rock slip from her fingers. Good, her father wasn't around, just Maureen and I. And the tattered board hadn't broken when the rock struck.

"Why do you have to shut the doors all up, Auntie Win?" we asked as our aunt placed the board over the chickens' exit, a hole cut into the wall beside the doorway, then kicked the rock against it. She closed the big door and shoved a stick into the clasp.

"We don't want a coyote to get the chickens, do we? And see that board over there? Covering the hole in those rotten old boards? Your grandpa nailed the board up just last week. Old Shep barked so hard the other night, he woke grandpa up, and it's a good thing he did, too, because there was a weasel trying to get into the chicken coop."

"What's a weasel? Why don't you want him in the chicken coop? Maybe he was just cold," wondered the two city kids.

"No, he wasn't just cold," laughed our aunt. "Those weasels, you know, they're just about this long, and so skinny they can get in almost anywhere. And then they go after the chickens, and they kill them all. And they don't even eat them. They seem to kill for the fun of it. Let's get in now, it's past your bedtime, and if your mother knew you were still awake, she'd skin us alive."

Winnie took one of our hands in each of her own, and we headed toward the house, reluctant to end this golden day, not quite ready to admit to being ready for sleep, wanting to soak up every minute.

After breakfast the next day, gran washed the dishes, Maureen and I brought in some firewood, and Winnie got out the broom and dustpan. She swept the living room and the kitchen, tossed the floor-dirt into the stove, and began to clean out the pantry.

"Ee-e-e-e-k," came my aunt's shriek from behind the pantry wall. The broom flew from her hands and knocked the saucers off their shelf onto the cookie tins below. The metal dustpan clattered against the big glass jars of white and brown sugar, and pushed the almost-empty corn syrup tin onto the floor where its loosened lid separated and let the syrup escape. By then, Winnie was nowhere to be seen. She'd raced across the kitchen, through the back kitchen, out the screen door and down the yard in her bare feet, oblivious to gravel and chicken poop, intent on only one thing – escaping the little grey mouse that had tried to scamper up her broom.

My sister and I stood open-mouthed, rooted to the spot beside the woodbox where we'd barely escaped a brush against the hot stove. Gran got up off her stool, her lips tightened into a thin line. " 'ark, is there a mouse in there?" Her displeasure was clearly evident. "It's a good thing your grandpa isn't in just now." She picked up the broom and dustpan and set them out of the way, covered her hands with a rag and went in after the mouse. Carefully, soundlessly, her hands swooped down to the floor between the flour barrels. "Out you go," she muttered, the errant mouse firmly trapped between her hands till she was outside. "Come on, Shep, take care of this mouse." The dog quickly followed her bidding.

Winnie returned, chastened by her mother's actions and withering glance. "I'll clean it up, Mum."

WINNIE IS THE ONLY THURSTON SIBLING born in Canada. When her birth became imminent, her father herded the other children into the front room, with instructions to sit quietly. They saw Dr. Greenburgh arrive, summoned by one of their older brothers, who must have ridden the three miles to town. The Thurston's had no telephone yet on that first day of March in 1930. The doctor would deliver the baby, as he usually did, right on the bed in which she had been conceived. A neighbour woman might have been with their mother for several hours already, perhaps Mrs. Barber or maybe Mrs. Smallwood – not even the Irma history book notes which women assisted in childbirth. The dark-haired baby arrived in due course. Her siblings listened in awe when that first baby cry penetrated the thin walls.

Although there is no longer anyone who can explain why, there is a family rumour that gran vowed to have no more children in Canada, after her one Canadian birthing experience…and she didn't.

MANY YEARS LATER, I asked Winnie to remember her youth and wondered if her stories would parallel those I'd heard from my mother and her other siblings. As Winnie told her stories, I shook my head in wonder – were her parents actually the same ones who raised my mother and Aunt Olive? The stories differed so markedly. How could Winnie have such totally joyful recollections, while Olive's memories were filled with fear of her father, Phyllis resented the treatment she'd received from that same man, and Ted maintained that "there was never a lick of trouble" between father and children? The complexities of family relationships continue to amaze and confound…

The Depression was just a few months old when Winnie was born. Did that terrible era mean anything to Winnie the child, I wonder? Probably precious little. She had lots of food in her tummy, few material needs, and apart from the pictures in the Eaton's catalogue, little concept of what she was missing. By the time Winnie was a teenager, the war was in full swing, farmers reaped good returns for their produce, mortgages were paid off, and personal bank accounts grew in size and quantity. Winnie never knew the economic hardships her older siblings had suffered. She never had to deal with the soul- and relationship-destroying impact of poverty. Her laughter burbled forth, fostered and encouraged by the siblings who surrounded her, unfettered by the realities with which the older ones had been forced to wrestle.

"Why shouldn't they have treated me well?" she said one day. "The more that came, the better they got!"

Top: Winnie at age three, c1933. Yet another photo taken in front of the farmhouse!

Bottom: With her brother Ivor, c1933 – he never stopped teasing her.

Is she going to feed that thing to the dog, or is she just teasing him? c1935

Perhaps their mother sewed those pet animals, as well as the clothes Olive and Winnie dressed them in.

Winnie was the only sibling who knew that everyone loved her. Perhaps she was also the only one able to accept that love without question.

Being the youngest had its downside though. As a child, Winnie never had much opportunity to know her two oldest sisters, Mary and Phyllis. Mary worked away from home most of the time, then moved to Ontario to marry Bert Russell in 1937. Phyllis left for Camrose Normal School in 1931, when Winnie was only a year old, then taught at Sunny Brae for five years before she moved to Edmonton.

Winnie's childhood memories of her two eldest brothers, Ted and Len, are of watching as they drove the big eight- or ten-horse teams to the barn, and her father sending her off to the house so she wouldn't startle the teams. And of visiting Ted and Len as they batched up on the quarter-section they were renting, a mile or so north of home.

When Len left for Ontario, ten-year-old Winnie's world collapsed. Then Ted married Molly Burton. And Ron, the next brother, was called up for the Army. "Mum, will we ever see him again?" she asked fearfully.

"Yes, I expect we will, God willing. You remember him in your prayers every night, now, pray that he comes home safely," instructed her mother.

"Mum and dad must have prayed hard for Ron, too," Winnie told me years later, as I attempted to understand my grandparents and their beliefs, the way they'd managed their lives and their family. "I remember seeing them kneeling down beside their bed, before they climbed in. I think they prayed like that every night."

"Did they often pray, Winnie? I remember they always said grace before meals – 'Lord, let us be thankful for what we are about to receive. Amen.' – but I don't remember seeing them praying."

"Well, maybe they stopped kneeling down as they got older! They sure did when I was growing up. They weren't what you'd call God-fearing, but they really had a strong faith, mum especially."

"It doesn't sound like they let their faith interfere too much with the pranks you guys got into! What did you do for fun, Winnie, when you were at home?" I asked.

"Oh, we always had lots to do. In the winter, Olive and Ivor and Leo and I went sledding on the big hill beside the house. The boys would make sleighs, and smooth the runners with sandpaper and sometimes put a bit of water on to ice them up. In the evenings we learned to knit, and we read everything we could get our hands on. We'd sit close to the fireplace and listen to the radio – remember that old battery-powered Viking™ radio that sat on the shelf behind the sofa? We loved to hear the Lux Radio Theatre at 7 o'clock Monday evening. Other times we'd hear Fibber McGee & Molly, or Amos & Andy. But when we heard Foster Hewitt's voice calling out "It's Hockey Night in Canada" on Saturday night, we knew we had to be quiet. We were really in trouble if dad missed a Toronto Maple Leaf goal because of our noise.

"Sometimes during the game we'd pick wool, you know, pick all the bits and pieces of brush and grass from our own sheep's fleeces. Grandpa and the boys sheared the sheep in the spring, they always kept a fleece or two to use at home, and we'd wash it and wash it – those fleeces get so dirty. We used to lay the fleece over the fence to dry, and then we'd put it away until we had time to pick it clean and card it. That got all the fibres separated, and then mum would spin it on that old wheel Cap Larsen made for her. She'd knit our hats and mitts and scarves and socks, and when we were old enough, we learned to knit and did some of our own knitting.

"And we'd darn the socks too, when holes got worn in the heels or soles. Hardly anybody darns socks any more, remember how we'd put a ball or something inside, then run yarn back and forth over the hole, and then weave up and down over the threads from the other side? We had to make the mend smooth or the boys would get blisters.

"Mum used to make quilts out of our own wool too. She'd card it and get it all clean and smooth, then she'd lay it out on some cotton flour sacks sewn together to the right size for the bed. She'd put a layer of flour sacks on top, and then over that she put the quilt top. She used up squares of melton cloth [a thick, closely-woven wool fabric] left over from when she made coats. Other times she used fabric samples all sewn together. She sewed all around the sides and fastened all the layers together every few inches with bits of bright yarn. I've still got one of those quilts, they last forever, and it's just as warm now as it was when she made it.

"We did all those things by the light of coal oil lamps or the old Aladdin™ lamp. They seem pretty dull now, but we didn't know any different then. I remember when they bought their first Aladdin lamp. We'd been using coal oil lamps like everyone did, the kind that had a wick and a glass chimney. Then these Aladdin lamps came out. They burned kerosene and they had a mantle, so you had to pump some air into the tank to increase the pressure, and then you lit a match close to the mantle, and it caught fire and gave a really bright light. You had to be a bit careful not to get too much air pumped in or you'd have the whole thing up in flames, but mostly they worked really well."

"Electric light switches seem pretty easy by comparison, don't they?" I laughed. "I remember seeing gran knit, Winnie, but I don't really remember her spinning. Maybe she spun mostly in the wintertime, and we were only at the farm in the summer. Whatever became of that old spinning wheel she used? I hope it didn't go into the auction." My grandparents had held an auction sale when they moved from their farm home to the seniors' lodge in Irma.

"I had that spinning wheel for a long time, but then it kind of got in the way, and I wasn't using it. Will's got it now," she said. I was relieved to hear that this aged, precious-but-valueless artifact was in her son's caring hands.

"What did you do for spending money when you were a kid, Winnie? There must have been some things you wanted but that grandpa couldn't afford or chose not to buy."

"Oh sure, there were a few things. I don't know, nobody had much money then, and we didn't seem to need much. But I remember my first money-making venture. Your grandpa bought eight or a dozen turkey poults for me, they were just a few days old when we picked them up from the train along with gran's chicks. We put them in a box behind the kitchen stove for a few days until it was warm enough out in the henhouse for them. We didn't have power in the chicken house

Top: That looks like sweet
corn growing in the garden.
Perhaps the family overcame
their initial rejection of corn
as good only for cows, and
learned to enjoy the juicy
kernels.

Right: Winnie learned to
handle horses as well as hens
and turkeys. c1943

in those days, so we couldn't run a heat lamp for them. Anyhow, I fed the birds all summer and made sure they stayed inside their fence so the coyotes couldn't get them. Then in the fall gran butchered them and helped me pluck and clean them. I sold them for eight dollars each and made a huge profit, even after I paid dad what he figured I owed him for the feed.

"That was the first year I had money to buy 'real' Christmas presents for everyone. Christmas was always a great time for us. There weren't any spruce trees to cut down, all we had were poplar trees. But we didn't care, one of the boys went out and cut down a little poplar tree and we wrapped it around with green crêpe paper, and decorated it with red and green streamers, and aluminum foil wrappers we'd saved all year. We used to beat some powdered Sunlight™ soap with water to make snow, and we used that to decorate the tree too. We always had a few real decorations – I still hang them in our cabin at Christmas time."

Winnie grew up surrounded by animals and birds. Although she sometimes made pets of them, their purpose was clear – they were livestock, raised for food or produce or revenue. Even the dogs and cats had jobs to do: round up the cattle or sheep, keep the mouse and vole population down. "Many's the tear I shed when one of our dogs died," Winnie remembers.

"And I remember dad waking me up in the morning. 'Come on, Win, hurry now, the sheep are over in Craig's [or Barber's, or Smallwood's or Yarr's or some other neighbour's field].' And I'd have to chase them home but they never wanted to go back to their own pasture. I shed lots of tears over those creatures. And then they'd rest up in their pasture all day so they could escape again the next morning. We had an electric fence, but if they wanted out, it was out they got.

"I always hated it when dad had to dock the lamb's tails, it seemed so cruel. I could never figure out why God gave them such long tails, they were such a nuisance. If they weren't docked they'd always be filthy and matted.

Top: This sheep would be shorn in the spring; Nellie and the girls would clean and comb the fleece, and ready it for spinning over the winter. c1934

Right:This sheep put up with a lot from the Thurston kids. c1935

"I hated sheep-shearing day too. Any other day, those sheep would follow my dad anywhere, but on shearing day it was as if they knew something was going to happen. They acted like they couldn't even see the barn door, let alone go into it and we'd spend hours trying to get them into the barn. Then dad and the boys would spend all day in that hot barn shearing the sheep with those big shears. They didn't often cut themselves or the sheep, I don't know how they did it. They packed the fleece into large bags, I guess they must have shipped the bags to somebody or maybe a buyer would come to the farm, I don't remember.

"We had a couple of nanny goats too. We believed the coyotes wouldn't bother the sheep if there were goats in with them. One of the goats lived for a long time. She got all crippled up, and I used to take special food to her and a bucket of water. Finally dad had to kill her. I remember him saying 'When you have livestock you can expect dead stock.' He told me later that he figured the old nanny knew what was going to happen when he went to get her that last time, she bleated so pitifully."

Not long after World War II ended, Winnie's brother Leo was accepted into St. John's Theological College at Winnipeg. Winnie watched, her heart heavy but her pride high, as Leo prepared to leave. She rode along when her father took Leo to the train station in Irma, and waved goodbye. Another beloved brother was gone.

"The family at home was really dwindling, wasn't it, by then?"

"Well, I was okay with that. I was thrilled that I was going to have a brother who was an Anglican church minister. Mum and dad had always lived their religion, you know. They read their Bible, and they prayed every night, we always said grace before meals, and we went to church every Sunday.

"When we were kids, Olive and I really looked forward to Sunday School by Post. We'd get papers in the mail and mum would help us fill them out, then we'd send them to Miss Camp. She marked the papers and sent them back to us in an envelope with our own name on it! And she always included some pretty stickers, or a pencil or some-

Winnie visited her brother while he was in Edson as a 'minister-in-training'; here at the rectory, summer 1949.

thing. She'd come to visit us nearly every year. There was Vacation Bible School in the summertime too, but I don't think that started until after I'd left home. We had a pretty close relationship with all those church people.

"The Anglican church minister would come for supper quite often, and that was great fun. The folks didn't have much company, really, apart from feeding the minister and of course, mum would have the W.A. [Women's Auxiliary of the Anglican church, later renamed the ACW or Anglican Church Women] to the house for their meetings. Sometime during the summer, mum and dad would put on a garden party to raise money for the church. Dad and the boys would build a shelter out of the small poplar trees that had leafed out, and they'd fix up a table under the shelter. I think everybody brought their own dishes and cutlery, but mum would do all the cooking and then serve dinner outside. She'd have cold chicken likely, and potato salad, maybe some cucumbers or cold beets from the garden, and last year's pickles.

Mum made wonderful pies, and she would have served dessert of saskatoon or rhubarb pie, or maybe raspberry pie if there were enough ripe ones, with lots of thick cream on top. And tea, of course. "

"Well, I didn't know about the garden parties, but I do remember that Sunday activities revolved around the church schedule. Sometimes the minister did Morning Prayer at 11:00 o'clock, sometimes Evensong in the afternoon or evening. I guess the churches in the parish took turns with the timing of their services, didn't they?

"I don't think Leo came home in the summer after he'd entered college, did he? I have photos of him when he worked for Len and Bert in Ontario. I have another photo of you too, Winnie, at Edson. I think the year would have been 1949, wouldn't it, it was the year Leo spent at the Edson mission and you went out to visit him.

"And here's another picture of you – as bridesmaid at Leo and Joyce's wedding. Now, that must have been quite an event, there you were, having grown up on the farm, and that wedding was quite an affair. The service was in the cathedral in Winnipeg – a bit bigger than St. Mary's in Irma!

"Joyce said in her diary that there were about two hundred people at the service, and about a hundred at the reception. And that it poured rain that day! How did you get the money to go, and to buy your dress and hat?"

"You know, I have no recollection of that wedding at all, Jeannie. You tell me it was in the cathedral, so that must have been a big church, but I can't remember a thing about the ceremony. I remember I went fishing with Joyce's dad the day after the wedding!

"There were quite a few of us bridesmaids, I think, and we wore matching outfits. I made my dress in class when I was going to Vermilion [the Vermilion School of Agriculture and Home Economics]. It was blue, I remember that, blue lace. And the hat was white, with a big brim.

"I think dad found the money for my train fare. He and mum had intended to go, but there was a big frost in early August, and it killed off the whole crop, so there was just no income at all that year. It must

Winnie sewed her own bridesmaid dress, then took the train to Winnipeg for Leo and Joyce's wedding. Winnie (l to r), with Joyce, Josy and Nancy; August 1950.

have been a big disappointment, especially for mum, because she and Leo had been so close."

Perhaps Fred sold a steer to raise the money for Winnie's fare to Winnipeg. He had a good cattle herd by then, big reddish-brown and white Herefords, prize-winning steers and fertile cows.

Grandpa had raised cattle in Wales before coming to Canada, dairy cattle not the beef cattle he raised in Irma. After they emigrated, he bought whatever cattle he could afford, initially to provide milk and dairy products for his family, range cattle with hair of any colour – white, red, brown, black, and even greyish blue. But Fred knew he could only build a good herd with good stock, and he set about breeding reliable cows with sturdy bulls. He soon developed a reputation for solid, heavy, registered Herefords.

While the whole family benefitted financially from the well-bred herd, Winnie's interest and efforts brought her special recognition. The 4-H Beef Club in Irma attracted many district youngsters, boys

Winnie's calf came from her father's herd; she won the 4-H Beef Club grand prize in 1954 and wept when the calf was sold to the packing plant.

and girls whose parents raised beef cattle. Usually, the 4-H member was given (or sometimes bought) a calf from the family herd, early in the spring. Then the boy or girl became responsible for raising the animal, making sure it was fed a balanced diet, received its inoculations against tuberculosis and Bangs disease, had access to water and to salt blocks. The little calves had to be handled too, gently but firmly, and trust built between the animal and its owner. In the spring, when the calf was a year old and weighed over a thousand pounds (454 kg), the young owners showed off their animals at the annual competition in the village show ring – otherwise known as the outdoor skating rink. Each year, the winning calf was not only awarded the blue ribbon, it was purchased by a packing company and the revenue was paid directly to the winning 4-H owner. Winnie's calf was declared Grand Champion in the 4-H competition of 1949. Winnie also won first place in the club's Grooming and Showmanship categories.

"I won," Winnie wrote to her parents, who were in Wales enjoying their first visit home since their departure twenty-two years earlier. "I've got the ribbon, and they gave me a cheque right there. I'll have money to pay for his feed, dad, when you get home."

Winnie didn't mention the tears she'd shed as her brother Ivor walked the calf to the train station and loaded it on the cattle car for shipment to its new owner – an Edmonton meat-packing company.

While Fred and Nellie were in Wales, the brothers and sisters were responsible for the farm operation, including Fred's garden. It covered a huge area, three or four acres, surrounded by the shelterbelt of carragana hedge, Manitoba maples, and spruce trees. "That was an immense garden to manage, Winnie. How did you do it?" I asked.

"Oh, my goodness, that was a BIG garden. We all helped. Lots of times I'd ride old Babe – you remember sitting on her, don't you, when you were little? – we'd go up and down the rows pulling a scuffler, sort of a cultivator with five or six bent tines that disturbed the soil so the weeds couldn't grow. There was always a patch of winter onions in that garden, and we'd look forward to getting the first ones. We'd take them in for gran to chop up and then we'd make cheese and onion sandwiches! Oh my, they were good.

"And dad would take a pail or two, early in the spring, and put them upside down over the rhubarb so it would come along faster. Then he'd pull the first stalks and take them in so mum could make stewed rhubarb or maybe a rhubarb pie. We always had lots of thick cream to pour over it, and you know, Ted always knew when the rhubarb was ripe and he'd be there waiting for his mother's first rhubarb pie of the season!

"All winter long, dad dumped manure on the garden, then early in the spring, he'd burn it. I don't know how he managed to get it to burn, it must have still been pretty wet, but he'd get it all going. He always said that the burn was what kept the cutworms out of the garden, and you know, I never did see a cutworm in the garden.

"That garden grew the best crop of anyone's in the neighbourhood, I think. In the fall we'd dig the carrots and beets and haul them

Winnie atop the wagonload of potatoes. The potato crop never failed, and grandpa killed any potato beetle that dared enter his garden.

into the cellar, dad hung the cabbages upside down on the basement posts, and the potatoes…!" Winnie laughed aloud as she remembered the potato harvest.

"Dad would designate a Saturday as potato-digging day, and the boys would hitch up one of the horses to a plow, and dad would plow out the potatoes. Us kids would pick them up into pails, dump them into burlap bags, the boys would load them into the horse-drawn wagon and then take them and dump them in the bin in the cellar. Mum would always have fresh baked potatoes for supper that night. I still blame those potato-picking days for my back trouble. Those fifteen-gallon pails full of potatoes were heavy, but I wasn't going to let anyone get ahead of me picking potatoes!

"We all worked together and somehow made it a fun day even though it was such hard work. We'd eat all the potatoes we wanted in the winter, there would be lots for seed the next spring, lots to eat until the next fall and lots left that had to be packed up out of the cellar and fed to the pigs so the cellar could be cleaned out for the next crop!"

"Oh brother, that really was huge work, wasn't it?" I asked. "And you didn't have running water yet then, did you, so you couldn't have had the luxury of soaking your stiff muscles in hot water. What would you have done to ease your aches?"

"Gosh, I don't remember, Jeannie, we just lived with them, I guess. If they were really bad, mum would make a Scotch emulsion to rub on our aching bones and muscles. It was a terrible-smelling concoction. I believe it had turpentine in it and maybe cream."

"But you know what mum used to do when we had a cold, or when dad's chest got bad? Well, she'd make a mustard plaster, one part flour to one part mustard, mixed with water, then spread on a flannel cloth. She'd put another flannel cloth on our chest and then put the mustard plaster over that, then a wool cloth, and talk about sweat – a real kill or cure treatment! Other times mum would boil up some onions and make a poultice and put it on our chest – not at the same time as the mustard plaster, of course. If we had a sliver that wouldn't come out, we'd put the wet skin of an egg shell on it and as it dried it would pull the sliver out. For bad pimples or boils she'd make a bread poultice – bread and hot water and put it on hot. For a burn we'd use butter – not recommended anymore, but it worked then."

"Mum always had Vicks Vapo-Rub™, and Pinex™ cough syrup, and a Vicks product she added to water. But the hot lemon and honey with a few teaspoons of dad's precious whiskey in a glass of water was a never-fail remedy. We had a small green knitted wool tam that was a family favourite and if we got sick we always wore that tam to bed, so our head would keep warm. I don't know what happened if more than one of us was sick at the same time. Ivor had that tam for years after I left home and kept it under his pillow to wear after he'd washed his hair."

"It sounds as if you seldom ever saw a doctor, Winnie. And what about dentists, what did you do to keep your teeth in good shape?" I asked.

"No, we never saw a doctor. Most everybody doctored themselves. There were lots of home remedies, and I guess people either got better

Winnie spent a year at the Vermilion School of Agriculture; she learned to type and to sew – essential skills.

or they died. I remember seeing a dentist though, old Dr. Hawke in Wainwright. I must have had something really wrong with my teeth, but the freezing wouldn't take, and he really had a bad time. Told me never to come back!"

After high school, Winnie spent a year at the Vermilion School of Agriculture and Home Economics. She lived in residence and came home on weekends, her tuition fees paid by her dad, her spending money the proceeds from the sale of her 4-H calf. She took secretarial courses so she could find a job – a temporary one – as all women then knew their real vocation was to get married, and they took sewing and other home-making classes to get ready for that eventuality.

Then Winnie came to Edmonton, where she lived with my family for the first few months of her employment with the Exams Branch of the Department of Education. She travelled with us on one of our two family vacations, when we went out to Banff and Jasper and Radium Hot Springs.

Winnie was with us that terrible night of March 28, 1951 when our father died. She gathered up the four of us children and took us down

Top: We kids loved having Winnie visit – perhaps she came to help out when Colleen was born in 1946.

Bottom: And perhaps she came back to help out when Mike was born in 1948 – she's becoming increasingly mature and attractive.

Winnie travelled to Banff and Jasper with us one summer; here we are at Athabasca Falls.

to her room in the basement. "I'll bring some hot chocolate," she said. Our dad had been injured in a vehicle collision four months previously and had been bed-ridden, then on crutches as his broken leg mended. Now he was dead. We knew our world would never be the same.

He was 71 years, 10 months and 13 days old when he died, although we kids didn't know his age then and even if we had known, we couldn't have understood the implications of the age difference between he and our mother. Neither could we picture our future.

Winnie kept us with her, curled up on her bed, her arms around us, until we fell asleep.

I've always remembered the care Winnie showed us that night, her protectiveness, and the loving way she held us during those first dreadful hours. But I didn't know why Winnie had taken us down to her bedroom, until years later: "Win, when we were kids, that night our father died, you called us down to your bedroom in the basement. Do you remember? Why did you do that?"

We used to write postcards – they only took a day or two to be delivered; Winnie sent this one to Florence, her brother Ron's wife. Dated July 6, 1948 – just a month before my brother Mike was born! Winnie had gone with us as we did the circuit through Banff and Jasper.

Miss F. Pugh
c/o Wainwright
Hospital
Wainwright
Alta

Hi Florence
Here we are at Jasper and this is the mountain which we can see when we look out of our cabin door. We are on our way now to see Maligne Canyon right now, but had a flat tire, so while Map is fixing it, I decided to drop this card to you. Don't work too hard will you.
Love
Winnie

"Oh, Jeannie, I didn't want you kids to see the undertaker come and take your dad's body away. No little kids should see that sort of thing." Winnie was only twenty-one-years-old herself at the time.

She stayed with us for a short time after our father died, then she moved to a boarding house closer to her office. She enjoyed the work and the people at the Exams Branch, but a short term of city life was all she wanted. Soon she returned to Irma, back to her parents' farm, and to a job at the village post office. She sorted mail and cancelled stamps, weighed parcels, deposited incoming mail in the villagers' individual post boxes or handed it directly to those who didn't have a box. Each customer received a warm smile and Winnie's cheerful greeting.

"Good morning, Mrs. Charter, how's Arthur today? I'll have your mail sorted in just about ten minutes, they've just brought the bag from the train and I'm not quite done with it yet." or "Well, hello there, Milt, you're going to need a whole box to carry all the Co-op's mail today."

Sometime during the years when Winnie worked at the Irma post office and, later, the Wainwright post office, a brown-eyed, curly-haired young man entered her life. His name was Bill Askin. He'd grown up just east of Irma in the Sunny Brae school district (although he attended that school long after Phyllis had resigned her teaching position). Bill and Winnie had known one another in high school, then they'd each gone away to work. Bill took Winnie home from a Saturday dance one warm June night at the Alma Mater hall, just east of Ted and Molly's home. And, as Winnie said: "We started to see each other. We got married on August 3rd, 1953." The young couple honeymooned at a little cottage on Mann Lake, near Ashmont, where Leo and Joyce were living.

Winnie and Bill bought the old Roan farm, about ten miles north of the Thurston farm and lived there for the first four or five years of their marriage. They raised pigs, big red Tamworth creatures, so fierce that a person couldn't walk among them. Bill dumped their feed from a wagon pulled behind his tractor.

Winnie's sister Mary on the left, Winnie and Bill and the unidentified best man, outside St. Mary's, Irma, August 1953.

Winnie wanted a family, so did Bill, and their wishes soon came to fruition. William Frederick was born on June 30th, 1954, a little boy who shared the same birthday as his Grandpa Thurston, and who grew to closely resemble his Uncle Ivor. He was born the day after Winnie's parents returned from their second trip to Wales.

"I can remember being stung by a bumblebee when we were living there at the Roan place," recalled my now tall and husky cousin Will. "I was playing on the porch, and the bee came up from underneath the floorboards, and stung me right here on my cheek. Mum was in the kitchen baking something, and right away she stuck baking soda on my face. Took out the stinger, I guess. I'm not afraid of bumblebees now, but I sure have a lot of respect for them."

Soon another son arrived. Robert Douglas was born on April 5, 1956, a poor little not-quite-right baby. Winnie and Bill were told their child would likely not survive beyond age six. There was no help available, no resources, little of the understanding we now have of patterning and physiotherapy, learning aids and community resources. Bobby's mother had little choice except to shelter the child in his crib while she helped her husband work their farm.

I remember watching gran patiently exercise Bobby's legs whenever he was left in her care. "There now," she'd say, "We'll just get those muscles working a little." By the time Bobby was three- or four-years old, his body was long and uncoordinated. Gran crooned softly and held him close to her as she spooned baby food into his mouth.

In 1957, a farm property close to Winnie's parents came on the market: the section abandoned by Winnie's sister Mary and brother-in-law Bert after a crop- and soul-destroying hail storm. Winnie urged Bill to move to the Russell place, with its well-built house, close to the Thurston homes. "Mum could sometimes help with the children, Bill, so I could get out on the farm with you more." Catherine Ann, Winnie and Bill's only daughter, had been born earlier that year, on May 5th. The family moved and developed the largest pig farm in the area. There were pigs, pigs, and more pigs, not the fierce Tamworths but ordinary pigs with pink skin from which sprang a few stiff white hairs.

"Winnie, what are you doing?" I asked in horror, as my aunt picked up a day-old baby pig, held its mouth open, and clipped the point off its incisor teeth. The baby shrieked and squealed and yelled in pain as only a baby pig can. It wriggled and struggled to be free, all four of its little legs churned, its body jerked and quivered.

"Well, you have to do that, Jeannie, or they hurt the sow when they suck her. These little teeth are just like razors." My aunt deftly clipped one tooth after another, returned the pig to its mother and picked up the next one. She repeated the process until each pig in the litter was done.

Winnie managed the day-to-day chores. There were a few boars and a hundred sows that each produced eight, ten or a dozen baby pigs several times a year. Bill worked the farm too, as well as working out on pipeline construction projects.

Pig farming is an up-and-down business, economically viable one year, a disaster the next, depending on world pork prices. By the mid-1960's, pork prices had dropped again; Winnie sought and found employment, this time at the old folks home in Wainwright.

Winnie and Bill agonized over their middle son, the little boy who needed so much more care than they were able to provide. They took Bobby to the Michener Centre in Red Deer, where he lived till he was thirty-four-years-old.

In 1971 Winnie and Bill sold their farm to Ivor, and bought another one at Plamondon, an hour or so northeast of Edmonton. "Why did you do that, Winnie?" I queried. "The Russell place had pretty good land, didn't it? And you were close to the family."

"Well, I know. But Bill felt there was getting to be too many people around, too much stuff going on. We were only at Plamondon for a while – less than a year – and then we bought a trapline and moved up to Steen River. Bill had been quite friendly with a guy at Plamondon who had done a lot of trapping, and he showed Bill lots about trapping and preparing the furs for market. We ended up spending eighteen years with our trap lines. The market was good then, remember, there was a real call for furs in those years."

"You know the difference between a cabin and a house?" Bill asked.

"Well, there could be a lot of differences," I said, "which ones are you thinking of?"

"You should know this now, the difference between a cabin and a house is that the door on a cabin is to let people in, and the door on a house in town is to keep people out."

"Bill never did like to be around people too much," my mother told me once. "He used to camp out in the coulee south of Irma during the summer, when he was a teenager, never went home unless he had to. I think maybe he used to trap coyotes then too."

Traplines are closely controlled by the provincial government in Alberta, as they are across the country. The trapper must buy a license to run a line, and in return is given exclusive rights to trap in a specific area. Bill and Winnie each bought a license to trap. Bill's trapline area was described as:

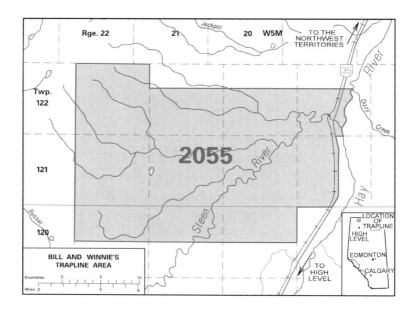

Commencing at the junction of the west bank of the Hay River and north boundary of township 121-19 proceed west to the McKenzie Highway, then south along the west side of the highway to the south boundary of township 121-19. Then west about three miles to the northwest corner of township 120-19, then three miles south, eighteen miles west and fifteen miles north to the northwest corner of township 122-22. Then six miles east, two miles south and about seventeen miles east to the west bank of the Hay River, then south along the west bank of the river to the point of commencement. All west of the 5th meridian, excluding from the above all privately owned or leased lands except those of the licencee.

Winnie's trapline was immediately south of Bill's. The traplines covered an area of about six townships – 216 square miles (559 sq km) of woods, bush, snow, and frozen muskeg.

They've been called the family's gypsies. They've moved around far more than have any of the other Thurston children. They spent one winter in Edson, a couple of hours west of Edmonton: "We loved it there, wonderful people, we made such good friends," Winnie said.

They spent another winter at the Little Buffalo Mission about 60 miles (96 km) from Peace River. Winnie looked after the fifteen or twenty girls at the mission school. Bill took care of the maintenance and upkeep of the school, its residence and outbuildings.

One summer, during the period when Winnie and Bill were heavily involved with the Alliance Church, they donated their time to the Ross Haven Bible Camp at Lac Ste. Anne, half an hour northwest of Edmonton. My own daughter Beth and her husband Greg have been managing the same camp since 1996.

We seldom saw either Winnie or Bill, or their children, during the trapline days. Every couple of years Winnie drove to Irma, or took the bus to Edmonton then drove to Irma, perhaps in her son's vehicle. Her father never got used to women driving.

"You know what your grandpa asked me, Jeannie?" There were crinkles at Winnie's eyes and mouth. "He asked me if I wanted one of the boys to drive me back to Edmonton! Can you imagine? I'd driven all the way from Steen River, more than six hundred miles, and he wants someone to drive back to Edmonton with me."

I've thought and thought about this conversation, over the years. It's just one more piece in the puzzle of life, mine and those of my aunts and uncles. Another piece of knowledge to help me understand why my mother places such credence on the men in her life, so little on women's abilities. Perhaps some day I'll learn to laugh as much about it as does my Aunt Winnie.

Winnie returned to her home in the north, back to her husband and their traplines. Will left home, Bobby was in Red Deer. Although Cathy moved to Steen River with her parents and completed her Grade 9 schoolwork by correspondence, she moved to Fairview and boarded with friends while she went to high school.

Winnie went home for funerals – her father's in 1978, her brother Ivor's in 1979, her mother's in 1981. After each one, she returned to her own reality: the silence of the north, the friendly but scattered population, the fertile plains with the Caribou Hills in the background.

"Tell me about the trapline, Winnie. I can't imagine what you two did out there all by yourselves. That's incredibly beautiful country I know, the Caribou Hills south of Steen River, the sky is so clear and you can watch the Northern Lights at night. But man, the winters are cold and the winter days are so short." I shivered at the concept of choosing to be outside all day, every day, through a northern Alberta winter. Or of using an outhouse rather than a nice warm bathroom. And of having no access to a shower or bathtub full of hot, scented water.

"Well, I guess all that's true," Winnie replied. "But we loved it, we loved our life out in the woods where the air is so good. It's healthy too, there was hardly any pollution up there, and it was so quiet – that was before there got to be so much oil exploration. We had about five or six cabins, and we stocked each of them with food staples – flour and baking powder, and powdered milk, sugar, salt and pepper. Dried apples and raisins, nuts maybe and sometimes chocolate or cocoa, tea and coffee. Nothing perishable, of course."

"And we'd ride our skidoos and pull a sort of sled behind each of them. We had our bedding and radios and that sort of stuff. It was beautiful on the trapline. The sky is so blue and clear up here in the winter, and when the trees are covered with hoar frost – well, it looks great but when you drive a skidoo underneath them and the ice particles drop down your collar it's not so good!"

"I remember one time, I got so cold I could hardly walk. My feet and my hands hurt so bad. And Bill – he made me go into the woods and get firewood. He shouted at me, and I thought he was being so cruel. But you know, he saved my life that time. If I hadn't got moving I might have died. By the time I got back with the wood, he already had a fire going, and I soon got warmed up. We didn't have many times like that, but I sure remember that day."

I marvelled at the independent life these two people led. The northern Alberta prairie stretches for miles and miles, with large farms and

Winnie on the trapline, 1975

Skidoos with enhanced windshields and loaded sleighs, December 1981. There's not another human being for miles around.

few people. Beyond that, where the boreal forest again takes hold, where black spruce and Labrador tea shrubs dominate acidic soils and the more basic lands produce white spruce / birch forests, you can travel for miles without seeing another human being. Or so it was in the 1970's and 1980's. Now, cut-lines race through the forest, 6m to 8m wide scars left behind by petroleum exploration and production activities. After-dark airplane flights between High Level on the prairie and Rainbow Lake in the boreal forest heartland of petroleum country reveal an all-encompassing pattern of follow-the-dot lights from drilling rigs, well-servicing outfits, and bush camps.

For close to twenty years, beginning in 1971, my aunt and her husband spent their winters in that bushland. They trapped beaver and muskrat, wolf and wolverine, coyote, mink, lynx, squirrel and weasel.

"The buyers loved that fur from northern Alberta," Winnie remembered. "We used to take bags, gunny bags, or special fur bags we'd get from the buyers to keep the furs in after we dressed them. We left the furs in wooden boxes or cleaned-out 45-gallon barrels, outside the cabins, until we were ready to haul them away. See, we usually left the first cabin, at Steen River, about the first of October, and we'd be gone till Christmas time."

"And the furs were safe? No-one ever bothered them, and the animals couldn't get at them, I guess?"

"Oh no. The buyers at High Level or Fort Vermilion liked our furs. I used to comb them," Winnie told me, "and then I'd vacuum them so they'd be all fluffed up. They were so beautiful. The buyers told me they always knew when a woman had handled the fur!"

"And you didn't see anyone else during that time?" I asked. "From October till Christmas?"

"Well, we'd see a few people. Nobody else could trap in our area, you know, we had a registered trapline – the government licensed it to us and we had to trap it, or we'd get a notice questioning why we weren't trapping and selling furs – but nobody else could use it. Oh, hunters could come in for moose and caribou and that sort of thing, and we'd see a few of those people. Then after we were finished for the season, we'd sometimes take our furs over to the Batts, our friends who lived close to Fort Vermilion, and get the fur ready for the buyers."

Winnie and Bill lived a life of immense quiet, without music or voices except on the radio, without vehicle noises or construction sounds. Only the murmurs of the bush, the whispers of frozen tree branches brushing against one another, the scurries of mice and voles in their tunnels under the snow, an occasional whoosh from a snowy owl's wing, the raucous screech of ever-present ravens, the high-pitched 'chick-a-dee-dee-dee' from the boreal or black-capped chickadees. The gentleness of snow falling, dropping down to cover already-in-place drifts. Occasional wind sounds, strong and harsh as the weather systems changed. Dark nights or bright nights, clouded skies or sparkling stars, brilliantly-coloured northern lights ribbon-dancing across the sky. A world in tune with its nature, harmony rather than battle, synchronicity instead of rivalry.

And then there were the other seasons...

"What did you do in the summer, Winnie?"

"Well you know, the days are so long up here from about May until September. The temperature gets pretty high and the mosquitoes come out in droves. I had to do something. I used to work sometimes in the restaurant at Indian Cabins or at Steen River. Some summers I cooked for the railway crews, or at a fishing lodge, one summer I worked for Poole Construction, cooking at their camp."

"I remember you writing to me, and telling me about the berries you'd picked and canned – jars and jars of saskatoons and wild rasp-berries, and those tiny little wild strawberries, high-bush cranberries for jelly. It's kind of a family thing, isn't it, canning all those fruits?" We laughed together, sharing remembered satisfaction at work well done, the beauty of fruit in quart sealers and jam or jelly in little jars.

"Oh, I did a lot of that. Still do. Have to eat, you know, and your own food is so much better than the store-bought stuff."

A few days after I'd asked my aunt to recall her trapping days, a parcel arrived in my mail box. Inside was Winnie's 5-year diary for the years 1976 to 1980, together with some photos. As I read Winnie's tiny hand-written entries – only 5 or 6 lines were provided for each day – the realities of the life they'd lead leapt from the pages.

1976:

January 4: -40° [F] all day. Will froze his nose. Got 1 fox, 1 marten, 1 beaver, 8 weasel, 8 squirrel.

January 8: I started homespun mitts for Bill.

January 9: I sewed canvas on Bill's moccasins.

February 7: Stayed at tent, I shot a squirrel, skinning wolverine tonight and finished baby sweater back.

Winnie also worked at the café in Steen River during the summer season, and, it appears in the post-Christmas winters of 1976 and 1977. Her diary entries for February 21 to 24, 1976 as well as February and March 1977 record "worked full shift" or "worked 12 hours" or "worked 2 –10".

The diary details where the couple lived during the trapping season – the "big tent" or the "little cabin" or the "big cabin". Each of the cabins was cleaned up in the fall and stocked with staples, ready for habitation as needed. Bill dug a 3 ½ ft (1 m) deep hole in the ground at each location, a storehouse for the root vegetables they'd need all winter, deep enough to protect the turnips, potatoes, and carrots from frost, as well as canned milk and even fresh eggs. Once the food was in place, it was covered with a deep layer of native hay, then tar paper; then the dirt was replaced, packed firmly and covered with snow. Each hole held a two-week supply of food.

For their meat supply, Bill shot moose and Winnie canned it, sometimes boiling the quart sealers in a large metal pan set on a grate over an open fire. Although I've never tasted canned moose meat, the thought of it reminds me of my most favourite of all suppers at my grandparents' farm – beef or chicken canned in quart jars, heated in a frying pan with a bit of onion, the gelatin thickened to make gravy, a little salt and pepper added. Only a few of us are lucky enough to remember that wonderful flavour...

1977:

September 22:Bill calling[47] moose, no answer. Left at 10:00. Bill
  dug hole to put vegetables.

September 26: Bill dug holes for vegetables.

September 27: Dried onions

1980:

September 6: Bill packing for bush.

September 8: Ice on water pails in a.m. Bill working on Elan
  [one of the snowmobiles]. Sunny day. I made sauerkraut and
  more beet pickle. Took skidoos across tracks.

September 14: Bill took load of stuff to bush.

September 19: Finished packing up and left at 3. No trouble
  getting here

September 20: Bill shot moose across river at first rapids.

September 22: Worked on meat all day, 7 qts. and 2 pts. canned.
  Fixed fire in ground and canned on it.

September 23: 3 inches snow. Terra[48] wouldn't start. Bill walked
  to Steen and got skidoos. Canned 12 qt. 2 pt. meat and rendered 2 cans fat[49].

Stacks of wood were needed at each cabin and tent, for warmth
and for cooking. Bill and Winnie spent hours each season felling and
hauling trees, cutting them into stove-length logs, and splitting the
logs.

1978:

September 29: Bill hauled green wood…

October 28: I split and piled wood…

Of course, roads into and along the trapline were non-existent.
The line travelled through boreal forest, across watery muskeg accessible only after freeze-up, over creeks and rivers crossed only on
hand-built bridges. Eventually, the oil companies stepped up their

exploration activities. They had been licensed to do so without consulting the trapline owners, and they created cutlines through the forest – straight-as-a-die lines up to 30 feet (9 m) wide, mile after mile through the forest. Meanwhile, transportation and haulage were a never-ending challenge for the trappers, the vagaries of skidoos and all-terrain vehicles often a man versus machine duel.

1978;
March 5: Skidoo caught fire, put it out with snow.

1979:
October 28: Left at 2:30, brought 3 skidoos part way to cabin.
October 29: Bill took my skidoo part way and then walked to Elan and brought it to cabin. I walked to my skidoo and brought it...
October 31: Left cabin with 2011, rough trip, clutch bolt came out of Bill's, I rode back in sleigh.
November 12: Ski on Bill's skidoo broke in muskeg.

1980:
October 17: Got stuck in muskeg close to home.
October 26: Away from little cabin at 10:00, rough trip, Bill's skidoo broke through ice. Got to tent at 7, all okay.

Those who run the traplines must be self-reliant – there are no machine shops in the woods. Neither are there doctors – only self-healing and self-treatment. The work of running the trapline continues regardless of pains or problems. Neither Bill or Winnie were youngsters – they were both closer to fifty than forty at this time.

1978:
February 2: Migraine so can't go home.

1979:

January 14: Woke up with migraine.

November 22: Up at 7, back to bed with migraine, till noon.

1980:

April 26: Bill sick during night, spent most of day in bed.

April 27: Bill some better. Got almost 2 pails of birch [birch
sap has always been used by the aboriginal peoples as a very
pleasant-tasting medicinal agent]

October 27: Both tired, I have bad stomach pains.

October 28: I'm still feeling really tough. Got 1 beaver, 1 rat,
1 weasel, 1 beaver, ice thin, Bill setting traps in walking
distance.

Both Bill and Winnie worked the traplines, setting traps and checking
them, pulling them and fixing them, moving the traps to new or different locations. Beaver skins were slit up the belly and removed; the
skin of most other animals was taken whole, turned inside out. Then
Winnie fleshed the hide – scraped it clean, and Bill stretched the hides
by nailing them to boards.

1976:

December 18: Working on beaver and other furs.

December 24: Bill working on beaver.

1977:

December 26: Worked on animals, then to Steen [they were
back in the cabin on the Steen River at that point].

December 27: Working on animals.

1978:

March 8: Skinned 3 beaver and fleshed 4.

November 22: Bill stretched lynx and fox, I stretched
5 marten.

1979:
December 7: Busy day dressing animals.

1980:
February 3: Skinned 1 mink, 12 squirrel, 1 weasel, and stretched
   1 lynx.
December 5: -50°, Bill skinned wolf, I skinned 4 animals.

Winnie's knitting travelled with her along the line. When she
wasn't working on furs, she knitted or baked:

1976:
December 9: Started pair of slippers.

1977:
November 18: Stayed home, cooked, knitted, wrote letters.
November 28: Cooked, dressed marten and weasels, knitted.
November 29: Finished helmet and mitts.

1978:
February 1: Knitted pair of socks.

1979:
February 13: Finished Ellen's sweater; started sweater for
   Nicole [Winnie's granddaughter].

1980:
December 3: -50°. I finished Nicole's sweater and started
   helmet.

Winnie's father, as well as her brother Ivor and her brother-in-law
Bert [her sister Mary's husband], died during the 1976 – 1980 period
covered by the diary Winnie loaned me. The entries for those days are
terse.

Her father, Fred, was hospitalized for several weeks before his death on April 28, 1978.

April 1978:
9th: Ride to Edmonton with friends of Ann.
10th: Bus to hospital. Phyl and mum there. Dad pretty good.
22nd: Ann will take me home tomorrow.
29th: Darrel brought message dad passed away yesterday. Quite cool out.
30th: Away on bus, leaves coming out on trees on hills. I'm knitting on Nicole's sweater.

May 1978:
2nd: My dad's funeral. Will left in evening.
3rd: Sad day packing up folks things.
4th: Did some more packing. Len and Phyllis there for dinner. Sad to leave mum.

Three days later, Winnie was back home:

7th: Working on beaver all day.
"Working on beaver" – the reality of trapping, a cover for grief, never-ending activity.

July 1979:
27th: Cut out another dress for Nicole. Jim and Steve came with news Ivor passed away.
30th: Sad day – Ivor's funeral…Mum pretty good.

In early April 1981, when Winnie and Bill were working at the Caribou Point fishing lodge where there was no telephone, Winnie's mother took a sudden turn for the worse.

Winnie's sister Olive telephoned the boss at the CNR camp outside Meander River where Winnie often worked in the summer. "Tony, do you know how I can reach Winnie? Our poor mum is so sick. I don't think she'll last much longer."

"I'll get to her," responded Tony. Within minutes, he was in his truck and on the way to Hay River, a distance of about 150 miles. He relayed the news to his friend, a pilot with Landa Air, who flew to the lodge and brought Winnie out to Hay River.

Winnie phoned her brother Ted. "No, Winnie, mum's doing better now. No, I don't think there's any need for you to come out just now."

Winnie returned to the lodge. "We all took care of one another, you know, we had to, there were so few of us in the north then. We thought nothing of driving a hundred miles or more to visit our friends, or to take messages."

Only on the frontier...

Finally, in 1990, Winnie and Bill sold the trapline and built a cabin in the bush a few miles east of High Level. Fifteen years later, Winnie and Bill showed me around their property, and told me more of their story.

"See, we're putting an addition on here – three more rooms! We're going to put a propane heater in here, then we'll be able to get away for more than a few hours in the wintertime, without having to take all the perishables with us so they don't freeze up. And we may even put a chemical toilet in this little room here, we'll see." Winnie laughed at the extent of their 'civilization'.

My mother and I had driven north from Edmonton, stayed over-night in Slave Lake, then travelled on through prairie and forest, along the straight-as-a-die Highway 35 into the town of High Level. It was a journey of over 500 miles (800 km) one way. After checking into our motel, we drove east, directions in hand, to find Winnie and Bill's home. "Just go east on the highway, across the river – it's just a little thing, not like the North Saskatchewan, up the hill and continue on for a few miles, then turn north. The entrance to our place is on your left-hand side, on the west side of the road."

We followed the directions carefully, and found the entrance we were looking for, not at all clearly marked, half-hidden with tall grasses. We maneuvered our way through the opening in the fence, along a dirt track, between tall poplars, past a sign warning trespassers to turn around and retreat, through another poplar bluff. A calmness crept over and through my car as we travelled that short distance, a peacefulness that seemed to emanate from the land itself.

There in front of us stood a wooden cabin with a porch across the front, a solar collector down the path a little way, an outhouse down another path. Winnie came outside, her face wreathed with that familiar grin. "Well, you got here, did you," she exclaimed. "I'll bet you'd like some tea."

Tea, the Thurston panacea for everything from social niceties to sore toes. Loving, familiar territory.

Over tea that day and the next, we caught up with family news, neighborhood gossip, future plans, and current affairs. And we walked Bill and Winnie's property.

"How much land do you have here?"

"Well, we have a quarter section. We built the cabin ourselves. A lot of the wood came from our trapline at Steen River, we had the logs cut down and then we had them milled into lumber. The frame is 2 x 6's stacked on top of one another. We did all that work ourselves. Will made my kitchen cupboards – aren't they beautiful?" Winnie stroked her cabinets, beautifully crafted poplar, sanded and varnished to a gentle sheen.

"And you have lights, Winnie. They must make the winters easier to take than if you had just kerosene lamps."

"They sure do. Bill's solar collector panel gives us enough power for the lights, and all the small tools Bill needs, or the ones I want to use. We can't use heating appliances, or an iron, but I never did like ironing anyway!" she chuckled.

"What a garden you have, Win. Oh look at the raspberries, where's your bowl, I'll get enough for supper from these canes in five minutes," directed my mother, and her youngest sister handed over the bowl she'd been carrying. My mother prided herself on being the

Winnie with her sister Phyllis, in front of the cabin in northern Alberta, autumn 2005.

fastest berry picker in the west – and all the berries went into the bowl, few went down her throat.

"What's this little house for, Bill?" I asked as we came upon a small, one-room version of the main cabin.

"Well, that's for people to stay in. Those that want peace and quiet and don't need a lot of water or city lights," was the reply. I wondered if he might have been referring to mom and me, who preferred a motel with a shower and a toilet.

"That's my work shed over there, built that ourselves too," Bill went on. "And I figure we've got enough wood to last the winter."

I looked around. Here and there, dotted over the property, were several wood stacks, each two stick-lengths deep, ten or fifteen feet wide, and four or five feet high. "Looks like enough wood here for five years, Bill," I laughed. "But you sure don't want to run out in the middle of a cold spell, do you?"

"Nope, that's for sure."

"You must get a few creatures coming through here, don't you?"

"Oh yeah, we get some, not like we used to. Some bear, we used to see more than we do now. Marten, and deer – this country has a lot of deer. We feed the birds all winter."

The talk went on, calmness prevailed, the sisters talked as sisters everywhere do, Bill wandered back to his project at the work shed. We all listened to the quiet. Then we took photographs, recorded images of our people and their place, before I started the car to begin our return journey to Edmonton.

Epilogue

What happens now?
Will the Thurston family ties hold, will cousins bond,
and second cousins and third-cousins-once-removed?
In what direction are we heading? Does it matter?

THIS YEAR, my sister sent a spur-of-the-moment email to our mother's grandchildren. Within hours she received responses from most of them. The occasion was Mother's Day, the messages were notes of thanks, admiration, respect, and love for their grandmother. My sister printed each one, tied it with a ribbon, and placed the scrolls in a gift bag. Our mother was as touched as our grandmother would have been.

I suspect each grandparent in this family would have felt the same.

The Thurston family, my family, is like but unlike all other families. Siblings care for one another, sometimes dislike or even hate other siblings, try to get along or not, are sometimes patient and other times short-tempered. There are rumours of sibling rivalries and quarrels in Wales prior to Fred and Nellie's emigration. In Canada, sisters sometimes refused to speak to one another for lengthy periods. Brothers may have been more able to resolve differences – or to ignore them. There are families in dispute today.

Regardless of the rivalries and jealousies, intended or unintentional slights, the photographs of family gatherings – beginning in the 1920's and carrying right through to the last family reunion in 2006 – show family members smiling and talking, laughing and playing and working together. I am amazed.

I observe the family and its photographs with wonder, with gratitude, and with joy. I cannot imagine life without this family.

None of the Thurston progeny became corner boys.

Rather, Fred and Nellie Thurston led their children and their grandchildren – indeed, all their descendants – into the ways and the cultures of their new world. They left behind the old ways – the class consciousness, the staid conservatism, the perception that only that way was right. But they retained the qualities that propelled them to seek adventure and a different sense of freedom – a willingness to work hard and long, a determination for economic independence even if that meant a period of extreme frugality, recognition that future success required long-term investments in land and livestock, and a strong sense of justice and equality. They imbued their children with honesty, love of family, acceptance of others, and a strong desire to succeed.

The new Canada was built by people such as the Thurston's. People who were involved both in their own families and in the life of the community; people who supported the church and who led the local 4-H groups, who marshalled the parades and initiated the local co-ops. Farmers whose children became lawyers and secretaries, entrepreneurs and administrators, sales representatives and mechanics. Or who stayed on the farm and bred pedigreed cattle, produced malt-quality barley, fine northern wheat, oats and rye and canola. People who did more than simply pass the potatoes.

Fred and Nellie Thurston wove and sustained the silken webs of family, strong ties among the new generations of aunts and uncles and cousins, siblings and children and grandchildren. The webs span the

Atlantic and the Pacific, cross borders between provinces and countries. Who knows if the silks will be tended? Who knows if tomorrow's generations will keep the ties firmly tethered?

Will each of us become the grandparents – the favoured aunt or uncle – the mentors that our own relatives were? Will the children of today's generation have the same sense of family that we had? Do they need to fit into a big extended family? Does it matter that they can send emails around the world and instantly receive replies, rather than write letters that travel by land or air and take days or weeks to reach their destination, more days or weeks for a response to be received?

Who knows, who knows? For today, and for the past, we are unbelievably fortunate.

Notes

1. "Thunder mug" was a name given to the crockery or enamel toilet pot used before plumbing was available. Occasionally the thunder mug had a lid. It was stored under the bed before and after use.

2. Divorce was extremely uncommon in Canada prior to WWII; the country had one of the lowest divorce rates in the Western world. Adultery was virtually the only grounds. Applications for divorce were heard by the federal Parliament until divorce courts were established in the provinces; Alberta, Saskatchewan and Ontario created their divorce courts in the period between the two World Wars. Canada's social and religious leaders of the time condemned divorce as a threat to the family, and the strength of this opinion prevented relaxation of Canadian divorce laws. [*Canadian Encyclopedia*, p. 1309]

3. The Lancaster was the most successful bomber used by the Royal Air Force and the Royal Canadian Air Force. Of the 7,377 Lancasters built for use in WWII, 430 were manufactured in Canada. The country at the time was still largely agrarian; the 500,000 manufacturing operations needed to create the 55,000 parts in each Lancaster was a huge challenge. It signalled the beginning of Ontario's industrial growth. The Canadian Lancasters were assembled by the Victory Aircraft Plant in Malton, Ontario. After the war, A. V. Roe Ltd. took over the Victory assets; and designed and built the well-known Avro Arrow.
    See *www.lancastermuseum.ca*

4. The *Concise Oxford Dictionary*, 7th ed., defines chilblain as: itching swelling on hand, foot, etc. from exposure to cold and poor blood circulation.

5   The British school system is quite different than the Canadian system.
     Here, only a tiny proportion of students attend privately-funded,
     fee-charging schools. The tax-supported Canadian school system is
     responsible for (and overall successful at) delivering a good education.
     In the United Kingdom of the early 20th century, the privately-operated
     schools (their 'public' schools) provided an education far superior to that
     offered by the municipally- or church-supported schools. Thus, while
     Phyllis's siblings were educationally accommodated at the Romilly Road
     School, the educational and social opportunities afforded through a
     scholarship to the Barry County Girls' School were enormous.

6   The eastbound Canadian National Railways (CNR) train left Edmonton
     every day at 9:00 a.m., arrived in Irma at 12:43 p.m., and at Wainwright
     at 1:20 p.m. The westbound train left Wainwright at 3:15 p.m., arrived in
     Irma at 4:00 p.m. and reached Edmonton at 7:47 p.m. Train travel was
     cheap, and the superintendent could review his reports as he travelled.

7   The Alberta Provincial Police force existed from 1917 until April 1, 1932;
     the Force was responsible for enforcement of provincial statutes. In 1932,
     essentially all policing activities outside the cities became the responsi-
     bility of the Royal Canadian Mounted Police (RCMP).

8   A dipper was a long-handled pot, similar to a saucepan, usually enam-
     elled. Often, the handle was bent at the end so it could hook over the
     edge of the water pail. Every farm home, and every school, had a water
     pail with a dipper. No-one ever seemed anxious about picking up
     viruses or bacteria from these communal drinking facilities.

9   The address noted on my birth registration was 9631 – 106A Avenue.

10   The Big Bend highway no longer exists – it was covered by the Mica
     Dam reservoir in the 1960's. Now, the Trans-Canada Highway #1 snakes
     through the mountains, along the valleys and hillsides past Golden,
     and connects with the Coquihalla to transport people and goods to
     Vancouver.

11   *Down Memory Lane, A History of Irma and District*. Compiled by Irma and
     District Historical Society. Irma, Alberta. 1985. 2 vols. 1036 pp.

12   *www.en.wikipedia.org* Cheyne-Stokes respiration is an abnormal pat-
     tern of breathing characterized by periods of breathing with gradually
     increasing and decreasing tidal volume interspersed with periods of
     apnea...

13   During the period before and immediately after World War I, the
     Canadian government mounted intense public relations campaigns to
     lure immigrants to Western Canada. Agents scoured Britain for likely

immigrants, and apparently made some highly unlikely promises – the agents were paid a fee for each immigrant who signed on the dotted line.

14   In Western Canada, even in the 1920's, a quarter section (160 acres) was barely enough land to support a family. But in Wales, where climatic conditions allow significantly greater yields per acre than is true on the prairies, a farm of 172 acres was considered a fairly large operation.

15   'Nob' was a term used to describe the 'hoity-toity' or aristocratic, wealthy landowners in Britain.

16   Pemmican was a staple food of the nomadic Cree peoples, who also supplied it to the early fur traders. The pemmican was made of dried and pounded meat (usually bison), mixed with melted fat and saskatoon berries, and formed into round balls. It lasted for years, and could be reconstituted by mixing with hot water.

17   Cream cans were five or ten-gallon stainless steel cans, with a lid and two handles, used by the farm wives to send cream to the creamery, usually by rail. The owner's name was painted in black, on top of the basic blue paint. Sometimes, a tag also noted the destination. The creamery returned the can to the owner, after emptying its contents for butter. Milk cans were the same as cream cans, only bigger – perhaps 15 or 20 gallons; I expect Ted may have hauled the water in milk, rather than cream, cans.

18   The *Irma Times* was a weekly newspaper, usually eight pages of both local and national news. Everyone subscribed to the newspaper in those days. Now, the Irma news is included as a column or two in the larger *Wainwright Star-Chronicle*.

19   *Down Memory Lane, A History of Irma and District*. Compiled by Irma and District Historical Society. Irma, Alberta. 1985. 2 vols. 1036 pp. p132.

20   4-H is an organization for rural young people; its motto is: "Learn to do by doing". Local clubs develop according to local interests such as calf, horse, or dairy clubs, sewing, music, visual arts, entrepreneur clubs. The 4 H's come from the pledge: "I pledge: My head to clearer thinking, My heart to greater loyalty, My hands to larger service, And my health to better living, For my club, my community, and my country." In the Irma area, the 4-H Calf Club was popular and successful; many of the Thurston kids belonged to it, and learned to raise, show, and breed good cattle. More information is available at: *www.4h.ab.ca*

21   The Hudson's Bay Co. was awarded sections 8 and 26 in every township of Western Canada, as compensation for relinquishing its control

over Rupert's Land – the lands that drained into Hudson's Bay – which had been assigned in the company's original charter of May 2, 1670. The company sold its land directly, or through a land agency, to new settlers. Sometimes the company built houses on the land to make it more attractive to immigrants; other times settlers bought house plans – and / or all the construction materials – directly from the company. The prairie landscape was dotted throughout with these houses.

22   There are no stone quarries in the Irma area; the entire landscape is covered with 50 to 100 feet (17 to 35 m) of soil, clay, and glacial till above the bedrock. The closest brick factory was miles away, close to Edmonton (110 miles, 200 km). Almost all houses in the Irma area were built of wood.

23   The first successful human trial of penicillin took place in 1942; it is estimated that the drug was responsible for a 10% to 15% reduction in Allied mortality during WWII, as well as countless anti-bacterial defenses since then.

24   Every day, the pigs were fed a measure of oats or barley that had been chopped in a mill. The chop was fairly fine, with a whitish powder that dusted everything. The pigs squealed loudly and climbed over one another to get at the chop when it was poured into their troughs.

25   www.classes.uleth.ca/200301/geog3225a/industrialLethbridge.html

26   Carter, David J. *POW: Behind Canadian Barbed Wire*. Elkwater, AB: Eagle Butte Press Co. Ltd. 1998.

27   Fooks, George Green. *Prairie Prisoners: POW's in Lethbridge during two world conflicts*. Lethbridge Historical Society Occasional Paper No. 34. Lethbridge: Historical Society of Alberta. 2002.

28   The Canadian Encyclopedia website: *www.tceplus.com* [National Resources Mobilization Act].

29   Douglas, W. A. B. and Brereton Greenhous. *Out of the Shadows: Canada in the Second World War*. Toronto: Oxford University Press. 1977. p. 245.

30   Carter, David J. *ibid*, p. 76.

31   Low-interest loans were available for returning service men and women, and could be used to purchase land for a home and/or farm.

32   Petrie, Anne. *Gone to an Aunt's: Remembering Canada's Homes for Unwed Mothers*. 1998. Toronto: McClelland & Stewart. 248 pp.

33   *When Coal was King* website: *www.coalking.ca/industry*

34   Canada. Library and Archives website: *www.lac-bac.gc.ca/sos*

35 Durant afficionados across North America have formed clubs – The Durant Motors Automobile Club in Fremont, Califorina maintains a website of information and photographs: *www.durantmotors.com*.

36 The mill at Hinton, about 175 miles west of Edmonton, used local timber to create rolls of kraft, the material needed in making glossy magazine pages.

37 That is, section number 14.

38 Muriel and Knute Gulbraa had three sons, Allan in 1958, Brian in 1959, and Kent in 1960.

39 "The 'Lodge of Sorrow' is a 138-year-old ritual performed at the funeral of each departed Elk Lodge member. All the departed's Brothers who are present bid that final farewell. Small twigs of ivy, spruce or other suitable greenery are given to arriving members prior to the ceremony and sequestered on their person until the conclusion. It is an element of the ceremony that ensures every Brother rightfully participates in saying adieu." This explanation provided by Mike Kelly, historian of the International Order of Elks, April 2006.

40 The Canada Agriculture Museum website (*www.agriculture.technomuses.ca*) includes the history and development of cream separators, with photographs and drawings of the mechanism.

41 *www.ualberta.ca* Corbett Hall was named after Edward Annand (Ned) Corbett (1882 to 1964), the second director of the university's Faculty of Extension (1928 to 1937). He played an important role in the establishment of Canada's first university radio station (CKUA), founded the Banff School of Fine Arts (now the Banff Centre) in 1933, and initiated the Farm Radio Forum and Citizens' Forum on CBC in the 1940's.

42 'Shank's mare' is a euphemism for 'on foot' – also called 'shank's pony, especially in UK.

43 The Model A Ford was the successor to Henry Ford's Model T – the first assembly-line vehicle. Model T's were produced from 1908 to 1927, then production lines were changed over. Ford manufactured 4,320,446 Model A's between 1928 and 1931, in several models, including the coupe George bought from his neighbour.

44 Doris taught at Giles school. The community buzzed with the news when she and one of her students fell in love, then married. They raised a family and farmed not far from the Pugh's for several years, until Doris's death.

45 Water-retention ponds are dug on most prairie farms, as holding places for snow-melt and rainwater; the cattle use the ponds for drinking water. In the winter, the children skate and play hockey on the ponds.

46 Excerpt from the poem *Do Not Stand at my Grave and Weep* written by Mary Frye in 1932.

47 Moose are solitary animals during most of the year. In the fall, during mating season, the males seek mates with a unique "call". The hunter tries to emulate that sound, either using his hands and mouth or by using a birch-bark megaphone-like instrument.

48 The Terrajet was an All Terrain Vehicle (ATV) with four balloon tires; if one of the tires went flat, the vehicle would still operate safely. The Terrajet was the only vehicle that could be used to get into the trapline cabins before the muskeg froze – the vehicle's big balloon tires allowed it to float over the soggy terrain.

49 Winnie rendered the fat from the moose or bears Bill shot; she used the fat as we would use lard or shortening.